BASIC CONTRACT DRAFTING ASSIGNMENTS

ASPEN COURSEBOOK SERIES

BASIC CONTRACT DRAFTING ASSIGNMENTS

A Narrative Approach

Sue Payne

Clinical Assistant Professor

Northwestern University School of Law

Wolters Kluwer

Law & Business

AUSTIN   BOSTON   CHICAGO   NEW YORK   THE NETHERLANDS

Aspen Publishers
Attn: Permissions Department
76 Ninth Avenue, 7th Floor
New York, NY 10011-5201

To contact Customer Care, e-mail customer.service@aspenpublishers.com, call 1-800-234-1660, fax 1-800-901-9075, or mail correspondence to:

Aspen Publishers
Attn: Order Department
PO Box 990
Frederick, MD 21705

Printed in the United States of America.

1 2 3 4 5 6 7 8 9 0

ISBN 978-0-7355-8925-4

Library of Congress Cataloging-in-Publication Data

Payne, Sue, 1953-
    Basic contract drafting assignments : a narrative approach / Sue Payne.
       p. cm.
    ISBN 978-0-7355-8925-4
    1. Contracts—United States. 2. Contracts—United States—Language. I. Title.

KF807.P39 2011
346.73'02—dc22

2010039047

About Wolters Kluwer Law & Business

Wolters Kluwer Law & Business is a leading provider of research information and workflow solutions in key specialty areas. The strengths of the individual brands of Aspen Publishers, CCH, Kluwer Law International and Loislaw are aligned within Wolters Kluwer Law & Business to provide comprehensive, in-depth solutions and expert-authored content for the legal, professional and education markets.

CCH was founded in 1913 and has served more than four generations of business professionals and their clients. The CCH products in the Wolters Kluwer Law & Business group are highly regarded electronic and print resources for legal, securities, antitrust and trade regulation, government contracting, banking, pension, payroll, employment and labor, and healthcare reimbursement and compliance professionals.

Aspen Publishers is a leading information provider for attorneys, business professionals and law students. Written by preeminent authorities, Aspen products offer analytical and practical information in a range of specialty practice areas from securities law and intellectual property to mergers and acquisitions and pension/benefits. Aspen's trusted legal education resources provide professors and students with high-quality, up-to-date and effective resources for successful instruction and study in all areas of the law.

Kluwer Law International supplies the global business community with comprehensive English-language international legal information. Legal practitioners, corporate counsel and business executives around the world rely on the Kluwer Law International journals, loose-leafs, books and electronic products for authoritative information in many areas of international legal practice.

Loislaw is a premier provider of digitized legal content to small law firm practitioners of various specializations. Loislaw provides attorneys with the ability to quickly and efficiently find the necessary legal information they need, when and where they need it, by facilitating access to primary law as well as state-specific law, records, forms and treatises.

Wolters Kluwer Law & Business, a unit of Wolters Kluwer, is headquartered in New York and Riverwoods, Illinois. Wolters Kluwer is a leading multinational publisher and information services company.

For my mother, Dorothy Payne, who taught me to love a good story.

Summary of Contents

The **TOY AND GAME INVENTOR** Sequence

APPENDICES

Contents

The **GOLFER** Sequence

The **ROCK BAND** Sequence

The **TOY AND GAME INVENTOR** Sequence

Introduction to Students

In this book, which contains contract drafting assignments grouped into four separate narrative sequences, I use storytelling to introduce you to clients, their businesses, and their needs. Through simulation, I ask you to deal with "real" characters, "real" situations, and "real" concerns.

Instead of teaching you about contract drafting concepts in the abstract, your professors can use the characters and situations in this book to bring those concepts to life. The main characters introduced in the initial client interview evolve and grow through the remaining assignments in each sequence. Narrative lends itself nicely to this progression. The characters move through life. Their businesses develop. And their needs change.

As you learn more about how to draft contracts during the course of the term, the characters enter into more complicated business deals, which require you to draft more complex contracts. The larger assignments in each sequence progress as follows:

Assignment 1	Assignment 2	Assignment 3
Level: Basic	Level: Intermediate	Level: Advanced
Purchase Contract	Services Contract	Fully Negotiated Services Contract

You will begin by learning to draft naked—that is, you will learn how to draft without relying on sample or form contracts, otherwise known as "precedent." For the final contract in each sequence, you will be permitted to search for precedent and use what you find, as long as you carefully scrutinize it and share it with the class, if your professor asks you to do so.

Assignment 1	Assignment 2	Assignment 3
No Precedent	Precedent Supplied ("Canned Precedent")	Open Precedent

Finally, unless your professor directs you otherwise, you will progress from drafting in a team (working with facts gleaned from a client interview), to drafting individually (working with facts contained in documents), to drafting with opposing counsel (working with facts you and your opposing counsel previously negotiated).

Assignment 1	Assignment 2	Assignment 3
Team	Self	Pair
Client Interview	Documents	Negotiated Facts

The common thread linking all of the assignments in each sequence — including the shorter assignments — is the narrative. What is happening in this client's story?

My primary purpose for using narrative to teach basic contract drafting is to give you context—that is, to give you a realistic setting within which to apply the abstract concepts you will learn in this course. I create characters to supply you with an audience other than your professors. You meet the clients, their counsel, and some of the other people involved in each deal. If all goes as planned, when you complete each assignment, you will remember to consider these characters, as well as the judges, arbitrators, mediators, and other third parties who may have a reason to read, interpret, implement, or enforce the contracts you draft.

I want you to have fun getting to know the characters in each sequence, decoding some of the colorful jargon associated with their professions, and transforming the raw terms of their business deals into polished contracts. Through storytelling, I help you imagine your clients as people and entities with real needs. I do this because I believe it will make you a better contract drafter.

Acknowledgments

I begin by thanking all of the students who have taken my *Basics of Contract Drafting* seminar. Working with them helped me understand how important it was to create engaging and challenging assignments.

Thank you to all of the teaching assistants and research assistants who have worked for me over the past five years, but especially Allison Grow, Micah Hughes, Vivian Lee, Kathryn Perry, Alice Vosmek, and Xiaoxiao Wang. Their support made it possible for me to continue creating new assignments until I had enough to fill this book.

I thank all of my colleagues in Northwestern's Communication and Legal Reasoning department. I am particularly grateful to Grace Dodier, Martha Kanter, Ellen Mulaney, Kathleen Dillon Narko, Sue Provenzano, Judy Rosenbaum, and Brian Silbernagel. They were enthusiastic about this project from the beginning and their encouragement has been a great gift.

Thank you to Helene Shapo, my legal writing professor, mentor, and friend.

Thank you also to Tina L. Stark, whose textbook, *Drafting Contracts: How and Why Lawyers Do What They Do*, has been invaluable to me. I deeply appreciate the help that Tina gave me when I first started teaching contract drafting five years ago. I am also grateful for the continued support she provides by working so hard to develop and promote transactional skills training.

I thank my development editor, Barbara Roth, and my production editor, Christie Rears. Both made working on this book a pleasure.

Thank you to my son, Nate Madden, for cherishing and sharing my creative spirit.

And, finally, thank you to my husband, Daniel Kirschenbaum, who inspires me every day.

BASIC CONTRACT DRAFTING ASSIGNMENTS

The
ARTIST
Sequence

Assignment *1*

The Paperweight Purchase Agreement

1A: ENGAGEMENT LETTER BETWEEN ATTORNEY AND CLIENT

Instructions

A. **Summary:** You will draft an engagement letter/retainer agreement between your law firm and a new client.

B. **Background:** You are an associate at the law firm of Bishop, Dickinson & Plath. Anna Claire Glass, an artist who creates glass sculptures, wants your firm to draft a contract for her. For the first time in her career, she is going to sell one of her sculptures—a glass paperweight—to an individual collector.

 Both of Ms. Glass's grandparents are retired attorneys. They advised Ms. Glass to seek counsel, but they also told her to be wary of engaging an attorney without having a written engagement letter or retainer agreement in place.

 To date, Bishop, Dickinson & Plath has not required its clients to sign an engagement letter or retainer agreement. The senior partner, Eliza Bishop, has resisted formalizing client relationships in this way. Eliza now wants you to draft an engagement letter that she can present to Ms. Glass to communicate basic information about how the attorney-client relationship between Ms. Glass and the firm is likely to work.

 Eliza wants the engagement letter to be a contract that both parties will sign, but she does not want it to be so formal that it frightens Ms. Glass away or causes her to ask her grandparents to review it and suggest changes.

C. **No Use of Precedent:** Eliza does not want you to use other engagement or retainer letters that you find through a library or Internet search or through any other means. She would like to see what you can draft without using any precedent. She believes that, if you are not influenced by what other firms have already done, you will produce something fresh, creative, well-written, and tailored to this particular client's needs.

D. **Legal Research:** In preparation for completing this assignment, please read *Brian Dowling v. Chicago Options Associates, Inc. et al. (DLA Piper Rudnick Gray Cary (US), LLP)*, 226 Ill. 2d 277, 875 N.E.2d 1012 (Ill. 2007).

E. Draft Specific to This Attorney-Client Relationship: Eliza does not want you to create a "form" engagement letter/retainer agreement to be used for all of the firm's clients. She wants you to focus on this particular client. If you do a good job, perhaps Eliza will ask you to create a "form" later. Right now, Eliza's main concern is that you cover the issues listed in the table included in Part F and that you capture the terms that Eliza already has communicated to Ms. Glass.

F. Table of Issues and Terms: Eliza prepared the following quick list of the issues that the engagement letter should cover and the terms upon which she and Ms. Glass have reached agreement. The issues appear in no particular order.

Issue	Terms
Security retainer (intended to secure payment of fees for future services the firm is expected to perform)	$500; will be applied to the first invoice
Trust account (separate from firm's property; remains client's property until firm applies it to charges for services actually rendered)	Will put the $500 security retainer in client trust account
Refund of unused fees	Will refund unused fees (if any)
Initial consultation (Eliza already met with Ms. Glass)	No charge, but clarify initial consultation already occurred
Fees	Senior Partner—$250 per hour Junior Partner—$200 per hour Associate (any level)—$125 per hour Paralegal (any level)—$80 per hour

Issue	Terms
Personnel assigned	Eliza Bishop (Senior Partner) No Junior Partners Associates (any student in this class) Paralegal (Walter Wittman)
When work will begin	Upon receipt of signed engagement letter and check for $500 security retainer
Who firm works for	Anna Claire Glass (individual)
Scope of services	Draft contract for sale of glass paperweight; no more than that; if she wants more, then must sign another engagement letter
Client's obligations to firm	Cooperate Tell us everything about the deal Provide any supporting documents needed Be available; reachable through multiple means Pay bill within 30 days of receipt
Business hours of firm	8 a.m. to 7 p.m.; but give her Eliza's cell phone number [make this number up]
Invoices	Sent out at end of month
Quarter hours	Bill out time in 15-minute increments
Expenses	Client pays for overnight mail; no markup, just a pass-through
Phone calls	We bill for time spent on calls received and made—at regular hourly rate
E-mails	We bill for reading and responding—at regular hourly rate
Termination by client	Can terminate at any time; no refund if the retainer has been spent; must pay fees for services already rendered; firm will prepare final invoice

Issue	Terms
Termination by firm	If client doesn't pay in timely fashion or if there's a breakdown in the attorney/client relationship (spell out what this means a bit—client fails to fulfill her obligations, other causes, such as client wanting attorney to do something that might violate ethical obligations)
Division of labor and billing	Associates will do initial client interview and first draft of contract We bill for associates' time, plus partner supervisory time Partner will not attend client interview but will review associates' work and communicate with client
Core billing	Time spent reviewing facts, creating drafts, reviewing drafts, communicating with clients, communicating with opposing counsel, all other activities related to representation
Beginning of representation	When both parties have signed the contract and Ms. Glass has paid the security retainer fee
End of representation	When final bill is paid; note that the $500 retainer is deducted from the first bill
Dowling v. Chicago Options	Include whatever the court requires about the security retainer to assure that the client is fully informed about how the money will be handled
Detail in bills	Will show who performed the work, how much time was spent (rounded up to the quarter hour), brief description of the work performed
Increase in hourly billing rates	Occurs at the beginning of each new year, but we will not raise billing rates for this client during the term of this letter
Changes to personnel	Can substitute associates but not Senior Partner, unless obtain client's consent
Disputing a bill	Must contact Senior Partner by mail or telephone within 14 days of receipt of invoice

Issue	Terms
Qualifications of attorneys	All will be licensed to practice law in Illinois We'll state that everyone working on the matter is competent; add in "with appropriate supervision" for associates and paralegals
Potential conflict of interest	We conducted a conflict search based on the info the client supplied and turned up no conflict
Overhead expenses	Not billed to client
Attorney/client privilege	Explain it briefly; make sure she knows not to share info with third parties and destroy privilege
Customer service	Can expect us to work hard and to keep client informed; let us know if we are not doing that
Governing law	Illinois
Signatures required	Eliza Bishop and Anna Claire Glass

G. **Further Instructions for Drafting Engagement Letter:** Eliza wants the engagement letter to come from Eliza herself. She would like you to draft it using a personal, somewhat informal tone, without including any slang and without sounding unprofessional. Unlike most other contracts you will draft, you may use personal pronouns in this letter. Refer to Eliza as "I" and to Ms. Glass as "you."

Remember that your main audience for the engagement letter is an artist who has very little experience in business and may never have entered into a similar arrangement with an attorney before. You must make sure that you communicate clearly so that she understands everything in the letter. Encourage her to ask Eliza questions before signing the letter if there is anything that she does not understand.

In order to keep the engagement letter from sounding too formal, you may use "will" instead of "shall" for covenants throughout the letter.

Please divide the letter up into sections and use boldfaced headings to help Ms. Glass. Think about how best to organize the information you convey.

> ***Note:*** You should not use a table, except perhaps to summarize information about the individuals working on the matter and their hourly rates.

After Eliza's signature (with her title and the date), include a statement from Ms. Glass, acknowledging that she has read the letter, understands it, and agrees to its terms. Then put in lines for Ms. Glass's signature and the date. Under her signature line, designate her as "Client."

One final word: Strive to keep the engagement letter simple, straightforward, and brief. This letter should provide you with an excellent opportunity to practice the skill of drafting in Plain English. Your main goal is to communicate clearly so that the client understands how the attorney/client relationship is supposed to work.

H. **Additional Instructions:** Your professor may provide you with additional instructions regarding this assignment.

1B: THE CLIENT INTERVIEW

Instructions

A. **Summary:** You are going to meet your client, Anna Claire Glass, an artist who would like to sell one of her glass sculptures (a paperweight) to an individual collector named Arthur Cole Lector. You will interview Ms. Glass in order to find out the terms of the deal that she has negotiated with Mr. Lector.

B. **Preparation for the Client Interview:** After you read the following Memorandum from Bishop, please read Appendix 1, Ten Tips for Interviewing a Client About a Transaction. Since your client's business and website are fictional, you will not be able to do any research about her or her business beforehand. However, you should do a small amount of research about glassmaking and glass sculpture as a backdrop for the client interview. Remember that you may not search for any purchase agreements regarding works of art, as that would violate the prohibition against using precedent on this assignment (see Section D, Precedent, below). Brainstorm about what provisions you think ought to be included in a contract for the sale of the glass paperweight. Then prepare a list of questions to ask your client.

C. **Legal Expertise and Research:** In practice, you should not draft a contract in an area in which you have no legal expertise unless you acquire the expertise or seek help from another attorney who possesses it. Rule 1.1 of the Model Rules of Professional Conduct states:

> **Competence.** A lawyer shall provide competent representation to a client. Competent representation requires the legal knowledge, skill, thoroughness and preparation reasonably necessary for the representation.

Comment 2 to MRPC Rule 1.1 clarifies that "[a] lawyer can provide adequate representation in a wholly novel field through necessary study" or "through the association of a lawyer of established competence in the field in question." For the purposes of this assignment, you may assume that your senior partner has the requisite legal expertise to serve as your guide. You may not do any legal research in connection with this assignment unless your professor authorizes you to do so.

D. **Precedent:** In preparation for the client interview, you may not use any sample contracts, forms, templates, or models (collectively, "precedent") other than any model contracts provided by your professor.

> **Note:** Because most transactional attorneys have some relevant precedent in hand when drafting a contract, you will be permitted to use precedent in some subsequent drafting assignments.

E. **Additional Access to Client:** After the in-class interview, you may need to obtain more information from Ms. Glass. Collect your questions and e-mail them to your professor, who may (a) pass them along to Ms. Glass, or (b) arrange for Ms. Glass to come into class for another interview.

F. **Additional Instructions:** Your professor may provide you with additional instructions regarding this assignment.

Bishop, Dickinson & Plath

MEMORANDUM

TO: Associates

FROM: Eliza Bishop

RE: New Client, Anna Claire Glass

DATE: September 6, 2012

As many of you know, I am a painter and had my first exhibition at The Mythical Beast Café last year. (Thanks to all of you, by the way, for coming to the opening.) While my work was on display, I frequented the Café every Saturday morning and struck up a friendship with Anna Claire Glass, a member of the wait staff who is also a glass sculptor. She displays her incredible glass paperweights on the top of the bagel case.

Anna is very excited about finding a purchaser for her largest glass paperweight, which she has entitled "Bulbous I." The purchaser is Arthur Cole Lector, a regular at the Mythical Beast. (I've seen him looking at my paintings, but he has never taken much interest in them.) Anna told me that Arthur offered her $20,000 for the paperweight. She was inclined to turn it over to him immediately so she could get her hands on the cash. However, her grandparents are both retired attorneys, which naturally makes her more cautious.

In brief, Anna has asked our firm to draft the contract for this deal. She can't really afford my rates, but she can afford yours! She will be coming into the office to meet with you about the details.

I don't know much about Arthur Cole Lector, except that he sells insurance and may also have some family money, which would permit him to pursue his interest in collecting art. I'm sure that Anna can tell you more about him. So far he is not represented by an attorney.

Please interview Anna and find out the terms of the deal that she has struck with Arthur.

1C: LETTER TO CLIENT RE POTENTIAL ETHICAL QUESTION

Instructions

A. **Summary:** Analyze the scenario presented below in order to determine whether you may be violating any ethical rules if your firm jointly represents Anna Claire Glass and Arthur Cole Lector in the paperweight purchase transaction that Ms. Glass described when you interviewed her as part of Assignment 1B. You must be able to explain your answer by citing specific portions of the Model Rules of Professional Conduct and the comments to those rules. Weigh also the business issues that representing both Anna and Arthur may present. Draft a letter to the client, informing her of your answer and its rationale.

B. **Scenario:** After your interview with Anna Claire Glass, she calls you to say that Arthur Cole Lector does not want to hire an attorney to represent him in connection with this deal. He told her that he thinks the deal is too simple to warrant the additional expense. Anna is a little bit uncomfortable about this, as she likes the idea of having your firm all to herself. Nevertheless, she sees the wisdom of Arthur's thinking and is willing to consider having you represent Arthur, too. Since she already has established a relationship with you, she knows that your first loyalty will always be to her.

C. **Format of Client Letter:** Begin the letter by summarizing the issue about which Anna has sought your advice. If you believe there is an ethical issue that prohibits the joint representation, tell Anna, but be sure to explain it in terms that a non-lawyer will understand. If you do not believe that this scenario presents an ethical issue but you do believe that it presents a business issue, explain the issue to Anna, providing enough information for her to give the business issue careful consideration.

D. **Tone of Client Letter:** Remember that the relationship between your firm and Anna Claire Glass is brand new. Your senior partner, Eliza Bishop, expects that Anna eventually will become a famous artist who will send the firm a lot of additional legal work. In your letter, use a business-like tone, but be sure to make the client feel that you have her best interests at heart. Remember to tell Anna that she can choose to waive any conflict of interest and that, if she does make that choice, she should let you know so that you can send her the appropriate Waiver of Conflict of Interest Agreement.

> **Note:** This assignment does not require you to draft the Waiver of Conflict of Interest Agreement.

E. **Additional Instructions:** Your professor may provide you with additional instructions regarding this assignment.

1D: MEMORANDUM TO SENIOR PARTNER RE SUMMARY OF DEAL TERMS

Instructions

A. **Summary:** Using the notes from your interview with your client, Anna Claire Glass, draft a memorandum to Eliza Bishop, summarizing the terms of the paperweight purchase transaction. Assume that Eliza was not present at the client interview.

B. **Format of Memorandum:** Set up your memo as follows—

Bishop, Dickinson & Plath

MEMORANDUM

CONFIDENTIAL

TO: Eliza Bishop

FROM: [Insert Your Name]

RE: Interview with Anna Claire Glass, September 9, 2012

SUBJECT: Paperweight Purchase Agreement

DATE: September 10, 2012

[Insert the text of the memo here, single-spaced. Use headings to help organize the material.]

C. **Collaboration:** If your professor permits, you and your classmates may share your client interview notes. Most likely, if you missed a deal fact, your classmate caught it. Through collaboration, you can fill in any information gaps you have, unless, of course, the client did not give you the information you need.

D. **Follow-Up Questions to Client:** In the course of writing this memo, you may find that you need to ask the client some additional questions. Please direct those questions to your professor, who will either consult the client and post the answers for the entire class or invite the client in for another interview.

E. **Identification of Legal Issues:** While drafting this memo, you may identify one or more legal issues that this transaction poses. If so, please identify those issues at the end of the memo so that Eliza becomes aware of them and can give you some direction regarding how to pursue them.

F. **Additional Instructions:** Your professor may provide you with additional instructions regarding this assignment.

1E: ASSEMBLING THE FRAME: DRAFTING THE TITLE, PREAMBLE, BACKGROUND, WORDS OF AGREEMENT, DEFINITIONS, AND SIGNATURE LINES

Instructions

A. **Summary:** Using the deal facts gathered from the client interview you conducted in Assignment 1B, you will draft the Paperweight Purchase Agreement's frame—the Title, Preamble, Background, Words of Agreement, Definitions, and Signature Lines.

B. **The "Frame" Metaphor:** Some parts of a contract are traditional and easily drafted using models. They create a "frame" for the business provisions of the contract. The Title, Preamble, Words of Agreement, and Signature Lines are rudimentary parts of the contract's frame. The Definitions and Background sections, while more difficult to draft, still should not contain covenants, conditions precedent, representations and warranties, and statements of discretionary authority—otherwise known as "operative" provisions. For that reason, the Background and Definitions sections are also part of the contract's frame, stabilizing it by adding more information about the deal and preparing the reader for the "picture" containing the operative provisions of the deal.

 Professors who teach contract drafting use various images to convey what contract drafters do. Therefore, you may hear someone else refer to the "frame" as the "skeleton" of the contract and the "picture" as the "meat on the bones." If it helps you to think of the contract that way, please feel free to do so. The purpose of these metaphors is to help you break down the drafting process into manageable parts.

C. **The Preamble—An Example of Learning from a Model:** Provided that you have the right information, you can draft a Preamble for the Paperweight Purchase Agreement by following the pattern of the Preamble in the model Leaf Disposal Services Agreement,[1] reprinted below.

---

1. The entire model Leaf Disposal Services Agreement is included in Appendix 2.

LEAF DISPOSAL SERVICES AGREEMENT

Leaf Disposal Services Agreement made this 10th day of October 2007, between SpinGazer, Inc., a Delaware corporation with its principal place of business located at 1200 Ridge Avenue, Evanston, Illinois 60201 (the "Company"), and Fallen Leaves, Inc., an Illinois corporation with its principal place of business located at 2025 North Clark Street, Chicago, Illinois 60614 (the "Provider").

Because both Anna and Arthur are individuals and not corporations, you obviously do not need to identify where they are incorporated and where their principal places of business are located. For individuals, you simply say "an individual residing at [insert address]."

You must still choose a shorthand nickname for the individual and place the parenthetical containing the shorthand name *after* all of the identifying information about the individual. Therefore, after Anna's address, you may insert "(the "Artist")," for example. If you call Anna *the Artist*, then you will want to give Arthur a nickname at the same level of generality. Perhaps for Arthur, you will insert "(the "Collector")" after his address.

The placement of the shorthand names you choose for the parties, which function like in-text definitions, is very important. Perhaps it is hard to believe, but there could be more than one Anna Claire Glass in the world. By placing the parenthetical after Anna's address, you make it more likely that you have clearly identified the "Anna Claire Glass" who is a party to this contract.

When you draft the Preamble of your contract, pay careful attention to punctuation. The Preamble contains a lot of information and is difficult to read if not punctuated properly. Moreover, aside from the Title, the Preamble is the very first thing that the reader will encounter in your contract. Even though it is formulaic, you can set a good tone by drafting it so that it reads smoothly. Proper punctuation helps.

Finally, you and your professor are likely to spend some time talking about what date you should insert in the Preamble. When is the contract "made"? Is it the same date on which the contract is signed? Is this date different from the effective date of the term? Also, sometimes the date in the Preamble is preceded by the words "as of." Under what circumstances is it appropriate to use those words? Even a formulaic Preamble can present interesting questions that you are likely to bandy about in class.

D. **Title, Words of Agreement, and Signature Lines:** You and your professor will discuss what to call this contract. For the sake of convenience, I have referred to it as the *Paperweight Purchase Agreement*, but you are not required to use that title.

The "Words of Agreement" used in the Leaf Disposal Services Agreement model are simple. After the Background section, insert "Accordingly, the parties agree as follows:". In most contracts, at about this point in the contract, you will see a lengthy "Consideration" provision that sounds like complete gobbledygook. You and your professor are likely to discuss whether a formal statement of consideration is necessary when the contract itself makes it amply clear that consideration for the transaction does exist. The drafter of the Leaf Disposal Services Agreement has concluded that the contract does not require a formal statement of consideration.

You can easily imitate the Signature lines and get them right. The Signature lines from the Leaf Disposal Services Agreement are reprinted below.

AGREED:

SPINGAZER, INC.   **FALLEN LEAVES, INC.**

By: _____   By: _____
     Jackie Spingazer   Leif E. Liminator

Title: Director of Operations   Title: Supervisor

Since both parties to the Paperweight Purchase Agreement are individuals, you will need to adapt this format a bit. The names in bold-faced, all caps, above the signature lines are the formal names of the parties to the contract—not the shorthand names that you chose in the Preamble and used throughout the rest of the contract. So, where you see **SPINGAZER, INC.** and **FALLEN LEAVES, INC.**, above, you would substitute **ANNA CLAIRE GLASS** and **ARTHUR COLE LECTOR**.

> **Note:** Generally, it is a good idea to put your client's signature line first. Believe it or not, this sometimes matters to the client.

Underneath the Signature Lines, type the names of the individuals signing the agreement. You do not need the word "By" if the individual signing is also the party. Just re-type "Anna Claire Glass" and "Arthur Cole Lector," in upper and lower case letters, below their Signature Lines. This may seem repetitious, but the names above the Signature Lines identify the parties to the contract and the names below the signature lines identify who signed the contract.

Finally, since Anna and Arthur are individuals and do not have titles, you can eliminate the "Title" lines.

E. **Background:** The purpose of the Background section is twofold—to put the agreement in context and to express the intentions of the parties.

You may be accustomed to seeing this section called "Recitals" and containing a list of "WHEREAS" clauses ending with the crescendo "NOW THEREFORE" clause. Plain English drafters avoid those clauses like the plague. Instead, draft the Background section in smooth prose. This is probably the only place in the contract where you will get to tell a little story. Use it well. Who are the parties? What do they do? Why are they entering into this deal? The Background section should not be too long or too lopsided (containing more information about one party than the other).

The Background section is a place where you should avoid following your models too closely. It is not as formulaic as the Preamble, for example. Ask yourself: What do my readers need to know about the parties? What do they need to know about what happened before (if anything) and about what is about to happen (this transaction)?

Remember that you should not include any operative provisions in the Background section. Be very careful not to include any covenants, conditions precedent, representations and warranties, or statements of discretionary authority here. The courts generally will not give effect to operative language contained in a Background section. And, if you include a covenant in the Background section, you run the risk of forgetting to include it in the body of the contract, where it would actually obligate a party to do something.

Sometimes the parties want to clarify their intentions early in a contract. Even though the Background section should not contain operative provisions, it can contain a statement of the parties' intentions. Sometimes, if there is a contractual dispute, the court will give effect to a statement of intentions included in the Background section instead of, or in addition to, admitting parol evidence of those intentions.

F. **Definitions:** The model Leaf Disposal Services Agreement gives you some limited guidance about how to draft the definitions. It contains the prefatory language below.

As used in this Agreement, the terms defined in the preamble have their assigned meanings and the following terms have the meanings assigned to them in this Article.

If you have defined any terms, in-text, in the Background section, you must add the words "and in the Background section" to the prefatory language after the words "in the preamble." That way, you will not have to include any cross-references to those definitions in the Definitions article itself.

By looking at the model agreement, you will see that most definitions use the verb "means" or "includes but does not include." You will also see that in-text definitions found in the body of the contract (but not in the Preamble or Background section) are cross-referenced in the Definitions article, using the verb phrase "has the meaning assigned in."

You and your professor will discuss how to choose what to define and how to draft the definitions. Remember that definitions are declarations and should not contain any operative language—no covenants, conditions precedent, representations and warranties, or statements of discretionary authority. Think of a definition as a statement of what a term means whenever it appears capitalized in the contract. If you want a party to undertake any kind of obligation, you must include it in the body of the contract rather than in a definition.

> **Important Note About Drafting Definitions as Part of the Frame:** In practice, lawyers hardly ever draft a complete Definitions article before they draft the rest of the contract. In a sense, asking you to draft the definitions before you draft the rest of the contract is an artificial exercise. Nevertheless, it is a good exercise and it may save you some time and energy. It forces you, as a novice contract drafter, to think in advance about what terms you may need to define. You can draft a definition for the paperweight, for example, because you know that you will need to refer to it over and over again. You also know that you have to find a way to specifically identify the paperweight so that it is always clear which paperweight you are talking about.

Moreover, drafting definitions in advance may prevent you from making the mistake of using too many in-text definitions. When a Definitions article contains too many cross-references to in-text definitions, the reader is forced to hop all over the contract to find out what things mean. Instead, by defining most terms in the Definitions article itself, you keep the reader happy by feeding her information. You also take the opportunity to educate her about the deal a bit before she launches into the contract. This idea of educating the reader may sound like a litigation drafting concept, but it holds true for contract drafting as well. As your reader moves into the contract, after reading a fully developed Definitions article, she is more likely to understand the rest of the contract.

If you remember to consider your audience(s), you will be more likely to achieve the goal of clear communication. Transactional attorneys who fail to consider their audience(s) give transactional attorneys a bad name.

G. **Additional Instructions:** Your professor may provide you with additional instructions regarding this assignment.

1F: FILLING IN THE PICTURE: DRAFTING THE CONTRACT'S OPERATIVE PROVISIONS

Instructions

A. **Summary:** Using the deal facts gathered from the client interview you conducted in Assignment 1B, draft all of the operative provisions of the Paperweight Purchase Agreement. The "operative" provisions do not include the "frame" of the contract—the Title, Preamble, Background, Words of Agreement, Definitions, and Signature Lines. This assignment assumes that you have already drafted the "frame" of the contract as part of Assignment 1E—or that your professor has asked you to skip that assignment and concentrate on "filling in the picture."

B. **Filling in the Picture:** To fill in the picture, you must draft all of the operative provisions of the contract and decide how to organize them. Your professor will help you develop the basic skills you need to take the terms of the deal and translate them into contract concepts—covenants, conditions precedent, representations and warranties, statements of discretionary authority, and declarations.[2]

In practice, some attorneys call this *memorializing* the terms of the deal, which basically means getting the terms of the deal down on paper so that they have a legal effect. The paper (or contract) is the *memorial.* The parties should be able to turn to the contract whenever they have any questions about their rights and duties with regard to the particular transaction.

C. **Organization—Naming and Ordering the Articles and Sections:** Some provisions are traditionally placed in certain spots. For example, after the Definitions article, some drafters include a brief article containing the main covenants of the deal. One leading contract drafting expert, Tina L. Stark, calls this brief article the "subject matter performance provision."[3] The subject matter performance provision in the model Leaf Disposal Services Agreement is reprinted below.

---

2. Tina L. Stark, *Drafting Contracts: How and Why Lawyers Do What They Do* 9-10 (Aspen 2007) (describes the contract concepts as the "building blocks" of the contract and the process of converting business terms into contract concepts as a "translation skill").

3. *Id.* at 39-40.

Article III. Summary of Services and Fees

Section 3.01 Services and Fees. Subject to the provisions of this Agreement, the Provider shall perform the Services described in Article IV. To compensate the Provider for performing the Services, the Company shall pay the Provider the fees and reimburse the Provider for the expenses described in Article V.

The drafter of the model Leaf Disposal Services Agreement put the subject matter performance provision after the Term article. While the exact order of these provisions sometimes varies, remember that the subject matter performance provision, the Term, and the Closing articles should appear near the beginning of the contract.

It is sometimes helpful to think of the subject matter performance provision as a thesis statement plus road map. It tells you the "main idea" (or "primary covenants") of the contract and points you to the places in the contract where you can find out more details about those covenants.

After the subject matter performance provision, the Term article, and the Closing article, the reader expects to find information about what the Artist is selling and how much the Collector is going to pay for the item. Therefore, you must put those articles close to the beginning of the contract.

At the end of the contract, right before the signature lines, place the contract's boilerplate provisions (sometimes called *General Provisions*). The Termination and Dispute Resolution articles generally come right before the boilerplate.

So, with the parts of the contract in their traditional places, and allowing for some flexibility in their exact order, your contract (not including the frame) will look something like this:

Summary of Sale and Purchase
Term
Closing (if any)
The Sale of the Paperweight
Compensation
[OTHER TOPICS TO BE COVERED]
Dispute Resolution
Termination
General Provisions

One of the biggest challenges that a drafter faces is how to organize the business provisions not specifically listed above—that is, how to organize those "other topics to be covered." Start by making a list of every deal term not addressed in the named articles. Then, group those deal terms by topic and select a good name for the article covering that topic. Remember that "Buyer's Obligations" and "Seller's Responsibilities" are contract concepts, not topics. Moreover, if you use a heading like "Buyer's Obligations," you are indicating to the reader that all of the Buyer's obligations are contained under that heading. More likely, the Buyer's obligations are scattered throughout the contract.

Choose article names (and section names as well) that are specific and clear. Instead of "Buyer's Obligations," for example, you may have articles called "Restrictions on Buyer's Right to Change or Sell the Paperweight" and "Public Exhibition of the Paperweight." Instead of "Seller's Responsibilities," you may have articles called "Care and Delivery of the Paperweight" and "Transfer of Ownership." These articles may contain obligations and responsibilities of one or both parties.

If you find that you have a number of miscellaneous deal terms that do not seem to fit anywhere, give them another look before deciding to create single-section articles. Single-section articles (other than the subject matter performance provision and the Term article) can make the particular topic seem like an undeveloped afterthought or, conversely, give the particular topic too much weight. It is better to put the miscellaneous deal term into the article it relates to the most, even if it is not a perfect fit.

Once you have found a place for every deal term and named the articles you want to include in the contract, decide what order to put them in. Generally, place the articles in order from most important topic to least important topic. However, if you are describing a process, it may make more sense to put some of the articles in chronological order. There is no magic bullet of contract organization. However, it is very important to remember your audience(s). Ask yourself what your reader needs to know and when your reader needs to know it. Also, remember the terms of the deal. For example, if your client stressed that the Buyer was very concerned about the security of the paperweight while it remained in your client's hands, then you may want to move that topic up near the beginning of the contract for emphasis.

D. Additional Instructions: Your professor may provide you with additional instructions regarding this assignment.

1G: PUTTING THE PICTURE IN THE FRAME: FINISHING THE DRAFT CONTRACT

Instructions

A. **Summary:** This assignment applies only if you have already completed Assignments 1E and 1F. You will now insert the "picture" that you drafted in response to Assignment 1F into the "frame" that you drafted in response to Assignment 1E. The result will be one completed draft of a Paperweight Purchase Agreement (with a title that you have selected).

B. **The Process:** Inserting the picture into the frame is not merely a mechanical process. Once you have merged the two documents together, you must make sure that the picture fits the frame properly; in other words, you must review the draft contract as a whole and ask yourself at least the following questions:

☐ Is the Title I chose for the contract still appropriate?

☐ Have I consistently referred to the parties to the contract using the shorthand names that I gave them in the Preamble?

☐ Do the full party names in the Preamble (not the shorthand names) match the full party names above the Signature Lines?

☐ Does the date in the Preamble reflect the date when the contract is made? If this date is different from the effective date of the contract, have I clarified that in the body of the contract?

☐ Do the addresses in the Preamble match the addresses in the "Notice" provision included in the boilerplate?

☐ Did I include enough information in the Background section? Is there anything else that I may want to add to that section? Is there anything I may want to take out?

☐ Do I use my defined terms whenever it is appropriate? [*Note:* This is called "letting your defined terms do their work."]

☐ Did I remember to capitalize my defined terms in the body of the contract?

☐ Are there any lengthy phrases that I repeat more than once that could perhaps be defined terms?

☐ Are there any concepts that I repeat in different ways each time that I should perhaps be saying the same way each time? Would a defined term help?

☐ Are there any defined terms that I never use or use only once? (If so, you probably do not need to define that term.)

☐ Have I included a cross-reference to every in-text definition in the Definitions article? Are my definitions still in alphabetical order?

☐ Whenever I use a cross-reference, have I referenced the correct article or section?

☐ Have I used cross-references in the body of the contract to help the reader understand the relationship between parts of the contract?

☐ Are all of my article and section numbers in order? Does each have an appropriate heading?

☐ In the "Survivability" boilerplate provision, have I listed all of the sections of the contract that will survive the early termination of the contract or the end of the term?

☐ Do all of the parts of the contract work well together?

Once you have answered all of these questions and made any necessary adjustments to the contract, you can move into the editing and proof-reading stage described below.

C. **Editing and Proofreading:** Using the Contract Drafting Checklist provided in Appendix 3, go back over your draft contract again. The checklist is set up to help you take the long view first. Think about the transaction. Have you captured all of the terms of the deal? Have you translated them into the correct contract concepts? Have you answered all questions about the rights and duties of the parties with regard to this transaction? Have you raised any questions without answering them? Is your contract well-organized, coherent, and coordinated? Does it read smoothly? Is it easy to follow?

The checklist then asks you to look at some formatting issues that are directly related to readability. Review those issues, remembering also that well-chosen headings and the judicious use of "white space" enhance the readability of a contract. Do not remove headings or white space in order to make sure that you do not exceed the page limit for this assignment. If you need guidance about how to avoid exceeding the page limit, seek your professor's help.

Following the checklist, now make sure that your contract contains all of the essential parts. Then review each part. Finally, under the broad heading "Plain English," the checklist directs you to make sure that you have not made any grammatical, mechanical, or typographical errors.

Once you have gone through the checklist, prepare your contract for submission by proofreading it carefully, using the proofreading tips and tricks contained in Appendix 5. Finally, review your professor's instructions and verify that you have followed all of the directions regarding submitting the contract to your professor. There is something particularly disturbing about a transactional attorney who fails to follow directions. Failing to follow directions indicates that you are not detail oriented, which, in practice, can make your supervisor and your client mistrust you. It can also lead to a dangerous loss of credibility with the attorney representing the other side.

D. **Submitting the Contract:** Do one final thing before you submit your contract: Make sure that you are turning in a clean copy. That is, make sure that you have eliminated any highlighting or comments to yourself that you may have inserted during the drafting process. Practicing attorneys, both litigators and deal lawyers alike, can tell many war stories about forgetting to delete comments or critiques before filing documents or sending drafts to the other side. You do not want to make such an embarrassing mistake. You may also want to make sure that your document does not contain any hidden personal or metadata, such as information about when you finished the assignment. Check the software you are using to figure out how to eliminate that information.

E. **Additional Instructions:** Your professor may provide you with additional instructions regarding this assignment.

1H: MAKING CHANGES TO THE DRAFT CONTRACT: REDLINING

Instructions

A. **Summary:** Using the facts contained in the following memorandum from Eliza Bishop, make the appropriate changes to the Paperweight Purchase Agreement. Apparently, Arthur Cole Lector is now represented by an attorney. Ms. Bishop's memorandum summarizes the conversation she had with Mr. Lector's attorney about the draft contract that she sent him. Ms. Bishop has consulted with your client, Anna Claire Glass, and determined that all of the changes are acceptable to Ms. Glass.

B. **Making Changes to a Draft Reviewed by Opposing Counsel:** Now that opposing counsel has reviewed your draft contract, you should not make any changes to it without redlining those changes. Find the "Track Changes" (or equivalent function) on your computer and learn how to use it. Ideally, every word you delete should be struck through and every word you add should appear in red.

Make the changes mentioned in Ms. Bishop's memo. Remember not to make any changes to the document without tracking them. In real life, you will quickly lose credibility with opposing counsel if you do not track all of your changes because you will be breaking the unwritten code of honor that transactional attorneys follow. Track even the smallest change—even the correction of a minor misspelling.

C. **Turning in the Redlined Contract:** After you have reviewed the redlined contract to make sure that you took into account all of the changes mentioned in Ms. Bishop's memo, submit it to your professor. This time, make sure that you submit the document *with* the changes showing. (This may be as simple as saving the document as "Final Showing Markup.") Remember to rename the document, using the date and the initials "RL" to indicate that it is a redlined version.

D. Additional Instructions: Your professor may provide you with additional instructions regarding this assignment.

Bishop, Dickinson & Plath

MEMORANDUM

TO:	Associates
FROM:	Eliza Bishop
RE:	Telephone Conference with Cash Inbank, Attorney for Arthur Cole Lector
DATE:	September 23, 2012

I spoke with Cash Inbank today and am writing out a summary of that conversation here. Would much rather meet with all of you in person right now, but I am sitting in the Elite Flyer Lounge at the airport, waiting for a flight to New York City to meet with a new potential client.

Anyway, Cash told me something I didn't know about our client. Apparently, she has become romantically involved with Arthur Cole Lector. She and Arthur talked about the contract and decided to make some changes. (I checked this out with Anna and she confirmed.)

Originally, Arthur was going to lend Anna his car as security for the second payment on the paperweight. As it turns out, Arthur can't part with his car because he needs it to drive to work. Anna says she'll instead take a painting Arthur has in his bedroom as security for the second payment. The painting, by a local artist named Constance Gardner, is called "Love in the Afternoon." Its appraised value, according to Arthur, is about $10,000. Here's how it's now supposed to work: Arthur will give Anna the painting when he makes the first payment; Anna will give Arthur the paperweight. Anna will keep the painting until Arthur makes the second payment. Then she will return the painting. If Arthur fails to make the second payment, then Anna gets to keep the painting and Arthur gets to keep the paperweight.

I told Anna that she had better be willing to take $10,000 plus the painting for the paperweight because Arthur may decide not to make the second payment after all. She does not believe that this is much of a risk because she knows how much Arthur loves the painting and does not believe he'll be willing to part with it permanently.

Arthur was not entirely honest with Anna about what he wants to do with the paperweight. After seeing his paperweight collection, she got him to tell her that he wants to exhibit the whole collection this year and he wants "Bulbous I" to be part of the exhibit. Anna has agreed to let "Bulbous I" be part of the exhibit. Arthur has asked Anna not to tell anyone about his plans; if she does, he could lose a lot of money because he's in the process of negotiating the deal with several different museums across the country. Anna agreed not to tell anyone but us. (Make sure you carve us out of any non-disclosure provision you put into the contract.)

Arthur's also afraid that he may have inadvertently shared other confidential information with Anna—information about his plans to open a gallery near Superior and Wells in Chicago. He took her there to see the space one night. Anna has agreed to promise that she won't disclose any information about his plans for the gallery. Since Arthur's not sure what else he told her, he'd also like her not to disclose any other confidential information regarding his business plans. Anna is amenable to that. (I would draft a mutual non-disclosure provision. Think about the kinds of confidential information that Anna may have disclosed to Arthur.)

Arthur's afraid to promise not to change the paperweight after he buys it. His attorney said Arthur fears that promise may keep him from cleaning and polishing it. This is simple. Just put in an exception so that he is clearly permitted to perform normal maintenance on the paperweight.

Anna asked Arthur if we could put something in the contract about his credentials. She said that this amused him and that he had no objection. Anna wants Arthur to state that he's a private collector, and not an agent or employee of a museum or gallery (understandable since he originally told her that he was just going to use the paperweight on his desk at the insurance agency). She also wants him to say that the painting "Love in the Afternoon," by Constance Gardner, belongs to him and that he is not under contract to sell it to anyone else. She wants him to show her a copy of the painting's most recent appraisal before she signs the contract. If he does not show her the copy or if the appraisal does not value the painting at $10,000 or more, then Anna is not going to sign the contract.

I agreed with Cash that we should attach to the contract (as exhibits) a copy of Anna's diploma showing her MFA from Chicago Fine Art University and a copy of the certificate showing her membership in the "Glass Media Arts

Association." Cash also agreed that we should attach to the contract (as an additional exhibit) a copy of the painting's most recent appraisal.

Anna and Arthur agreed that Anna may borrow the paperweight back to exhibit it at a gallery or museum or in a show each year and that Arthur will not charge her a rental fee. Arthur wants her to keep his name out of it, so Anna has agreed to exhibit it without identifying him as the paperweight's owner. Apparently, Arthur is afraid that identifying him as the owner might tip people off to his plans to exhibit his paperweight collection. In the contract, Arthur wants Anna to say that she will not identify him as the owner during any exhibition. However, to protect his interests, he would like the paperweight to have a sign attached that says "Not for Sale." Anna understands his concerns and has agreed to do what he asks.

While I'm away, please put these changes into the contract. I'll take a look at the redlined agreement when I return. Thank you. With any luck, I'll be bringing home some more business.

Assignment 2

The Consignment Agreement

2A: THE WAIVER OF CONFLICT OF INTEREST AGREEMENT

Instructions

A. **Summary:** After reading the scenario below, you will draft a Waiver of Conflict of Interest Agreement, which you will ask your former client, Anna Claire Glass, to sign.

B. **Scenario:** It is now September 2015. Your new client is The Cole Lector Gallery, Inc., a corporation formed by Arthur Cole Lector (the "Company"). The Company owns and operates The Cole Lector Art Gallery (the "Gallery"). Arthur is the president of the Company and the senior curator of the Gallery. You may remember him from a deal you handled approximately three years ago, in which you represented Anna Claire Glass, an up-and-coming artist who sold him a paperweight for his personal collection. Since drafting the Paperweight Purchase Agreement three years ago, you have not performed any additional legal work for Ms. Glass. Nevertheless, you have kept in touch with her and taken her out to lunch at least once a year in order to maintain contact in case she finds herself in a position to send your firm additional business.

   The Company now wants to enter into a consignment agreement with Ms. Glass, so that it can exhibit, market, and sell her work for a commission. You remind your senior partner, Eliza Bishop, that you may not be able to represent the Company in this new transaction, given that you represented Ms. Glass against Mr. Lector in the paperweight purchase deal. Even though three years have passed since that deal, Eliza asks you to talk to your firm's conflicts administrator, who will help you determine if a conflict exists. The conflicts administrator determines that a conflict does exist.

   Arthur and Ms. Glass are friends. Arthur tells you that he has already told Ms. Glass that he intended to contact your firm to seek representation in this deal. He believes that Ms. Glass does not object to your firm representing the Company in this deal.

C. **The Waiver of Conflict of Interest Agreement:** Eliza has asked you to do two things: (1) write a cover letter to Ms. Glass, explaining why you need her written consent to the firm's representation of the Company in this deal; and (2) draft a Waiver of Conflict of Interest Agreement, a copy of which you will enclose with your cover letter.

D. **Preparation for Drafting:** Your firm's conflicts administrator is new at the job and does not have a form Waiver of Conflict of Interest Agreement to give you. *You must complete this assignment without using any models, templates, or forms.*

Begin by looking at any guidance provided by the Model Rules of Professional Conduct regarding the "Client-Lawyer Relationship." More than one rule may be relevant to this issue. However, you are likely to find that Model Rule 1.9 ("Duties to Former Clients") and its associated Comments, are right on point. Determine what constitutes "informed consent" and how best to confirm that you have obtained that informed consent in writing. Then draft the letter and the Waiver of Conflict of Interest Agreement (the "Waiver").

E. **Content of the Waiver:** Make sure that the Waiver contains a signature line for Eliza Bishop and a signature line for Anna Claire Glass. Use all of the basic contract drafting principles you have learned when you draft the Waiver. Do not forget about using contract drafting concepts like covenants and representations and warranties and expressing them with the appropriate verbs. For example, you may be tempted to have Ms. Glass "acknowledge" that she has been informed of a potential conflict and that she "understands" what it means. Consider having her "represent" and "warrant" these things instead. One exception: You may use the word "waives" instead of "shall waive" to capture Ms. Glass's covenant to waive the conflict.

Think carefully about how your cover letter and your Waiver work together. Are you going to include the information about the potential conflict in the cover letter and then refer to the letter in the Waiver? Will you be attaching the cover letter to the Waiver as an exhibit? Or, do you want to inform the client of the conflict in the Waiver itself, so that attaching the cover letter is unnecessary? Use your best judgment, keeping in mind that the client must understand everything that you draft.

F. **Additional Consideration Re the Company:** Think about whether you should also write a letter to the Company, reminding them that you represented Anna Claire Glass against Arthur Cole Lector in the paperweight purchase transaction and letting them know that you have sought Ms. Glass's waiver of any conflict of interest associated with the firm now representing the Company in the consignment agreement deal. You may also want to consider whether to remind your new client that you are bound not to reveal any confidential information about your former client, Ms. Glass.

G. **Additional Instructions:** Your professor may provide you with additional instructions regarding this assignment.

2B: MEMORANDUM TO SENIOR PARTNER RE SUMMARY OF DEAL TERMS

Instructions

A. **Summary:** Each of you must read and digest the following fact pattern and memorandum from your client contact, Arthur Cole Lector, regarding the consignment agreement that his company, The Cole Lector Gallery, Inc., wants you to draft. Your senior partner, Eliza Bishop, has decided to ask one of the other senior partners in the firm, Emory Dickinson, to supervise your work on this transaction. Eliza is busy with another transaction and wants The Cole Lector Art Gallery, Inc. and Mr. Lector to get the attention they deserve. Therefore, Eliza has introduced Emory to Mr. Lector. Emory and Arthur get along famously and are pleased to be working together on the consignment agreement.

   Emory is very busy, too, and he would like you to draft a Memorandum summarizing the terms of the deal for him.

B. **Format of Memorandum:** Set up your memo as follows—

Bishop, Dickinson & Plath

MEMORANDUM

CONFIDENTIAL

TO:	Emory Dickinson
FROM:	[Insert Your Name]
RE:	Summary of Deal Terms
SUBJECT:	Consignment Agreement Between The Cole Lector Gallery, Inc. and Anna Claire Glass
DATE:	September 14, 2015

[Insert the text of the memo, single-spaced. Note that Emory would like this memo to be organized a specific way. First, he wants you to summarize the deal facts. Then, he wants you to list any legal issues that you think it may be necessary to research before drafting the contract. Finally, he wants you to make a list of additional questions that you want him to ask the client.]

To satisfy Emory's expectations, the main headings in your memo should be:

I. Known Deal Facts
II. Potential Legal Issues
III. Additional Questions for the Client

You may want to break up any one of the main sections into subsections with headings. This might be especially helpful to Emory in Section I.

C. **Collaboration:** If your professor permits, you and your classmates may draft this memo (or parts of it) in pairs or in teams. Alternatively, you and your classmates may brainstorm about Parts II and III of the memo in class. Your professor will guide you regarding how much collaboration (if any) is appropriate on this assignment.

D. **Additional Instructions:** Your professor may provide you with additional instructions regarding this assignment.

Fact Pattern for Consignment Agreement

It is September 2015.

Approximately three years have gone by since the artist, Anna Claire Glass, sold one of her original paperweights to Arthur Cole Lector, a man she met at The Mythical Beast Café. Anna Claire and Arthur signed a contract regarding the paperweight; Anna Claire delivered the paperweight to Arthur at the closing, as planned, and Arthur paid the initial down payment and the final payment on time. There were no contractual disputes. Arthur still owns the paperweight, which he displays as part of his personal collection in a well-lit case located in the upstairs ballroom of his mansion on Lake Michigan. He admits that he paid way too much for it because he was smitten with Anna Claire. Although Anna Claire used to "borrow" the paperweight in order to exhibit it at a museum or gallery for two weeks each year, she no longer does so.

Anna Claire and Arthur dated for about eight months after they met. They parted amicably when Anna Claire decided that she wanted to dedicate herself more seriously to her art. Arthur, who knew a lot of creative people, understood Anna Claire's need to go into isolation for a while. Besides, he had recently been admitted to Chicago Fine Art University, where he was going to pursue an MBA with an "arts" focus. He was glad that his romance with Anna Claire would not impede his studies.

Over the years, Arthur and Anna Claire remained friends, seeing each other at art shows approximately every other month and having dinner together every year on the anniversary of their breakup. They liked to celebrate their breakup because it was like a creative re-birth for each of them. Arthur had gone on to get his MBA and open a successful art gallery called The Cole Lector Art Gallery, located at 2400 Great Artist's Lane, in Chicago. Anna Claire developed her skills as an artist, working primarily with glass. She entered her glass sculptures in numerous local and national juried shows and won several prizes, including five "firsts," five "seconds," and three "thirds." She exhibited her work at some major galleries. And, she opened her own small studio, where she displayed and occasionally sold her work.

Even though Anna Claire now has an impressive "artist's résumé," she has not yet established a regular relationship with a gallery or an art dealer to help market and sell her work. Recently, over their annual dinner, Arthur and Anna Claire agreed that it was time for her to consign her glass sculptures to The Cole Lector Art Gallery so that Arthur could help her sell them. During dinner, Anna Claire and Arthur worked out the business terms of their deal.

Up until this point, with its other artists, The Cole Lector Art Gallery has been using a one-page, bare-bones consignment/exhibition agreement drafted by one of Arthur's non-lawyer classmates at Chicago Fine Art University. Last month, at a meeting of the We Sell Art Association ("WSAA"), Arthur ran into Eliza Bishop, the attorney whose firm had drafted the Paperweight Purchase Agreement between him and Anna Claire Glass. Although he understands that Bishop's firm is high-priced, he wants Bishop, Dickinson & Plath to draft the consignment/exhibition agreement between The Cole Lector Art Gallery, Inc. and Anna Claire Glass. Arthur plans to ask the firm to draft the agreement from scratch. (He refuses to show the firm the one-page agreement he has used with artists in the past because he does not want the firm to be influenced by its contents.)

You work as an associate attorney at Bishop, Dickinson & Plath. Last week, Arthur called your senior partner, Eliza Bishop, and asked her to have one of her associates draft a consignment/exhibition contract between Anna Claire Glass and The Cole Lector Art Gallery, Inc. Eliza, who is busy working on another transaction, invited Arthur to the firm to meet her partner, Emory Dickinson. Arthur agreed to work with Emory and the firm's associates on this agreement. Emory assured Arthur that his associates' hourly rate would be considerably lower than his own.

In order to save time (and thus, money) Emory asked Arthur to write him a memo describing the terms of the deal. Today, Emory received a copy of Arthur's memo in the mail. He has passed it along to you and asked you to draft the contract. You're overworked and exhausted, but you don't want to disappoint Emory (or Eliza), so you get to work immediately.

MEMORANDUM

TO: Emory Dickinson (Bishop, Dickinson & Plath)

FROM: Arthur Cole Lector

RE: Consignment Agreement with Anna Claire Glass

DATE: September 10, 2015

As you know, I'm an art dealer who sells fine art, primarily by exhibiting it at The Cole Lector Art Gallery at 2400 Great Artist's Lane, Chicago, Illinois 60611. I own and operate The Cole Lector Art Gallery through my corporation, The Cole Lector Art Gallery, Inc., which is incorporated in Illinois. I tend to use the word "Gallery" to refer to my corporation, so forgive me if that gets confusing. My friend, Anna Claire Glass, creates beautiful glass sculptures and has finally agreed to consign her work to the Gallery so I can help her sell it. (By the way, Anna Claire is not incorporated. She lives above her studio, which is located at 6213 Georgia O'Keefe Avenue, Chicago, Illinois 60614. She sometimes sells her work at her studio.)

Starting on November 1, 2015, and for the next two years (ending on October 31, 2017), the Gallery will be Anna Claire's exclusive agent for the exhibition and sale of her glass sculptures. The contract will cover the glass sculptures that Anna Claire has already created but not yet sold and any other glass sculptures that she creates during the two-year period, or longer, if we extend the contract. I would like the option to extend the contract for another year if I notify Anna Claire no later than 30 days before the end of that first two years.

Once the contract is in force, at any one time, the Gallery is to have in its possession at least five of Anna Claire's glass sculptures. Descriptions of the first five glass sculptures that Anna Claire will deliver to the Gallery are attached to this memo. (She has assured me that she won't change those five sculptures between now and then and that these are accurate descriptions of the sculptures she will deliver after she signs the contract.) Anna Claire will cover the costs of packing the sculptures, insuring them for transport, and shipping them to the Gallery. Anna Claire and I have assessed and agreed upon the value of each of the first five glass sculptures and set a Retail Price equal to that value. Once we sell one of Anna Claire's sculptures and it leaves the Gallery to be delivered to the new owner, Anna Claire will provide us with another glass sculpture to exhibit.

Anna Claire will pay the costs of any special materials needed to "frame" or "mount" her glass sculptures, with the exception of special lighting, which the Gallery will supply. For example, sometimes Anna Claire uses a wooden base or stand to display one of her pieces. She would have to supply and pay for that base or stand.

I am surprising myself by how much I sound like an attorney!

The Gallery will prepare and sign a Consignment Record for the initial five pieces and update and re-sign this record and send Anna Claire a copy of it each time that Anna Claire sends the Gallery a new piece. The Consignment Record will contain the standard stuff, clearly identifying each piece by title, description, medium, and retail price, as well as the date of delivery to the Gallery. In a sense, the Consignment Record will serve as a receipt.

As I may have mentioned, Anna Claire and I will agree upon the value of each work and set the Retail Price at that amount. In fact, I will visit her studio before we sign the agreement, and we will assign Retail Prices to all of her existing glass sculptures. (I guess she needs to verify in the agreement that she hasn't changed those Retail Prices that we previously set.) Each time she creates a new piece, Anna Claire and I will meet at her studio again to set the Retail Price. Once every six months, Anna Claire and I will review the Retail Prices set for her glass sculptures and make any adjustments necessary to bring the Retail Prices in line with the market and with Anna Claire's growing reputation.

I will keep all five of Anna Claire's glass sculptures on display in the Gallery at all times, except when we mount a solo exhibition for another artist. While Anna Claire's work is being displayed with the work of other artists, she will have no artistic control. I think she trusts that I will do it justice. During the solo exhibitions of other artists, I will carefully move Anna Claire's sculptures to the storage area of the Gallery.

The Gallery is going to market, promote, advertise, and sell Anna Claire's glass sculptures. Anna Claire knows that we'll need her to supply us with high-quality photographs of her work and authorize us to use these photographs as well as her name, biographical material, and likeness on our website and in any print materials we use to promote and sell her work. Anna Claire has also agreed to do at least three personal appearances a year in connection with our promotions of her artwork, as long as we pay any expenses she might incur in connection with these appearances. I expect that we'll be asking her to come to the gallery for her solo exhibit and to show up at the gallery at certain other times of the year.

Each time the Gallery sells one of Anna Claire's glass sculptures, the Gallery will get a commission equal to 50% of the Retail Price. Sometimes I give discounts of 15% off of the Retail Price to my regular clients or to clients who buy more than one piece by a particular artist. I do this primarily to make the clients feel appreciated, which is for the greater good of the Gallery. Therefore, even though some of my fellow gallery owners think I'm crazy, I deduct these discounts from my own commission rather than charging them to the artist.

Each time we sell one of Anna Claire's works, the Gallery will present the purchaser with an Artist Sales Contract ("ASC") for signature. The ASC will show the Retail Price of the work, the actual price paid, and any discounts given. Moreover, I promised Anna Claire that the ASC will identify the purchaser and remind the purchaser that he or she cannot alter, reproduce, or restore the work without the artist's permission. (You don't have to draft the ASC—just make sure my promise to Anna Claire goes into the agreement you are drafting.)

The Gallery will pay Anna Claire her portion of the Retail Price of any work sold within 30 days after receipt of payment. Naturally, she'll retain title in each work until the work is sold and paid for in full. Sometimes, we will allow a client to pay for the work in installments. If we do that, then the money from the installments will first be applied to pay any balance due to Anna Claire. If we accept a deposit from a client, then we will pay Anna Claire any amount due to her after the deposit turns into an actual payment for the work. The Gallery will be responsible for collecting the client's payments and will pay for any costs associated with collection. If a client defaults and doesn't pay, the Gallery will pay Anna Claire the remaining Retail Price of the item, less the Gallery's commission.

I don't intend to engage in any shenanigans. I will live up to my commitment to sell Anna Claire's glass sculptures at the Retail Price specified on the Consignment Record, unless I give a standard discount, as previously mentioned.

If Anna Claire sells any glass sculptures from her studio, then Anna Claire will pay the Gallery a commission of 40% of the Retail Price. She understands this because I explained to her that it is part of what it means to "work with a gallery." She and I will determine and set the Retail Prices of the glass sculptures at her studio. Anna Claire will sell the glass sculptures at the set Retail Price, unless she gives a discount, which will come out of her 60%. Anna Claire need not pay the Gallery a commission if anyone specifically requests her (i.e., "commissions" her) to create a new glass sculpture for him or her. Anna Claire has agreed to use an ASC for each studio deal and to send copies of all ASCs to me at the Gallery on a monthly basis. At that time, she will also pay the Gallery any commissions owed on glass sculptures sold from her studio.

Anna Claire does not want the Gallery to allow a potential purchaser to take any of her works home "on approval." Sometimes we do that in order to allow the potential purchaser to see the work at home and determine whether he or she can live with it. Because this "take-home-on-approval" practice makes Anna Claire especially nervous, I have promised her that I will not use it with regard to any of her works.

It goes without saying that Anna Claire does not have the power to veto any purchaser.

On the last day of each month, the Gallery will give Anna Claire copies of all ASCs for her work, along with a summary accounting sheet. The summary will state which of her works have been sold, to whom (name and address), at what price, and at what discount, if any. The summary will also state the current whereabouts of each of the other glass sculptures consigned to the Gallery. The first accounting will be due on November 30, 2015. If the agreement terminates for any reason, the Gallery will give Anna Claire an accounting no later than the end of the fifth business day after the effective termination date. If Anna Claire ever gets antsy and wants to inspect our books, I have no problem with that, as long as she does it privately during the Gallery's business hours and as long as she doesn't do it too often.

I've agreed to purchase an all-risk insurance policy to cover Anna Claire's glass sculptures while they are in the Gallery. This policy will cover fire, flood, theft, and any other damage to the work while it is in the Gallery's possession. I've agreed to insure each work for 60% of its Retail Price. I've agreed to be responsible for all loss or damage of any consigned work from the date we get it until it is returned to Anna Claire or delivered to a purchaser. If something happens to a work and it needs restoration, I'll give Anna Claire the first right to restore the work and, if she refuses or doesn't have time, I'll give her the right to approve any outside restorer I might engage.

I know you'll ask me if we talked about termination provisions. I have to admit that we really didn't want to envision a bad end to the relationship. Anna Claire did mention that, if she dies, she'd like the Gallery to continue exhibiting and selling her glass sculptures until all of them are disposed of. During this part of our dinner conversation, I learned for the first time that Anna Claire has an heir—a son named Cole L. Glass. She wants Cole to reap the benefits of the contract after her death.

Now that I think about it, it's pretty standard for both Anna Claire and the Gallery to be able to terminate the contract for any reason by giving 60 days prior written notice to the other party. And I want the right to terminate the contract within 10 days if Anna Claire fails to deliver glass sculptures to replace those that the Gallery has sold or, worse yet, if Anna Claire stops creating glass sculptures altogether. I don't think she'll ever stop working in glass, but stranger things have happened. Some artists who work in glass have been so seriously burned on their hands and arms that they are unable to continue working in the medium. Others totally switch mediums on a whim.

I haven't guaranteed Anna Claire that the Gallery will sell any of her work. However, I suppose she should have the right to terminate the contract if we fail to sell a certain number of pieces in a contract year. I want to set that number very low—let's say we have to sell at least two. We ought to be able to do that with our eyes closed. Oh, and Anna Claire's been reading the gallery news. She heard about the gallery down the street from us going bankrupt a few months ago. I think I want to let her terminate the contract if we go bankrupt or become insolvent. A provision like that might ease her mind some.

Anna Claire's a bit of a fatalist. She also wants to be protected if I happen to die during the contract's term. She'd like to be able to terminate within 30 days because she doesn't want to work with any other agent. I'm flattered, but I'm also in great health and am not too concerned about this.

Once the contract is terminated, or if I don't renew before the end of that first two years, the Gallery will return all of the consigned work to Anna Claire at its own expense. Please put in any other termination provisions you think are reasonable. Anna Claire and I will consider them.

Before I forget, I want you to make sure that you put in whatever language is necessary, if any, to protect Anna Claire's rights under the Visual Artists Rights Act. It's my understanding that Anna Claire has not registered the copyrights in any of her glass sculptures. She believes that the registration process is tedious and useless. Nevertheless, the Gallery will do whatever is necessary to make sure that Anna Claire's copyrights in the consigned works are protected, including making sure that copyright notices appear on all reproductions of the works used in publications such as our catalogs or advertising materials.

Also, please make sure the contract contains whatever is required for compliance with the Illinois Consignment of Art Act. As a longstanding member of the WSAA ("We Sell Art Association"), I've pledged to uphold that statute.

Once a year, as we do for all of our artists, we will mount a solo exhibition of Anna Claire's work. Anna Claire will provide us with a sufficient number of additional glass sculptures for the exhibition, which will take place in May or June of 2016 and last three weeks (21 days). Anna Claire asked me if she could have total artistic control over the solo exhibition and over the quality of the photographs used for advertising, but I did not totally yield. I explained that she needs to trust me and value my experience in this area. However, I will give her the opportunity to see the solo exhibition 7 days before it begins. I'll grant any of her reasonable requests to change how the work is mounted, but I will have the discretion to decide whether each request is reasonable. Anna Claire's very picky about how her work is displayed, especially because it's glass and must have appropriate lighting to show well. I will yield total control of the quality of the photographs used for advertising to Anna Claire, but she will have to pay for the photographs.

It was tough to work out who would pay the rest of the expenses for the solo exhibition. Anna Claire will pay for all of the expenses of packing, insuring for transport, and shipping her work to the Gallery for the exhibition. The Gallery will pay to pack, insure for transport, and ship all of her unsold work (less the 5 sculptures that remain in the Gallery) back to Anna Claire. Of course, the Gallery will also pay to pack, insure for transport, and ship Anna Claire's work to any purchasers.

With regard to the other costs of mounting the exhibition, Anna Claire and the Gallery will split the expenses as follows:

Expense	The Gallery	Anna Claire Glass
advertising	100%	
catalogs	100%	
announcements	100%	
postage	75%	25%
pedestals/framing		100%
lighting	100%	
photos		100%
party for opening	100%	
all other expenses	80%	20%

Anna Claire will supply the Gallery with her personal mailing list. The Gallery will agree to keep it confidential. Come to think of it, we need Anna Claire to agree not to disclose any of the Gallery's Confidential Information she learns by virtue of her association with the Gallery. For example, she should not be permitted to tell anyone how she and I arrive at Retail Prices for the glass sculptures or who the Gallery's clients are. I'm sure you can come up with a list of similar things.

It has taken me a very long time to draft this memo, and I am trying not to forget anything important. I expect that you'll put in something standard about Anna Claire representing that she's a professional artist who has exhibited at galleries and won awards and such. Also, I'd like to see the contract state that I am a member in good standing of WSAA and that I have owned and operated the Gallery for 2 years. It also seems important to mention that Anna Claire and I have known each other for so many years and that I purchased the first glass sculpture that she ever sold to anyone (that paperweight). I'm not sure whether that should go in the contract.

Anna Claire and I would like to sign this contract on October 1, 2015, even though it won't go into effect until November 1, 2015. We can have the closing at the Gallery at 9 a.m. on October 1. I suppose I need the right to walk away from the deal if Anna Claire doesn't deliver the first five glass sculptures by November 1st. Or if she significantly alters any of those five sculptures between the closing date and November 1st.

I guess you'll add in all of the necessary fine print. Make sure she doesn't have the right to delegate her duty to create the sculptures to some apprentice or something. Anna Claire is unique. No one else can supply me with glass sculptures as incredible as hers. If we get into a dispute—which I highly doubt will ever happen—we'd rather go to arbitration than to court. And I know we both want some flexibility to amend the agreement if things change. Since we're both in Illinois, it sure seems like Illinois law ought to apply. But I'll leave that up to you and your associates. After all, you're the experts!

2C: E-MAIL TO CLIENT RE POTENTIAL ETHICAL QUESTION

Instructions

A. **Summary:** You will analyze the scenario below in order to determine whether your firm may be violating any ethical rules if you include a provision like the one that Arthur Cole Lector has requested in the contract. You will also decide whether the provision that Arthur is requesting violates the Illinois Consignment of Art Act, 815 ILCS 320 ("ICAA").

B. **Scenario:** As a member of the We Sell Art Association, Arthur Cole Lector (on behalf of The Cole Lector Gallery, Inc.) has agreed to abide by the ICAA. In fact, Arthur has asked you to put everything in the contract that is necessary for him to live up to this pledge.

Recently, Arthur learned about a mental patient entering a nearby art gallery and completely destroying the consigned paintings of 25 artists by spraying them with a fire extinguisher containing chemicals that dissolved the paint. The owner's insurance did not cover this scenario. The owner— who, by the way, had overpriced all of the work—wound up having to pay the artists the purchase price (previously recorded in the consignment agreement) of every destroyed piece.

This story really frightened Arthur. While he intends to reasonably price Anna Claire's sculptures and to record those prices in the Consignment Agreement, he would like to pay Anna only 50% of the purchase price if the glass sculptures are destroyed and the destruction is not covered by his insurance. Arthur wants you to put this provision in the contract.

C. **Preparing the E-Mail to Client:** Determine whether the provision that Arthur wants included in the contract violates the ICAA. Review the Model Rules of Professional Conduct and the Comments to those rules for guidance about whether you should include the provision in the contract.

Draft an e-mail to the client in which you explain any risks associated with putting the requested provision in the contract. Emphasize the legal and business risks for the client over any potential ethical risks to you, the attorney. Use your judgment about how much to include regarding the potential ethical risks. Perhaps you will have to explain those risks to convince the client to change his position.

Take every step you can take to assure that your e-mail remains confidential and protected by the attorney/client privilege. Send it only to Arthur Cole Lector. Mark it "Confidential: Attorney/Client Privilege." Explicitly request that Arthur not forward the e-mail to anyone else, which could destroy the e-mail's privileged status. At the end of the e-mail, include a standard notification-to-unintended-recipients box like the following:

This communication is from Bishop, Dickinson & Plath. E-mail text or attachments may contain information that is confidential and may also be privileged. This communication is for the exclusive use of the intended recipient(s). If you have received this communication in error, please return it with the title "received in error" to Emory Dickinson at Bishop, Dickinson & Plath. Then delete the e-mail and destroy any copies of it.

D. **Tone of Client E-Mail:** Remember that you are drafting an e-mail to the client, not to your best friend. Draft the e-mail in Plain English, using a professional tone. Do not use abbreviations or acronyms (like "OMG") and do not type in all caps for emphasis or insert any emoticons. Your e-mail to the client should be only slightly less formal than a letter to the client. You are writing the e-mail presumably because it's faster to write and send via this method. While it might be better to communicate the results of your investigation via telephone, your client wants a written record for his files.

Remember to always keep your audience in mind. Arthur is a businessperson and art collector. Explain everything in terms that he may be able to understand.

E. **Additional Instructions:** Your professor may provide you with additional instructions regarding this assignment.

2D: ASSEMBLING THE FRAME: DRAFTING THE TITLE, PREAMBLE, BACKGROUND, WORDS OF AGREEMENT, DEFINITIONS, AND SIGNATURE LINES

Instructions

A. **Summary:** Using the deal facts contained in the fact pattern and memorandum to Emory Dickinson (following Assignment 2B), draft the Consignment Agreement's frame—the Title, Preamble, Background, Words of Agreement, Definitions, and Signature Lines. In preparation for this assignment, you may also review the sample agreements referenced under "Precedent," below.

B. **Precedent:** For this assignment, you may use the sample contracts cited below and only those sample contracts. This is a "canned precedent" assignment. In other words, in order to keep you focused on drafting rather than on searching for precedent, you are prohibited from using anything but the limited body (or "can") of precedent listed below. These are examples of the precedent you would be likely to find if you did your own search for artist-gallery consignment agreements on the Internet. You may not use any precedent other than the sample contracts listed here and any model contracts that your professor provides. If you do adapt or adopt any language from the samples provided, then you must cite your source, even if you have not quoted it directly. Your professor will tell you what citation format she requires.

> *Caution # 1:* Remember that every contract "breaks the mold." That is, each contract memorializes the terms of a particular deal. If you rely too heavily on precedent, you are bound to make some serious mistakes.
>
> *Caution # 2:* View each sample contract with a critical eye, applying all of the contract drafting principles that you have learned so far.

Can of Precedent[4]

http://www.artmarketing.com/artoffice/artist-agent.html
http://www.lehmannstrobel.com/files/pdfs/artist-agreement.pdf
http://www.enchantedcreek.com/Art/Contracts/artist-gallery.html
http://glitterworkshop.com/docs/consignment.pdf

C. **The "Frame" Metaphor:** Some parts of a contract are traditional and easily drafted using models. They create a "frame" for the business provisions of the contract. The Title, Preamble, Words of Agreement, and Signature Lines are rudimentary parts of the contract's frame. The Definitions and Background sections, while more difficult to draft, still should not contain covenants, conditions precedent, representations and warranties, and statements of discretionary authority—otherwise known as "operative" provisions. For that reason, the Background and Definitions sections are also part of the contract's frame, stabilizing it by adding more information about the deal and preparing the reader for the "picture" containing the operative provisions of the deal.

A "model" contract is different from a "sample" contract in that a "model" is a contract worth imitating. Applying the basic contract drafting principles that you have learned so far, you may examine the samples in the "Can of Precedent," above, in order to determine if any elements of their frames are worthy of imitation. However, in drafting the frame of the Consignment Agreement, you are most likely going to rely on the model Leaf Disposal Services Agreement or any other "model" agreement that your professor has supplied. The precedent will become more useful when you fill in the picture of the contract, as required by Assignment 2E.

Professors who teach contract drafting use various images to convey what contracts drafters do. Therefore, you may hear someone else refer to the "frame" as the "skeleton" of the contract and the "picture" as the "meat on the bones." If it helps you to think of the contract that way, please feel free to do so. The purpose of these metaphors is to help you break down the drafting process into manageable parts.

D. **The Preamble: An Example of Learning from a Model:** Provided that you have the right information, you can draft a Preamble for the Consignment Agreement by following the pattern of the Preamble in the model Leaf Disposal Services Agreement, reprinted below.

---

4. Your professor may substitute other citations for the ones included here.

LEAF DISPOSAL SERVICES AGREEMENT

Leaf Disposal Services Agreement made this 10th day of October 2007, between SpinGazer, Inc., a Delaware corporation with its principal place of business located at 1200 Ridge Avenue, Evanston, Illinois 60201 (the "Company"), and Fallen Leaves, Inc., an Illinois corporation with its principal place of business located at 2025 North Clark Street, Chicago, Illinois 60614 (the "Provider").

Ask yourself: Who are the parties to this contract? One is a corporation and one is an individual. For Anna Claire Glass, you obviously do not need to identify where she is incorporated and where her principal place of business is located. Simply say "an individual residing at [insert address]." In this case, you may also want to add that Anna has a studio at that same address, since she does occasionally sell sculptures from her studio.

You must choose a shorthand nickname for the individual and place the parenthetical containing the shorthand name *after* all of the identifying information about the individual. Therefore, after Anna's address, you may insert "(the "Artist")," for example. If you call Anna "the Artist," then you will want to give The Cole Lector Art Gallery, Inc. a nickname at the same level of generality. Perhaps for The Cole Lector Art Gallery, Inc., you will insert "(the "Gallery")" after the address of its principal place of business. Be careful here. Remember that later you must refer to the premises of The Cole Lector Art Gallery—and "the Gallery" makes more sense when you are referring to a place. Consider whether you may want to refer to The Cole Lector Art Gallery, Inc. as "the Company."

The placement of the shorthand names you choose for the parties, which function like in-text definitions, is very important. Perhaps it is hard to believe, but there could be more than one Anna Claire Glass in the world. By placing the parenthetical after her address, you make it more likely that you have clearly identified the "Anna Claire Glass" who is a party to this contract. The same goes for The Cole Lector Art Gallery, Inc. Clearly identify the party by placing the shorthand name for that party after the identifying information about that party.

When you draft the Preamble of your contract, pay careful attention to punctuation. The Preamble contains a lot of information and is difficult to read if not punctuated properly. Moreover, aside from the title, the Preamble is the very first thing that the reader will encounter in your contract. Even though it is formulaic, you can set a good tone by drafting it so that it reads smoothly. Proper punctuation helps.

Finally, you and your professor are likely to spend some time talking about what date you should insert in the Preamble. When is the contract "made"? Is it the same date when the contract is signed? Is this date different from the effective date of the term? Also, sometimes the date in the Preamble is preceded by the words "as of." Under what circumstances is it appropriate to use those words? Even a formulaic Preamble can present interesting questions that you are likely to bandy about in class.

E. **Title, Words of Agreement, and Signature Lines:** You and your professor will discuss what to call this contract. For the sake of convenience, I have referred to it as the *Consignment Agreement*, but you are not required to use that title.

The "Words of Agreement" used in the Leaf Disposal Services Agreement model are simple. After the Background section, insert "Accordingly, the parties agree as follows:". In most contracts, at about this point in the contract, you will see a lengthy "consideration" provision that sounds like complete gobbledygook. You and your professor are likely to discuss whether a formal statement of consideration is necessary if the contract itself makes it amply clear that consideration for the transaction does exist. The drafter of the Leaf Disposal Services Agreement has concluded that the contract does not require a formal statement of consideration.

You can easily imitate the Signature Lines and get them right. The Signature Lines from the Leaf Disposal Services Agreement are reprinted below.

AGREED:

SPINGAZER, INC.   **FALLEN LEAVES, INC.**

By: _____   By: _____
     Jackie Spingazer   Leif E. Liminator

Title: Director of Operations   Title: Supervisor

Since one party to the Consignment Agreement is an individual, you will need to adapt this format a bit. The names in boldface, all capital letters, above the signature lines are the formal names of the parties to the contract—not the shorthand names that you chose in the Preamble and used throughout the rest of the contract. So, where you see **SPINGAZER, INC.** and **FALLEN LEAVES, INC.**, above, you would substitute **THE COLE LECTOR ART GALLERY, INC.** and **ANNA CLAIRE GLASS**.

> **Note:** Generally, it is a good idea to put your client's Signature Line first. Believe it or not, this sometimes matters to the client.

Underneath the Signature Lines, type the names of the individuals signing the agreement. You do not need the word "By" if the individual signing is also the party. Just re-type "Anna Claire Glass" under her Signature Line, in upper and lowercase letters. Arthur will sign on behalf of The Cole Lector Art Gallery, Inc. Therefore, you *will* need the word "By" before his Signature Line.

Finally, do not forget to insert Arthur's title. Since Anna is an individual, you do not need to insert a "title" line for her.

F. **Background:** The purpose of the Background section is twofold—to put the agreement in context and to express the intentions of the parties.

You may be accustomed to seeing this section called "Recitals" and containing a list of "WHEREAS" clauses ending with the crescendo "NOW THEREFORE" clause. Plain English drafters avoid those clauses like the plague. Instead, draft the Background section in smooth prose. This is probably the only place in the contract where you get to tell a little story. Use it well. Who are the parties? What do they do? Why are they entering into this deal? The Background section should not be too long or too lopsided (containing more information about one party than the other).

The Background section is a place where you should avoid following your models too closely. It is not as formulaic as the Preamble, for example. Ask yourself: What do my readers need to know about the parties? About what happened before (if anything) and about what is about to happen (this transaction)?

Remember that you should not include any operative provisions in the Background section. Be very careful not to include any covenants, conditions precedent, representations and warranties, or statements of discretionary authority here. The courts generally will not give effect to operative language contained in a Background section. And, if you include a covenant in the Background section, you run the risk of forgetting to include it in the body of the contract, where it would actually obligate a party to do something.

Sometimes the parties want to clarify their intentions early in a contract. Even though the Background section should not contain operative provisions, it can contain a statement of the parties' intentions. Sometimes, if there is a contractual dispute, the court will give effect to a statement of intentions included in the Background section instead of, or in addition to, admitting parol evidence of those intentions.

G. **Definitions:** The model Leaf Disposal Services Agreement gives you some limited guidance about how to draft the definitions. It contains the prefatory language below.

As used in this Agreement, the terms defined in the preamble have their assigned meanings and the following terms have the meanings assigned to them in this Article.

If you have defined any terms, in-text, in the Background section, you must add the words "and in the Background section" to the prefatory language after the words "in the preamble." That way, you will not have to include any cross-references to those definitions in the Definitions article itself.

By looking at the model, you will see that most definitions use the verb "means" or "includes but does not include." You will also see that in-text definitions found in the body of the contract (but not in the Preamble or Background section) are cross-referenced here, using the verb phrase "has the meaning assigned in."

You and your professor will discuss how to choose what to define and how to draft the definitions. Remember that definitions are declarations and should not contain any operative language—no covenants, conditions, representations and warranties, or statements of discretionary authority. Think of a definition as a statement of what a term means whenever you encounter it used with a capital letter in the contract. If you want a party to undertake any kind of obligation, you must include it in the body of the contract rather than in a definition.

Important Note About Drafting Definitions as Part of the Frame: In practice, lawyers hardly ever draft a complete Definitions article before they draft the rest of the contract. In a sense, asking you to draft the Definitions before you draft the rest of the contract is an artificial exercise. Nevertheless, it is a good exercise and it may save you some time and energy. It forces you, as a novice contract drafter, to think in advance about what terms you may need to define. You can draft a definition for "the Gallery," for example, because you know that you will need to refer to it over and over again. You also know that you have to find a way to specifically identify the sculptures that Anna Claire Glass consigns to the Gallery so that it is always clear which sculptures you are talking about.

Moreover, drafting definitions in advance will prevent you from making the mistake of using too many in-text definitions. When a Definitions article contains too many cross-references to in-text definitions, the reader is forced to hop all over the contract to find out what things mean. Instead, by defining most terms in the Definitions article itself, you keep the reader happy by feeding her information. You also take the opportunity to educate her about the deal a bit before she launches into the contract. This may sound like a litigation drafting concept, but it holds true for contract drafting as well. As your reader moves into the contract, after reading a fully developed Definitions article, she is more likely to understand the rest of the contract.

If you remember to consider your audience(s), you will be more likely to achieve the goal of clear communication. Transactional attorneys who fail to consider their audience(s) give transactional attorneys a bad name.

H. **Additional Instructions:** Your professor may provide you with additional instructions regarding this assignment.

2E: FILLING IN THE PICTURE: DRAFTING THE CONTRACT'S OPERATIVE PROVISIONS

Instructions

A. **Summary:** This assignment assumes that you have already drafted the "frame" of the contract as required by Assignment 2D—or that your professor has asked you to skip that assignment and concentrate on "filling in the picture." Using the deal facts contained in the Fact Pattern and Memorandum to Emory Dickinson (following Assignment 2B, above), draft all of the operative provisions of the Consignment Agreement. The "operative" provisions do not include the "frame" of the contract— the Title, Preamble, Background, Words of Agreement, Definitions, and Signature Lines.

B. **Preparation for Filling in the Picture:** Before you begin to fill in the picture, you must do two things. First, review the Can of Precedent identified in Assignment 2D. Determine which topics are generally covered in a consignment agreement and evaluate each contract to see if it contains any language that you think you may be able to adapt or adopt for use in your contract.

Second, you must research any legal issues that you have identified so far. By now you know that you must at least read the Visual Artists Rights Act, 17 USCS § 106A ("VARA") and the Illinois Consignment of Art Act, 815 ILCS 320 ("ICAA").

> **Note:** Assume that the glass objects Anna Claire Glass is consigning to The Cole Lector Art Gallery, Inc. are all "sculptures."

If you have identified other legal issues that you feel you must explore in order to draft the contract, please seek direction from your professor. You should not spend too much time on legal research. Focus instead on drafting the contract.

C. **Filling in the Picture:** To fill in the picture, you must draft all of the operative provisions of the contract and decide how to organize them. Your professor will help you develop the basic skills you need to take the terms of the deal and translate them into contract concepts—covenants, conditions precedent, representations and warranties, statements of discretionary authority, and declarations.[5]

In practice, some call this *memorializing* the terms of the deal, which basically means getting the terms of the deal down on paper so that they have a legal effect. The paper (or contract) is the *memorial*. The parties should be able to turn to the contract whenever they have any questions about their rights and duties with regard to the particular transaction.

D. **Organization—Naming and Ordering the Articles and Sections:** Some provisions are traditionally placed in certain spots. For example, after the Definitions article, some drafters include a brief article containing the main covenants of the deal. One contract drafting expert, Tina L. Stark, calls this brief article the "subject matter performance provision."[6] The subject matter performance provision in the model Leaf Disposal Services Agreement is reprinted below.

Article III. Summary of Services and Fees

Section 3.01 Services and Fees. Subject to the provisions of this Agreement, the Provider shall perform the Services described in Article IV. To compensate the Provider for performing the Services, the Company shall pay the Provider the fees and reimburse the Provider for the expenses described in Article V.

---

5. Tina L. Stark, *Drafting Contracts: How and Why Lawyers Do What They Do* 9-10 (Aspen 2007) (describes the contract concepts as the "building blocks" of the contract and the process of converting business terms into contract concepts as a "translation skill").
    6. *Id.* at 39-40.

The drafter of the model Leaf Disposal Services Agreement put the subject matter performance provision after the Term article. While the exact order of these provisions sometimes varies, remember that the subject matter performance provision, the Term, and the Closing articles should appear near the beginning of the contract.

It is sometimes helpful to think of the subject matter performance provision as a thesis statement plus roadmap. It tells you the "main idea" (or "primary covenants") of the contract and points you to the places in the contract where you can find out more details about those covenants.

After the subject matter performance provision, the Term article, and the Closing article, the reader expects to find information about what the Artist is going to consign and what services the Company is going to provide, as well as how much money is going to exchange hands. Therefore, you must put the articles covering those topics close to the beginning of the contract.

At the end of the contract, right before the Signature Lines, place the contract's boilerplate provisions (sometimes called *General Provisions*). The Termination and Dispute Resolution articles generally come immediately before the boilerplate.

So, with the parts of the contract in their traditional places, and allowing for some flexibility in their exact order, your contract (not including the frame) will look something like this:

Summary of Services and Compensation
Term
Closing [if any]
The Consignment
Exhibition, Marketing, and Sale of Consigned Works
Commissions, Fees, and Expenses
[OTHER TOPICS TO BE COVERED]
Dispute Resolution
Termination
General Provisions

Note that the above italicized headings are offered as an example only. They are not set in stone. You are encouraged to draft your own appropriate headings for the articles you include in the contract.

One of the biggest challenges that a drafter faces is how to organize the business provisions not specifically listed above—that is, how to organize those "other topics to be covered." Start by making a list of every deal term not addressed in the named articles. Then, group those deal terms by topic and select a good name for the article covering that topic. Remember that "Artist's Obligations" and "Company's Responsibilities" are contract concepts, not topics. If you use a heading like "Artist's Obligations," you are indicating to the reader that all of the Artist's obligations are contained under that heading. More likely, the Artist's obligations are scattered throughout the contract.

Choose article names (and section names as well) that are specific and clear. Instead of "Artist's Obligations," for example, you may have articles or sections called "Joint Marketing Efforts" or "Replenishment of Consigned Works." Instead of "Company's Responsibilities," you may have articles called "Promotion of Consigned Works" or "Display and Maintenance of Consigned Works." Any of these articles or sections may contain obligations and responsibilities of one or both parties.

If you find that you have a number of miscellaneous deal terms that do not seem to fit anywhere, give them another look before deciding to create single-section articles. Single-section articles (other than the subject matter performance provision and the Term article) can make the particular topic seem like an undeveloped afterthought or, conversely, give the particular topic too much weight. It is better to put the miscellaneous deal term into the article it relates to the most, even if it is not a perfect fit.

Once you have found a place for every deal term and named the articles you want to include in the contract, decide what order to put them in. Generally, place the articles in order from most important topic to least important topic. However, if you are describing a process, it may make more sense to put some of the articles in chronological order. There is no magic bullet of contract organization. However, it is very important to remember your audience(s). Ask yourself what your reader needs to know and when your reader needs to know it. Also, remember the terms of the deal. For example, if your client stressed that the Company was very concerned about maintaining enough inventory of the consigned works, then you may want to move that topic up near the beginning of the contract for emphasis.

E. **Boilerplate Provisions:** The fact pattern and the memo from your client contact may not contain all of the facts you need in order to select the appropriate boilerplate provisions to include in your contract. Follow your professor's instructions regarding which boilerplate to include. A valuable resource to help you understand the history and evolution of various boilerplate provisions is the book *Negotiating and Drafting Contract Boilerplate*, edited and co-authored by Tina L. Stark (American Lawyer Media 2003). Your professor may also ask you to complete Assignment 2G, which requires you to think about both parties' concerns regarding the inclusion of certain boilerplate in the contract.

F. **Additional Instructions:** Your professor may provide you with additional instructions about this assignment.

2F: PUTTING THE PICTURE IN THE FRAME: FINISHING THE DRAFT CONTRACT

Instructions

A. **Summary:** You will now insert the "picture" that you drafted in response to Assignment 2E into the "frame" that you drafted in response to Assignment 2D. The result will be one completed draft of a Consignment Agreement (with a title that you have selected).

B. **The Process:** Inserting the picture into the frame is not merely a mechanical process. Once you have merged the two documents together, you must make sure that the picture fits the frame properly; in other words, you must review the draft contract as a whole and ask yourself at least the following questions:

- ☐ Is the Title I chose for the contract still appropriate?
- ☐ Have I consistently referred to the parties to the contract using the shorthand names that I gave them in the Preamble?
- ☐ Do the full party names in the Preamble (not the shorthand names) match the full party names above the Signature Lines?
- ☐ Does the date in the Preamble reflect the date when the contract is made? If this is different from the effective date of the contract, have I clarified that in the body of the contract?
- ☐ Do the addresses in the Preamble match the addresses in the "Notice" provision included in the boilerplate?
- ☐ Did I include enough information in the Background section? Is there anything else that I may want to add to that section? Is there anything I may want to take out?
- ☐ Do I use my defined terms whenever it is appropriate? [*Note:* This is called "letting your defined terms do their work."]
- ☐ Did I remember to capitalize my defined terms in the body of the contract?
- ☐ Are there any lengthy phrases that I repeat more than once that could perhaps be defined terms?
- ☐ Are there any concepts that I repeat in different ways each time that I should perhaps be saying the same way each time? Would a defined term help?
- ☐ Are there any defined terms that I never use or use only once? (If so, you probably do not need to define that term.)
- ☐ Have I included a cross-reference to every in-text definition in the Definitions article? Are my definitions still in alphabetical order?
- ☐ Whenever I use a cross-reference, have I referenced the correct article or section?
- ☐ Have I used cross-references in the body of the contract to help the reader understand the relationship between parts of the contract?

☐ Are all of my article and section numbers in order? Does each have an appropriate heading?

☐ In the "Survivability" boilerplate provision, have I listed all of the sections of the contract that will survive the early termination of the contract or the end of the term?

☐ Do all of the parts of the contract work well together?

Once you have answered all of these questions and made any necessary adjustments to the contract, you can move into the editing and proofreading stage described below.

C. **Editing and Proofreading:** Using the Contract Drafting Checklist provided in Appendix 3, go back over your draft contract again. The checklist is set up to help you take the long view first. Think about the transaction. Have you captured all of the terms of the deal? Have you translated them into the right contract concepts? Have you answered all questions about the rights and duties of the parties with regard to this transaction? Have you raised any questions without answering them? Is your contract well organized, coherent, and coordinated? Does it read smoothly? Is it easy to follow?

The checklist then asks you to look at some formatting issues that are directly related to readability. Review those issues, remembering also that well-chosen headings and the judicious use of "white space" enhance the readability of a contract. Do not remove headings or white space in order to make sure you do not exceed the page limit for this assignment. If you need guidance about how to avoid exceeding the page limit, seek your professor's help.

Following the checklist, now make sure that your contract contains all of the essential parts. Then review each part. Finally, under the broad heading "Plain English," the checklist directs you to make sure that you have not made any grammatical, mechanical, or typographical errors.

Once you have gone through the checklist, prepare your contract for submission by proofreading it carefully, using the proofreading tips and tricks contained in Appendix 5. Finally, go back to the original assignment sheet and verify that you have followed all of the directions regarding submitting the contract to your professor. There is something particularly disturbing about a transactional attorney who fails to follow directions. Failing to follow directions indicates that you are not detail oriented, which, in practice, can make your supervisor and your client mistrust you. It can also lead to a dangerous loss of credibility with the attorney representing the other side.

D. **Submitting the Contract:** Do one final thing before you submit your contract: Make sure that you are turning in a clean copy. That is, make sure that you have eliminated any highlighting or comments to yourself that you may have used during the drafting process. Practicing attorneys, both litigators and deal lawyers, can tell many war stories about forgetting to delete comments or critiques before filing documents or sending drafts to the other side. You do not want to make such an embarrassing mistake. You may also want to make sure that your document does not contain any hidden personal or metadata, such as information about when you finished the assignment. Check the software you are using to figure out how to eliminate that information.

E. Additional Instructions: Your professor may provide you with additional instructions about this assignment.

2G: CONSIDERING THE BOILERPLATE PROVISIONS

Instructions

A. Summary: You will work with your classmates to review the standard boilerplate provisions and determine whether your client, The Cole Lector Art Gallery, Inc. (the "Company"), has any particular concerns that can be addressed by altering the standard boilerplate language in the Consignment Agreement. Ultimately, you will draft the boilerplate that you will include in the final Consignment Agreement.

B. The Nature of Boilerplate: Boilerplate is not engraved in stone. Do not make the mistake of believing that boilerplate is language that has been tested in court and therefore cannot be changed. Always read the fine print carefully and remember that you can negotiate for and draft changes to any boilerplate provision.

C. Filling in the Chart:[7] Think about what positions both the Company and the Artist would be likely to take with regard to each standard boilerplate provision. Make a good attempt to walk in each party's shoes. Complete the chart by filling in columns 3 and 4. Note that the provisions in this chart do not appear in any particular order. You must decide what order to put them in when you draft the contract. Note also that, although "Confidentiality" and "Dispute Resolution" provisions are sometimes considered to be boilerplate, those provisions do not appear on this chart. You should draft separate articles to cover those issues—articles that precede the boilerplate provisions.

> *Caveat:* This exercise does not cover every boilerplate provision that you should include in your contract.

---

7. The descriptions of boilerplate provisions included in the chart are derived from Tina L. Stark, *Drafting Contracts: How and Why Lawyers Do What They Do* 167-180 (Aspen 2007).

D. **Drafting the Boilerplate for the Consignment Agreement:** Once you
have completed the chart, refer to your textbook for some standard boilerplate language. Re-draft that language, taking into account your client's
concerns. For example, the Company may want the right to assign the
contract if the Company is sold. Since standard boilerplate language
provides for no assignment without the written consent of the other
party, you will re-draft that language to carve out an exception for
when (or if) the Company is sold.

E. **Additional Instructions:** Your professor may provide you with additional
instructions about this assignment.

Boilerplate Provision	Description	The Company's Concerns	The Artist's Concerns
Assignment	A transfer of rights to a third party		
Delegation	Appointment of another person or entity to perform either a duty or a condition		
Choice of Law and Forum Selection	Prevents disputes as to the governing law; parties choose which law will govern; parties also agree that a particular court will have jurisdiction over them with respect to disputes about the contract		
Notice	Provides that parties may give notice by fax, personally, or by overnight carrier; notice is effective only upon receipt		
Severability	Expresses parties' intent that the court enforce the valid provisions of a contract, even if it finds one or more other provisions to be illegal or invalid		

Boilerplate Provision	Description	The Company's Concerns	The Artist's Concerns
Amendment	Provides that no oral amendments will be enforceable; states parties may amend only by written agreement		
Merger/ Integration	Says the contract is the final and exclusive expression of the parties' intent (i.e., the contract is fully integrated)		
Force Majeure	Parties are relieved of the burden of performing because an event has rendered performance impossible		

2H: SIDE LETTER RE SPECIAL EXHIBITION

Instructions

A. **Summary:** Your client, The Cole Lector Art Gallery, Inc. (the "Company"), has asked you to draft a "side letter" memorializing a new, but not completely unrelated, agreement it has struck with the artist, Anna Claire Glass. Your client does not want to terminate the Consignment Agreement already in place (the "Agreement"); nor does it want to push the Artist into terminating the Agreement.

B. **Scenario:** Anna Claire Glass has been invited to be one of the headliner artists at an international exhibition at the Museum of Contemporary Glass Sculpture in Stockholm, Sweden. She has written to Arthur Cole Lector about this opportunity. Read the following letter from Anna Claire Glass to Arthur Cole Lector. Read also the following e-mail string between Arthur and your senior partner, Emory Dickinson.

In brief, Anna wants to borrow back the five sculptures currently on consignment with the Company and take a brief hiatus from supplying the Company with additional sculptures. The Company is willing to agree to Anna's request, as long as the Company can protect its investment and assure an ongoing interest in Anna's work.

C. **Side Letters, in General:** Do not look for an example of a "side letter" on the Internet or in forms books. Instead, with your professor's guidance, think this through.

Side letters are generally used to clarify an issue in a contract or to address an issue that the parties failed to cover in the contract. Collective bargaining agreements, for example, often have numerous side letters that become a part of the main agreement.

Clients like The Cole Lector Art Gallery, Inc. will sometimes request that you draft a side letter because they believe that it will take you less time than drafting a separate contract and will therefore cost them less money (since you generally are billing them by the hour).

D. **Drafting the Side Letter:** Address the side letter from your client to Anna Claire Glass. (You have verified that she is not represented by an attorney; therefore, your client may contact her directly.)

It is a good idea to think about a side letter as being a contract in its own right. Ask yourself what the consideration is for the Company's agreement to allow the Artist to include the consigned work in the international exhibition. Make sure that you clarify that the side letter concerns a bargained-for exchange by describing that exchange in the body of the letter.

> **Note:** You can accomplish this without including an archaic statement of consideration that is full of meaningless gobbledygook!

Think first about the Agreement and how the side letter will work with the Agreement. Include language clarifying that the side letter does not override the Agreement; nor is the side letter superseded by the Agreement. The side letter is, in effect, a written agreement amending the Agreement in certain limited ways.

In order to make sure that the side letter does not get lost or overlooked, make sure that you provide for it to be attached to and incorporated into the Agreement. Then follow through, making sure that both your client and the Artist receive new copies of the Agreement with the signed side letter attached as an exhibit. (This is what you would do in real life. Your professor will let you know whether he wants you to do this for purposes of this assignment.)

Remember to include language stating that this side letter is the only amendment to the Agreement and that the remainder of the Agreement's provisions will remain in effect. Include signature and date lines for both parties (and a title line for Arthur Cole Lector). Arthur will sign and date the letter, fill in his title, and mail it to Anna Claire Glass for her signature. The letter should include instructions for her to sign and return the letter to Arthur as soon as possible. Remember to inform Ms. Glass that the side letter is not effective until it is signed by both parties.

E. **Additional Instructions:** Your professor may provide you with additional instructions about this assignment.

Anna Claire Glass
6213 Georgia O'Keefe Avenue
Chicago, Illinois 60614

June 30, 2016
Attn: Arthur Cole Lector
The Cole Lector Art Gallery, Inc.
2400 Great Artist's Lane
Chicago, Illinois 60611

My Dear Artie:

I just received a letter inviting me to participate in the international exhibition at the Museum of Contemporary Glass Sculpture in Stockholm, Sweden, three months from now. I know you'll be as excited as I am that they want me to be one of the featured artists in a show they are calling "Imaginative Modern Artistic Glass Extraordinaire" or "IMAGE," for short. The only problem is that the curators want me to send them at least 20 pieces and I only have 15 completed sculptures here at my studio.

Would it be possible for you to loan me the 5 sculptures that you have in the Gallery right now? I know that I consigned them to you and that our contract says that I have to supply you with 5 sculptures at all times. Would you be willing to let me out of that part of the contract for 40 days or so? IMAGE lasts from October 1, 2016, through October 30, 2016. I would need the ten additional days for shipping my work to and from Sweden.

If you agree to this, I'll pay for packaging and shipping everything both ways. I'll also buy additional insurance to cover all the sculptures for the entire time period. You can come to my studio and we can go over the retail prices of everything one more time. If I sell anything while it's on exhibit in Sweden or afterwards, as a direct result of the IMAGE exhibition, I will pay you your regular commission as if the particular sculpture was on display at the Gallery (as opposed to the lower commission you get if I sell it out of my studio).

I think that this can be a win/win situation for both of us. My work will get a lot of exposure and, in addition to what I sell during the exhibit, I am sure to sell even more work after I return home. I want to continue our business relationship. I have no intention of terminating the contract, though I guess that will be one of my options if you should refuse this request. So, please, please let me know if you can do something like write me a letter giving me permission to borrow the sculptures currently on display at the Gallery. If you want to have your lawyer put a bunch of stuff in there that makes you feel better about this arrangement, please do. I'll agree to whatever is reasonable so that we can continue to work together and prosper.

Sincerely yours,

Anna Claire Glass
Anna Claire Glass

E-Mail String Between Arthur Cole Lector and Emory Dickinson

From: Arthur Cole Lector   Sent: 7/10/2016, 7:30 a.m.

To: Emory Dickinson

Cc:

Subject: Side Letter to Consignment Agreement with Anna Claire Glass

Dear Emory:

By now you've had a chance to read Anna's letter. I agree with her that this could be a win/win for us, but I'm pretty concerned about not having any of her sculptures on display during the IMAGE exhibition. Anna seems amenable to you putting some things in the letter that will make me feel comfy with this arrangement. Please add that she will provide me with high-resolution, actual size color photos of the five sculptures that she removes from the Gallery. I can then put those photos in their place with a sign saying that the actual sculptures are currently on display at the prestigious IMAGE exhibition in Sweden. What do you think?

* * *

From: Emory Dickinson   Sent: 7/10/2016, 7:45 a.m.

To: Arthur Cole Lector

Cc:

Subject: Side Letter to Consignment Agreement with Anna Claire Glass

Arthur:

Good idea. Let's also put in a certain amount for the insurance Anna carries. What do you think will be the total retail value of all 20 sculptures that she displays at IMAGE?

Emory

This communication is from Bishop, Dickinson & Plath. E-mail text or attachments may contain information that is confidential and may also be privileged. This communication is for the exclusive use of the intended recipient(s). If you have received this communication in error, please return it with the title "received in error" to Emory Dickinson at Bishop, Dickinson & Plath. Then delete the e-mail and destroy any copies of it.

*   *   *

From:	Arthur Cole Lector	Sent: 7/10/2016, 8:45 a.m.
To:	Emory Dickinson	
Cc:		
Subject:	Side Letter to Consignment Agreement with Anna Claire Glass	

Emory—I added up all of the retail prices we last set (some of which may be out of date) and it came to about $842,000. Let's ask her to insure them for a million and a half or so. That way we get a little cushion in case Anna and I decide to raise the retail prices when we re-examine them before she goes off to Sweden. Do you have any other thoughts about how I can safeguard my investment?

Art

*   *   *

From:	Emory Dickinson	Sent: 7/10, 2016, 10:42 a.m.
To:	Arthur Cole Lector	
Cc:		
Subject:	Side Letter to Consignment Agreement with Anna Claire Glass	

Art—

Sorry it took me so long to respond. Was in a meeting I couldn't avoid. Maybe you can use this IMAGE thing as leverage to get Anna to agree to allow you to extend the contract for two years instead of the one year provided for in the Consignment Agreement. I also suggest that you ask her to agree to advertise your gallery by having cards available that identify The Cole Lector Art Gallery, Inc. as her exclusive sales agent. Try to get some publicity for the Gallery out of this—maybe she can even post a sign if the IMAGE rules permit.

Emory

P.S. I'll ask my associates to see what other safeguards they can come up with.

* * *

From:	Arthur Cole Lector	Sent: 7/10/2016, 11:16 a.m.
To:	Emory Dickinson	
Cc:		
Subject:	Side Letter to Consignment Agreement with Anna Claire Glass	

E—

I like your ideas! Yes, please do get your team of associates thinking about this little side letter. They're a pretty smart bunch. Remind them, though, that Anna is my friend and I don't want to even tempt her to think of terminating the contract. Can you send the draft by the end of the day?

ACL

* * *

From:	Emory Dickinson	Sent: 7/10/2016, 11:22 a.m.
To:	Arthur Cole Lector	

Cc:

Subject: Side Letter to Consignment Agreement with Anna Claire
                  Glass

A—

No problem. Just send me a list of the names of the 5 sculptures you now have
on site so we can identify them in the contract. You'll also have to create a list
of the 15 she has in her studio. We can attach that to the side letter later. Send
the list of 5 right away.

E.

*   *   *

From: Arthur Cole Lector   Sent: 7/10/2016,
                                                   11:29 a.m.

To: Emory Dickinson

Cc:

Subject: Side Letter to Consignment Agreement with Anna Claire
               Glass

E—

Fast enough for you? They also have I.D. Nos.

1. Hideous Ice Cap, No. 859
2. Inside a Dreamsickle, No. 860
3. Memory Cube, No. 861
4. Portrait of an Empty Head, No. 862
5. See-Through Soccer Ball with Goldfish, No. 863

ACL
P.S. Please add that Anna will pay for me to travel to the IMAGE exhibit—
business class airline ticket and overnight accommodations for three nights.
Seriously! Just got off the phone with her and she liked the idea.

Assignment *3*

The Public Art Commission Agreement

3A: NON-DISCLOSURE AGREEMENT: DRAFTING THE DEFINITIONS OF CONFIDENTIAL INFORMATION

Instructions

A. **Summary:** In Assignment 3E, you will be assigned to represent either the City of Chicago (the "City") or Anna Claire Glass (the "Artist"). The City wants to commission the Artist to create a glass sculpture commemorating the Great Chicago Fire. Ultimately, you will negotiate and draft a public art commission agreement embodying the negotiated terms of the deal. (Read the General Information for Both Parties, below.)

Before the parties can negotiate further, they need a non-disclosure agreement ("NDA") to protect any confidential information that they may disclose to each other during the course of the negotiations. This assignment requires you to draft the definitions of "Artist's Confidential Information" and "City's Confidential Information." You will later incorporate these definitions into the NDA (as part of Assignment 3B).

B. **Using Precedent:** You may review any NDAs you can locate in order to determine how "Confidential Information" is generally defined. However, definitions of Confidential Information contained in NDAs are notoriously full of meaningless language that does not take into account what information actually is going to be disclosed by each party during the course of their negotiations. You must closely examine any precedent you find, tailor it to the terms of your deal (that is, to what kinds of confidential information the parties to this deal are likely to disclose to each other), and translate it into Plain English.

C. **Focus:** The purpose of this brief exercise is to make you focus on who is going to disclose what to whom. In law practice, as in-house counsel at a corporation, for example, you may find the vice president of sales standing at your office door five minutes before a scheduled meeting, demanding that you prepare an NDA. You may have most of the NDA already prepared in a template. But the most important thing is for you to identify what information your client is going to disclose and for what purpose. You would not want your client to reveal a marketing strategy, for example, if you have not included "marketing strategy" in the list of things considered Client's Confidential Information. Nor would you want the other side to use the information about your client's marketing strategy for any purpose other than the particular project about which the parties are negotiating.

You must also be very careful to describe as specifically and narrowly as possible the information that the other party is going to reveal to your client. Parties will frequently bring their own NDAs to meetings and attempt to get other parties to agree not to disclose a wide range of information, much of which is simply not confidential. Limit your client's risk by limiting the kind of information your client agrees not to disclose.

D. **Procedure and Format:** Think about what you know about the transaction. What confidential information has your client most likely already disclosed to the other side? What confidential information is your client likely to disclose to the other side during the course of the continuing negotiation? Make a list of these specific items. Your goal is to avoid using a vague definition like "any information that has commercial value to the Artist [or City]."

Draft two separate definitions as described below:

"Artist's Confidential Information" includes [insert list of specific items], and [catchall phrase].

"City's Confidential Information" includes [insert list of specific items], and [catchall phrase].

The "catchall phrase" is designed to make sure that your definition covers things that you have not listed but that are similar to the items in your list. For example, your catchall phrase could be something like "and any other similarly sensitive or proprietary information revealed by the City to the Artist during the negotiations." You can do better than that! Look at the precedent you have gathered to see if you can find a definition of Confidential Information that employs a better catchall phrase.

After you say what each party's Confidential Information includes, you must put in the standard exceptions to the definition of Confidential Information, which generally cover things like "information that has previously entered the public domain." You can easily find out what these standard exceptions are by looking at almost any NDA.

Introduce these exceptions by stating: "Neither the Artist's nor the City's Confidential Information includes [insert standard exceptions.]"

E. **Additional Instructions:** Your professor may provide you with additional instructions about this assignment.

General Information for Both Parties

It is now September 2021.

Anna Claire Glass and Arthur Cole Lector are married. Their son, Cole, was the best man at their small wedding, which took place at the Art Institute of Chicago, in the alcove housing its glass paperweight collection. (Anna did not change her name.)

Right before the wedding, Anna and Arthur mutually agreed to terminate the Glass Sculpture Consignment and Exhibition Agreement between Anna and The Cole Lector Art Gallery, Inc. Subsequently, Arthur sold the gallery, dissolved The Cole Lector Art Gallery, Inc., and retired.

Anna is now a world-famous glass sculptor who markets her work primarily through her website (www.aclaireglass.com). A few months ago, to Anna's delight, the City of Chicago contacted her to see if she would be interested in designing a large glass sculpture commemorating the Great Chicago Fire of 1871. The city wants to place this sculpture in Millennium Park on a green expanse that is empty, but for a number of mature trees.

Anna has already met once with the city's Director of Commemorative Art, Sean B. O'Leary, who asked her to call him "Sean." Coincidentally, Sean is a direct descendant of the legendary Mrs. O'Leary whose cow allegedly started the Chicago Fire by kicking over a lantern in the O'Leary's barn. During their meeting, Anna presented her idea for the sculpture and Sean conditionally approved it.

In grade school, while studying the Chicago Fire, Anna was impressed by the role that the wind had played in the conflagration. Thus, she envisions a glass sculpture of red, orange, yellow, and metallic gold flames flying sideways rather than going straight up. The flames will create an irregularly shaped "wall" surrounding (or "engulfing") the trunks of the mature trees on the site in Millennium Park. Furthermore, the sculpture will have strategically placed openings that will allow the wind to play it like a flute. On a particularly windy Chicago day, Anna expects the sculpture to emit a "howl" resembling the cries of the hundreds of people who died in the fire. At night, the sculpture will be lit from within and will be visible from Columbus Drive.

Sean told Anna that the city would like the sculpture to be designed, created, and fully installed no later than June 20, 2022, just in time for the annual "Taste of Chicago" celebration.

3B: NON-DISCLOSURE AGREEMENT: DRAFTING THE OPERATIVE PROVISIONS

Instructions

A. **Summary:** This assignment assumes that you have completed Assignment 3A and that you now have in hand the definitions of Artist's Confidential Information and City's Confidential Information. Using those definitions, you will complete the Non-Disclosure Agreement ("NDA") that the parties will sign before they begin negotiating the terms of the Public Art Commission Agreement. The attorneys for the Artist and the City have met and agreed upon the operative terms that they want to include in the NDA. The City's corporate counsel assigned a junior attorney to take notes during this meeting (copy attached). The City has read the notes and believes that they accurately represent what the parties agreed to at the meeting.

B. **Using Precedent:** You may review any NDAs you can locate in order to help you determine how NDAs look and what provisions they generally contain. (You may want to refer to the same NDAs you used when drafting the definitions of Confidential Information in Assignment 3A.) You must apply everything you know about good contract drafting to any language you adopt or adapt from the available precedent. For example, remember to use "shall" for covenants and to draft in the active voice. Say "The City shall not disclose the Artist's Confidential Information" as opposed to "The Artist's Confidential Information shall not be disclosed by the City."

Remember, also, to eliminate all legalese from any precedent you use. Do not develop the lawyerly bad habit of using two or even three words when one strong word will do. For example, say "The Artist shall not disclose the City's Confidential Information" as opposed to "The Artist shall not reveal, disseminate, or disclose the City's Confidential Information."

> **Note:** Reasonable people may disagree about whether "disseminate" carries a different meaning from "reveal" and "disclose" and should therefore be included. Always ask yourself if all of the words in your list are necessary to carry your meaning. (Certainly "reveal" and "disclose" are synonymous. Eliminate one of them.)

C. **Organization of the Non-Disclosure Agreement:** Draft a Preamble for the NDA, just as you would for any other contract. Follow the model Leaf Disposal Services Agreement Preamble shown below.

LEAF DISPOSAL SERVICES AGREEMENT

Leaf Disposal Services Agreement made this 10th day of October 2007, between SpinGazer, Inc., a Delaware corporation with its principal place of business located at 1200 Ridge Avenue, Evanston, Illinois 60201 (the "Company"), and Fallen Leaves, Inc., an Illinois corporation with its principal place of business located at 2025 North Clark Street, Chicago, Illinois 60614 (the "Provider").

The tricky part about the Preamble for your NDA (as well as for the Public Art Commission Agreement that you will draft after you complete your negotiation) is that you have to know how to identify the City of Chicago. This may require a little research. Look online for a City contract. There you will find the "buzz words" you need. You do not have to put in an address for the City, although you will include an address in the "Notice" boilerplate provision. (You can make up that address.) The Artist is acting as an individual, so you simply say "an individual residing at [insert address]."

For the Background section in your NDA, do not succumb to blindly following precedent by inserting a number of "WHEREAS" clauses culminating in the big "NOW, THEREFORE" clause. Instead, simply insert a brief description of why the parties are going to be revealing confidential information to each other. What does the City want to discuss with the Artist? In the Background section, you may want to create an in-text definition of "Project" that you can use throughout the NDA. Remember that your client is entering into an NDA to protect information revealed to your client during the negotiations about the Project.

After the Preamble, you should include the words, "Accordingly, the parties agree as follows," unless you determine that it may be important to use a fuller statement of consideration in this NDA. Since both parties are exchanging Confidential Information, and both parties are agreeing not to disclose that information, the consideration for the contract is inherent in the contract itself. But, because the consideration for an NDA may not be as obvious as it is for a purchase or services agreement, you may want to include a statement like, "Accordingly, in consideration of the mutual promises contained in this Agreement, the parties agree as follows." Do not revert to gobbledygook by adding the words "and other good and valuable consideration, the receipt and sufficiency of which is hereby mutually acknowledged." Keep it simple.

After the statement of consideration, organize the remainder of the NDA as follows:

Definitions
Term
Basic Non-Disclosure Obligations
[Other Operative Provisions]
General Provisions
Signature Lines

Draft the basic non-disclosure obligations before you cover any other operative provisions. You will find precedent in which the drafters describe both parties' non-disclosure obligations in one section or paragraph. In order to avoid the difficulties of the "Both parties shall not" construction—including having to define "Disclosing Party" and "Recipient"—try drafting one section containing the City's non-disclosure obligations and another section containing the Artist's non-disclosure obligations.

After you draft the parties' basic non-disclosure obligations, you must decide what other operative provisions you need to cover and organize them in a logical way. For example, you will want to talk about what happens to the Confidential Information when the term of the NDA ends. You may want to cover this topic near the end of the contract, since it addresses what is to happen at the end of the parties' relationship. When considering how to organize the "other operative provisions," keep your audience in mind. You still have to consider an audience wider than just the parties' signators and the parties' attorneys. Remember that other City executives who have a "need to know" the Artist's Confidential Information, for example, may have to see the NDA so that they understand their own non-disclosure obligations.

Next, look at the precedent you have located to determine what kind of boilerplate provisions generally appear in an NDA. Most NDAs have merger/integration and choice-of-law provisions, for example. Some have severability provisions as well. Think about your client's needs. If you believe that any other boilerplate should be included to address your client's needs, put it in. For example, perhaps several years after signing the NDA, your client will need to disclose the other party's Confidential Information to a third party. If you think that might happen, you may want to include an amendment and modification clause so that it might be possible to shorten the NDA's term.

D. **Formatting the Non-Disclosure Agreement:** After the Definitions article, you can use simple numbered paragraphs with headings to format the NDA. So, for example, the Term and Non-Disclosure Obligations sections might look like this:

1. **Term.** This Agreement begins on [insert date] and ends [insert date].
2. **City's Duty Not to Disclose Artist's Confidential Information.** [insert body of provision].
3. **Artist's Duty Not to Disclose City's Confidential Information.** [insert body of provision].

E. **One Final Note About the Nature of Confidential Information:** Remember that parties can reveal confidential information both orally and in writing. In other words, much of what the parties say to each other may never be put down in a document but may still constitute confidential information. Do not make the mistake of assuming that confidential information is only contained in written documents. Be sure that your NDA takes this into account.

F. **Additional Instructions:** Your professor may provide you with additional instructions about this assignment.

From the desk of:

Willa C. Williams

Subject: Notes of Meeting Between Anna Claire Glass and the City of Chicago

Re: Terms of Non-Disclosure Agreement (Public Art Commission Negotiations)

Date: October 1, 2021

The Artist asked that the City stamp any document considered to contain the City's Confidential Information with the word "Confidential." The City explained that it would not be possible to ensure that all of its employees involved in the negotiation (and preparation for the negotiation) remember to stamp documents "Confidential." The City has a broad universe of people to control. Therefore, the City does not want to accept the risk that some of the City's Confidential Information might not be considered confidential just because someone forgot to stamp it.

Since the Artist is self-employed and likely to be the only one who handles documents containing the Artist's Confidential Information, she can easily stamp any documents containing the Artist's Confidential Information with the word "Confidential" in the upper right-hand corner. She agreed to do this.

The Artist asked that the City only share the Artist's Confidential Information (whether contained in documents or otherwise) with people in the City's employ who have some genuine need to know what the documents contain.

The City agreed. Both parties agreed that those City employees with a "need to know" include at least the Director of Commemorative Art, the City's attorneys, and the City's Chief Accountant. At this time, it is not possible for the City to identify exactly who else may need to see the documents containing the Artist's Confidential Information.

The City knows that the Artist will want to share some of the City's Confidential Information with her spouse, Arthur Cole Lector, who is retired but still helps the Artist market her work. She may also need to share the City's Confidential Information with her attorneys, and, of course, her financial advisors. The Artist agreed not to disclose the City's Confidential Information to anyone else unless she gets the City's written permission first. (She anticipates perhaps needing to consult a civil engineer regarding how to construct a sound internal structure for a glass sculpture this large. She agreed that she would seek the City's written permission before doing that because it would most likely involve disclosing the City's Confidential Information.)

Both the City and the Artist agree that they will show the NDA to everyone on the permitted list and get those individuals to sign an acknowledgment stating that they have read the NDA and understand that they are undertaking the same obligations as the signators. Both the City and the Artist also agreed that, if they have to show the other party's Confidential Information to anyone not on the permitted list, they will get that person to agree not to disclose the information and have that person sign a similar acknowledgment.

The Artist wants to make sure that entering into this NDA does not bind her to enter into a contract with the City to create the sculpture. The City has the same concern—i.e., that the NDA not bind the City to engage the Artist to create the sculpture—and would like to include some language to that effect in the NDA. Both parties want this language to be prominent in the NDA.

There was much discussion about how long the duties not to disclose should last. The parties finally agreed that the non-disclosure obligations should last for five years after the negotiation is completed, if the negotiation does not result in a contract. If the negotiation does result in a contract, then the parties want the non-disclosure obligations to last for the life of the contract plus five years and not to be superseded by the contract.

For both parties, the duties not to disclose the Confidential Information will include the obvious—not disclosing to anyone but those on the permitted list—as well as protecting the other party's Confidential Information just as the recipient would protect its own. Also, the parties are only going to use the Confidential Information in connection with the project at hand—the City's commissioning of the Artist to create a glass sculpture commemorating the Chicago Fire. Both parties want the NDA to state the reason why they are disclosing the information to each other—to evaluate whether or not to enter into that commission agreement.

After the parties finish negotiating, if they decide not to enter into a contract, both parties must return each other's Confidential Information immediately. The parties agreed to deliver the Confidential Information contained in documents by messenger. If the parties do enter into a contract, a party can keep the documents containing the Confidential Information until the other party requests its return. All Confidential Information must be returned by messenger within five business days of the other party's request. Alternatively, the party holding the Confidential Information may destroy the documents and provide an Affidavit of Destruction, signed by the Artist or the Director of Commemorative Art, as appropriate.

If either the City or the Artist is compelled to produce the other party's Confidential Information by a court order or subpoena, then the compelled party will let the other party know right away by telephone and e-mail. That way the owner of the Confidential Information can decide whether to move for a protective order or take some other action to prevent its disclosure. The City was particularly adamant about this point.

Finally, both parties want the existence of the NDA and its contents to remain confidential, except that the parties may show it to people on the permitted list, who will also agree to keep its existence and contents confidential.

3C: PREPARATION FOR THE NEGOTIATION OF THE PUBLIC ART COMMISSION AGREEMENT

Part I: Finding, Evaluating, and Using the Relevant Precedent

Instructions

A. **Summary:** Re-read the General Information for Both Parties included in Assignment 3A. You will now search for contracts that will be likely to help you draft a Public Art Commission Agreement. Once you locate the relevant precedent, you will review it and begin creating a negotiation prep sheet.

B. **Resources:** You may look for precedent in the library and on the Internet. *You may not contact the City of Chicago or any other city or entity in order to locate precedent.* You may not purchase any forms, whether from a store or online. You may not use any precedent in your own files (from a previous job or a summer position) or any precedent you obtain from an attorney. Finally, you may not use any contracts obtained from other students who have taken this class. Pretend that the library and the Internet are your only resources.

C. **What to Look For:** When you look for precedent in the litigation context, you try to find cases that are as close to your case as possible. If your case is about intentional infliction of emotional distress and involves one neighbor terrorizing another by putting dead insects and snakes on the other neighbor's doorstep, you would be very happy to find another case with nearly identical facts. If that case turns out to be in the same jurisdiction as yours, you would be even happier. Most likely, you will have to settle for cases with similar or analogous facts—and you may need to look beyond your jurisdiction.

In the transactional context, when you look for precedent, focus first on what kind of contract you are being asked to draft. For the purpose of this assignment, you want to find public art commission agreements. While it may be helpful to find a public art commission agreement about a large glass sculpture that is destined to be placed in a public park, it is not as important to find a contract with nearly identical facts as it might be if you were trying to prove a case in the litigation context. Moreover, while searching for precedent in the transactional context, you do not have to be as conscious of jurisdictional issues, though you do have to familiarize yourself with any laws that affect your deal (as you will do in Assignment 3D).

Is it important to find a public art commission agreement in which the City of Chicago is a party? Of course! If you find a City of Chicago public art commission agreement, you can use it like any other precedent (after the appropriate review and evaluation). Additionally, it may also help you with Assignment 3D, which requires you to find out if there are any provisions that a City public art commission agreement must contain in order to comply with City regulations and ordinances.

More likely, you will find public art commission agreements from other cities—the equivalent of finding similar or analogous cases in the litigation context.

D. **How to Find It:** If you love books and libraries, you may be tempted to start looking for precedent there. However, unless you do not own a computer or cannot connect to the Internet, looking for books in the library would not be the most efficient way to begin.

Begin by surfing the Web. You may choose to do a general search, using the search engine of your choice, or to go to LEXIS or WEST-LAW to see what forms are available there. One very good online source of sample contracts is www.onecle.com (click on Business Contracts). There, you will find thousands of actual contracts used by businesses for various purposes. Another good online source of sample contracts is Findlaw.com (click on Learn about the Law; Small Business; and then Business Forms and Contracts). Remember that the samples you find on these sites are "samples," not "models."

For more about what that distinction means, see "Reviewing and Evaluating Precedent," below.

When you surf the Web seeking relevant precedent, start with a narrow search and then broaden it out. For example, you may want to start by searching for "City of Chicago public art commission agreement." From there, you might move on to "public art commission agreement." If you still do not feel as if you have found enough precedent, ask yourself what kinds of contracts are similar to a public art commission agreement. Perhaps searching for "art commission agreements" will reveal some commission agreements between artists and private entities containing useful provisions. Since "agreement" and "contract" are used interchangeably, be sure to search for both terms.

Do not forget to search LEXIS and WESTLAW. Both have databases containing contract forms.

If you prefer working with actual books, go to your law library and locate the "Forms" books. Skim through the table of contents or indexes to determine if the books contain any relevant forms.

E. **Reviewing and Evaluating Precedent:** Once you have located eight or ten relevant contracts, begin to review them. Ask yourself at least the following questions about each contract:

☐ How relevant is the precedent?
    ☐ Is it a public art commission agreement?
    ☐ Is it a private art commission agreement?
    ☐ Is it a commission agreement about a work of visual art (as opposed to, say, about a book)?
    ☐ Is it a contract from the United States (as opposed to the United Kingdom or another country, with different contract drafting methods and formats)?
☐ How is the agreement formatted?
    ☐ Does it contain all of the essential parts of a contract?
    ☐ If it does not contain all of the essential parts, what is omitted?
☐ What topics are covered?
    ☐ Does the agreement cover any topics that you would not have thought to cover?
☐ How is the agreement organized?
    ☐ What appears to be the organizing principle behind the placement of topics in the agreement? Importance? Chronology? Something else?
☐ Is it easy to find things in the agreement?
☐ Does the agreement read smoothly?
☐ Did the drafters use the appropriate verbs to express contract concepts?
☐ Did the drafters use the active voice?
☐ Did the drafters use Plain English throughout? In parts?

☐ Are there any places in the agreement that are heavy with legalese?

☐ Does anything in the agreement strike you as being particularly well drafted or handled?

After you finish reading through all of the relevant precedent you have found, rate the agreements on a scale of 1 to 5, with 1 signifying "best" and 5 signifying "useless." Make a note of which contracts contain "good language" about particular topics. The "good language" standard does not necessarily mean "well-drafted" language; you may just appreciate the way the drafters handle a particular issue as opposed to the way they write about it. Perhaps, for example, you find an agreement that requires the buyer to allow the artist to re-purchase the artwork if the buyer decides to sell it. The drafters may be the worst culprits when it comes to using legalese. Nevertheless, make a note of the language because it contains an interesting idea that you may want to include in your own contract.

After you have rated the contracts, look at the entire batch of precedent once again and make a list of the main topics covered in the agreements. If most of the agreements cover "Maintenance of the Artwork," for example, then you will most likely need to cover that topic when you negotiate and draft the Public Art Commission Agreement between the Artist and the City. If one agreement contains a provision that none of the other agreements contains, you may have found a provision particular to the transaction at issue in that agreement.

F. **Using the Relevant Precedent:** When you draft your contract, you may decide to adopt or adapt some language from the relevant precedent you found. If so, you must remember the following principles:

1. **Every deal is its own deal.** This means that no matter how close the relevant precedent seems to the deal you are negotiating, your deal is a different deal. On the surface level, the parties' names and addresses are different. On a deeper level, your deal may include many facts that are different from the deal memorialized in the precedent. Maybe, for example, the City is going to engage and pay the subcontractors rather than allow the Artist to engage and pay the subcontractors and be reimbursed, as provided in the precedent you have chosen to use. Remember to tailor the precedent to the facts of your deal.

2. **Cutting and pasting numbs the mind.** It is tempting to cut and paste. Resist the temptation. If you re-type the language instead, you are more likely to notice things about how it is drafted—like the way the drafters used "null and void" instead of just "void." Or the fact that none of the parties is mentioned in a sentence purporting to obligate one of the parties to do something. If you simply cut and paste the language and

rely on yourself to catch and fix those things in the editing and proof-reading stage, you are missing a golden, immediate opportunity. The best example of the way cutting and pasting numbs the mind is this: Many students make the mistake of cutting and pasting a piece of precedent from another contract and forgetting to change the names of the parties. When the reader used to seeing the "the City" and "the Artist" suddenly comes across "the Buyer" and "the Seller," she stumbles. If she is grading the contract, she takes off points.

3. **The naked drafter rules the world.** No, I am not advocating that you draft in the nude. I am advocating that you learn how to draft without relying on precedent. If you master the skill of translating deal terms into contract concepts (covenants, conditions precedent, representations and warranties, declarations, and statements of discretionary authority), then you will be able to draft a contract without having any precedent at hand. When your client asks you to put a unique provision in the contract, you will be the "can-do" lawyer—that is, the lawyer who can draft the provision on the spot without needing a precedential crutch. Exercising your "naked drafting" skills will make you feel smart, efficient, creative, and, yes, powerful! Moreover, when you decide to use precedent, you will have the skills necessary to help you analyze and improve the language in the provisions you decide to adopt or adapt.

4. **Mine the precedent for ideas, not language.** The best way to use precedent is to help you "see" how a contract like the one you are attempting to draft generally "looks." Reviewing some relevant precedent is a good way to get started on a drafting a contract that seems daunting. In other words, with the facts of your own deal foremost in your mind, you can use precedent to help you figure out what terms to define, what topics to cover, and what order to cover them in. You can also use precedent to help you discover whether you ought to include certain provisions because they are traditionally included in this type of contract or because they are required by law. (Of course, you must still do enough legal research to satisfy yourself that you have covered any legal issues the contract raises.)

Finally, ask your professor if he wants you to cite to any precedent you use. If so, find out what citation format he prefers.

G. **The Negotiation Prep Sheet:** After you have located some good, relevant precedent, use it to help you prepare for the negotiation of the Public Art Commission Agreement between the City and the Artist. Create a three-column table entitled *Negotiation Prep Sheet*. Label the first column "Topic," the second column "Description," and the third column "Position." Since you do not yet know which client you represent, leave the third column blank. In the first column, list the topics covered in the precedent. In the second column, insert some details about each topic. Your negotiation prep sheet will look something like this:

NEGOTIATION PREP SHEET

Topic	Description	Position
Maintenance of Artwork	Obligation to care for the Artwork after installation; method of maintenance, including cleaning solutions; distinction between regular maintenance and extraordinary repairs.	
Etc.	Etc.	

When you finish filling in columns 1 and 2 of your negotiation prep sheet, you will have a living document that you can revise in light of the legal research you do in response to Assignment 3D and the confidential instructions you receive from your client as part of Assignment 3E.

H. **Collaboration:** Your professor may permit you to collaborate with your classmates in locating, reviewing, and evaluating precedent as well as in creating the first negotiation prep sheet. If you do collaborate with your classmates on this assignment, you will get to see how different people approach the task of finding precedent. Which search engines do your classmates use? How do they word their first search? Their second search? Their third? Do they begin with LEXIS or WESTLAW? When they find something useful, how do they record it? Do they bookmark it? Copy the URL into a Word document? Print it out in hard copy? Do they make any spot judgments about the quality of the precedent they find? Do they dwell on one contract or continue searching until they have gathered a number of relevant contracts? And so on. . . . You will inevitably get some great ideas from your classmates. But the most valuable part of the collaboration lies in observing someone else's "process." It may open your mind!

I. **Additional Instructions:** Your professor may provide you with additional instructions about this assignment.

3D: CONTINUED PREPARATION FOR THE NEGOTIATION OF THE PUBLIC ART COMMISSION AGREEMENT

Part II: Researching the Legal Issues

Instructions

A. **Summary:** This assignment assumes that you have completed Assignment 3C. First, re-read the General Information for Both Parties included in Assignment 3A. In further preparation for your negotiation, you will now research the legal issues impacting the Public Art Commission Agreement between the City and the Artist. You will research the legal issues that you identified when locating, reviewing, and evaluating the relevant precedent as well as research any other legal issues that you have identified yourself or that your professor has identified for you. You will then revise the negotiation prep sheet, adding new topics and descriptions that address these legal issues.

B. **What to Look For:** When you reviewed and evaluated the relevant precedent, you may have found that several sample contracts contained references to particular statutes or municipal ordinances. Begin there. For example, if you have found any public art commission agreements involving a city, you probably noticed that those agreements contain boilerplate (or other provisions) that appear to address specific city ordinances or policies such as equal employment opportunity or conflict of interest. You must determine whether the City of Chicago requires its public art commission agreements to contain any similar provisions.

   You probably also noticed that most of the relevant precedent addresses copyright issues such as ownership and something called "moral rights." You must figure out what the copyright issues are. Although you need not become an intellectual property rights guru, you must do enough research to grasp what copyright issues arise when an entity commissions an artist to create a work of art. The relevant precedent will help you understand how drafters generally address those issues.

   Do not hesitate to research other legal issues that you or your professor have identified, even if you do not find them addressed in the relevant precedent. Remember that you have located "sample contracts," not models. Perhaps the additional legal research you do will uncover some key points that the sample contracts simply failed to cover.

> **Caveat:** Do not let yourself get too caught up in legal research. You are not striving to become an expert. Do enough research to satisfy yourself that you are competent to draft the contract—and rely on your professor to supply additional expertise, if need be.

C. **How to Find It:** By now, you know how to find statutes and municipal ordinances. Start with the primary sources: the statutes and municipal ordinances cited in any City of Chicago contracts that you have found.

Then, to locate the City of Chicago's policies regarding public art commission agreements or contracts in general, peruse the City of Chicago's website. I say "peruse" rather than "look at" because I want you to examine the website very carefully. In other words, you will have to spend some time there! Click on anything that appears to be relevant. Use the internal search function as well. If the website quotes from a particular statute or ordinance that you think may be relevant to the Public Art Commission Agreement, look it up and read it.

To research the "moral rights" issue, you can start with the U.S. Copyright Office's website or do a more general search, using the search engine of your choice. *Above all, remember to read the relevant portions of the statute itself.*

D. **The Negotiation Prep Sheet:** When you feel you have a pretty good grasp of the legal issues you have identified, add them to the negotiation prep sheet. Remember to include citations in your descriptions, since you may want to revisit these issues when you are negotiating or drafting.

E. **Collaboration:** Your professor may permit you to collaborate with your classmates in conducting the legal research this assignment requires. If so, you will benefit from seeing how someone else approaches a problem. Observing your classmates' "process" may make you decide to change your own way of doing things. Even if watching your classmates in action merely confirms that your own process is more effective, you are still likely to benefit from talking about the legal issues while you are researching them. In a good collaborative environment, participants take turns being the striker and the flint. When a striker is applied to flint, sparks fly. Sometimes you will raise a question (acting as the striker) and your classmate will propose an answer (acting as the flint). And sometimes, vice versa. You will both benefit from the sparks!

F. **Additional Instructions:** Your professor may provide you with additional instructions about this assignment.

3E: NEGOTIATION OF THE PUBLIC ART COMMISSION AGREEMENT: LETTER OF INTENT AND TERM SHEET

Instructions

A. **Summary:** For this assignment, you will represent either Anna Claire Glass (the "Artist") or the City of Chicago (the "City"). As you know from reading the General Information for Both Parties included in

Assignment 3A, the City wants to commission the Artist to create a large glass sculpture commemorating the Great Chicago Fire of 1871. The Artist wants to accept the commission. Your task is to negotiate the deal and draft the contract between the City and the Artist.

B. **Assume No Conflict of Interest:** If you represent the City of Chicago in this deal, you can assume that there is no conflict of interest in your representing the City against the Artist, even though you may have represented the Artist in connection with a previous deal. Alternatively, you may pretend that you have never represented the Artist in the past.

C. **The Negotiation:** Your professor will tell you which party you represent and which of your classmates will be your opposing counsel. Your professor will also give you some Confidential Instructions from your client.

Logistics:

1. Begin by re-reading the General Information for Both Parties included in Assignment 3A and reading the Confidential Instructions from your client.
2. After carefully reviewing the Confidential Instructions from your client, revise the negotiation prep sheet you prepared in response to Assignments 3C and 3D to add any topics mentioned in the Confidential Instructions but not listed on your negotiation prep sheet. If you know what your client's position is with regard to a particular issue, insert that information in the "Position" column.

> **Note:** If you do not know what your client's position is with regard to a particular issue—and you believe it is an issue that the contract ought to cover—make a note to ask your client about it.

3. Complete your negotiation prep sheet by asking your professor to answer any questions you have about your client's position on the issues. Your professor may choose to tell you what your client's position is, or allow you to decide what your client's position ought to be. Either way, be sure to complete the negotiation prep sheet before moving on to the next step.
4. Prepare to negotiate. Study your negotiation prep sheet and tweak it, if necessary. You will bring this sheet with you to the negotiation.
5. Talk to your opposing counsel to schedule a mutually convenient time and place for the negotiation. Make sure that you find a quiet place where you will not be disturbed and will not encounter other pairs of negotiators from your class. Allow at least two hours for your first negotiation session.
6. Do not show your negotiation prep sheet or the Confidential Instructions you received from your client to your opposing counsel (or to any

other students who represent the opposing party) at any time before, during, or after the negotiation. During the negotiation, you will use the information in your Confidential Instructions as your guide to your client's wishes. You will naturally and judiciously reveal some of the information to your opposing counsel during the course of the negotiation in order to achieve your client's objectives.

7. Your Confidential Instructions may or may not contain information about your client's wishes regarding every issue you need to cover in the contract. For example, your Confidential Instructions do not address every boilerplate provision that you may want to include in the contract. If you do not know what your client wants, ask your professor or negotiate for what you believe will be in your client's best interests.

8. During the negotiation, you and your opposing counsel should prepare a "Term Sheet," which will ultimately be attached to your Letter of Intent ("LOI") and should look something like this:

**ATTACHMENT A
TO LETTER OF INTENT**

Issue	Terms

---

9. In this negotiation, you MUST reach an agreement. While the negotiation itself is not graded, you will receive extra points for being especially thorough and for devising creative solutions to disputed issues between the parties.

10. If you need access to your client during the negotiation, please contact your professor. If you and your opposing counsel reach a stalemate on any issues, please contact your professor.

11. If you do not finish your negotiation in one sitting, schedule another mutually convenient time to meet. Remember that you are likely to continue negotiating during the drafting process.

D. **Drafting the Letter of Intent:** Once you have completed your negotiation, you and your opposing counsel must draft one LOI and submit it to your professor. Your professor will decide whether to grade the LOI itself, but he may simply want to refer to the LOI when grading your contract. Therefore, if you and your opposing counsel change any significant terms contained in the LOI during subsequent negotiations, your professor may ask you to revise the LOI and re-submit it.

DRAFTING THE LETTER OF INTENT

(A Mini-Assignment within the Negotiation Assignment)

1. Draft an LOI. You will attach the term sheet that you created during your negotiation to the LOI as Exhibit A.

2. Address the LOI to your professor.

3. Do not use any precedent to draft the LOI. Draft in Plain English. Do not include anything that looks like a covenant. This is not a contract. See No. 4, below.

4. The most important thing to keep in mind is that you do not want your opposing counsel to be able to say that the LOI is a binding contract whether your negotiations fall through or your negotiations result in a signed contract. The LOI contains preliminary terms, some of which are likely to change over time. Make sure that you emphasize that the LOI is not a binding contract by featuring this point prominently in the LOI.

5. State that the letter describes the terms that the City and the Artist have discussed about the project and include a brief description of the project. Mention that the terms are attached in Exhibit A.

6. Clarify that the parties are not bound by any of the terms in the term sheet unless they sign a contract including those terms.

7. Clarify that when the parties sign the letter they are not acquiring any rights or undertaking any obligations, and, especially, that they are not promising to enter into a contract with the other party.

8. Include a paragraph reminding the Artist and the City that they are bound by the Non-Disclosure Agreement ("NDA") they signed before they began negotiating this deal and that the NDA prohibits them from disclosing the existence or terms of this LOI. Alternatively, you can include non-disclosure obligations in the LOI. (However, since the LOI is not a contract, any covenants you include in it arguably are not enforceable.)

9. Insert signature lines for both parties. This is another reason to include the language about the LOI not being a contract. The LOI is likely to look like a contract because both parties sign it.

10. Remember to attach the term sheet to the LOI before submitting the LOI to your professor.

E. **Additional Instructions:** Your professor may provide you with additional instructions regarding this assignment.

3F: PREPARATION OF TALKING POINTS FOR MEETING WITH THE CITY'S GENERAL COUNSEL RE POTENTIAL ETHICAL QUESTION

Instructions

A. **Summary:** For the purposes of this assignment, pretend that you represent the City of Chicago. You must analyze the scenario presented below to determine whether you would be violating the Model Rules of Professional Conduct if you allowed the omission to stand. The City's General Counsel heard about the situation from the Director of Commemorative Art, who presented the omission to the City's General Counsel as a happy mistake that works in the City's favor.

B. **Scenario:** After negotiating the terms of the Public Art Commission Agreement with the attorney for Anna Claire Glass, you agreed that her attorney would prepare the first draft of the contract. You now have that first draft in hand.

Ms. Glass's attorney did a pretty good job; however, she left out one key term: The parties agreed that the sculpture would remain in place at its original site in Millennium Park for at least three years. As the attorney for the City, you recognize that the omission of this fact favors the City. If the glass sculpture is not well received by the public, then the City would like to be able to move it immediately to another less conspicuous location or to a warehouse. In truth, when you agreed to the three-year moratorium on moving the sculpture, you felt like you had conceded too much.

Given that Ms. Glass's attorney left the three-year moratorium provision out of the contract entirely, you must decide whether you are required to bring this omission to her attention.

C. **Analysis:** Analyze this scenario to determine whether you may be violating any ethical rules if you do not bring the omission of the three-year moratorium provision to the attention of Ms. Glass's attorney. Determine whether any specific portions of the Model Rules of Professional Conduct and the comments to those rules are applicable.

If you decide that failing to inform Ms. Glass's attorney of the omission would not violate the MRPC, are there any other reasons why it might not be a good idea to withhold this information?

Does the Visual Artist Rights Act, 17 USCS § 106A ("VARA") make the three-year moratorium provision unnecessary? In other words, is it possible that the City will be violating VARA if it ever moves the sculpture from its original Millennium Park site? Could the Artist's attorney have strategically omitted the three-year moratorium on moving the sculpture?

D. **Preparation of Talking Points:** "Talking Points" are simply notes that you prepare for yourself to structure your discussion with the City's General Counsel. You do not have to draft them using any particular format. That being said, it is a good idea to use headings and bullet points to keep yourself on track—especially if you get nervous talking to your supervisor. Include a brief statement of the issue. Then summarize what you have concluded and how you reached those conclusions. Conclude with "action points" in which you recommend how to proceed. Do not forget to cover how to manage the Director of Commemorative Art's gleeful reaction to the omission.

E. **Additional Instructions:** Your professor may provide you with additional instructions regarding this assignment.

3G: DRAFTING THE PUBLIC ART COMMISSION AGREEMENT

The Frame and the Picture

Instructions

A. **Summary:** Once you have completed your negotiations and drafted and submitted your LOI (as described in Assignment 3E), you will draft the Public Art Commission Agreement memorializing the terms of the deal that you negotiated with your opposing counsel. The two of you will turn in one completed contract.

B. **The Frame and the Picture:** Unlike what you did with the Paperweight Purchase Agreement and the Consignment Agreement in this sequence, you will not draft the frame and the picture of the contract separately. Since we will not repeat the instructions for drafting the frame and the picture here, you may want to review Assignments 1E and 1F or Assignments 2D and 2E.

C. **The Drafting Process:** In the real world, one of you would probably prepare the entire first draft and submit it to your opposing counsel, who would edit it and redline the changes. You would review her edits and decide whether to accept or reject each of them. You might then send another redlined version to her, showing additional edits that you have made. This back-and-forth process may carry you through many drafts.

For this assignment, I recommend that you and your opposing counsel consider operating as you would in the real world. This can work in the law school context if one of you has more time and fewer pending deadlines than the other. Ideally, the least busy person would prepare the entire first draft and submit it to the busier person for review. The back-and-forth editing and redlining process can then proceed.

Realistically, you and your opposing counsel are more likely to divide up the work of preparing the first draft so that the bulk of it does not fall on one student's shoulders. If you do divide the contract into parts, you will have to allow a lot of extra time before the contract is due for the two of you to make sure that the parts work together well. For example, you will need to make sure that both of you have used the same defined terms and that you have used them to mean the same things. This is trickier than you think, so you should try to complete a full draft as early in the process as possible. That way, the two of you can review, edit, redline, and repeat as often as you need to in order to produce a seamless, polished product.

Remember that your goal is to produce a contract that sounds as if it were written by one person, not two. If one of you drafts in Plain English and the other peppers his language with legalese, your contract will be split into two distinct halves. Alternatively, if the two of you have divided up the work so that you each have responsibility for drafting alternating articles within the contract, the reader is likely to feel like she is on a seesaw. Strive to draft with a consistent voice. To accomplish this, both of you will have to read the entire contract more than once. I recommend reading it out loud to each other and listening for the places where the language becomes more elevated or slips into legalese. The two of you can then work together to translate those passages into Plain English.

D. **Incomplete Confidential Instructions:** You may not have received any confidential instructions from your clients about some of the topics in your negotiation prep sheet (see Assignments 3C and 3D). Address any questions about your client's position on particular issues to your professor, who will either provide you with additional confidential instructions or give you permission to decide what would be in your client's best interests. Because this is a "simulated assignment," you may have to use your imagination. Do not go so far as to make up wildly improbable deal facts, but do feel free to be a little creative.

Include any boilerplate provisions appropriate for this particular deal as well as any boilerplate provisions that your professor suggests are necessary. Remember to negotiate about the language of the boilerplate provisions. While you may not have confidential instructions addressing every piece of boilerplate, you can imagine what your clients' concerns might be and address them. For example, if you represent the City and do not have any confidential instructions about delegation of performance, think about whether the City would want the Artist to be able to delegate her performance to another party. Most likely the City recognizes that the Artist is unique; only she can produce the sculpture that the City envisions. Therefore, you may want to negotiate to adjust the standard anti-delegation language (which allows a party to delegate only with the written consent of the other party) to address the City's concern. In other words, you may want to draft stronger anti-delegation language to indicate that the City would never even entertain the Artist's request for permission to delegate.

E. **Use of Precedent for Drafting the Public Art Commission Agreement:** As you know if you completed Assignment 3C, you may use any forms or templates you can find in the library or on the Internet. *You may not contact the City of Chicago or any other city or entity in order to locate precedent.* You may not purchase any forms, whether from a store or online. You may not use any precedent in your own files (from a previous job or a summer position) or any precedent you obtain from an attorney. *Finally, you may not use any contracts obtained from other students who have taken this class.* Pretend that the library and the Internet are your only resources.

  See Assignment 3C for some tips on how to locate, review, evaluate, and use the available precedent.

F. **Provisions Addressing Legal Issues:** Be sure to address in the contract any specific things that the parties must do in order to comply with the law. If you know that you need to address copyright issues, for example, spell out the parties' specific rights and obligations. Avoid the easy cop-out of saying, "The City and the Artists shall abide by the Copyright Act," or words to that effect. As the City's attorney, if you try to simplify your task by saying "The Artist shall abide by all City ordinances," it will be apparent that you did not take the time and care necessary to determine which city ordinances are relevant to this deal. Moreover, the Artist's lawyer might refuse to include that language in the contract because it is, in effect, redundant; that is, it simply amounts to her client's promise to obey the law, which the Artist must do even if she is not contractually bound. If there is a legal issue that you must address, include specific provisions that give the parties clear guidance about their rights and duties.

G. **Grading:** Unless your professor tells you otherwise, both you and your opposing counsel will receive the same grade on the contract you submit.

H. **Additional Instructions:** Your professor may provide you with additional instructions regarding this assignment.

The
GOLFER
Sequence

Assignment 1

The Putting Green Purchase Agreement

1A: ENGAGEMENT LETTER BETWEEN ATTORNEY AND CLIENT

Instructions

A. **Summary:** You will draft an engagement letter/retainer agreement between your law firm and a new client.

B. **Background:** You are an associate at the law firm of Payne & Associates. Betsy Bennett, an up-and-coming professional golfer, has asked your firm to draft a contract for her. She wants to purchase a customized putting green for the large backyard of her new home. The vendor she has selected for the job wants to do business with only a handshake. Ms. Bennett wants to get it in writing.

Both of Ms. Bennett's grandparents are retired attorneys. They advised Ms. Bennett to seek counsel, but they also told her to be wary of engaging an attorney without having a written engagement letter or retainer agreement in place.

To date, Payne & Associates has not required its clients to sign an engagement letter or retainer agreement. The senior partner, Sue Payne, has resisted formalizing client relationships in this way. Sue now wants you to draft an engagement letter that she can present to Ms. Bennett to communicate basic information about how the attorney/client relationship between Ms. Bennett and the firm is likely to work.

Sue wants the engagement letter to be a contract that both parties will sign, but she does not want it to be so formal that it frightens Ms. Bennett away or causes her to ask her grandparents to review it and suggest changes.

C. **No Use of Precedent:** Sue does not want you to use other engagement or retainer letters that you find through a library or Internet search or any other means. She would like to see what you can draft without using any precedent. She believes that, if you are not influenced by what other firms have already done, you will produce something fresh, creative, well-written, and tailored to this particular client's needs.

D. **Legal Research:** In preparation for completing this assignment, please read *Brian Dowling v. Chicago Options Associates, Inc. et al. (DLA Piper*

Rudnick Gray Cary (US), LLP), 226 Ill. 2d 277, 875 N.E.2d 1012 (Ill. 2007).

E. **Draft Specific to This Attorney/Client Relationship:** Sue does not want you to create a "form" engagement letter/retainer agreement to be used for all of the firm's clients. She wants you to focus on this particular client. If you do a good job, perhaps Sue will ask you to create a "form" later. Right now, Sue's main concern is that you cover the issues listed in the table below and that you capture the terms that Sue already has communicated to Ms. Bennett.

F. **Table of Issues and Terms:** Sue prepared this quick list of the issues that the engagement letter should cover and the terms upon which she and Ms. Bennett have reached agreement. The issues appear in no particular order.

Issue	Terms
Potential conflict of interest	We conducted a conflict search based on the info the client supplied and turned up no conflict
Personnel assigned	Sue Payne (senior partner) No junior partners Associates (any student in this class) Paralegal (Joanna Keets)
Division of labor and billing	Associates will do initial client interview and first draft of contract We bill for associates' time, plus partner supervisory time Partner will not attend client interview but will review associates' work and communicate with client
Refund of unused fees	Will refund unused fees (if any)
Initial consultation (Sue already met with Ms. Bennett)	No charge, but clarify initial consultation already occurred
Fees	Senior Partner—$450 per hour Junior Partner—$300 per hour Associate (any level)—$175 per hour Paralegal (any level)—$95 per hour

Issue	Terms
Security retainer (intended to secure payment of fees for future services the firm is expected to perform)	$1,500; will be applied to the first invoice
Trust account (separate from firm's property; remains client's property until firm applies it to charges for services actually rendered)	Will put the $1,500 security retainer in client trust account
When work will begin	Upon receipt of signed engagement letter and check for $1,500 security retainer
Who firm works for	Betsy Bennett (individual) [Note: This is her formal name (she is not "Elizabeth").]
Scope of services	Draft contract for purchase of putting green for Ms. Bennett's backyard; no more than that; if she wants more, then must sign another engagement letter
Client's obligations to firm	Cooperate Tell us everything about the deal Provide any supporting documents needed Be available; reachable through multiple means Pay bill within 30 days of receipt
Business hours of firm	7 a.m. to 8 p.m.; but give her Sue's cell phone number [make up this number]
Invoices	Sent out at end of each month
Quarter hours	Bill out time in 15-minute increments
Expenses	Client pays for overnight mail; no markup, just a pass-through
Phone calls	We bill for time spent on calls received and made—at regular hourly rate

Issue	Terms
E-mails	We bill for reading and responding at regular hourly rate
Termination by client	Can terminate at any time; no refund if the retainer has been spent; must pay fees for services already rendered; firm will prepare final invoice
Termination by firm	If client doesn't pay in timely fashion or if there's a breakdown in the attorney/client relationship (spell out what this means a bit—client fails to fulfill her obligations, other causes, such as client wanting attorney to do something that might violate ethical obligations)
Core billing	Time spent reviewing facts, creating drafts, reviewing drafts, communicating with clients, communicating with opposing counsel, all other activities related to representation
Beginning of representation	When both parties have signed the contract and Ms. Bennett has paid the security retainer fee
End of representation	When final bill is paid; note that the $1,500 retainer is deducted from the first bill
Dowling v. Chicago Options	Include whatever the court requires about the security retainer to assure that the client is fully informed about how the money will be handled
Detail in bills	Will show who performed the work, how much time was spent (rounded up to the quarter hour), brief description of the work performed
Increase in hourly billing rates	Occurs at the beginning of each new year, but we will not raise billing rates for this client during the term of this letter

Issue	Terms
Changes to personnel	Can substitute associates but not senior partner, unless obtain client's consent
Disputing a bill	Must contact senior partner by mail or telephone within 14 days of receipt of invoice
Qualifications of attorneys	All will be licensed to practice law in Illinois We'll state that everyone working on the matter is competent; add in "with appropriate supervision" for associates and paralegals
Paralegal role	Help with gathering information from vendor, obtaining permits, documentation, and miscellaneous other tasks not appropriate for attorney time
Overhead expenses	Not billed to client
Attorney/client privilege	Explain it briefly; make sure she knows not to share info with third parties and destroy privilege
Customer service	Can expect us to work hard and to keep client informed; let us know if we are not doing that
Governing law	Illinois
Signatures required	Betsy Bennett and Sue Payne

G. **Further Instructions for Drafting Engagement Letter:** Sue wants the engagement letter to come from Sue herself. She would like you to draft it using a personal, somewhat informal tone, without including any slang and without sounding unprofessional. Unlike most other contracts you will draft, you may use personal pronouns in this letter. Refer to Sue as "I" and to Ms. Glass as "you."

Remember that your main audience for the engagement letter is a new professional golfer who thus far has very little experience in business and may never have entered into a similar arrangement with an attorney before. You must make sure that you communicate clearly so that she understands everything in the letter. Encourage her to ask Sue questions before signing the letter if there is anything that she does not understand.

In order to keep the engagement letter from sounding too formal, you may use "will" instead of "shall" for covenants throughout the letter.

Please divide up the letter into sections and use boldfaced headings to help Ms. Bennett. Think about how best to organize the information you convey.

> **Note:** You should not use a table, except perhaps to summarize the information about the individuals working on the matter and their hourly rates.

After Sue's signature (with her title and the date), include a statement from Ms. Bennett, acknowledging that she has read the letter, understands it, and agrees to its terms. Then put lines for Ms. Bennett's signature and the date. Under her signature line, designate her as "Client."

One final word: Strive to keep the engagement letter simple, straightforward, and brief. This letter should provide you with an excellent opportunity to practice the skill of drafting in Plain English. Your main goal is to communicate clearly so that the client understands how the attorney/client relationship is supposed to work.

H. Additional Instructions: Your professor may provide you with additional instructions regarding this assignment.

1B: THE CLIENT INTERVIEW

Instructions

A. Summary: You are going to meet your client, Betsy Bennett, a professional golfer who wants to purchase a putting green for her backyard. You will interview Ms. Bennett in order to find out the terms of the deal that she has negotiated with The Village Green Society, Inc., a private company that she has engaged to design, supply, and install the putting green.

B. Preparation for the Client Interview: After you read the following memorandum from your senior partner, Sue Payne, please read Appendix 1, Ten Tips for Interviewing a Client About a Transaction. Since your client is a fictional character, you will not be able to do any research about her or her golf career beforehand. Nevertheless, you should make an effort to learn something about the business of professional golf and, specifically, the Ladies Professional Golf Association. Prior to the client interview, you may conduct Internet or library searches to learn about professional golf in general. However, remember that you may not search for any purchase agreements regarding putting greens, as that would violate the prohibition against using precedent on this assignment (see Section D, Precedent, below). Brainstorm about what provisions you think ought to be included in a putting green purchase agreement. Then prepare a list of questions to ask your client.

C. **Legal Expertise and Research:** In practice, you should not draft a contract in an area in which you have no legal expertise unless you acquire the expertise or seek help from another attorney who possesses it. Rule 1.1 of the Model Rules of Professional Conduct states:

> *Competence.* A lawyer shall provide competent representation to a client. Competent representation requires the legal knowledge, skill, thoroughness and preparation reasonably necessary for the representation.

> Comment 2 to MRPC Rule 1.1 clarifies that "[a] lawyer can provide adequate representation in a wholly novel field through necessary study" or "through the association of a lawyer of established competence in the field in question." For the purposes of this assignment, you may assume that your senior partner has the requisite legal expertise to serve as your guide. You may not do any legal research in connection with this assignment unless your professor authorizes you to do so.

D. **Precedent:** In preparation for the client interview, you may not use any sample contracts, forms, templates, or models (collectively, "precedent") other than any model contracts provided by your professor.

> **Note:** Because most transactional attorneys have some relevant precedent in hand when drafting a contract, you will be permitted to use precedent in some subsequent drafting assignments.

E. **Additional Access to Client:** After the in-class interview, you may need to obtain more information from Ms. Bennett. Collect your questions and e-mail them to your professor, who may (a) pass them along to Ms. Bennett, or (b) arrange for Ms. Bennett to come into class for another interview.

F. **Additional Instructions:** Your professor may provide you with additional instructions regarding this assignment.

Payne & Associates, Attorneys-At-Law

MEMORANDUM

CONFIDENTIAL

FROM: Sue Payne, Senior Partner

TO: Associates

RE: Betsy Bennett (New Client)

DATE: January 2, 2012

I hope when I tell you how I met our new client you will recognize how important networking is to client development. I was looking at golf equipment in the pro shop at Longbourn Park Country Club when I struck up a conversation with another customer, Chip Mulligan, who talked me out of buying a particularly expensive new putter. He seemed so knowledgeable that I asked him what he did for a living and he told me that he caddies for a professional golfer named Betsy Bennett. We chatted for awhile longer, mainly about our mutual love of the game.

Later, I ran into Chip in the Club's restaurant, where he and Ms. Bennett were eating a light lunch. He invited me to join them and I did, thinking that I might be able to get some good advice about my golf swing. They asked me what I do for a living and rolled their eyes when I told them. Chip spouted off a few pretty good lawyer jokes. Ms. Bennett and I laughed . . . and the rest is history.

Betsy (we were on a first-name basis at that point) was very excited about her plans to buy a putting green for her backyard. Then, as if a lightbulb went off in her head, she asked me if our firm might be interested in drafting the contract.

So, here is what I know about the client and the deal so far. Betsy Bennett is a professional golfer on the LPGA Tour. She is 25 years old and has been on the Tour for three years. She is not married (though I don't think that matters) and she attended Ohio State University on a golf scholarship.

Although Betsy spends much of her time in Florida, she really misses the Chicago area and her hometown of Longbourn, Illinois, an exurb of Chicago. So, she has purchased a house on 30 acres of land at 2005 Eagle Lane, in Longbourn. Needless to say, Betsy has a very large back yard.

LPGA fans have nicknamed Betsy Bennett "the Killer B" because of her tendency to "sting" her opponents by coming from behind to win and because of her initials ("BB") and her ever-present yellow and black cap. (Betsy, who is very superstitious about this cap, wears it whenever she plays in a tournament.) But I am getting rather far afield.

As I said before, Betsy wants to purchase a putting green for her backyard in Longbourn. On the recommendation of some local pros, Betsy wants to buy the putting green from The Village Green Society, Inc. ("VGSI"), who will also design and install it. In recent weeks, Betsy has had extensive discussions with Ray Bunker, the president and chief executive officer of VGSI. Betsy and Mr. Bunker have worked out most of the deal terms. I wasn't able to delve into the details at lunch since Betsy and Chip had to dash off to catch a plane. When Ms. Bennett returns, she will come into our office to meet with us and talk about the deal. Please be prepared to interview Ms. Bennett.

1C: LETTER TO CLIENT RE POTENTIAL ETHICAL QUESTION

Instructions

A. **Summary:** Analyze the scenario presented below in order to determine whether you may be violating any ethical rules if you contact Ray Bunker directly, as your client, Betsy Bennett, has requested. You must be able to explain your answer by citing specific portions of the Model Rules of Professional Conduct and the Comments to those rules. Weigh also the business issues that contacting Mr. Bunker directly may present. Draft a letter to the client, informing her of your answer and its rationale.

B. **Scenario:** After your interview with Betsy Bennett, you call her to clarify some of the deal terms. She is fuzzy on some issues and is too busy working on her golf swing to talk to you at length. She asks you if you can call Ray Bunker, at The Village Green Society, Inc. ("VGSI"), in order to get some answers. She also mentions that she thinks VGSI may have hired an attorney to review the contract, but she is not sure.

C. **Format of Client Letter:** Begin the letter by summarizing the issue that Ms. Bennett's request raises. If you believe there is an ethical issue that prohibits you from contacting Ray Bunker directly, tell Ms. Bennett, but be sure to explain it in terms that a non-lawyer will understand. If you do not believe that this scenario presents an ethical issue but you do believe that it presents a business issue, explain the issue to Ms. Bennett, providing enough information for her to give the business issue careful consideration.

D. **Tone of Client Letter:** Remember that the relationship between your firm and Betsy Bennett is brand new. Your senior partner, Sue Payne, expects that Ms. Bennett eventually will become a very successful professional golfer who will send the firm a lot of additional legal work. In your letter, use a businesslike tone, but be sure to make the client feel that you have her best interests at heart.

E. **Additional Instructions:** Your professor may provide you with additional instructions regarding this assignment.

1D: MEMORANDUM TO SENIOR PARTNER RE SUMMARY OF DEAL TERMS

Instructions

A. **Summary:** Using the notes from your interview with your client, Betsy Bennett, draft a memorandum to Sue Payne, summarizing the terms of the putting green purchase transaction. Assume that Ms. Payne was not present at the client interview.

B. **Format of Memorandum:** Set up your memo as follows—

Payne & Associates, Attorneys-At-Law

MEMORANDUM

CONFIDENTIAL

TO: Sue Payne

FROM: [Insert Your Name]

RE: Interview with Betsy Bennett, January 8, 2012

SUBJECT: Putting Green Purchase Agreement

DATE: January 9, 2012

[Insert the text of the memo here, single-spaced. Use headings to help organize the material.]

C. **Collaboration:** If your professor permits, you and your classmates may share your client interview notes. Most likely, if you missed a deal fact, your classmate caught it. Through collaboration, you can fill in any information gaps you have, unless, of course, the client did not give you the information you need.

D. **Follow-Up Questions to Client:** In the course of writing this memo, you may find that you need to ask the client some additional questions. Please direct those questions to your professor, who will either consult the client and post the answers for the entire class or invite the client in for another interview.

E. **Identification of Legal Issues:** While drafting this memo, you may identify one or more legal issues that this transaction poses. If so, please identify those issues at the end of the memo so that Sue becomes aware of them and can give you some direction regarding how to pursue them.

F. **Additional Instructions:** Your professor may provide you with additional instructions regarding this assignment.

1E: ASSEMBLING THE FRAME: DRAFTING THE TITLE, PREAMBLE, BACKGROUND, WORDS OF AGREEMENT, DEFINITIONS, AND SIGNATURE LINES

Instructions

A. **Summary:** Using the deal facts gathered from the client interview you conducted in Assignment 1B, you will draft the Putting Green Purchase Agreement's frame—the Title, Preamble, Background, Words of Agreement, Definitions, and Signature Lines.

B. **The "Frame" Metaphor:** Some parts of a contract are traditional and easily drafted using models. They create a "frame" for the business provisions of the contract. The Title, Preamble, Words of Agreement, and Signature Lines are rudimentary parts of the contract's frame. The Definitions and Background sections, while more difficult to draft, still should not contain covenants, conditions precedent, representations and warranties, and statements of discretionary authority—otherwise known as "operative" provisions. For that reason, the Background and Definitions sections are also part of the contract's frame, stabilizing it by adding more information about the deal and preparing the reader for the "picture" containing the operative provisions of the deal.

Professors who teach contract drafting use various images to convey what contract drafters do. Therefore, you may hear someone else refer to the "frame" as the "skeleton" of the contract and the "picture" as the "meat on the bones." If it helps you to think of the contract that way, please feel free to do so. The purpose of these metaphors is to help you break down the drafting process into manageable parts.

C. **The Preamble—An Example of Learning from a Model:** Provided that you have the correct information, you can draft a Preamble for the Putting Green Purchase Agreement by following the pattern of the Preamble in the model Leaf Disposal Services Agreement,[1] reprinted below.

LEAF DISPOSAL SERVICES AGREEMENT

Leaf Disposal Services Agreement made this 10th day of October 2007, between SpinGazer, Inc., a Delaware corporation with its principal place of business located at 1200 Ridge Avenue, Evanston, Illinois 60201 (the "Company"), and Fallen Leaves, Inc., an Illinois corporation with its principal place of business located at 2025 North Clark Street, Chicago, Illinois 60614 (the "Provider").

Because Betsy Bennett is an individual and not a corporation, you obviously do not need to identify where she is incorporated and where her principal place of business is located. For an individual, you simply say "an individual residing at [insert address]."

You must still choose a shorthand nickname for the individual and place the parenthetical containing the shorthand name *after* all of the identifying information about the individual. Therefore, after Betsy's address, you may insert (the "Golfer"), for example. If you call Betsy "the Golfer," then you will want to give The Village Green Society, Inc. a nickname at the same level of generality. Perhaps for The Village Green Society, Inc. you will insert (the "Contractor") or ("the Company") after its identifying information.

The placement of the shorthand names you choose for the parties, which function like in-text definitions, is very important. Perhaps it is hard to believe, but there could be more than one Betsy Bennett in the world. By placing the parenthetical after Betsy's address, you make it more likely that you have clearly identified the "Betsy Bennett" who is a party to this contract.

When you draft the Preamble of your contract, pay careful attention to punctuation. The Preamble contains a lot of information and is

---

1. The entire model Leaf Disposal Services Agreement is included in Appendix 2.

difficult to read if not punctuated properly. Moreover, aside from the title, the Preamble is the very first thing that the reader will encounter in your contract. Even though it is formulaic, you can set a good tone by drafting it so that it reads smoothly. Proper punctuation helps.

Finally, you and your professor are likely to spend some time talking about what date you should insert in the Preamble. When is the contract "made"? Is it the same date when the contract is signed? Is this date different from the effective date of the term? Also, sometimes the date in the Preamble is preceded by the words "as of." Under what circumstances is it appropriate to use those words? Even a formulaic Preamble can present interesting questions that you are likely to bandy about in class.

D. **Title, Words of Agreement, and Signature Lines:** You and your professor will discuss what to call this contract. For convenience sake, I have referred to it as the *Putting Green Purchase Agreement*, but you are not required to use that as a title.

The Words of Agreement used in the model Leaf Disposal Services Agreement are simple. After the Background section, insert "Accordingly, the parties agree as follows:". In most contracts, at about this point in the contract, you will see a lengthy "consideration" provision that sounds like complete gobbledygook. You and your professor are likely to discuss whether a formal statement of consideration is necessary when the contract itself makes it amply clear that consideration for the transaction does exist. The drafter of the Leaf Disposal Services Agreement has concluded that the contract does not require a formal statement of consideration.

You can easily imitate the Signature Lines and get them right. The Signature Lines from the Leaf Disposal Services Agreement are reprinted below.

AGREED:

SPINGAZER, INC.	**FALLEN LEAVES, INC.**
By: _____	By: _____
Jackie Spingazer	Leif E. Liminator
Title: Director of Operations	Title: Supervisor

Since one of the parties to the Putting Green Purchase Agreement is an individual, you will need to adapt this format a bit. The names in boldface, all capital letters, above the Signature Lines are the formal names of the parties to the contract—not the shorthand names that you chose in the Preamble and used throughout the rest of the contract. So, where you see **SPINGAZER, INC.** and **FALLEN LEAVES, INC.**, above, you would substitute **BETSY BENNETT** and **THE VILLAGE GREEN SOCIETY, INC.**

> **Note:** Generally, it is a good idea to put your client's signature line first. Believe it or not, this sometimes matters to the client.

Underneath the Signature Lines, type the names of the individuals signing the agreement. You do not need the word "By" if the individual signing is also the party. Just re-type "Betsy Bennett," in upper and lowercase letters, below her Signature Line. This may seem repetitious, but the names above the Signature Lines identify the parties to the contract and the names below the Signature Lines identify who signed the contract.

Finally, since Betsy is an individual and does not have a title, you can eliminate the "Title" line from her signature block. Under the Signature Line for The Village Green Society, Inc., type the name of the individual signing on behalf of the corporation. Then insert that individual's title.

E. **Background:** The purpose of the Background section is twofold—to put the Agreement in context and to express the intentions of the parties.

You may be accustomed to seeing this section called "Recitals" and containing a list of "WHEREAS" clauses ending with the crescendo "NOW THEREFORE" clause. Plain English drafters avoid those clauses like the plague. Instead, draft the Background section in smooth prose. This is probably the only place in the contract where you will get to tell a little story. Use it well. Who are the parties? What do they do? Why are they entering into this deal? The Background section should not be too long or too lopsided (containing more information about one party than the other).

The Background section is a place where you should avoid following your models too closely. It is not as formulaic as the Preamble, for example. Ask yourself: What do my readers need to know about the parties? About what happened before (if anything) and about what is about to happen (this transaction)?

Remember that you should not include any operative provisions in the Background section. Be very careful not to include any covenants, conditions precedent, representations and warranties, or statements of discretionary authority here. The courts generally will not give effect to operative language contained in a Background section. And, if you include a covenant in the Background section, you run the risk of forgetting to include it in the body of the contract, where it would actually obligate a party to do something.

Sometimes the parties want to clarify their intentions early in a contract. Even though the Background section should not contain operative provisions, it can contain a statement of the parties' intentions. Sometimes, if there is a contractual dispute, the court will give effect to a statement of intentions included in the Background section instead of, or in addition to, admitting parol evidence of those intentions.

F. **Definitions:** The model Leaf Disposal Services Agreement gives you some limited guidance about how to draft the definitions. It contains the prefatory language below.

As used in this Agreement, the terms defined in the preamble have their assigned meanings and the following terms have the meanings assigned to them in this Article.

If you have defined any terms, in-text, in the Background section, you must add the words "and in the Background section" to the prefatory language after the words "in the preamble." That way, you will not have to include any cross-references to those definitions in the Definitions article itself.

By looking at the model agreement, you will see that most definitions use the verb "means" or "includes but does not include." You will also see that in-text definitions found in the body of the contract (but not in the Preamble or Background section) are cross-referenced in the Definitions article, using the verb phrase "has the meaning assigned in."

You and your professor will discuss how to choose what to define and how to draft the definitions. Remember that definitions are declarations and should not contain any operative language—no covenants, conditions precedent, representations and warranties, or statements of discretionary authority. Think of a definition as a statement of what a term means whenever it appears capitalized in the contract. If you want a party to undertake any kind of obligation, you must include it in the body of the contract rather than in a definition.

Important Note About Drafting Definitions as Part of the Frame: In practice, lawyers hardly ever draft a complete Definitions article before they draft the rest of the contract. In a sense, asking you to draft the Definitions before you draft the rest of the contract is an artificial exercise. Nevertheless, it is a good exercise and it may save you some time and energy. It forces you, as a novice contract drafter, to think in advance about what terms you may need to define. You can draft a definition for the putting green, for example, because you know that you will need to refer to it over and over again.

Moreover, drafting definitions in advance may prevent you from making the mistake of using too many in-text definitions. When a Definitions article contains too many cross-references to in-text definitions, the reader is forced to hop all over the contract to find out what things mean. Instead, by defining most terms in the Definitions article itself, you keep the reader happy by feeding her information. You also take the opportunity to educate her about the deal a bit before she launches into the contract. This idea of educating the reader may sound like a litigation drafting concept, but it holds true for contract drafting as well. As your reader moves into the contract, after reading a fully developed Definitions article, she is more likely to understand the rest of the contract.

If you remember to consider your audience(s), you will be more likely to achieve the goal of clear communication. Transactional attorneys who fail to consider their audience(s) give transactional attorneys a bad name.

G. **Additional Instructions:** Your professor may provide you with additional instructions regarding this assignment.

1F: FILLING IN THE PICTURE: DRAFTING THE CONTRACT'S OPERATIVE PROVISIONS

Instructions

A. **Summary:** Using the deal facts gathered from the client interview you conducted in Assignment 1B, draft all of the operative provisions of the Putting Green Purchase Agreement. The "operative" provisions do not include the "frame" of the contract—the Title, Preamble, Background, Words of Agreement, Definitions, and Signature Lines. This assignment assumes that you have already drafted the "frame" of the contract as part of Assignment 1E—or that your professor has asked you to skip that assignment and concentrate on "filling in the picture."

B. **Filling in the Picture:** To fill in the picture, you must draft all of the operative provisions of the contract and decide how to organize them.

Your professor will help you develop the basic skills you need to take the terms of the deal and translate them into contract concepts—covenants, conditions precedent, representations and warranties, statements of discretionary authority, and declarations.[2]

In practice, some attorneys call this *memorializing* the terms of the deal, which basically means getting the terms of the deal down on paper so that they have a legal effect. The paper (or contract) is the *memorial*. The parties should be able to turn to the contract whenever they have any questions about their rights and duties with regard to the particular transaction.

C. **Organization—Naming and Ordering the Articles and Sections:** Some provisions are traditionally placed in certain spots. For example, after the Definitions article, some drafters include a brief article containing the main covenants of the deal. One leading contract drafting expert, Tina L. Stark, calls this brief article the "subject matter performance provision."[3] The subject matter performance provision in the model Leaf Disposal Services Agreement is reprinted below.

Article III. Summary of Services and Fees

Section 3.01 Services and Fees. Subject to the provisions of this Agreement, the Provider shall perform the Services described in Article IV. To compensate the Provider for performing the Services, the Company shall pay the Provider the fees and reimburse the Provider for the expenses described in Article V.

The drafter of the model Leaf Disposal Services Agreement put the subject matter performance provision after the Term article. While the exact order of these provisions sometimes varies, remember that the subject matter performance provision, the Term, and the Closing articles should appear near the beginning of the contract.

It is sometimes helpful to think of the subject matter performance provision as a thesis statement plus roadmap. It tells you the "main idea" (or "primary covenants") of the contract and points you to the

---

2. Tina L. Stark, *Drafting Contracts: How and Why Lawyers Do What They Do* 9-10 (Aspen 2007) (describes the contract concepts as the "building blocks" of the contract and the process of converting business terms into contract concepts as a "translation skill").
3. *Id.* at 39-40.

places in the contract where you can find out more details about those covenants.

After the subject matter performance provision, the Term article, and the Closing article, the reader expects to find information about what the Golfer is purchasing and how much she is going to pay for it. Therefore, you must put those articles close to the beginning of the contract.

At the end of the contract, right before the signature lines, place the contract's boilerplate provisions (sometimes called *General Provisions*). The Termination and Dispute Resolution articles generally come right before the boilerplate.

So, with the parts of the contract in their traditional places, and allowing for some flexibility in their exact order, your contract (not including the frame) will look something like this:

Summary of Purchase and Sale
Term
Closing (if any)
Design of the Putting Green
Installation of the Putting Green
Payments and Other Compensation
[OTHER TOPICS TO BE COVERED]
Dispute Resolution
Termination
General Provisions

One of the biggest challenges that a drafter faces is how to organize the business provisions not specifically listed above—that is, how to organize those "other topics to be covered." Start by making a list of every deal term not addressed in the named articles. Then, group those deal terms by topic and select a good name for the article covering that topic. Remember that "Golfer's Obligations" and "Contractor's Responsibilities" are contract concepts, not topics. Moreover, if you use a heading like "Golfer's Obligations," you are indicating to the reader that all of the Golfer's obligations are contained under that heading. More likely, the Golfer's obligations are scattered throughout the contract.

If you find that you have a number of miscellaneous deal terms that do not seem to fit anywhere, give them another look before deciding to create single-section articles. Single-section articles (other than the subject matter performance provision and the Term article) can make the particular topic seem like an undeveloped afterthought or, conversely, give the particular topic too much weight. It is better to put the miscellaneous deal term into the article it relates to the most, even if it is not a perfect fit.

Once you have found a place for every deal term and named the articles you want to include in the contract, decide what order to put them in. Generally, place the articles in order from most important topic to least important topic. However, if you are describing a process, it may make more sense to put some of the articles in chronological order. There is no magic bullet of contract organization. However, it is very important to remember your audience(s). Ask yourself what your reader needs to know and when your reader needs to know it. Also, remember the terms of the deal. For example, if your client stressed that the Contractor was very concerned about the ownership of the property where the Contractor is to install the putting green, then you may want to move that topic up near the beginning of the contract for emphasis.

D. **Additional Instructions:** Your professor may provide you with additional instructions regarding this assignment.

1G: PUTTING THE PICTURE IN THE FRAME: FINISHING THE DRAFT CONTRACT

Instructions

A. **Summary:** This assignment applies only if you have already completed Assignment 1E and 1F. You will now insert the "picture" that you drafted in response to Assignment 1F into the "frame" that you drafted in response to Assignment 1E. The result will be one completed draft of a Putting Green Purchase Agreement (with a title that you have selected).

B. **The Process:** Inserting the picture into the frame is not merely a mechanical process. Once you have merged the two documents together, you must make sure that the picture fits the frame properly; in other words, you must review the draft contract as a whole and ask yourself at least the following questions:

- ☐ Is the Title I chose for the contract still appropriate?
- ☐ Have I consistently referred to the parties to the contract using the shorthand names that I gave them in the Preamble?
- ☐ Do the full party names in the Preamble (not the shorthand names) match the full party names above the Signature Lines?
- ☐ Does the date in the Preamble reflect the date when the contract is made? If this date is different from the effective date of the contract, have I clarified that in the body of the contract?
- ☐ Do the addresses in the Preamble match the addresses in the "Notice" provision included in the boilerplate?
- ☐ Did I include enough information in the Background section? Is there anything else that I may want to add to that section? Is there anything I may want to take out?

☐ Do I use my defined terms whenever it is appropriate? [*Note:* This is called "letting your defined terms do their work."]

☐ Did I remember to capitalize my defined terms in the body of the contract?

☐ Are there any lengthy phrases that I repeat more than once that could perhaps be defined terms?

☐ Are there any concepts that I repeat in different ways each time that I should perhaps be saying the same way each time? Would a defined term help?

☐ Are there any defined terms that I never use or use only once? (If so, you probably do not need to define that term.)

☐ Have I included a cross-reference to every in-text definition in the Definitions article? Are my definitions still in alphabetical order?

☐ Whenever I use a cross-reference, have I referenced the correct article or section?

☐ Have I used cross-references in the body of the contract to help the reader understand the relationship between parts of the contract?

☐ Are all of my article and section numbers in order? Does each have an appropriate heading?

☐ In the "Survivability" boilerplate provision, have I listed all of the sections of the contract that will survive the early termination of the contract or the end of the term?

☐ Do all of the parts of the contract work well together?

Once you have answered all of these questions and made any necessary adjustments to the contract, you can move into the editing and proofreading stage described next.

C. **Editing and Proofreading:** Using the Contract Drafting Checklist provided in Appendix 3, go back over your draft contract again. The checklist is set up to help you take the long view first. Think about the transaction. Have you captured all of the terms of the deal? Have you translated them into the correct contract concepts? Have you answered all questions about the rights and duties of the parties with regard to this transaction? Have you raised any questions without answering them? Is your contract well organized, coherent, and coordinated? Does it read smoothly? Is it easy to follow?

The checklist then asks you to look at some formatting issues that are directly related to readability. Review those issues, remembering also that well-chosen headings and the judicious use of "white space" enhance the readability of a contract. Do not remove headings or white space in order to make sure that you do not exceed the page limit for this assignment. If you need guidance about how to avoid exceeding the page limit, seek your professor's help.

Following the checklist, now make sure that your contract contains all of the essential parts. Then, review each part. Finally, under the broad heading "Plain English," the checklist directs you to make sure that you have not made any grammatical, mechanical, or typographical errors.

Once you have gone through the checklist, prepare your contract for submission by proofreading it carefully, using the proofreading tips and tricks contained in Appendix 5. Finally, review your professor's instructions and verify that you have followed all of the directions regarding submitting the contract to your professor. There is something particularly disturbing about a transactional attorney who fails to follow directions. Failing to follow directions indicates that you are not detail oriented, which, in practice, can make your supervisor and your client mistrust you. It can also lead to a dangerous loss of credibility with the attorney representing the other side.

D. **Submitting the Contract:** Do one final thing before you submit your contract: Make sure that you are turning in a clean copy. That is, make sure that you have eliminated any highlighting or comments to yourself that you may have inserted during the drafting process. Practicing attorneys, both litigators and deal lawyers alike, can tell many war stories about forgetting to delete comments or critiques before filing documents or sending drafts to the other side. You do not want to make such an embarrassing mistake. You may also want to make sure that your document does not contain any hidden personal or metadata, such as information about when you finished the assignment. Check the software you are using to figure out how to eliminate that information.

E. **Additional Instructions:** Your professor may provide you with additional instructions regarding this assignment.

1H: MAKING CHANGES TO THE DRAFT CONTRACT: REDLINING

Instructions

A. **Summary:** Using the facts contained in the following memorandum from Sue Payne, make the appropriate changes to the Putting Green Purchase Agreement. Apparently, The Village Green Society, Inc. ("VGSI") is now represented by an attorney. Ms. Payne's memorandum summarizes the conversation she had with VGSI's attorney about the draft contract that she sent him. Ms. Payne has consulted with your client,

Betsy Bennett, and determined that all of the changes are acceptable to Ms. Bennett.

B. **Making Changes to a Draft Reviewed by Opposing Counsel:** Now that opposing counsel has reviewed your draft contract, you should not make any changes to it without redlining those changes. Find the "Track Changes" (or equivalent function) on your computer and learn how to use it. Ideally, every word you delete should be struck through and every word you add should appear in red.

Make the changes mentioned in Ms. Payne's memo. Remember not to make any changes to the document without tracking them. In real life, you will quickly lose credibility with opposing counsel if you do not track all of your changes because you will be breaking the unwritten code of honor that transactional attorneys follow. Track even the smallest change—even the correction of a minor misspelling.

C. **Turning in the Redlined Contract:** After you have reviewed the redlined contract to make sure that you took into account all of the changes mentioned in Ms. Bishop's memo, submit it to your professor. This time, make sure that you submit the document *with* the changes showing. (This may be as simple as saving the document as "Final Showing Markup.") Remember to rename the document, using the date and the initials "RL" to indicate that it is a redlined version.

D. **Additional Instructions:** Your professor may provide you with additional instructions regarding this assignment.

Payne & Associates, Attorneys-At-Law

MEMORANDUM

CONFIDENTIAL

FROM: Sue Payne, Senior Partner

TO: Associates

RE: Changes to Putting Green Purchase Agreement

DATE: February 2, 2012

As you all know, VGSI hired an attorney, Louis Majors. I sent your draft Putting Green Purchase Agreement to Louis and he called me to discuss some requested changes. He told me that Betsy and Ray Bunker had a long lunch last week and, apparently, the horse is already out of the barn. That is, Betsy has agreed to these changes without consulting us!

I double-checked with Betsy by phone today and she confirmed that she wants us to make all of the changes that Louis related to me. Please remember to redline these changes and review the entire agreement to make sure you make any other changes that become necessary as a result. Rather than asking Louis to put the changes in himself, I told him that we wanted to maintain control of the document, so please make sure you do a thorough job.

VGSI had two main concerns that Ray brought to Betsy. First, they did not want to risk traumatizing her dogs during the installation phase. And, second, they did not want to risk trampling her beloved "Queen Bee" rose bed. In the first go-round, Betsy had been very firm about getting VGSI to guarantee not to traumatize her dogs and not to trample her roses.

Now, Betsy has agreed that she will remove her dogs from the premises during the installation phase. She may keep them at her other home in Florida or put them in a kennel near her Longbourn property. The contract need not specify where she puts the dogs, but rather merely that she will remove them for the entire installation phase.

Betsy has also agreed to move her garden—the one containing her beloved "Queen Bee" roses—to another part of the property, far enough away from the putting green site so that VGSI's work will not disturb them. Oddly enough, VGSI has agreed to provide the labor for this move at no extra cost to Betsy.

The rose garden is to be moved to another part of Betsy's Longbourn property as part of the putting green site preparation.

Betsy agreed to some other changes as well. She agreed to permit VGSI to subcontract out the lighting system—but no other part of the design and installation. She also promised to install a video camera or hire a security guard to make sure that the site is protected at night. Apparently, there is a local gang of high school kids that has been vandalizing swimming pools and construction sites in the area. Betsy wants the option to either install the camera or hire the guard and to change from the camera to the security guard or vice versa as often as she likes. Meanwhile, VGSI promised to do what it can to secure the site—with temporary fencing and canvas and ropes. All of these measures should take effect as soon as VGSI begins preparing the site. (You'll have to clarify whether site preparation is part of the installation phase.)

Finally, Betsy found out that she could lower the price of the putting green by eliminating her desire for one of the greens to be a "turtle-back." This lowers the total price from $15,000 to $13,500. Bunker told her she could have the option to add the turtle-back later for a cost of no more than $1,500.

Please put the changes into the contract and send me a redlined version ASAP.

Assignment 2

The Sport Psychologist Consulting Agreement

2A: THE WAIVER OF CONFLICT OF INTEREST AGREEMENT

Instructions

A. **Summary:** After reading the scenario below, you will draft a Waiver of Conflict of Interest Agreement, which you will ask your former client, Dr. Hope Bowker, to sign.

B. **Scenario:** It is now March 2013. Betsy Bennett has a wonderful putting green in her backyard. Now she wants to engage a sport psychologist, Dr. Hope Bowker, to help her with her golf game. She has asked your firm to draft the contract. You do a conflicts check and discover that, six years ago, your firm represented Dr. Hope Bowker when she purchased her personal residence. Since then, your firm has performed no additional legal work for Dr. Bowker. Nevertheless, you have kept in touch with her and taken her out to lunch at least once a year in order to maintain contact in case she finds herself in a position to send your firm additional business.

Your firm now wants to represent Betsy Bennett with regard to her consulting agreement with Dr. Bowker. You remind your senior partner, Sue Payne, that you may not be able to represent Ms. Bennett in this new transaction, given that you represented Dr. Bowker in the past. Even though six years have passed since your firm represented Dr. Bowker with regard to the purchase of her personal residence, Sue asks you to talk to your firm's conflicts administrator, who will help you determine if a conflict exists. The conflicts administrator determines that a conflict may exist.

Betsy and Dr. Bowker have already developed a relationship. Betsy tells you that she told Dr. Bowker that she intended to contact your firm to seek representation in this deal. Betsy believes that Dr. Bowker does not object to your firm representing Betsy in this deal.

C. **The Waiver of Conflict of Interest Agreement:** Sue has asked you to do two things: (1) Write a cover letter to Dr. Bowker, explaining why you need her written consent to the firm's representation of Betsy Bennett in this deal; and (2) draft a Waiver of Conflict of Interest Agreement, a copy of which you will enclose with your cover letter.

D. **Preparation for Drafting:** Your firm's conflicts administrator is new at the job and does not have a form Waiver of Conflict of Interest Agreement to give you. *You must complete this assignment without using any models, templates, or forms.*

Begin by looking at any guidance provided by the Model Rules of Professional Conduct regarding the "Client-Lawyer Relationship." More than one rule may be relevant to this issue. However, you are likely to find that Model Rule 1.9 ("Duties to Former Clients"), and its associated Comments, are right on point. Determine what constitutes "informed consent" and how best to confirm that you have obtained that informed consent in writing. Then draft the letter and the Waiver of Conflict of Interest Agreement (the "Waiver").

E. **Content of the Waiver:** Make sure that the Waiver contains a signature line for Sue Payne and a signature line for Dr. Hope Bowker. Use all of the basic contract drafting principles you have learned when you draft the Waiver. Do not forget about using contract drafting concepts like covenants and representations and warranties and expressing them with the appropriate verbs. For example, you may be tempted to have Dr. Bowker "acknowledge" that she has been informed of a potential conflict and that she "understands" what it means. Consider having her "represent" and "warrant" these things instead. One exception: You may use the word "waives" instead of "shall waive" to capture Dr. Bowker's covenant to waive the conflict.

Think carefully about how your cover letter and your Waiver work together. Are you going to include the information about the potential conflict in the cover letter and then refer to the letter in the Waiver? Will you be attaching the cover letter to the Waiver as an Exhibit? Or, do you want to inform the client of the conflict in the Waiver itself, so that attaching the cover letter is unnecessary? Use your best judgment, keeping in mind that the client must understand everything that you draft.

F. **Additional Consideration Re the Company:** Think about whether you should also write a letter to Betsy Bennett, reminding her that you previously represented Dr. Hope Bowker in a totally unrelated transaction and letting her know that you have sought Dr. Bowker's waiver of any conflict of interest associated with the firm now representing Ms. Bennett in the sport psychologist consulting agreement transaction. You may also want to consider whether to remind Ms. Bennett that you are bound not to reveal any confidential information about your former client, Dr. Hope Bowker.

G. **Additional Instructions:** Your professor may provide you with additional instructions regarding this assignment.

2B: MEMORANDUM TO SENIOR PARTNER RE SUMMARY OF DEAL TERMS

Instructions

A. **Summary:** Each of you must read and digest the attached memorandum from your senior partner, Sue Payne, and letter from your client, Betsy Bennett, regarding the sport psychologist consulting agreement that Ms. Bennett wants you to draft. Dr. Hope Bowker has provided Ms. Bennett with a draft agreement, which you must also review. Since Ms. Payne is very busy right now, she would like you to draft a memorandum summarizing the terms of the deal for her.

B. **Format of Memorandum:** Set up your memo as follows—

Payne & Associates, Attorneys-At-Law

MEMORANDUM

CONFIDENTIAL

FROM: [Insert Your Name]

TO: Sue Payne

RE: Betsy Bennett—Terms of Sport Psychologist Consulting Agreement

DATE: March 30, 2013

[Insert the text of the memo, single-spaced. Note that Sue would like this memo to be organized a specific way. First, she wants you to summarize the deal facts. Then she wants you to list any legal issues that you think it may be necessary to research before drafting the contract. Finally, she wants you to make a list of additional questions that you want her to ask the client.]

To satisfy Sue's expectations, the main headings in your memo should be:

I. Known Deal Facts
II. Potential Legal Issues
III. Additional Questions for the Client

You may want to break up any one of the main sections into subsections with headings. This might be especially helpful to Sue in Section I.

C. **Collaboration:** If your professor permits, you and your classmates may draft this memo (or parts of it) in pairs or in teams. Alternatively, you and your classmates may brainstorm about Parts II and III of the memo in class. Your professor will guide you regarding how much collaboration (if any) is appropriate on this assignment.

D. **Additional Instructions:** Your professor may provide you with additional instructions regarding this assignment.

Payne & Associates, Attorneys-At-Law

MEMORANDUM

CONFIDENTIAL

FROM: Sue Payne, Senior Partner

TO: Associates

RE: The Killer Bee (Betsy Bennett) Strikes Again

DATE: March 18, 2013

Thanks to all of you for your good work on Betsy Bennett's putting green contract. As you can see from the enclosed letter, good work generates more work.

Please read Betsy's letter. I gather she wants to retain a sport psychologist, Dr. Hope Bowker, to help her with her golf game. They've already agreed to many of the terms and Betsy has tried to summarize them for you. Dr. Bowker also presented her with a draft contract.

I need you to help me get my head around the facts of this deal. Please prepare a memo summarizing the terms of the deal. While you are working on the memo, please consider whether there is any other information we need from Betsy. I can set up a conference call with her once we have a final list of questions.

Your work on this transaction is crucial to maintaining our relationship with a professional golfer who is predicted to become quite successful in the near future. Betsy's fellow golfers in the LPGA are so impressed with her that they call her "the Killer Bee." Who knows how much additional business your work will generate for the firm?

The Killer Bee

Betsy Bennett
2005 Eagle Lane
Longbourn, IL 65432

March 16, 2013
Sue Payne
Payne & Associates, LLP
357 East Chicago Avenue
Chicago, IL 60611

Dear Sue,

First of all, I want to thank you for the great job you and your associates did drafting my contract with The Village Green Society, Inc. Ray Bunker and his crew installed a wonderful putting green, and I have been practicing my putting on it ever since.

Unfortunately, all of that practice has not helped much. In truth, I've been having a lot of trouble with my game lately. I'm afraid I have a bad case of what we golfers call the "yips." Oddly enough, it is mainly affecting my putting. I go through my pre-shot routine—get behind the ball, crouch down to see which way the green breaks, get a feel for the distance, pick an intermediate target, align the clubface, move to the side of the ball, take a rehearsal swing, address the ball, and then—I freeze. It's so bad that sometimes I can't even bring the putter back and hit the ball. Usually, when I do manage to hit the ball, it doesn't go quite where I want it to go.

I also need some additional help focusing on the rest of my game. Lately, when I tee off, I am easily distracted by the crowd or by other players or by something so simple as the branch of a tree moving in the wind. Then, if I make a mistake, I obsess about it, and that inevitably leads me to make more mistakes.

After talking this all over with my trusted caddy, Chip Mulligan, I've decided to see a sport psychologist, Dr. Hope Bowker. She and I have already met several times. She has charged me $200 per hour, which is her regular hourly fee. After our last meeting, I decided that I want to consult Dr. Bowker on a regular basis at her office, in my home, and at my local golf course, the Longbourn Park Country Club (located at 3000 Falcon Drive). I also want her to be with me whenever I play in a major tournament on the LPGA tour.

Dr. Bowker, who is an avid amateur golfer herself, has agreed to give me the help I need. That's where you come in. We figured we'd have to have a contract, so she sent me the enclosed draft. She readily admitted that she wrote it herself and invited me to have my lawyers tear it apart. I'm no lawyer, but I can see that this thing needs a lot of work! I'm hoping that you and the same team of associates that helped you with my putting green contract can either rewrite it or draft an entirely new contract in the next few weeks.

I'll try to summarize everything Dr. Bowker and I discussed about our arrangement. Feel free to pass this letter along to your associates, as I know you will be delegating most of the work to them. Actually, I prefer their lower hourly billing rates to yours!

Dr. Bowker's office address is 18 S. Waterhazard Avenue, Suite 1536, Chicago, Illinois 61231. She has her own practice there. She's in the process of looking for a lawyer to review whatever draft we present, so please don't call her directly. I'll get her lawyer's name as soon as we are ready to send her our draft.

We'd like the contract to begin on April 10, 2013, and end one year later, unless we decide to extend it. She agreed that, at least 30 days before the contract ends, I should let her know if I want to extend it. She isn't required to agree to the extension; however, if she does agree to it, she will not increase her rates.

I'll be skipping the first major LPGA tournament this year—the Kraft-Nabisco Championship on April 4-7, 2013. It's being held at Mission Hills Country Club, in Rancho Mirage, California. I used to date a man who lives in Rancho Mirage and, since we broke up, I have never much liked that part of the country. I have also never had much luck in previous tournaments at Mission Hills. Besides, skipping Kraft-Nabisco will give me some time to work with Dr. Bowker before competing in the next major tournament.

From April 10, 2013, through June 3, 2013, Dr. Bowker will meet with me two times a week in her office. We'll have sessions on Monday and Wednesday from 10:00 a.m. until 12:30 p.m. Each one of these sessions will last 2½ hours—and that doesn't mean "psychologist" hours, which I know are usually just 50 minutes long. Dr. Bowker agreed to make each session a full 150 minutes long. These sessions will consist of regular talk therapy, focusing on problems with the mental side of my golf game. Sometimes, I may choose to have Chip attend these sessions with me. Dr. Bowker is okay with that.

Also, from April 10, 2013, through June 3, 2013, Dr. Bowker will come to my home every Friday to assist me with my practice sessions on my putting green from 10:00 a.m. until 12:30 p.m. Moreover, on Saturdays during that same time period, if the weather is good, Dr. Bowker will play 18 holes of golf with me at the Longbourn Park Country Club. She has agreed that Chip may also be present during any practice sessions at my home or at the Club.

For this initial phase of my therapy, I'll pay Dr. Bowker a flat fee of $20,000 (by personal check) divided into two equal installments, the first due in Dr. Bowker's office on April 18, 2013, and the second due in Dr. Bowker's office on May 30, 2013.

I gave Dr. Bowker the schedule for the three major LPGA Tour events that I'll be playing in during 2013. She's agreed to travel with me to each of them. They are:

> McDonald's LPGA Championship Presented by Coca-Cola, June 6-June 9
> U.S. Women's Open, June 27-June 30
> Evian Masters, July 18-July 21

She'll consult with me on the airplane on the way there, over breakfast in my hotel room before each match, and in my hotel room over dinner after each match. She'll follow along with me as I golf each day in order to closely observe my game. Sometimes, instead of using Chip as my caddy, I may use Dr. Bowker, though there are some pretty strict rules about getting a sport psychologist's advice during a tournament. I'm permitted to switch caddies during a round, as long as I don't do it to get specific advice about how to make a particular shot. I would only ask Chip to switch with Dr. Bowker if he gets too nervous (as he sometimes does) and I feel the need to have a more soothing companion by my side for the rest of that round.

Dr. Bowker wants to make sure that nothing in my contract with Chip prevents me from entering into this contract with her, and, especially, from substituting Dr. Bowker for Chip as my caddy from time to time. I have assured

Dr. Bowker that Chip's contract says nothing that would interfere with my plans for using her services.

In addition to all of the other duties that Dr. Bowker will perform while traveling with me, I may sometimes call upon her at night when I am having trouble sleeping. If necessary, she will lead me through a progressive relaxation therapy session before bedtime.

For accompanying me and advising me while on tour, I've agreed to pay Dr. Bowker $1,700 per day on tour, plus travel, food, and lodging expenses (if she gives me the receipts). Each tournament begins on a Thursday and ends on a Sunday. Since Dr. Bowker will be advising me on the plane on the way there, I will count Wednesday as a tour day. Dr. Bowker has agreed that she will not be paid for the day after I have finished playing in each tournament and she travels home.

Usually, I play well enough to make the cut and play for the entire tournament. If I don't make the cut, then I finish playing on Friday and travel home on Saturday. Therefore, when I don't make the cut, I will pay Dr. Bowker for three tour days—Wednesday, Thursday, and Friday. When I do make the cut, I will pay Dr. Bowker for Wednesday, Thursday, Friday, Saturday, and Sunday. I'll pay her for her tour services and expenses by the Friday following the day we return from each tournament. She'll accept my personal check, as long as it's in her hands by the due date.

In between the three major LPGA Tour events in which I'll be competing, I won't play in any other tournaments. I'll rest and relax. I don't require Dr. Bowker to be available to me during those interim periods, as long as she shows up at the airport ready to travel with me on the Wednesday before each major.

During the period after the Evian Masters tournament until October 31, 2013, Dr. Bowker will counsel me as I practice at the Club. She's agreed to join me there every Tuesday and Thursday at 10:00 a.m. to play 18 holes of golf. She'll advise me about focusing, dealing with mistakes, and overcoming the yips. In bad weather, if Dr. Bowker thinks it's a good idea, we can use the video-camera/simulation facility inside the Club to record and analyze my swing and the speed, distance, and placement of my shots. Chip may be present during these golf games and indoor sessions.

For counseling me while golfing at the Club from July 29 through October 30, 2013, I'll pay Dr. Bowker a flat fee of $25,000 in two equal installments, one on September 5th, and one on October 31st, both by personal check due in her office on those dates.

Since the weather gets pretty crummy after October 30th, I'll start going to Dr. Bowker's office for therapy two times a week, on Monday and Wednesday, for 60-minute sessions. I will pay her $250 per session by personal check at the end of each session.

After the Evian Masters tournament, I may decide to play in some minor tournaments. Dr. Bowker will try to clear her schedule and attend those tournaments with me if I ask her to. In that case, I'll pay her $1,200 per day for touring, including one travel day. I will also reimburse her for travel, food, and lodging expenses, just as I do for major tournaments. If I miss any sessions at the Club with Dr. Bowker because I am playing in a minor tournament, I will still have to pay her the full fee for those sessions, even if she is traveling with me. However, if I miss any in-office sessions with Dr. Bowker because I am playing in a minor tournament, I won't have to pay her for those in-office sessions if she is traveling with me.

Oh, I almost forgot. I'm sure you won't like this, but I also agreed to pay Dr. Bowker 4% of the money I win while she's on tour with me, after taxes. This applies to all major and minor tournaments she attends with me. I'll pay Dr. Bowker her cut of my winnings on the 30th day after I receive them. Again, she trusts my personal check, as long as it arrives in her office on time.

That's the money stuff. Except that I want Dr. Bowker to agree to fill out any necessary insurance forms in case I can get reimbursed for some of her fees since I am essentially seeking mental health services.

I guess I will also need Dr. Bowker to state in the contract that she is qualified to serve as a caddy so that I don't have to worry about her not knowing what to do if I substitute her for Chip during a tournament. She told me that she received training from the PCA—that's the Professional Caddies Association— and I am relying on that.

By the way, I know of this golfer who got into some trouble with the IRS because they said that his coach, sport psychologist, driver, and personal assistant were his employees and not independent contractors as their contracts said. He had to pay all kinds of back payroll taxes and penalties and he also had to pay for workers compensation and unemployment compensation insurance. I don't want this to happen to me. I'm trusting you guys to put stuff in the contract that makes it clear that Dr. Bowker isn't my employee.

While I definitely want to work on the issues with my "mental game" that I've mentioned, Dr. Bowker is the expert and she will be directing the sessions. Also, I know she has lots of other clients, so how could I be considered her "employer"? It baffles me. I expect her to continue seeing her other clients, and she may even work with them by phone while we are traveling, as long as it doesn't interfere with our tour routine. Oh, yes, and she's assured me that none of her current clients is an LPGA golfer. I guess I want her to verify that again on the day that we sign the contract. If she does turn out to have an LPGA golfer as a client, I won't want to sign the contract.

And that does raise one other thing that Dr. Bowker and I discussed. She has agreed that, during our contract and for six months after it ends, she will not take on any other golfers in the LPGA as clients. I really pressed for that because I am very concerned about her leaking confidential information about my game to one of my competitors. I know you'll put in a strong confidentiality provision to prevent that. And it occurs to me now that I need her to say that she doesn't have any other agreements with anyone that would prevent her from doing what she's agreed to do. That is, no agreements that would prevent her from treating me or that would interfere with our tour travel.

Oh, and this time I remembered to talk with Dr. Bowker about what happens if things don't work out! (You and your associates have trained me well.) I want the right to terminate the agreement at any time and for any reason, as long as I give her 30 days prior written notice. She can terminate at any time and for any reason with 30 days prior written notice, too, as long as she agrees to help me find a comparably qualified sport psychologist who meets with my approval. If the new sport psychologist charges more for services than I've agreed to pay Dr. Bowker, then Dr. Bowker will have to pay me the difference between her fees and the replacement's fees. She agreed readily to this because I think she's very confident that our relationship will go well.

I also told Dr. Bowker that I want to be able to terminate the contract immediately if she does something terribly wrong—like if she discloses that she's counseling me, or if she badmouths me to the media. (I guess that means she has to promise not to say bad things about me; I don't mind agreeing not to say bad things about her either.) I also want to be able to terminate if she loses her license for some reason or is sanctioned for ethics violations. You read about stuff like that in the newspapers all the time.

I know I haven't thought of all the horrors that might lead me to want to terminate immediately. I hope you and your associates can help me with that. I'm also not sure how to handle the money issues if one of us terminates the contract. Can you help with that, too? And, what if we get into a dispute but neither of us wants to terminate? I think we'd like some time to fix things or some informal process that requires us to sit down over dinner to work out the problem. If that doesn't work, I suppose we could have a formal mediation, as long as I can still go to court if I choose to.

Both of us definitely want a confidentiality provision in the contract. I don't want Dr. Bowker to be able to tell anyone about the content of our sessions, or even to let anyone know that she's treating me. (Probably, her professional ethics will prevent her from doing that, don't you think?) I don't want her to talk to Chip when I'm not around and I especially don't want her to tell him how much I'm paying her. It's a bit more than he gets, and he's been with me for years.

You should know that Dr. Bowker is working on a book containing some of the innovative techniques that she'll be using in my therapy, so she doesn't want me to be able to pass those techniques along to other golfers, writers, or reporters. (I've guaranteed that I am not planning to write a book based on my work with her. I promised that Chip won't reveal any of Dr. Bowker's confidential information either.) In exchange, I certainly want Dr. Bowker to assure me that she won't identify me in her book.

Although Dr. Bowker comes highly recommended, she doesn't have her diplomas posted on her office wall the way some doctors do. She tells me that she has a Ph.D. in sport psychology from the University of Iowa and is a member of the Association for the Advancement of Applied Sport Psychology. I'd like to have written proof of her degree and her membership in the AAASP in my hand when I sign the contract. She understands my concerns and realizes that I won't sign the contract at all if she doesn't provide me with these documents.

I think Dr. Bowker originally wanted some written proof from me that I'm a member of the LPGA. After all, we're talking about some big sums of money that I've promised to pay her. She needs to make sure I at least have some earning potential. I told her I'd put a statement confirming that I'm an LPGA member in the contract. I lost my LPGA certificate and it's a hassle to get another one, so I can't promise to produce it.

Which brings me to the final item: We want to have a signing ceremony on April 4, 2013, even though the contract doesn't really become effective until April 10, 2013. We'd like to get together for a special lunch at "Bistro 110" that day. I'll foot the bill. We'll have a champagne toast, and then we'll sign the contract. And, of course, Sue, you may choose some of your associates to attend the lunch with you.

I hope this letter spells everything out clearly. I'm pretty tired after writing it! If I left some things out, please have your associates compile a list of questions for me. Then, you can contact me by e-mail or we can set up a conference call.

Now it's time for me to catch my plane. I'm going on a brief vacation in California, where I plan to play 36 holes of golf every day. I'll check in with you when I return.

Sincerely yours,

Betsy Bennett
Betsy Bennett

CONFIDENTIAL

Consulting/Contracting Agreement Between Therapist/Psychologist and Client

This Consulting Agreement, hereinafter referred to below as "Agreement," is entered into by and between Dr. Hope A. Bowker, who has an office in downtown Chicago, and Betsy Bennett, a female professional golfer in the LPGA, and shall expire one year from the signing ceremony date.

 WHEREAS Ms. Bennett needs a lot of assistance with the mental part of her deteriorating golf game; and

 WHEREAS Dr. Bowker is an eminent sport psychologist who works primarily with elite athletes all over the world; and

 WHEREAS Dr. Bowker agrees to assist Ms. Bennett by utilizing her proprietary psychological techniques to improve Ms. Bennett's performance.

 NOW THEREFORE, in consideration of the mutual covenants and promises described herein and for other good and valuable consideration in money exchanged, the receipt and sufficiency of which is hereby agreed upon and acknowledged, the parties undertake, assume responsibility for, and verify in good faith the following covenants, premises, conditions and terms, subject to, without limitation, the provisions below:

• Dr. Bowker provides the agreed upon therapy to Bennett in Bowker's office, at Bennett's home, at Bennett's golf club, and on tour (some major tournaments, some minor tournaments).

• Dr. Bowker is to be paid for her services by Ms. Bennett by personal check delivered to Bowker's office before the agreed-upon due dates, which Bennett will meet.

• Dr. Bowker is not Bennett's employee, but rather is an independent contractor.

• Betsy will not reveal the innovative sport psychology techniques that Dr. Bowker is using since Dr. Bowker is going to include them in a book to be published soon.

• Dr. Bowker can terminate the contract with 30 days notice as long as she finds a replacement sport psychologist who does not charge more than Dr. Bowker does.

- Dr. Bowker agrees not to tell Chip Mulligan how much money she is being paid by Betsy. Chip Mulligan can be present during therapy as long as he does not interfere in any way.

- Dr. Bowker will help Bennett with medical insurance claims.

- Dr. Bowker has already provided Bennett with the information she is required to provide under the HIPAA statute about the confidentiality of Personal Health Information.

- Ms. Bennett agrees never to say anything bad about Dr. Bowker, no matter what happens.

- Bennett certifies that she has enough money in the Bank to pay Dr. Bowker the fees she has agreed to pay.

- Ms. Bennett knows that psychotherapy has risks and that Bowker can't guarantee a good outcome.

- Dr. Bowker has revealed to Betsy that Dr. Bowker is a competent golfer and a trained caddy. Betsy has accepted these facts.

- We will have a signing ceremony for this contract on April 4, 2013.

    IN WITNESS WHEREOF, the parties affix their signatures hereto as of the dates set forth below, though the term of the Agreement does not begin until April 10, 2013.

SIGNATURE: _____
                    Betsy Bennett

DATE: _____

SIGNATURE: _____
                    Dr. Hope A. Bowker

DATE: _____

2C: E-MAIL TO CLIENT RE ANSWER TO POTENTIAL ETHICAL QUESTION

Instructions

A. **Summary:** Analyze the scenario presented below in order to determine whether you may be violating any ethical rules if you include the representation and warranty that Betsy Bennett wants you to include in the Sport Psychologist Consulting Agreement that you are going to draft. You must be able to explain your answer by citing specific portions of the Model Rules of Professional Conduct and the Comments to those rules. Weigh also any business issues that Ms. Bennett should consider. Draft a brief e-mail to the client, informing her of your decision about whether you can include in the contract the specific representation and warranty that she has made.

B. **Scenario:** Betsy has told Dr. Bowker that nothing in Betsy's contract with Chip Mulligan (Betsy's caddy) prevents Betsy from entering into this contract with Dr. Bowker. Betsy wants you to put a statement in the contract to that effect. She says that Dr. Bowker would not agree to be her sport psychologist until Betsy gave her that assurance.

Recently, Betsy told you that her statement to Dr. Bowker was a "little white lie." She says that Chip's contract contains a provision stating that she will not hire anyone else as a consultant to assist her with her golf game unless she pays that person less than she is paying Chip. Betsy thinks that Chip has forgotten about this provision, which his attorney added in at the last minute when they were negotiating Chip's contract.

Betsy wants you to put a representation and warranty in Dr. Bowker's contract, stating that nothing in Chip Mulligan's contract will interfere with Betsy entering into this Sport Psychologist Consulting Agreement with Dr. Bowker. (Of course, she has secured Dr. Bowker's promise not to tell Chip how much Betsy is paying her.) Betsy is pretty sure that Chip won't remember his contractual provision requiring that she pay him more than any other consultant assisting her with her golf game.

C. **Preparing the E-Mail to Client:** Begin the e-mail by summarizing the issue about the representation and warranty that Betsy has asked you to include in the contract. Then tell Betsy why you can or cannot include the representation and warranty in the contract. First explain any business or legal reasons for not including the representation and warranty. Then, since Betsy is adamant that it be included, go on to explain any ethical considerations that come into play. Explain your answer by citing specific portions of the Model Rules of Professional Conduct and the Comments to those rules. Be sure to add the firm's standard confidentiality language at the end of the e-mail, just in case the e-mail gets into the wrong hands. (See the sample, below.)

This communication is from Payne & Associates. E-mail text or attachments may contain information that is confidential and may also be privileged. This communication is for the exclusive use of the intended recipient(s). If you have received this communication in error, please return it with the title "received in error" to Payne & Associates. Then delete the e-mail and destroy any copies of it.

Also, remember to warn your client that she should not show or forward the e-mail to anyone else because she could make it impossible for the firm to assert attorney/client privilege on her behalf if the e-mail later becomes discoverable in litigation.

D. **Tone of Client E-Mail:** Remember that the relationship between your firm and Betsy Bennett is relatively new. Your senior partner, Sue Payne, expects that Betsy eventually will become a very successful professional golfer who will send the firm a lot of additional legal work. In your e-mail, use a business-like tone, but be sure to make the client feel that you have her best interests at heart. Even though you may have difficult information to impart, you have to work hard to make the client understand you are on her side.

Remember that you are not drafting an e-mail or text message to a friend. Do not use abbreviations or emoticons. Do not emphasize a statement by putting it in all capital letters. Consider this e-mail just a cut below a formal letter. In fact, the main difference between the e-mail and the formal letter is probably its length. (The e-mail is shorter.)

Remember to always keep your audience in mind. Betsy is a professional golfer. Explain everything in terms that she will be able to understand.

E. **Additional Instructions:** Your professor may provide you with additional instructions regarding this assignment.

2D: ASSEMBLING THE FRAME: DRAFTING THE TITLE, PREAMBLE, BACKGROUND, WORDS OF AGREEMENT, DEFINITIONS, AND SIGNATURE LINES

Instructions

A. **Summary:** Using the deal facts contained in the letter from Betsy Bennett and the draft contract from Dr. Bowker (attached to Assignment 2B), draft the Sport Psychologist Consulting Contract's frame—the Title, Preamble, Background, Words of Agreement, Definitions, and Signature Lines. In preparation for this assignment, you may also review the sample agreements referenced in Section C, Precedent, below.

B. **Legal Research:** As you may know, in practice, you should not draft a contract in an area in which you have no legal expertise unless you acquire the expertise or seek help from another attorney who possesses it. See the Model Rules of Professional Conduct, Rule 1.1, Competence (with Comment). For the purposes of this assignment, you will focus on contract drafting rather than on legal research. However, you must read the documents cited below, which address two of the legal issues this contract raises.

> *Issue # 1: What's the difference between an employee and an independent contractor?* Publication 15-A (2009), Employer's Supplemental Tax Guide (Supplement to Publication 15 *(circular E)*, Employer's Tax Guide).
>   http://www.irs.gov/publications/p15a/index.html.
>
> *Issue # 2: Is a non-compete restricting a psychologist from practicing her profession valid?* Jyoti Mohanty, M.D., et al. v. St. John Heart Clinic, S.C., et. al., 225 Ill. 2d 52, 866 N.E.2d 85 (Ill. 2006).

> **Note:** If you identify other legal issues that you feel you must explore in order to draft the contract, please seek direction from your professor.

C. **Precedent:** For this assignment, you may use the sample contracts cited below and only those sample contracts. This is a "canned precedent" assignment. In other words, in order to keep you focused on drafting rather than on searching for precedent, you are prohibited from using anything but the limited body (or "can") of precedent listed below. These are examples of the precedent you would be likely to find if you did your own search for sport psychologist consulting agreements or analogous agreements on the Internet. You may not use any precedent other than the sample contracts listed here, and any model contracts that your professor provides. If you do adapt or adopt any language from the samples provided, then you must cite your source, even if you have not quoted it directly. Your professor will tell you what citation format he requires.

> *Caution # 1:* Remember that every contract "breaks the mold." That is, each contract memorializes the terms of a particular deal. If you rely too heavily on precedent, you are bound to make some serious mistakes.
>
> *Caution # 2:* View each sample contract with a critical eye, applying all of the contract drafting principles that you have learned so far.

Can of Precedent[4]

7 Ill. Forms Legal & Bus. § 20:69. (Consultant)
Nichols Cyclopedia of Legal forms Annotated, Vol. 5A, Part One, § 5.2162 (General form of independent contractor agreement—Consulting services at hourly rate plus expenses.)
http://contracts.onecle.com/coyote-sports/paragon.consult.1998.10.07.shtml
2 Am. Jur. Legal Forms 2d § 19:294 (Employment contract—coach of university sports team)
www.apait.org/apait/applications/inf.doc.pdf

D. **The "Frame" Metaphor:** Some parts of a contract are traditional and easily drafted using models. They create a "frame" for the business provisions of the contract. The Title, Preamble, Words of Agreement, and Signature Lines are rudimentary parts of the contract's frame. The Definitions and Background sections, while more difficult to draft, still should not contain covenants, conditions precedent, representations and warranties, and statements of discretionary authority—otherwise known as "operative" provisions. For that reason, the Background and Definitions sections are also part of the contract's frame, stabilizing it by adding more information about the deal and preparing

---

4. Your professor may substitute other citations for the ones included here.

the Reader for the "picture" containing the operative provisions of the deal.

A "model" contract is different from a "sample" contract in that a "model" is a contract worth imitating. Applying the basic contract drafting principles that you have learned so far, you may examine the samples in the "Can of Precedent," above, in order to determine if any elements of their frames are worthy of imitation. However, in drafting the frame of the Sport Psychologist Consulting Agreement, you are most likely going to rely on the model Leaf Disposal Services Agreement or any other model agreement your professor supplies. The precedent will become more useful when you fill in the picture of the contract, as required by Assignment 2E.

Professors who teach contract drafting use various images to convey what contracts drafters do. Therefore, you may hear someone else refer to the "frame" as the "skeleton" of the contract and the "picture" as the "meat on the bones." If it helps you to think of the contract that way, please feel free to do so. The purpose of these metaphors is to help you break down the drafting process into manageable parts.

E. **The Preamble—An Example of Learning from a Model:** Provided that you have the correct information, you can draft a Preamble for the Sport Psychologist Consulting Agreement by following the pattern of the Preamble in the model Leaf Disposal Services Agreement, reprinted below.

LEAF DISPOSAL SERVICES AGREEMENT

Leaf Disposal Services Agreement made this 10th day of October 2007, between SpinGazer, Inc., a Delaware corporation with its principal place of business located at 1200 Ridge Avenue, Evanston, Illinois 60201 (the "Company"), and Fallen Leaves, Inc., an Illinois corporation with its principal place of business located at 2025 North Clark Street, Chicago, Illinois 60614 (the "Provider").

Ask yourself: Who are the parties to this contract? Both Betsy Bennett and Dr. Hope Bowker are individuals, not corporations. For Betsy Bennett, you obviously do not need to identify where she is incorporated and where her principal place of business is located. Simply say "an individual residing at [insert address]." For Dr. Bowker, you may want to say "an individual with her office located at [insert address]."

You must choose a shorthand nickname for each individual and place the parenthetical containing the shorthand name *after* all of the identifying information about that individual. Therefore, after Betsy's address, you may insert (the "Golfer"), for example. If you call Betsy the "Golfer," then you will want to give Dr. Hope Bowker, a nickname at the same level of generality. Perhaps for Dr. Hope Bowker, you will insert (the "Psychologist") after her office address. You may even want to choose nicknames that are more general, such as the "Athlete" and the "Consultant."

The placement of the shorthand names you choose for the parties, which function like in-text definitions, is very important. Perhaps it is hard to believe, but there could be more than one Betsy Bennett in the world. By placing the parenthetical after her address, you make it more likely that you have clearly identified the "Betsy Bennett" who is a party to this contract. The same goes for Dr. Hope Bowker. Clearly identify the party by placing the shorthand name for that party after the identifying information about that party.

When you draft the Preamble of your contract, pay careful attention to punctuation. The Preamble contains a lot of information and is difficult to read if not punctuated properly. Moreover, aside from the Title, the Preamble is the very first thing that the reader will encounter in your contract. Even though it is formulaic, you can set a good tone by drafting it so that it reads smoothly. Proper punctuation helps.

Finally, you and your professor are likely to spend some time talking about what date you should insert in the Preamble. When is the contract "made"? Is it the same date when the contract is signed? Is this date different from the effective date of the term? Also, sometimes the date in the Preamble is preceded by the words "as of." Under what circumstances is it appropriate to use those words? Even a formulaic Preamble can present interesting questions that you are likely to bandy about in class.

F. **Title, Words of Agreement, and Signature Lines:** You and your professor will discuss what to call this contract. For convenience sake, I have referred to it as the *Sport Psychologist Consulting Agreement*, but you are not required to use that title.

The Words of Agreement used in the model Leaf Disposal Services Agreement are simple. After the Background section, insert "Accordingly, the parties agree as follows:". In most contracts, at about this point in the contract, you will see a lengthy "consideration" provision that sounds like complete gobbledygook. You and your professor are likely to discuss whether a formal statement of consideration is necessary if the contract itself makes it amply clear that consideration for the transaction does exist. The drafter of the Leaf Disposal Services Agreement has concluded that the contract does not require a formal statement of consideration.

You can easily imitate the Signature Lines and get them right. The Signature Lines from the Leaf Disposal Services Agreement are reprinted below.

AGREED:

SPINGAZER, INC.   **FALLEN LEAVES, INC.**

By: _____   By: _____
    Jackie Spingazer   Leif E. Liminator

Title: Director of Operations   Title: Supervisor

Since both parties to the Sport Psychologist Consulting Agreement are individuals, you will need to adapt this format a bit. The names in bold-faced, all capital letters above the Signature Lines are the formal names of the parties to the contract—not the shorthand names that you chose in the Preamble and used throughout the rest of the contract. So, where you see **SPINGAZER, INC.** and **FALLEN LEAVES, INC.**, above, you would substitute **BETSY BENNETT** and **DR. HOPE BOWKER.**

> *Note:* Generally, it is a good idea to put your client's signature line first. Believe it or not, this sometimes matters to the client.

Underneath the Signature Lines, type the names of the individuals signing the agreement. You do not need the word "By" if the individual signing is also the party. Just re-type "Betsy Bennett" under her signature line, in upper and lowercase letters. Do the same for Dr. Hope Bowker.

Finally, since both parties are individuals who do not work for any entity, they do not have titles.

G. **Background:** The purpose of the Background section is twofold—to put the Agreement in context and to express the intentions of the parties.

You may be accustomed to seeing this section called "Recitals" and containing a list of "WHEREAS" clauses ending with the crescendo "NOW THEREFORE" clause. Plain English drafters avoid those clauses like the plague. Instead, draft the Background section in smooth prose. This is probably the only place in the contract where you will get to tell a little story. Use it well. Who are the parties? What do they do? Why are they entering into this deal? The Background section should not be too long or too lopsided (containing more information about one party than the other).

The Background section is a place where you should avoid following your models too closely. It is not as formulaic as the Preamble, for example. Ask yourself: What do my readers need to know about the parties? About what happened before (if anything) and about what is about to happen (this transaction)?

Remember that you should not include any operative provisions in the Background section. Be very careful not to include any covenants, conditions precedent, representations and warranties, or statements of discretionary authority here. The courts generally will not give effect to operative language contained in a Background section. And, if you include a covenant in the Background section, you run the risk of forgetting to include it in the body of the contract, where it would actually obligate a party to do something.

Sometimes the parties want to clarify their intentions early in a contract. Even though the Background section should not contain operative provisions, it can contain a statement of the parties' intentions. Sometimes, if there is a contractual dispute, the court will give effect to a statement of intentions included in the Background section instead of, or in addition to, admitting parol evidence of those intentions.

H. Definitions: The model Leaf Disposal Services Agreement gives you some limited guidance about how to draft the definitions. It contains the prefatory language below.

> As used in this Agreement, the terms defined in the preamble have their assigned meanings and the following terms have the meanings assigned to them in this Article.

If you have defined any terms, in-text, in the Background section, you must add the words "and in the Background section" to the prefatory language after the words "in the preamble." That way, you will not have to include any cross-references to those definitions in the Definitions article itself.

By looking at the model, you will see that most definitions use the verb "means" or "includes but does not include." You will also see that in-text definitions found in the body of the contract (but not in the Preamble or Background section) are cross-referenced here, using the verb phrase "has the meaning assigned in."

You and your professor will discuss how to choose what to define and how to draft the definitions. Remember that definitions are declarations and should not contain any operative language—no covenants, conditions, representations and warranties, or statements of discretionary authority. Think of a definition as a statement of what a term means whenever you encounter it used with a capital letter in the contract. If you want a party to undertake any kind of obligation, you must include it in the body of the contract rather than in a definition.

> *Important Note About Drafting Definitions:* In practice, lawyers hardly ever draft a complete Definitions article before they draft the rest of the contract. In a sense, asking you to draft the Definitions before you draft the rest of the contract is an artificial exercise. Nevertheless, it is a good exercise and it may save you some time and energy. It forces you, as a novice contract drafter, to think in advance about what terms you may need to define. You can draft a definition for "major tournament," for example, because you know that you will need to refer to it over and over again.
>
> Moreover, drafting definitions in advance will prevent you from making the mistake of using too many in-text definitions. When a Definitions article contains too many cross-references to in-text definitions, the reader is forced to hop all over the contract to find out what things mean. Instead, by defining most terms in the Definitions article itself, you keep the reader happy by feeding her information. You also take the opportunity to educate her about the deal a bit before she launches into the contract. This may sound like a litigation drafting concept, but it holds true for contract drafting as well. As your reader moves into the contract, after reading a fully developed Definitions article, she is more likely to understand the rest of the contract.

If you remember to consider your audience(s), you will be more likely to achieve the goal of clear communication. Transactional attorneys who fail to consider their audience(s) give transactional attorneys a bad name.

I. **Additional Instructions:** Your professor may provide you with additional instructions regarding this assignment.

2E: FILLING IN THE PICTURE: DRAFTING THE CONTRACT'S OPERATIVE PROVISIONS

Instructions

A. **Summary:** This assignment assumes that you have already drafted the "frame" of the contract as required by Assignment 2D—or that your professor has asked you to skip that assignment and concentrate on "filling in the picture." Using the deal facts contained in the letter from Betsy Bennett and the draft contract from Dr. Hope Bowker (in Assignment 2B, above), draft all of the operative provisions of the Sport Psychologist Consulting Agreement. The "operative" provisions do not include the "frame" of the contract—the Title, Preamble, Background, Words of Agreement, Definitions, and Signature Lines.

B. **Preparation for Filling in the Picture:** Before you begin to fill in the picture, you must do two things. First, review the Can of Precedent identified in Assignment 2D. Determine which topics are generally covered in a sport psychologist (or analogous) consulting agreement and evaluate each contract to see if it contains any language that you think you may be able to adapt or adopt for use in your contract.

Second, you must research the legal issues described in Assignment 2D. If you have identified any other legal issues that you feel you must explore in order to draft the contract, please seek direction from your professor. You should not spend too much time on legal research. Focus instead on drafting the contract.

C. **Filling in the Picture:** To fill in the picture, you must draft all of the operative provisions of the contract and decide how to organize them. Your professor will help you develop the basic skills you need to take the terms of the deal and translate them into contract concepts—covenants, conditions precedent, representations and warranties, statements of discretionary authority, and declarations.[5]

In practice, some call this *memorializing* the terms of the deal, which basically means getting the terms of the deal down on paper so that they have a legal effect. The paper (or contract) is the *memorial.* The parties should be able to turn to the contract whenever they have any questions about their rights and duties with regard to the particular transaction.

D. **Organization—Naming and Ordering the Articles and Sections:** Some provisions are traditionally placed in certain spots. For example, after the Definitions article, some drafters include a brief article containing the main covenants of the deal. One contract drafting expert, Tina L. Stark, calls this brief article the "subject matter performance provision."[6]

---

5. Tina L. Stark, *Drafting Contracts: How and Why Lawyers Do What They Do* 9-10 (Aspen 2007) (describes the contract concepts as the "building blocks" of the contract and the process of converting business terms into contract concepts as a "translation skill").
6. *Id.* at 39-40.

The subject matter performance provision in the model Leaf Disposal Services Agreement is reprinted below.

Article III. Summary of Services and Fees

Section 3.01 Services and Fees. Subject to the provisions of this Agreement, the Provider shall perform the Services described in Article IV. To compensate the Provider for performing the Services, the Company shall pay the Provider the fees and reimburse the Provider for the expenses described in Article V.

The drafter of the model Leaf Disposal Services Agreement put the subject matter performance provision after the Term article. While the exact order of these provisions sometimes varies, remember that the subject matter performance provision, the Term, and the Closing articles should appear near the beginning of the contract.

It is sometimes helpful to think of the subject matter performance provision as a thesis statement plus roadmap. It tells you the "main idea" (or "primary covenants") of the contract and points you to the places in the contract where you can find out more details about those covenants.

After the subject matter performance provision, the Term article, and the Closing article, the reader expects to find information about what services the Psychologist is going to provide and how much the Golfer is going to pay for them. Therefore, you must put the articles covering those topics close to the beginning of the contract.

At the end of the contract, right before the Signature Lines, place the contract's boilerplate provisions (sometimes called *General Provisions*). The Termination and Dispute Resolution articles generally come right before the boilerplate.

So, with the parts of the contract in their traditional places, and allowing for some flexibility in their exact order, your contract (not including the frame) will look something like this:

Summary of Services and Fees
Term
Closing (if any)
In-Office Therapy
Practice Therapy
Major Tournament Therapy
Fees and Expenses

[OTHER TOPICS TO BE COVERED]
Dispute Resolution
Termination
General Provisions

Note that the above italicized headings are offered as an example only. They are not set in stone. You are encouraged to draft your own appropriate headings for the articles you include in the contract.

One of the biggest challenges that a drafter faces is how to organize the business provisions not specifically listed above—that is, how to organize those "other topics to be covered." Start by making a list of every deal term not addressed in the named articles. Then, group those deal terms by "topic" and select a good name for the article covering that topic. Remember that "Golfer's Obligations" and "Psychologist's Responsibilities" are contract concepts, not topics. If you use a heading like "Golfer's Obligations," you are indicating to the reader that all of the Golfer's obligations are contained under that heading. More likely, the Golfer's obligations are scattered throughout the contract.

Choose article names (and section names as well) that are specific and clear. Instead of "Golfer's Obligations," and "Psychologist's Responsibilities," for example, you may have articles or sections called "In-Office Therapy" or "Substitution for Caddy." Either of these articles or sections may contain obligations and responsibilities of one or both parties.

If you find that you have a number of miscellaneous deal terms that do not seem to fit anywhere, give them another look before deciding to create single-section articles. Single-section articles (other than the subject matter performance provision and the Term article) can make the particular topic seem like an undeveloped afterthought, or, conversely, give the particular topic too much weight. It is better to put the miscellaneous deal term into the article it relates to the most, even if it is not a perfect fit.

Once you have found a place for every deal term and named the articles you want to include in the contract, decide what order to put them in. Generally, place the articles in order from most important topic to least important topic. However, if you are describing a process, it may make more sense to put some of the articles in chronological order. There is no magic bullet of contract organization. However, it is very important to remember your audience(s). Ask yourself what your reader needs to know and when your reader needs to know it. Also, remember the terms of the deal. For example, if your client stressed that she was very concerned about Dr. Bowker's attendance at major tournaments, then you may want to move that topic up near the beginning of the contract for emphasis.

E. **Boilerplate Provisions:** The letter from Betsy Bennett and the draft contract from Dr. Bowker may not contain all of the facts you need in order to select the appropriate boilerplate provisions to include in your contract. Follow your professor's instructions regarding which boilerplate to include. A valuable resource to help you understand the history and evolution of various boilerplate provisions is the book *Negotiating and Drafting Contract Boilerplate*, edited and co-authored by Tina L. Stark (American Lawyer Media 2003). Your professor may also ask you to complete Assignment 2G, which requires you to digest some new deal facts and adjust the standard boilerplate language accordingly.

F. **Additional Instructions:** Your professor may provide you with additional instructions about this assignment.

2F: PUTTING THE PICTURE IN THE FRAME: FINISHING THE DRAFT CONTRACT

Instructions

A. **Summary:** You will now insert the "picture" that you drafted in response to Assignment 2E into the "frame" that you drafted in response to Assignment 2D. The result will be one completed draft of a Sport Psychologist Consulting Agreement (with a title that you have selected).

B. **The Process:** Inserting the picture into the frame is not merely a mechanical process. Once you have merged the two documents together, you must make sure that the picture fits the frame properly; in other words, you must review the draft contract as a whole and ask yourself at least the following questions:

☐ Is the Title I chose for the contract still appropriate?

☐ Have I consistently referred to the parties to the contract using the shorthand names that I gave them in the Preamble?

☐ Do the full party names in the Preamble (not the shorthand names) match the full party names above the Signature Lines?

☐ Does the date in the Preamble reflect the date when the contract is made? If this is different from the effective date of the contract, have I clarified that in the body of the contract?

☐ Do the addresses in the Preamble match the addresses in the "Notice" provision included in the boilerplate?

☐ Did I include enough information in the Background section? Is there anything else that I may want to add to that section? Is there anything I may want to take out?

☐ Do I use my defined terms whenever it is appropriate? [*Note:* This is called "letting your defined terms do their work."]

☐ Did I remember to capitalize my defined terms in the body of the contract?

☐ Are there any lengthy phrases that I repeat more than once that could perhaps be defined terms?

☐ Are there any concepts that I repeat in different ways each time that I should perhaps be saying the same way each time? Would a defined term help?

☐ Are there any defined terms that I never use or use only once? (If so, you probably do not need to define that term.)

☐ Have I included a cross-reference to every in-text definition in the Definitions article? Are my definitions still in alphabetical order?

☐ Whenever I use a cross-reference, have I referenced the correct article or section?

☐ Have I used cross-references in the body of the contract to help the reader understand the relationship between parts of the contract?

☐ Are all of my article and section numbers in order? Does each have an appropriate heading?

☐ In the "Survivability" boilerplate provision, have I listed all of the sections of the contract that will survive the early termination of the contract or the end of the term?

☐ Do all of the parts of the contract work well together?

Once you have answered all of these questions and made any necessary adjustments to the contract, you can move into the editing and proofreading stage described below.

C. **Editing and Proofreading:** Using the Contract Drafting Checklist provided in Appendix 3, go back over your draft contract again. The checklist is set up to help you take the long view first. Think about the transaction. Have you captured all of the terms of the deal? Have you translated them into the correct contract concepts? Have you answered all questions about the rights and duties of the parties with regard to this transaction? Have you raised any questions without answering them? Is your contract well organized, coherent, and coordinated? Does it read smoothly? Is it easy to follow?

The checklist then asks you to look at some formatting issues that are directly related to readability. Review those issues, remembering also that well-chosen headings and the judicious use of "white space" enhance the readability of a contract. Do not remove headings or white space in order to make sure that you do not exceed the page limit for this assignment. If you need guidance about how to avoid exceeding the page limit, seek your professor's help.

Following the checklist, now make sure that your contract contains all of the essential parts. Then, review each part. Finally, under the broad heading "Plain English," the checklist directs you to make sure that you have not made any grammatical, mechanical, or typographical errors.

Once you have gone through the checklist, prepare your contract for submission by proofreading it carefully, using the proofreading tips and tricks contained in Appendix 5. Finally, go back to the original assignment sheet and verify that you have followed all of the directions regarding submitting the contract to your professor. There is something particularly disturbing about a transactional attorney who fails to follow directions. Failing to follow directions indicates that you are not detail-oriented, which, in practice, can make your supervisor and your client mistrust you. It can also lead to a dangerous loss of credibility with the attorney representing the other side.

D. Submitting the Contract: Do one final thing before you submit your contract: Make sure that you are turning in a clean copy. That is, make sure that you have eliminated any highlighting or comments to yourself that you may have used during the drafting process. Practicing attorneys, both litigators and deal lawyers, can tell many war stories about forgetting to delete comments or critiques before filing documents or sending drafts to the other side. You do not want to make such an embarrassing mistake. You may also want to make sure that your document does not contain any hidden personal or metadata, such as information about when you finished the assignment. Check the software you are using to figure out how to eliminate that information.

E. Additional Instructions: Your professor may provide you with additional instructions about this assignment.

2G: IN-CLASS WORKSHOP: BOILERPLATE PROVISIONS

Instructions

A. Summary: In pairs, triads, or larger teams (as directed by your professor), consider each business issue presented. Re-draft each basic boilerplate provision to address the business issue. You may sometimes decide that re-drafting the provision is not the best solution. If so, please suggest another solution.

B. New Deal Facts: This workshop introduces some new facts regarding the Sport Psychologist Consulting Agreement that you are drafting. You must incorporate these new deal facts into the final draft of your contract.

C. Caveat: This workshop does not address all of the boilerplate provisions that you should include in the contract.

D. **Source of the Basic Boilerplate Provisions:** Each basic boilerplate provision is taken from *Drafting Contracts: How and Why Lawyers Do What They Do*, by Tina L. Stark (Aspen 2007), cited as "Stark, *Drafting Contracts*." Remember that, in Tina Stark's words, the standard provisions "are not paradigms of perfect drafting." Rather, they are "intended to give you a sense of the provisions that you will typically see." Stark, *Drafting Contracts* 167. In drafting your answer, you may also wish to consult *Negotiating and Drafting Contract Boilerplate*, edited and co-authored by Tina L. Stark (American Lawyer Media 2003).

E. **Additional Instructions:** Your professor may provide you with additional instructions about this assignment.

EXERCISE I: ASSIGNMENT AND DELEGATION

BUSINESS ISSUE: We know that Bennett wants to give Bowker the right to terminate the Agreement with 30 days prior written notice as long as Bowker finds a comparably qualified sport psychologist to take Bowker's place. (Bennett must also approve of the substitute sport psychologist.) Under these circumstances, Bowker must be able to assign her rights and delegate her duties, as long as the substitute psychologist agrees to assume Bowker's obligation to perform.

Additionally, Bennett is considering forming a corporation called "Killer Bee Golf, Inc." ("KB Golf," for short.) Bennett wants to be able to delegate her duty to pay Dr. Bowker (or the substitute doctor, as the case may be) to KB Golf.

BASIC PROVISION:

> ***Assignment and Delegation.*** This Agreement cannot be assigned or delegated by the parties. (Stark, *Drafting Contracts* 168.)

REVISED PROVISION (OR OTHER SOLUTION):

EXERCISE II: GOVERNING LAW

BUSINESS ISSUE: Neither party is currently incorporated. Both parties reside in Illinois. When Bennett forms KB Golf, she expects it to be an Illinois corporation. Bowker insists that she wants California law to apply to this contract.

You suspect that Bowker may be looking for a way out of the non-competition provision. Assign one of your team members to do a quick

Internet search right now in order to determine if non-competition agreements are enforceable in California.

If Bowker continues to insist on California law and your client really wants Illinois law to apply, what are your options?

BASIC PROVISION:

Governing Law. This Agreement is to be governed by and construed in accordance with the laws of [insert name of state], without regard to its conflict of law principles. (Stark, *Drafting Contracts* 173-174.)

REVISED PROVISION (OR OTHER SOLUTION):

_____

EXERCISE III: NOTICE

BUSINESS ISSUE: Both parties want to be able to terminate the Agreement immediately upon verbal notice (by telephone or in person) if the other party materially breaches the Agreement. They would follow up with written confirmation either by e-mail or by U.S. mail. Both parties agree that all other notices should be in writing.

BASIC PROVISION:

Notice. All notices under this Agreement shall be given in writing. (Stark, *Drafting Contracts* 175-176.)

REVISED PROVISION (OR OTHER SOLUTION):

_____

EXERCISE IV: SEVERABILITY

BUSINESS ISSUE: The LPGA is in the process of reviewing its rules regarding whether to permit a substitute caddy to have sport psychologist credentials. In fact, the LGPA is expected to radically change its rules and to prohibit LPGA golfers from having any contact with their sport psychologists during the four days of play in any major or minor tournament. If this happens, or if the LPGA passes any other regulation that prohibits Bennett from receiving certain of Bowker's services, Bennett wants to sever the "illegal" provisions but keep the rest of the contract in force.

There is also the remote possibility that the LPGA will determine that its members may not seek the advice of a sport psychologist at all. Consider what effect that would have on the contract as well.

BASIC PROVISION:

    Severability. If any provision of this Agreement is illegal or unenforceable, that provision is severed from this Agreement and the other provisions remain in force. (Stark, *Drafting Contracts* 176-177.)

REVISED PROVISION (OR OTHER SOLUTION):

EXERCISE V: MERGER/INTEGRATION CLAUSE

BUSINESS ISSUE: Before deciding to engage Bowker as her regular sport psychologist, Bennett met with her in her office five times and paid her $200 per hour. Before their first session, Bennett asked Bowker to promise in writing not to reveal that Bennett had consulted her. Bowker signed the following Confidentiality Agreement.

Confidentiality Agreement
dated December 15, 2012

I, Dr. Hope Bowker, agree never to disclose to anyone that Betsy Bennett is consulting me in my capacity as sport psychologist. I shall personally prepare and mail her invoices to her. I shall also personally record her payments to me. I shall also treat all of these documents and the terms and conditions of this Agreement as confidential.

Dr. Hope Bowker

    Setting aside any issues about the validity of the above agreement or about the quality of its drafting, please help your client make sure that the contract you are now drafting does not supersede it. Bennett wants to make sure that those early visits to Bowker remain secret.

BASIC PROVISION:

    Merger. This Agreement states the full agreement between the parties and supersedes all prior negotiations and agreements. (Stark, *Drafting Contracts* 178-179.)

REVISED PROVISION (OR OTHER SOLUTION):

EXERCISE VI: WAIVER OF JURY TRIAL

BUSINESS ISSUE: If Bennett and Bowker have a dispute that is not resolved through informal means or through arbitration, Bennett wants to make sure that Bowker has no right to a jury trial.

Courts tend to frown on "Waiver of Jury Trial" provisions. Redraft the basic provision in order to make it more likely to be enforceable.

> **Note:** If your textbook does not contain any information about how to draft a Waiver of Jury Trial, you may need to do a small amount of legal research on this issue.

BASIC PROVISION:

Waiver of Jury Trial. [Insert Party Name] waives her right to trial by jury in all matters involving this Agreement. (Stark, *Drafting Contracts* 175.)

REVISED PROVISION:

2H: SIDE LETTER RE SPECIAL GOLF LESSONS FOR DR. BOWKER

Instructions

A. **Summary:** Your client, Betsy Bennett, has asked you to draft a "side letter" memorializing a new, but not completely unrelated agreement she has struck with the sport psychologist, Dr. Hope Bowker. Your client wants to keep in place the Sport Psychologist Consulting Agreement (the "Agreement") that you drafted. In effect, the side letter will qualify as a written agreement signed by both parties that amends or modifies the Agreement.

B. **Scenario:** Dr. Bowker has expressed an interest in becoming a better golfer, for the reasons described in the attached e-mail string between Betsy and Dr. Bowker. In brief, Dr. Bowker wants Betsy to give her some golf lessons in exchange for Dr. Bowker discounting some of the fees that Betsy is required to pay Dr. Bowker pursuant to the Agreement.

C. **Side Letters, in General:** Do not look for an example of a "side letter" on the Internet or in forms books. Instead, with your professor's guidance, think this through.

Side letters are generally used to clarify an issue in a contract or to address an issue that the parties have failed to cover in the contract.

Collective bargaining agreements, for example, often have numerous side letters that become a part of the main agreement.

Clients like Betsy Bennett will sometimes request that you draft a side letter because they believe that it will take you less time than drafting an amendment to the contract or drafting a separate contract. They believe that a side letter is less formal and will therefore take you less time and cost them less money (since you are billing them by the hour).

D. **Drafting the Side Letter:** Address the side letter from your client to Dr. Bowker. (You have verified that Dr. Bowker is not represented by an attorney; therefore, your client may contact her directly.)

It is a good idea to think about a side letter as being a contract in its own right. Ask yourself what the consideration is for Betsy Bennett's agreement to provide Dr. Bowker with golf lessons. Make sure that you clarify that the side letter concerns a bargained-for exchange by describing that exchange in the body of the letter.

> **Note:** You can accomplish this without including an archaic statement of consideration that is full of meaningless gobbledygook!

Think first about the Agreement and how the side letter will work with it. Include language clarifying that the side letter does not override the Agreement; nor is the side letter superseded by the Agreement. The side letter is, in effect, a written agreement amending the Agreement in certain limited ways.

In order to make sure that the side letter does not get lost or overlooked, make sure that you provide for it to be attached to and incorporated into the Agreement. Then follow through, making sure that both your client and Dr. Bowker receive new copies of the Agreement with the signed Side Letter attached as an exhibit. (This is what you would do in real life. Your professor will let you know whether he wants you to do this for purposes of this assignment.)

Remember to include language stating that this side letter is the only amendment to the Agreement and that the remainder of the Agreement's provisions will remain in effect. Include signature and date lines for both parties. Betsy Bennett will sign and date the letter and mail it to Dr. Bowker for her signature. The letter should include instructions for Dr. Bowker to sign and return the letter to Betsy as soon as possible. Remember to inform Betsy that the side letter is not effective until it is signed by both parties.

E. **Additional Instructions:** Your professor may provide you with additional instructions about this assignment.

E-Mail String Between Betsy Bennett and Dr. Hope Bowker

From: Dr. Hope Bowker   Sent: April 30, 2013; 9:00 a.m

To: Betsy Bennett

Cc:

Subject: Golf Lessons?

Dear Betsy:

During one of our practice sessions this week, I told you about my new relationship with Charles A. Choker, a golf pro at the Mystical Marco Island Resort in Florida. I feel certain that Chuck and I will get married eventually. But, as you know, my golf game is merely average. I want to get better so that we can honeymoon in Scotland and play at all of those fantastic courses that you have already conquered. Would you be willing to help me by giving me some golf lessons in the month of May? If so, I would be willing to lower the $10,000 payment due under our contract on May 30th. What say you?

Hope

* * *

From: Betsy Bennett   Sent: April 30, 2013; 9:28 a.m.

To: Dr. Hope Bowker

Cc:

Subject: Golf Lessons

Dear Hope:

Why Hope, I would say that your game is more than average, but I would be happy to give you some lessons during the month of May. Since we are working together on Monday, Wednesday, Friday, and Saturday every week until June 3rd, I'd like the lessons to be on Sunday mornings at Longbourn Country Club, if that would work for you. I can give you an hour and a half lesson (8:00 to 9:30 a.m.) before I hit the gym for my regular session with my personal trainer. How much would you be willing to take off of the $10,000 payment due on the 30th? Does $2,000 sound reasonable?

Betsy

* * *

From: Dr. Hope Bowker   Sent: April 30, 2013; 10:02 a.m

To: Betsy Bennett

Cc:

Subject: Golf Lessons

I'm so happy that you're willing to give me lessons. I'm honored. The day, time, and place sound great. I hate to sound ungrateful, but I wonder if I could deduct $1,500 instead of the $2,000 you suggested. I've had to cut back a bit on my practice to accommodate all of the time I'm spending with you and I can't really afford a $2,000 discount. Would $1,500 work?

Hope

*   *   *

From: Betsy Bennett   Sent: April 30, 2013; 11:11 a.m.

To: Dr. Hope Bowker

Cc:

Subject: Golf Lessons

Hope:

Okay, we can do $1,500, but only if you're willing to agree that Chip Mulligan can substitute for me if I get sick or have another important engagement on the day of one of our lessons. I don't imagine that happening more than once; in fact, we can limit it to one time if that would make you more comfortable. Also, I have to be totally in charge of what we work on during the lesson. Does that sit right with you?

Betsy

*   *   *

From: Dr. Hope Bowker   Sent: April 30, 2013; 11:27 a.m

To: Betsy Bennett

Cc:

Subject: Golf Lessons

Betsy:

I can deal with one of the lessons being given by Chip. And, yes, you're the boss. You've seen enough of my game to know what I need to work on. So,

I guess we've got a deal. Can you get your lawyers to write up a letter we can both sign? I'd appreciate that so much. I still don't have a lawyer, though I should probably think about getting one sometime in the next few years as my practice continues to grow.

Thank you very much!

Hope

Assignment 3

The Athlete Endorsement Agreement

3A: NON-DISCLOSURE AGREEMENT—DRAFTING THE DEFINITIONS OF CONFIDENTIAL INFORMATION

Instructions

A. **Summary**: In Assignment 3E, you will be assigned to represent either Betsy Bennett (the "Athlete") or Grace-Under-Pressure, Inc., a company that designs, manufactures, distributes, and sells women's golf equipment and women's golf clothing (the "Company"). The Company wants the Athlete to endorse its products; the Athlete wants to endorse the Company's products in exchange for money and free products. Ultimately, you will negotiate and draft an athlete endorsement agreement embodying the negotiated terms of the deal. (Read the General Information for Both Parties, below.)

Before the parties can negotiate further, they need a non-disclosure agreement ("NDA") to protect any confidential information that they may disclose to each other during the course of the negotiations. This assignment requires you to draft the definitions of "Athlete's Confidential Information" and "Company's Confidential Information." You will later incorporate these definitions into the NDA (as part of Assignment 3B).

B. **Using Precedent**: You may review any NDAs you can locate in order to determine how "Confidential Information" is generally defined. However, definitions of Confidential Information contained in NDAs are notoriously full of meaningless language that does not take into account what information actually is going to be disclosed by each party during the course of their negotiations. You must closely examine any precedent you find, tailor it to the terms of your deal (that is, to what kinds of confidential information the parties to this deal are likely to disclose to each other), and translate it into Plain English.

C. **Focus:** The purpose of this brief exercise is to make you focus on who is going to disclose what to whom. In law practice, as in-house counsel at a corporation, for example, you may find the vice president of sales standing at your office door five minutes before a scheduled meeting, demanding that you prepare an NDA. You may have most of the NDA already prepared in a template. But the most important thing is for you to identify what information your client is going to disclose and for what purpose. You would not want your client to reveal a marketing strategy, for example, if you have not included "marketing strategy" in the list of things considered Client's Confidential Information. Nor would you want the other side to use the information about your client's marketing strategy for any purpose other than the particular project about which the parties are negotiating.

You must also be very careful to describe as specifically and narrowly as possible the information that the other party is going to reveal to your client. Parties will frequently bring their own NDAs to meetings and attempt to get other parties to agree not to disclose a wide range of information, much of which is simply not confidential. Limit your client's risk by limiting the kind of information your client agrees not to disclose.

D. **Procedure and Format:** Think about what you know about the transaction. What confidential information has your client most likely already disclosed to the other side? What confidential information is your client likely to disclose to the other side during the course of the continuing negotiation? Make a list of these specific items. Your goal is to avoid using a vague definition like "any information that has commercial value to the Athlete [or the Company]."

Draft two separate definitions as described below:

"Athlete's Confidential Information" includes [insert list of specific items], and [catchall phrase].

"Company's Confidential Information" includes [insert list of specific items], and [catchall phrase].

The "catchall phrase" is designed to make sure that your definition covers things that you have not listed but that are similar to the items in your list. For example, your catchall phrase could be something like "and any other similarly sensitive or proprietary information revealed by the Athlete to the Company during the negotiations." You can do better than that! Look at the precedent you have gathered to see if you can find a definition of Confidential Information that employs a better catchall phrase.

After you say what each party's Confidential Information includes, you must put in the standard exceptions to the definition of Confidential Information, which generally cover things like "information that has previously entered the public domain." You can easily find out what these standard exceptions are by looking at almost any NDA.

Introduce these exceptions by stating: "Neither the Athlete's nor the Company's Confidential Information includes [insert standard exceptions]."

E. **Additional Instructions:** Your professor may provide you with additional instructions about this assignment.

General Information for Both Parties

I. Background

It is December 2016.

More than three years have passed since Ray Bunker, then President of The Village Green Society, Inc., oversaw the installation of a putting green in Betsy Bennett's backyard. During the negotiation of the putting green contract, Ray and Betsy got along quite well. Afterward, they dated seriously for several months.

Although Ray and Betsy loved each other very much, Betsy's career intruded. When she wasn't practicing or participating in LGPA tour events, she was "in session" with her sport psychologist. Eventually, Ray felt like he spent more time with Betsy's dog, Birdie, than he did with Betsy. Ray pleaded with Betsy to go into couples' therapy with him, but she refused. Sadly, Ray ended the relationship.

II. Betsy Bennett's Promising Career

Since Betsy got her backyard putting green, her career has taken off. The table below details her significant winnings and accomplishments over the past three years. (*Note:* An asterisk indicates a major LPGA Tour Event.)

Year	Tournament	Placement	Winnings	Comments
2013	Evian Masters* Navistar LPGA Classic Korea Championship, Presented By Sema	Fourth First Third	$173,000 $195,000 $100,000	Media touted her as one of the top ten rising stars
2014	MasterCard Classic Kraft Nabisco Championship* McDonald's LGPA Championship* Mizuno Classic—Japan	First Second First First	$195,000 $140,000 $300,000 $180,000	Breakthrough year; in contention for LGPA Player of the Year

Year	Tournament	Placement	Winnings	Comments
2015	Fields Open in Hawaii	Second	$195,000	Fourth-
	Michelob's ULTRA Open	First	$165,000	highest
	U.S. Women's Open Championship*	First	$560,000	money winner in
	RICOH Women's British Open*	First	$320,000	the LPGA; among the
	Samsung World Championship	Second	$156,000	top ten players in the world

III. Grace-Under-Pressure, Inc.

Shortly after Ray broke up with Betsy, he left The Village Green Society, Inc. and became a marketing associate for Grace-Under-Pressure, Inc. (known as "Guppy"), a designer, manufacturer, distributor, and seller of women's golf equipment and women's golf clothing. Ray, who still carries a torch for Betsy, has continued to follow her professional golf career. Whenever he hears a sportscaster hail Betsy as the next Annika Sorenstam, Ray elbows any person who happens to be next to him and says, "I almost married Betsy Bennett."

Ray's current employer, Guppy, is the brainchild of Sally Striker and her husband, Walt Wormburner. They formed the Company in January 2010, after they both decided to turn their hobby—playing golf—into a money-making venture.

Sally, Guppy's president, is a mechanical engineer who has always wanted to design golf clubs for women. In particular, she dreamed of creating a putter with a range of special grip sizes designed to fit a woman's hand. Walt, Guppy's director of marketing, is a women's clothing designer intent on making "functional yet feminine" clothing for women golfers; specifically, he wants to redress what he calls the "frump factor" in women's golf apparel.

Guppy, a privately held company incorporated in Illinois, has grown from 25 full-time employees in 2010 to 250 full-time employees in 2016. Its sales volume has increased from $5 million to $30 million. The Company has a wide, international customer base and a distinct competitive advantage—its "Amazin' Grace" putter is a unique product, as no other company has yet offered a putter with a range of putting grips designed to fit a woman's hand. Recently, the Illinois Chamber of Commerce named Guppy to the list of 100 fastest-growing privately held companies in Illinois. Guppy is in 99th place. The Illinois Chamber of Commerce applauds Guppy for its solid financials, job-generation potential, and contribution to promoting Illinois as a premier economic development center.

Because Sally and Walt want Guppy to continue to thrive, they have decided it is time to seek out an LPGA golfer to endorse their products.

> **Note:** As of today, Guppy has no other endorsement contracts with any athletes or celebrities. Guppy has confined its marketing efforts to full-page print ads published in *Golf for Women* magazine. Generally, Guppy has had a good reputation for producing high-quality equipment and clothing.

IV. Guppy's Initial Contact with Betsy Bennett

Having recently learned of Ray's prior relationship with Betsy Bennett, Sally suggested that Ray contact Betsy to tell her about Guppy's products and encourage her to try them. Ray was happy to have this opportunity to re-establish his connection with Betsy as well as to advance his own career.

Betsy was not unhappy to hear from Ray. She remembered him fondly, especially because her dog, Birdie, had been so attached to him. In the course of their lengthy telephone conversation, Ray learned that Betsy is still single but occasionally dates men she meets on the Internet through lovematch.com. Birdie now has a sister, a golden doodle puppy named "Fairway." Betsy also told Ray that she has never endorsed any products and she does not have an agent. She thinks most agents are "creepy" but acknowledges that she will have to hire one someday.

At Ray's suggestion and at Guppy's expense, Betsy agreed to try some of Guppy's products, including some clothing Ray would pick out for her, as well as one of Guppy's top-of-the-line putters, the Amazin' Grace. She agreed to wear the clothes while practicing at the Longbourn Country Club and to try out the putter on the putting green in her backyard.

Remembering that Betsy loves the color yellow, Ray chose a yellow outfit from Guppy's summer line, including yellow capri pants, a yellow golf shirt, a yellow windbreaker, a yellow sun visor, and yellow suede golf shoes. He also selected an Amazin' Grace putter in Betsy's size (based on her height) with a special grip designed to fit Betsy's tiny hands. (He remembered that he used to read her the e. e. cummings poem with the lovely line "Nobody, not even the rain, has such small hands.") Ray messengered the package of Guppy products to Betsy at her home in Longbourn, Illinois, along with a note that said: "Compliments of Grace-Under-Pressure, Inc. and your dear old friend, Ray Bunker."

Thus began Guppy's courtship of Betsy Bennett.

V. The Endorsement Contract Between Bennett and Guppy

About a month after Ray sent the package of Guppy products to Betsy, Sally Striker contacted Betsy directly and introduced herself. She invited Betsy to dine with her at Charley Trotter's restaurant in Chicago. Over a $300 bottle of wine, Betsy tentatively agreed to endorse Guppy's products. Sally told Betsy that she would have Guppy's attorney call Betsy's attorney in order to get the ball rolling.

VI. LPGA Restrictions on Endorsement Contracts

The LPGA permits its members to endorse any "reputable" products. The organization does not define "reputable." LPGA members are permitted to identify themselves as LPGA members, but they are not permitted to imply that the LPGA endorses any particular products.

> **Note:** Do not conduct any research on this issue. Assume that all of the products that Guppy wants Bennett to endorse are reputable products. Also assume that Guppy does not want Betsy to imply that the LPGA endorses any of its products.

3B: NON-DISCLOSURE AGREEMENT: DRAFTING THE OPERATIVE PROVISIONS

Instructions

A. **Summary:** This assignment assumes that you have completed Assignment 3A and that you now have in hand the definitions of Athlete's Confidential Information and Company's Confidential Information. Using those definitions, you will complete the Non-Disclosure Agreement ("NDA") that the parties will sign before they begin negotiating the terms of the Athlete Endorsement Agreement. The attorneys for the Athlete and the Company have met and agreed upon the operative terms that they want to include in the NDA. The Company's attorney assigned a junior associate to take notes during this meeting (copy attached). The parties have reviewed the notes and believe that they accurately represent what the parties agreed to at the meeting.

B. **Using Precedent:** You may review any NDAs you can locate in order to help you determine how NDAs look and what provisions they generally contain. (You may want to refer to the same NDAs you used when drafting the definitions of Confidential Information in Assignment 3A.) You must apply everything you know about good contract drafting to any language you adopt or adapt from the available precedent. For example, remember to use "shall" for covenants and to draft in the active voice. Say "The Company shall not disclose the Athlete's Confidential Information" as opposed to "The Athlete's Confidential Information shall not be disclosed by the Company."

Remember, also, to eliminate all legalese from any precedent you use. Do not develop the lawyerly bad habit of using two or even three words when one strong word will do. For example, say "The Athlete shall not disclose the Company's Confidential Information" as opposed to "The Athlete shall not reveal, disseminate, or disclose the Company's Confidential Information."

> **Note:** Reasonable people may disagree about whether "disseminate" carries a different meaning from "reveal" and "disclose" and should therefore be included. Always ask yourself if all of the words in your list are necessary to carry your meaning. (Certainly "reveal" and "disclose" are synonymous. Eliminate one of them.)

C. **Organization of the Non-Disclosure Agreement:** Draft a Preamble for the NDA, just as you would for any other contract. Follow the model Leaf Disposal Services Agreement Preamble shown below.

LEAF DISPOSAL SERVICES AGREEMENT

Leaf Disposal Services Agreement made this 10th day of October 2007, between SpinGazer, Inc., a Delaware corporation with its principal place of business located at 1200 Ridge Avenue, Evanston, Illinois 60201 (the "Company"), and Fallen Leaves, Inc., an Illinois corporation with its principal place of business located at 2025 North Clark Street, Chicago, Illinois 60614 (the "Provider").

For the Background section in your NDA, do not succumb to blindly following precedent by inserting a number of "WHEREAS" clauses culminating in the big "NOW, THEREFORE" clause. Instead, simply insert a brief description of why the parties are going to be revealing confidential information to each other. What does the Company want to discuss with the Athlete? In the Background section, you may want to create an in-text definition of "Project" that you can use throughout the NDA. Remember that your client is entering into an NDA to protect information revealed during the negotiations about the Project.

After the Preamble, you should include the words, "Accordingly, the parties agree as follows" unless you determine that it may be important to use a fuller statement of consideration in this NDA. Since both parties are exchanging Confidential Information, and both parties are agreeing not to disclose that information, the consideration for the contract is inherent in the contract itself. But, because the consideration for an NDA may not be as obvious as it is for a purchase or services agreement, you may want to include a statement like "Accordingly, in consideration of the mutual promises contained in this Agreement, the parties agree as follows." Do not revert to gobbledygook by adding the words "and other good and valuable consideration, the receipt and sufficiency of which is hereby mutually acknowledged." Keep it simple.

After the statement of consideration, organize the remainder of the NDA as follows:

Definitions
Term
Basic Non-Disclosure Obligations
[Other Operative Provisions]
General Provisions
Signature Lines

Draft the basic non-disclosure obligations before you cover any other operative provisions. You will find precedent in which the drafters describe both parties' non-disclosure obligations in one section or paragraph. In order to avoid the difficulties of the "Both parties shall not" construction—including having to define "Disclosing Party" and "Recipient"—try drafting one section containing the Company's non-disclosure obligations and another section containing the Athlete's non-disclosure obligations.

After you draft the parties' basic non-disclosure obligations, you must decide what other operative provisions you need to cover and organize them in a logical way. For example, you will want to talk about what happens to the Confidential Information when the term of the NDA ends. You may want to cover this topic near the end of the contract, since it addresses what is to happen at the end of the parties' relationship. When considering how to organize the "other operative provisions," keep your audience in mind. You still have to consider an audience wider than just the parties' signators and the parties' attorneys. Remember that Company executives other than the person signing on behalf of the Company may legitimately have a "need to know" the Athlete's Confidential Information. Therefore, these executives may have to see the NDA in order to understand their own non-disclosure obligations.

Next, look at the precedent you have located to determine what kind of boilerplate provisions generally appear in an NDA. Most NDAs have merger/integration and choice-of-law provisions, for example. Some have severability provisions as well. Think about your client's needs. If you believe that any other boilerplate should be included to address your client's needs, put it in. For example, perhaps several years after signing the NDA, your client will need to disclose the other party's Confidential

Information to a third party. If you think that might happen, you may want to include an amendment and modification clause so that it might be possible to shorten the NDA's term.

D. **Formatting the Non-Disclosure Agreement:** After the Definitions article, you can use simple numbered paragraphs with headings to format the NDA. So, for example, the "Term" and "Non-Disclosure Obligations" sections might look like this:

1. **Term.** This Agreement begins on [insert date] and ends [insert date].
2. **Company's Duty Not to Disclose Athlete's Confidential Information.** [Insert body of provision].
3. **Athlete's Duty Not to Disclose Company's Confidential Information.** [Insert body of provision].

E. **One Final Note About the Nature of Confidential Information:** Remember that parties can reveal confidential information both orally and in writing. In other words, much of what the parties say to each other may never be put down in a document but may still constitute confidential information. Do not make the mistake of assuming that confidential information is only contained in written documents. Be sure that your NDA takes this into account.

F. **Additional Instructions:** Your professor may provide you with additional instructions about this assignment.

Redford, Newman & McQueen

                                          Audra Hepburn, Junior Associate

Subject: Notes of Meeting Between Grace Under Pressure, Inc. and
                    Betsy Bennett

Re: Terms of Non-Disclosure Agreement (Athlete Endorse-
                    ment Agreement Negotiations)

Date: January 2, 2017

The Athlete asked that the Company stamp any document considered to contain the Company's Confidential Information with the word "Confidential." The Company explained that it would not be possible to ensure that all of its employees involved in the negotiation (and preparation for the negotiation) remember to stamp documents "Confidential." The Company has a broad universe of people to control. Therefore, the Company does not want to accept the risk that some of the Company's Confidential Information might not be considered confidential just because someone forgot to stamp it.

Since the Athlete is self-employed and likely to be the only one who handles documents containing the Athlete's Confidential Information, she can easily stamp any documents containing the Athlete's Confidential Information with the word "Confidential" in the upper right-hand corner. She agreed to do this.

The Athlete asked that the Company only share the Athlete's Confidential Information (whether contained in documents or otherwise) with its attorneys and people in the Company's employ who have some genuine need to know what the documents contain. The Company agreed. Both parties agreed that those Company employees with a "need to know" include at least the Company's President, Director of Marketing, and Director of Accounting. At this time, it is not possible for the Company to identify exactly who else may need to see the documents containing the Athlete's Confidential Information.

The Company knows that the Athlete will want to share some of the Company's Confidential Information with her caddy, Chip Mulligan, who sometimes helps manage her career. She may also need to share the Company's Confidential Information with her attorneys, and, of course, her financial advisors. The Athlete agreed not to disclose the Company's Confidential Information to anyone else unless she gets the Company's written permission first. (She anticipates perhaps hiring a manager some time during the next few years. She agreed that she would seek the Company's written permission before disclosing any of the Company's Confidential Information to the person she hires.)

Both the Company and the Athlete agree that they will show the NDA to everyone on the permitted list and get those individuals to sign an acknowledgment stating that they have read the NDA and understand that they are undertaking the same obligations as the signators. Both the Company and the Athlete also agreed that, if they have to show the other party's Confidential Information to anyone not on the permitted list, they will get that person to agree not to disclose the information and have that person sign a similar acknowledgment.

The Athlete wants to make sure that entering into this NDA does not bind her to enter into a contract with the Company. The Company has the same concern—i.e., that the NDA not bind the Company to engage the Athlete to endorse its products—and would like to include some language to that effect in the NDA. Both parties want this language to be prominent in the NDA.

There was much discussion about how long the duties not to disclose should last. The parties finally agreed that the non-disclosure obligations should last for five years after the negotiation is completed, if the negotiation does not result in a contract. If the negotiation does result in a contract, then the parties want the non-disclosure obligations to last for the life of the contract plus five years. They both want to make sure that the endorsement contract does not supersede the NDA.

For both parties, the duties not to disclose the Confidential Information will include the obvious—not disclosing to anyone but those on the permitted list—as well as protecting the other party's Confidential Information just as the recipient would protect its own. Also, the parties are only going to use the Confidential Information in connection with the project at hand—the Athlete's endorsement of the Company's equipment and clothing. Both parties want the NDA to state the reason why they are disclosing the information to each other—to evaluate whether or not to enter into an athlete endorsement agreement.

After the parties finish negotiating, if they decide not to enter into a contract, both parties must return each other's Confidential Information immediately. The parties agreed to deliver the Confidential Information contained in documents by messenger. If the parties do enter into a contract, a party can keep the documents containing the Confidential Information until the other party requests its return. All Confidential Information must be returned by messenger within five business days of the other party's request. Alternatively, the party holding the Confidential Information party may destroy the documents and provide an Affidavit of Destruction, signed by the Athlete or the Company's President, as appropriate.

If either the Company or the Athlete is compelled to produce the other party's Confidential Information by a court order or subpoena, then the compelled party will let the other party know right away by telephone and e-mail. That way the owner of the Confidential Information can decide whether to move for a protective order or take some other action to prevent its disclosure. The Company was particularly adamant about this point.

Finally, both parties want the existence of the NDA and its contents to remain confidential, except that the parties may show it to people on the permitted list, who will also agree to keep its existence and contents confidential.

3C: PREPARATION FOR THE NEGOTIATION OF THE ATHLETE ENDORSEMENT AGREEMENT

Part I: Finding, Evaluating, and Using the Relevant Precedent

Instructions

A. **Summary:** Re-read the General Information for Both Parties included in Assignment 3A. You will now search for contracts that will be likely to help you draft an Athlete Endorsement Agreement. Once you locate the relevant precedent, you will review it and begin creating a negotiation prep sheet.

B. **Resources:** You may look for precedent in the library and on the Internet. You may not purchase any forms, whether from a store or online. You may not use any precedent in your own files (from a previous job or a summer position) or any precedent you obtain from an attorney. Finally, you may not use any contracts obtained from other students who have taken this class. Pretend that the library and the Internet are your only resources.

C. **What to Look For:** When you look for precedent in the litigation context, you try to find cases that are as close to your case as possible. If your case is about intentional infliction of emotional distress and involves one neighbor terrorizing another by putting dead insects and snakes on the other neighbor's doorstep, you would be very happy to find another case with nearly identical facts. If that case turns out to be in the same jurisdiction as yours, you would be even happier. Most likely, you will have to settle for cases with similar or analogous facts—and you may need to look beyond your jurisdiction.

In the transactional context, when you look for precedent, focus first on what kind of contract you are being asked to draft. For the purposes of this assignment, you want to find endorsement agreements. While it may be helpful to find an endorsement agreement in which a golfer agrees to endorse golf equipment and clothing, it is not as important to find a contract with nearly identical facts as it might be if you were trying to prove a case in the litigation context. Moreover, while searching for precedent in the transactional context, you do not have to be as conscious of jurisdictional issues, though you do have to familiarize yourself with any laws that affect your deal (as you will do in Assignment 3D).

Would an endorsement agreement in which a celebrity endorses a particular brand of luxury watches be relevant precedent? Of course! If that celebrity happens to be a professional athlete, even better. But do not expect to find a contract that is precisely on point.

D. **How to Find It:** If you love books and libraries, you may be tempted to start looking for precedent there. However, unless you do not own a computer or cannot connect to the Internet, looking for books in the library would not be the most efficient way to begin.

Begin by surfing the Web. You may choose to do a general search, using the search engine of your choice, or to go to LEXIS or WESTLAW to see what forms are available there. One very good online source of sample contracts is www.onecle.com (click on Business Contracts). There, you will find thousands of actual contracts used by businesses for various purposes. Another good online source of sample contracts is Findlaw.com (click on Learn about the Law; then Small Business; then Business Forms and Contracts). Remember that the "samples" you find on these sites are "samples," and not "models." For more about what that distinction means, see Section E, Reviewing and Evaluating Precedent, below.

When you surf the Web seeking relevant precedent, start with a narrow search and then broaden it out. For example, you may want to start by searching for "golfer endorsement of product and equipment." From there, you might move on to "athlete endorsement agreement." If you still do not feel as if you have found enough precedent, ask yourself what kinds of contracts are similar to an athlete endorsement agreement. Perhaps searching for "endorsement agreement" will reveal some endorsement agreements between athletes and companies that contain useful provisions. Since "agreement" and "contract" are used interchangeably, be sure to search for both terms.

Do not forget to search LEXIS and WESTLAW. Both have databases containing contract forms.

If you prefer working with actual books, go to your law library and locate the "forms" books. Skim through the tables of contents or indexes to determine if the books contain any relevant forms.

E. **Reviewing and Evaluating Precedent:** Once you have located eight or ten relevant contracts, begin to review them. Ask yourself at least the following questions about each contract:

- ☐ How relevant is the precedent?
    - ☐ Is it an athlete endorsement agreement?
    - ☐ Is it a celebrity endorsement agreement?
    - ☐ Does the athlete or celebrity endorse clothing? Equipment?
- ☐ Is it a contract from the United States (as opposed to the United Kingdom or another country, with different contract drafting methods and formats)?
- ☐ How is the agreement formatted?
    - ☐ Does it contain all of the essential parts of a contract?
    - ☐ If it does not contain all of the essential parts, what is omitted?
- ☐ What topics are covered?

□ Does the agreement cover any topics that you would not have thought to cover?

□ How is the agreement organized?

□ What appears to be the organizing principle behind the placement of topics in the agreement? Importance? Chronology? Something else?

□ Is it easy to find things in the agreement?

□ Does the agreement read smoothly?

□ Did the drafters use the appropriate verbs to express contract concepts?

□ Did the drafters use the active voice?

□ Did the drafters use Plain English throughout? In parts?

□ Are there any places in the agreement that are heavy with legalese?

□ Does anything in the agreement strike you as being particularly well drafted or handled?

After you finish reading through all of the relevant precedent you have found, rate the agreements on a scale of 1 to 5, with 1 signifying "best" and 5 signifying "useless." Make a note of which contracts contain "good language" about particular topics. The "good language" standard does not necessarily mean "well-drafted" language; you may just appreciate the way the drafters handle a particular issue as opposed to the way they write about it. Perhaps, for example, you find an agreement that contains a clause requiring both the athlete and the company to behave with integrity and abide by the moral standards of the community (traditionally known as a "morals" clause). Even if the drafters speak legalese, mark the language because it contains an interesting concept (a morals clause binding *both* parties) that you may want to include in your own contract.

After you have rated the contracts, look at the entire batch of precedent once again and make a list of the main topics covered in the agreements. If most of the agreements cover "Logos on Clothing and Equipment," for example, then you will most likely need to cover that topic when you negotiate and draft the endorsement agreement between the Athlete and the Company. If one agreement contains a provision that none of the other agreements contains, you may have found a provision particular to the transaction at issue in that agreement.

F. **Using the Relevant Precedent:** When you draft your contract, you may decide to adopt or adapt some language from the relevant precedent you found. If so, you must remember the following principles.

1. **Every deal is its own deal.** This means that no matter how close the relevant precedent seems to the deal you are negotiating, your deal is a different deal. On the surface level, the parties' names and addresses are different. On a deeper level, your deal may include many facts that are different from the deal memorialized in the precedent. Maybe, for

example, in your deal, the Company is going to allow the Athlete to keep all of the clothing and equipment she tests rather than requiring her to pay for it, as provided in the precedent you have chosen to use. Remember to tailor the precedent to the facts of your deal.

2. **Cutting and pasting numbs the mind.** It is tempting to cut and paste. Resist the temptation. If you re-type the language instead, you are more likely to notice things about how it is drafted—like the way the drafters used "null and void" instead of just "void." Or the fact that none of the parties is mentioned in a sentence purporting to obligate one of the parties to do something. If you simply cut and paste the language and rely on yourself to catch and fix those things in the editing and proofreading stage, you are missing a golden, immediate opportunity. The best example of the way cutting and pasting numbs the mind is this: Many students make the mistake of cutting and pasting a piece of precedent from another contract and forgetting to change the names of the parties. When the reader, used to seeing the "the Athlete" and "the Company," suddenly comes across "the Buyer" and "the Seller," she stumbles. If she is grading the contract, she takes off points.

3. **The naked drafter rules the world.** No, I am not advocating that you draft in the nude. I am advocating that you learn how to draft without relying on precedent. If you master the skill of translating deal terms into contract concepts (covenants, conditions precedent, representations and warranties, declarations, and statements of discretionary authority), then you will be able to draft a contract without having any precedent at hand. When your client asks you to put a unique provision in the contract, you will be the "can-do" lawyer—that is, the lawyer who can draft the provision on the spot without needing a precedential crutch. Exercising your naked drafting skills will make you feel smart, efficient, creative, and, yes, powerful! Moreover, when you decide to use precedent, you will have the skills necessary to help you analyze and improve the language in the provisions you decide to adopt or adapt.

4. **Mine the precedent for ideas, not language.** The best way to use precedent is to help you "see" how a contract like the one you are attempting to draft generally "looks." Reviewing some relevant precedent is a good way to get started on a drafting a contract that seems daunting. In other words, with the facts of your own deal foremost in your mind, you can use precedent to help you figure out what terms to define, what topics to cover, and what order to cover them in. You can also use precedent to help you discover whether you ought to include certain provisions because they are traditionally included in this type of contract or because they are required by law. (Of course, you must still do enough legal research to satisfy yourself that you have covered any legal issues the contract raises.)

Finally, ask your professor if he wants you to cite to any precedent you use. If so, find out what citation format he prefers.

G. **The Negotiation Prep Sheet:** After you have located some good, relevant precedent, use it to help you prepare for the negotiation of the endorsement agreement between the Athlete and the Company. Create a three column table entitled *Negotiation Prep Sheet.* Label the first column "Topic," the second column "Description," and the third column "Position." Since you do not yet know which client you represent, leave the third column blank. In the first column, list the topics covered in the precedent. In the second column, insert some details about each topic. Your negotiation prep sheet will look something like this:

NEGOTIATION PREP SHEET

Topic	Description	Position
Logos on Clothing and Equipment	Size, placement—front and back? Number of logos displayed. Athlete's obligation not to cover or deface.	
Etc.	Etc.	

When you finish filling in columns 1 and 2 of your negotiation prep sheet, you will have a living document that you can revise in light of the legal research you do in response to Assignment 3D and the confidential instructions you receive from your client as part of Assignment 3E.

H. **Collaboration:** Your professor may permit you to collaborate with your classmates in locating, reviewing, and evaluating precedent as well as in creating the first negotiation prep sheet. If you do collaborate with your classmates on this assignment, you will get to see how different people approach the task of finding precedent. Which search engines do your classmates use? How do they word their first search? Their second search? Their third? Do they begin with LEXIS? WESTLAW? When they find something useful, how do they record it? Do they bookmark it? Copy the URL into a Word document? Print it out in hard copy? Do they make any spot judgments about the quality of the precedent they find? Do they dwell on one contract or continue searching until they have gathered a number of relevant contracts? And so on. . . . You will inevitably get some great ideas from your classmates. But the most valuable part of the collaboration lies in observing someone else's "process." It may open your mind!

I. **Additional Instructions:** Your professor may provide you with additional instructions about this assignment.

3D: CONTINUED PREPARATION FOR THE NEGOTIATION OF THE ATHLETE ENDORSEMENT AGREEMENT

Part II: Researching the Legal Issues

Instructions

A. **Summary:** This assignment assumes that you have completed Assignment 3C. First, re-read the General Information for Both Parties included in Assignment 3A. In further preparation for your negotiation, you will now research the legal issues impacting the Athlete Endorsement Agreement between Betsy Bennett and Grace-Under-Pressure, Inc. You will research the legal issues that you identified when locating, reviewing, and evaluating the relevant precedent as well as research any other legal issues that you have identified yourself or that your professor has identified for you. You will then revise the negotiation prep sheet, adding new topics and descriptions that address these legal issues.

B. **What to Look For:** When you reviewed and evaluated the relevant precedent, you may have found that several sample contracts contained references to particular statutes, ordinances, or regulations. Begin there. For example, if you have found any endorsement agreements that refer to the Federal Trade Commission's regulations regarding truth in advertising, you will want to know what those regulations say. You may also want to find out if there are any similar state laws regulating advertising. What is an individual who endorses a product allowed to say? Does she actually have to use the product that she endorses?

Do not hesitate to research other legal issues that you or your professor have identified, even if you do not find them addressed in the relevant precedent. Remember that you have located "sample contracts," not models. Perhaps the additional legal research you do will uncover some key points that the sample contracts simply failed to cover.

> *Caveat:* Do not let yourself get too caught up in legal research. You are not striving to become an expert. Do enough research to satisfy yourself that you are competent to draft the contract—and rely on your professor to supply additional expertise, if need be.

C. **How to Find It:** By now, you know how to find statutes and regulations. Start with the primary sources: the statutes and regulations cited in the precedent. Then do some more general searches, using the search engine of your choice or using LEXIS or WESTLAW. Regardless of which party you wind up representing, you will want to know about any restrictions on the Athlete's ability to endorse the products *before* you begin negotiating the contract.

D. **The Negotiation Prep Sheet:** When you feel you have a pretty good grasp of the legal issues you have identified, add them to the negotiation prep sheet. Remember to include citations in your descriptions, since you may want to revisit these issues when you are negotiating or drafting.

E. **Collaboration:** Your professor may permit you to collaborate with your classmates in conducting the legal research this assignment requires. If so, you will benefit from seeing how someone else approaches a problem. Observing your classmates' "process" may make you decide to change your own way of doing things. Even if watching your classmates in action merely confirms that your own process is more effective, you are still likely to benefit from talking about the legal issues while you are researching them. In a good collaborative environment, participants take turns being the striker and the flint. When a striker is applied to flint, sparks fly. Sometimes you will raise a question (acting as the striker) and your class-mate will propose an answer (acting as the flint). And sometimes, vice versa. You will both benefit from the sparks!

F. **Additional Instructions:** Your professor may provide you with additional instructions about this assignment.

3E: NEGOTIATION OF THE ATHLETE ENDORSEMENT AGREEMENT: LETTER OF INTENT AND TERM SHEET

Instructions

A. **Summary:** For this assignment, you will represent either Betsy Bennett (the "Athlete") or Grace-Under-Pressure, Inc. (the "Company"). As you know from reading the General Information for Both Parties included in Assignment 3A, the Company wants to engage the Athlete to endorse its clothing and equipment. The Athlete wants to endorse the Company's clothing and equipment for a fee. Your task is to negotiate the deal and draft the contract between the Athlete and the Company.

B. **Assume No Conflict of Interest:** If you represent the Company in this deal, you can assume that there is no conflict of interest in your representing the Company against the Athlete, even though you may have represented the Athlete in connection with a previous deal. Alternatively, you may pretend that you have never represented the Athlete in the past.

C. **The Negotiation:** Your professor will tell you which party you represent and which of your classmates will be your opposing counsel. Your professor will also give you some Confidential Instructions from your client.

Logistics:

1. Begin by re-reading the General Information for Both Parties included in Assignment 3A and reading the Confidential Instructions from your client.

2. After carefully reviewing the Confidential Instructions from your client, revise the negotiation prep sheet you prepared in response to Assignments 3C and 3D to add any topics mentioned in the Confidential Instructions but not listed on your negotiation prep sheet. If you know what your client's position is with regard to a particular issue, insert that information in the "Position" column.

> **Note:** If you do not know what your client's position is with regard to a particular issue—and you believe it is an issue that the contract ought to cover—make a note to ask your client about it.

3. Complete your negotiation prep sheet by asking your professor to answer any questions you have about your client's position on the issues. Your professor may choose to tell you what your client's position is, or allow you to decide what your client's position ought to be. Either way, be sure to complete the negotiation prep sheet before moving on to the next step.

4. Prepare to negotiate. Study your negotiation prep sheet and tweak it, if necessary. You will bring this sheet with you to the negotiation.

5. Talk to your opposing counsel to schedule a mutually convenient time and place for the negotiation. Make sure that you find a quiet place where you will not be disturbed and will not encounter other pairs of negotiators from your class. Allow at least two hours for your first negotiation session.

6. Do not show your negotiation prep sheet or the Confidential Instructions you received from your client to your opposing counsel (or any other students who represent the opposing party) at any time before, during, or after the negotiation. During the negotiation, you will use the information in your Confidential Instructions as your guide to your client's wishes. You will naturally and judiciously reveal some of the information to your opposing counsel during

the course of the negotiation in order to achieve your client's objectives.

7. Your Confidential Instructions may or may not contain information about your client's wishes regarding every issue you need to cover in the contract. For example, your Confidential Instructions do not address every boilerplate provision that you may want to include in the contract. If you do not know what your client wants, ask your professor or negotiate for what you believe will be in your client's best interests.

8. During the negotiation, you and your opposing counsel should prepare a "Term Sheet" which will ultimately be attached to your Letter of Intent ("LOI") and should look something like this:

ATTACHMENT A TO LETTER OF INTENT

Issue	Terms

---

9. In this negotiation, you MUST reach an agreement. While the negotiation itself is not graded, you will receive extra points for being especially thorough and for devising creative solutions to disputed issues between the parties.

10. If you need access to your client during the negotiation, please contact your professor. If you and your opposing counsel reach a stalemate on any issues, please contact your professor.

11. If you do not finish your negotiation in one sitting, schedule another mutually convenient time to meet. Remember that you are likely to continue negotiating during the drafting process.

D. **Drafting the Letter of Intent:** Once you have completed your negotiation, you and your opposing counsel must draft one LOI and submit it to your professor. Your professor will decide whether to grade the LOI itself, but he may simply want to refer to the LOI when grading your contract. Therefore, if you and your opposing counsel change any significant terms contained in the LOI during subsequent negotiations, your professor may ask you to revise the LOI and re-submit it.

DRAFTING THE LETTER OF INTENT

(A Mini-Assignment within the Negotiation Assignment)

1. Draft an LOI. You will attach the term sheet that you created during your negotiation to the LOI as Exhibit A.

2. Address the LOI to your professor.

3. Do not use any precedent to draft the LOI. Draft in Plain English. Do not include anything that looks like a covenant. This is not a contract. See No. 4, below.

4. The most important thing to keep in mind is that you do not want your opposing counsel to be able to say that the LOI is a binding contract whether your negotiations fall through or your negotiations result in a signed contract. The LOI contains preliminary terms, some of which are likely to change over time. Make sure that you emphasize that the LOI is not a binding contract by featuring this point prominently in the LOI.

5. State that the letter describes the terms that the Athlete and the Company have discussed about the transaction and include a brief description of the transaction. Mention that the terms are attached in Exhibit A.

6. Clarify that the parties are not bound by any of the terms in the term sheet unless they sign a contract including those terms.

7. Clarify that when the parties sign the letter they are not acquiring any rights or undertaking any obligations, and, especially, that they are not promising to enter into a contract with the other party.

8. Include a paragraph reminding the Athlete and the Company that they are bound by the Non-Disclosure Agreement ("NDA") they signed before they began negotiating this deal and that the NDA prohibits them from disclosing the existence or terms of this LOI. Alternatively, you can include non-disclosure obligations in the LOI. (However, since the LOI is not a contract, any covenants you include in it arguably are not enforceable.)

9. Insert signature lines for both parties. This is another reason to include the language about the LOI not being a contract. The LOI is likely to look like a contract because both parties sign it.

10. Remember to attach the term sheet to the LOI before submitting the LOI to your professor.

E. **Additional Instructions:** Your professor may provide you with additional instructions regarding this assignment.

3F: PREPARATION OF TALKING POINTS FOR MEETING WITH SENIOR PARTNER RE POTENTIAL ETHICAL QUESTION

Instructions

A. **Summary:** For the purposes of this assignment, pretend that you represent Grace-Under-Pressure, Inc. ("Guppy"). You must analyze the scenario presented below to determine whether you violated the Model Rules of Professional Conduct by agreeing to pay Ray Bunker the finder's fee demanded by Betsy Bennett's attorney. You must then draft "Talking Points" to guide you when you present the issue to your senior partner, Paula Newman.

B. **Scenario:** During your negotiations with Betsy Bennett's attorney, Bennett's attorney proposed that Guppy agree to pay Ray Bunker a "finder's fee" of $50,000 since he was the one who ultimately convinced Betsy to endorse Guppy's products. Betsy's attorney said that Betsy was not likely to go through with the deal unless Guppy agreed to pay Bunker the finder's fee. (In other words, the finder's fee was a deal breaker.)

   By this point in the negotiation, you were very tired. You knew that you did not have the authority to agree to the $50,000 finder's fee, but you also knew how much your client valued Betsy's endorsement. It was 3:30 a.m. on a Saturday morning and you doubted that you would be able to reach Guppy's president, Sally Striker, who was most likely safely ensconced in bed with her husband Walt Wormburner, Guppy's director of marketing.

   Rubbing your eyes and shaking your head, you agreed that Guppy would make the $50,000 payment. You believed that your client would want to pay the money rather than lose Betsy's endorsement. Indeed, on more than one occasion, Sally had informed you that she viewed signing Betsy as "crucial" to Guppy's future.

C. **Analysis:** Analyze this scenario to determine whether you may have violated any ethical rules by agreeing that Guppy would pay Bunker the $50,000 finder's fee. Review the Model Rules of Professional Conduct and the associated Comments to those rules. Additionally, ask yourself how you are going to tell your client that you agreed to the finder's fee. What client-relations issue have you created and how are you going to handle it? What if the client refuses to pay the finder's fee?

D. **Preparation of Talking Points:** "Talking Points" are simply notes that you prepare for yourself to structure your discussion with your senior partner. You do not have to draft them using any particular format. That said, it is a good idea to use headings and bullet points to keep yourself on track—especially if you get nervous talking to your supervisor. Include a brief statement of the issue. Then summarize what you have concluded and how you reached those conclusions. Conclude with "action points" in which you recommend how to proceed.

E. **Additional Instructions:** Your professor may provide you with additional instructions regarding this assignment.

3G: DRAFTING THE ATHLETE ENDORSEMENT AGREEMENT

The Frame and the Picture

Instructions

A. **Summary:** Once you have completed your negotiations and drafted and submitted your LOI (as described in Assignment 3E), you will draft the Athlete Endorsement Agreement memorializing the terms of the deal that you negotiated with your opposing counsel. The two of you will turn in one completed contract.

B. **The Frame and the Picture:** Unlike what you did with the Putting Green Purchase Agreement and the Sport Psychologist Consulting Agreement in this sequence, you will not draft the frame and the picture of the contract separately. Since we will not repeat the instructions for drafting the frame and the picture here, you may want to review Assignments 1E and 1F or Assignments 2D and 2E.

C. **The Drafting Process:** In the real world, one of you would probably prepare the entire first draft and submit it to your opposing counsel, who would edit it and redline the changes. You would review her edits and decide whether to accept or reject each of them. You might then send another redlined version to her, showing additional edits that you have made. This back-and-forth process may carry you through many drafts.

  For this assignment, I recommend that you and your opposing counsel consider operating as you would in the real world. This can work in the law school context if one of you has more time and fewer pending deadlines than the other. Ideally, the least busy person would prepare the entire first draft and submit it to the busier person for review. The back-and-forth editing and redlining process can then proceed.

  Realistically, you and your opposing counsel are more likely to divide up the work of preparing the first draft so that the bulk of it does not fall on one student's shoulders. If you do divide the contract into parts, you will have to allow a lot of extra time before the contract is due for the two of you to make sure that the parts work together well. For example, you will need to make sure that both of you have used the same defined terms and that you have used them to mean the same things. This is trickier than you think, so you should try to complete a full draft as early in the process as possible. That way, the two of you can review, edit, redline, and repeat as often as you need to in order to produce a seamless, polished product.

Remember that your goal is to produce a contract that sounds as if it were written by one person, not two. If one of you drafts in Plain English and the other peppers his language with legalese, your contract will be split into two distinct halves. Alternatively, if the two of you have divided up the work so that you each have responsibility for drafting alternating articles within the contract, the Reader is likely to feel like she is on a seesaw. Strive to draft with a consistent voice. To accomplish this, both of you will have to read the entire contract more than once. I recommend reading it out loud to each other and listening for the places where the language becomes more elevated or slips into legalese. The two of you can then work together to translate those passages into Plain English.

D. **Incomplete Confidential Instructions:** You may not have received any confidential instructions from your clients about some of the topics in your negotiation prep sheet (see Assignments 3C and 3D). Address any questions about your client's position on particular issues to your professor, who will either provide you with additional confidential instructions or give you permission to decide what would be in your client's best interests. Because this is a "simulated assignment," you may have to use your imagination. Do not go so far as to make up wildly improbable deal facts, but do feel free to be a little creative.

Include any boilerplate provisions appropriate for this particular deal as well as any boilerplate provisions that your professor suggests are necessary. Remember to negotiate about the language of the boilerplate provisions. While you may not have confidential instructions addressing every piece of boilerplate, you can imagine what your clients' concerns might be and address them. For example, if you represent the Company and do not have any confidential instructions about delegation of performance, think about whether the Company wants the Athlete to be able to delegate her performance to another party. Most likely the Company recognizes that the Athlete is unique; only she can endorse the Company's clothing and equipment to achieve the desired result. Therefore, you may want to negotiate to adjust the standard anti-delegation language (which allows a party to delegate only with the written consent of the other party) to address the Company's concern. In other words, you may want to draft stronger anti-delegation language to indicate that the Company would never even entertain the Athlete's request for permission to delegate.

E. **Use of Precedent for Drafting the Athlete Endorsement Agreement:** As you know if you completed Assignment 3C, you may use any forms or templates you can find in the library or on the Internet. You may not purchase any forms, whether from a store or online. You may not use any precedent in your own files (from a previous job or a summer position) or any precedent you obtain from an attorney. *Finally, you may not use any contracts obtained from other students who have taken this class.* Pretend that the library and the Internet are your only resources.

See Assignment 3C for some tips on how to locate, review, evaluate, and use the available precedent.

F. **Provisions Addressing Legal Issues:** Be sure to address in the contract any specific things that the parties must do in order to comply with the law. If you know that you need to address advertising restrictions imposed by the Federal Trade Commission, for example, spell out the parties' specific rights and obligations. Avoid the easy cop-out of saying, "The Athlete shall abide by all of the Federal Trade Commission's rules and regulations regarding false advertising," or words to that effect. The Athlete's lawyer might refuse to include that language in the contract because it is, in effect, redundant; that is, it simply amounts to her client's promise to obey the law, which the Athlete must do even if she is not contractually bound. If there is a legal issue that you must address, include specific provisions that give the parties clear guidance about their rights and duties.

G. **Grading:** Unless your professor tells you otherwise, both you and your opposing counsel will receive the same grade on the contract you submit.

H. **Additional Instructions:** Your professor may provide you with additional instructions regarding this assignment.

The
ROCK BAND
Sequence

Assignment *1*

The Band Logo Purchase Agreement

1A: ENGAGEMENT LETTER BETWEEN ATTORNEY AND CLIENT

Instructions

A. **Summary:** You will draft an engagement letter/retainer agreement between your law firm and a new client.

B. **Background:** You are an associate at the law firm of Hawthorn, Melville & Poe. "One Art," a rock band whose lead singer and lead guitarist is Marisa Treadwell, wants your firm to draft a band logo purchase agreement. "One Art Partnership"—the entity under which the band operates—is going to purchase a band logo from Vincent Van Logo, a tattoo artist and freelance logo designer.

Ms. Treadwell has entered into some contracts on behalf of the One Art Partnership (the "Partnership") before and believes that she has finally learned her lesson. She wants to stop pretending she's a lawyer and turn the legal work over to the professionals. She's read a bit about attorney/client relationships and has decided that she wants to have an engagement letter in place before your firm starts working on the contract.

Hawthorn, Melville & Poe, being a bit behind the times, has never required its clients to sign an engagement letter or retainer agreement. The senior partner, Nate Hawthorn, has resisted formalizing client relationships in this way. Nate now wants you to draft an engagement letter that he can present to Ms. Treadwell to communicate basic information about how the attorney/client relationship between the Partnership and the firm is likely to work.

Nate wants the engagement letter to be a contract that both parties will sign, but he does not want it to be so formal that it frightens Ms. Treadwell or the Partnership away. He wants you to strike just the right tone— businesslike with a touch of warmth.

C. **No Use of Precedent:** Nate does not want you to use other engagement or retainer letters that you find through a library or Internet search or through any other means. He would like to see what you can draft without using any precedent. He believes that, if you are not influenced by what other firms have already done, you will produce something fresh, creative, well written, and tailored to this particular client's needs.

D. **Legal Research:** In preparation for completing this assignment, please read *Brian Dowling v. Chicago Options Associates, Inc. et al. (DLA Piper Rudnick Gray Cary (US), LLP)*, 226 Ill. 2d 277, 875 N.E.2d 1012 (Ill. 2007).

E. **Draft Specific to This Attorney/Client Relationship:** Nate does not want you to create a "form" engagement letter/retainer agreement to be used for all of the firm's clients. He wants you to focus on this particular client. If you do a good job, perhaps Nate will ask you to create a "form" later. Right now, Nate's main concern is that you cover the issues listed in the table below and that you capture the terms that Nate already has communicated to Ms. Treadwell.

F. **Table of Issues and Terms:** Nate prepared this quick list of the issues that the engagement letter should cover and the terms upon which he and the Partnership have reached agreement. The issues appear in no particular order.

Issue	Terms
Who firm works for	One Art Partnership (Marisa Treadwell is general partner)
End of representation	When final bill is paid; note that the $1,000 retainer is deducted 1/2 from the first bill and 1/2 from the second bill
When work will begin	Upon receipt of signed engagement letter and check for $1,000 security retainer
Initial consultation (Nate already met with Ms. Treadwell)	Charge Nate's regular rate; they met for one hour; Ms. Treadwell knows about this charge
Fees	Senior Partner Hawthorn—$215 per hour Senior Partner Melville—$200 per hour Senior Partner Poe—$175 per hour Associate (any level)—$120 per hour Paralegal (any level)—$70 per hour

Issue	Terms
Refund of unused fees	Will refund unused fees (if any)
Security retainer (intended to secure payment of fees for future services the firm is expected to perform)	$1,000; will apply 1/2 to first bill and 1/2 to second bill
Trust account (separate from firm's property; remains client's property until firm applies it to charges for services actually rendered)	Will put the $1,000 security retainer in client trust account
Business hours of firm	9 a.m. to 5 p.m.; but give her Nate's cell phone number [make up this number]
Phone calls	We bill for time spent on calls received and made—at reduced hourly rate (reduce attorney or paralegal's rate by 5%)
Scope of services	Draft contract for purchase of band logo; no more than that; if she wants more, then we must draft an amendment to the engagement letter or she must sign another engagement letter
Attorney/client privilege	Explain it briefly; make sure she knows that she and the other band members should not share info with third parties and destroy privilege; especially note that she must not forward e-mails to anyone other than One Art partners and the Partnership's financial advisor
Client's obligations to firm	Cooperate Tell us everything about the deal Provide any supporting documents needed Be available; reachable through multiple means Pay bill within 30 days of receipt

Issue	Terms
Termination by firm	If client doesn't pay in timely fashion or if there's a breakdown in the attorney/client relationship (spell out what this means a bit—client fails to fulfill its obligations, other causes, such as client wanting attorney to do something that might violate ethical obligations)
Invoices	Sent out on the 15th of each month
Quarter hours	Bill out time in tenths of an hour
Expenses	Client pays for overnight mail; no markup, just a pass-through
Overhead expenses	Not billed to client
E-mails	We bill for reading and responding at regular hourly rate
Termination by client	Can terminate at any time; no refund if the retainer has been spent; must pay fees for services already rendered; firm will prepare final invoice
Division of labor and billing	Associates will do initial client interview and first draft of contract We bill for associates' time, plus partner supervisory time Partner will not attend client interview but will review associates' work and communicate with client (partner assigned to this task is Edwin Poe)
Core billing	Time spent reviewing facts, creating drafts, reviewing drafts, communicating with clients, communicating with opposing counsel, all other activities related to representation
Qualifications of attorneys	All will be licensed to practice law in Illinois We'll state that everyone working on the matter is competent; add in "with appropriate supervision" for associates and paralegals

Issue	Terms
Dowling v. Chicago Options	Include whatever the court requires about the security retainer to assure that the client is fully informed about how the money will be handled
Detail in bills	Will show who performed the work, how much time was spent (rounded up to the tenth of an hour), brief description of the work performed
Increase in hourly billing rates	Occurs at the beginning of each new year, no matter what; will apply to the Band if services are still being rendered at beginning of year
Changes to personnel	Can substitute associates and senior partners, without client's consent
Disputing a bill	Must contact Nate Hawthorn by mail or telephone within 14 days of receipt of invoice
Potential conflict of interest	We conducted a conflict search based on the info the client supplied and turned up no conflict
Overhead expenses	Not billed to client
Customer service	Can expect us to work hard and to keep client informed; let us know if we are not doing that
Governing law	Illinois
Signatures required	Marisa Treadwell (on behalf of One Art Partnership) and Nate Hawthorn (on behalf of your firm)

G. **Further Instructions for Drafting Engagement Letter:** Nate wants the engagement letter to come from Nate himself. He would like you to draft it using a personal, somewhat informal tone, without including any slang and without sounding unprofessional. Unlike most other contracts you will draft, you may use personal pronouns in this letter. Refer to Nate as "I" and to One Art Partnership as "you." Marisa Treadwell will sign on behalf of the partnership. *Note:* One Art Partnership's address is the same as Marisa Treadwell's current address—4323 W. Bishop Street, Chicago, Illinois 62901.

Remember that your main audience for the engagement letter is the partners of One Art Partnership—a group with very little experience in business and almost no experience with attorney/client relationships. You must make sure that you communicate clearly so that the partners understand everything in the letter. Encourage the partners to ask Nate questions before Marisa signs the letter if there is anything that they do not understand.

To keep the engagement letter from sounding too formal, you may use "will" instead of "shall" for covenants throughout the letter.

Please divide the letter up into sections and use boldfaced headings to help the Partnership. Think about how best to organize the information you convey.

> **Note:** You may not use a table, except perhaps to summarize the information about the individuals working on the matter and their hourly rates.

After Nate's signature (with his title and the date), include a statement from Ms. Treadwell, acknowledging that she and all of the other partners have read the letter, understand it, and agree to its terms. Include, also, a representation and warranty from the Partnership, stating that Marisa Treadwell is authorized to sign this engagement letter on behalf of the Partnership. Then, put lines for the Partnership's signature and the date. Under the signature line for One Art Partnership, spell out Marisa Treadwell's name, in upper and lowercase letters. Put the word "By" in front of her signature line. Under Marisa's name, put her title, "General Partner."

One final word: Strive to keep the engagement letter simple, straightforward, and brief. This letter should provide you with an excellent opportunity to practice the skill of drafting in Plain English. Your main goal is to communicate clearly so that the client understands how the attorney/client relationship is supposed to work.

H. **Additional Instructions:** Your professor may provide you with additional instructions regarding this assignment.

1B: THE CLIENT INTERVIEW

Instructions

A. **Summary:** You are going to meet One Art Partnership's general partner, Marisa Treadwell, the lead singer and guitarist of the band called *One Art*.

One Art wants to purchase a band logo from Vincent Van Logo, a tattoo artist and experienced logo designer. You will interview Ms. Treadwell in order to find out the terms of the deal that she has negotiated between One Art Partnership and Mr. Van Logo.

B. **Preparation for the Client Interview:** After you read the following memorandum from Edwin Poe, please read Appendix 1, Ten Tips for Interviewing a Client About a Transaction. Since your client's business and website are fictional, you will not be able to do any research about One Art Partnership, One Art, or Marisa Treadwell beforehand. However, as a backdrop for the client interview, you should do a small amount of research about rock bands and the design of logos. Remember that you may not search for any purchase agreements regarding logos, as that would violate the prohibition against using precedent on this assignment (see Section D, Precedent, below). Brainstorm about what provisions you think ought to be included in a contract for the purchase of a band logo. Then, prepare a list of questions to ask your client.

C. **Legal Expertise and Research:** In practice, you should not draft a contract in an area in which you have no legal expertise unless you acquire the expertise or seek help from another attorney who possesses it. Rule 1.1 of the Model Rules of Professional Conduct states:

> *Competence.* A lawyer shall provide competent representation to a client. Competent representation requires the legal knowledge, skill, thoroughness and preparation reasonably necessary for the representation.

Comment 2 to MRPC Rule 1.1 clarifies that "[a] lawyer can provide adequate representation in a wholly novel field through necessary study" or "through the association of a lawyer of established competence in the field in question." For the purposes of this assignment, you may assume that your senior partners have the requisite legal expertise to serve as your guides. You may not do any legal research in connection with this assignment unless your professor authorizes you to do so.

D. **Precedent:** In preparation for the client interview, you may not use any sample contracts, forms, templates, or models (collectively, "precedent") other than any model contracts provided by your professor.

> **Note:** Because most transactional attorneys have some relevant precedent in hand when drafting a contract, you will be permitted to use precedent in some subsequent drafting assignments.

E. **Additional Access to Client:** After the in-class interview, you may need to obtain more information from Ms. Treadwell. Collect your questions and e-mail them to your professor, who may (a) pass them along to Ms. Treadwell, or (b) arrange for Ms. Treadwell to come into class for another interview.

F. **Additional Instructions:** Your professor may provide you with additional instructions regarding this assignment.

Hawthorn, Melville & Poe

MEMORANDUM

TO:	Associates
FROM:	Edwin Poe
RE:	New Client (One Art)
DATE:	September 23, 2013

As many of you know, I have a rock band called *Nevermore.* We played at the firm's holiday party last year. Nevermore has practice space in a warehouse west of downtown Chicago. One day, while we were on a break from practicing, I met the band who uses the practice space above us—a band called *One Art,* with lead singer and guitarist, Marisa Treadwell. Marisa and her bandmates mentioned that they needed some legal help with a contract for the purchase of a band logo. I decided to offer her our firm's services.

One Art Partnership—the entity under which One Art operates—has asked our firm to draft a band logo purchase agreement between the Partnership and Vincent Van Logo, the artist who is going to design the logo. The Partnership can't really afford my rates, but they can afford yours. Therefore, Marisa Treadwell will be coming into the office to meet with you about the details.

I don't know much about Vincent Van Logo, except that he is a tattoo artist by trade. He has not incorporated his business; nor does he have any partners. On the side, Van Logo designs logos, primarily for musical groups. I'm sure that Marisa can tell you more about him. So far he is not represented by an attorney.

Please interview Marisa and find out the terms of the deal that she has struck between One Art Partnership and Vincent Van Logo.

1C: LETTER TO CLIENT RE POTENTIAL ETHICAL QUESTION

Instructions

A. **Summary:** Analyze the scenario presented below in order to determine what your obligations are regarding communicating with your client, One Art Partnership, and with Vincent Van Logo, who is not represented by an attorney. First read the statute cited in Section B, below. Then review the Model Rules of Professional Conduct and the Comments to those rules. Draft a letter to the Partnership, explaining the ramifications of altering the logo. If you feel that you need to inform Vincent Van Logo of his rights, explain that as well. Support your conclusions with specific quotes from the Model Rules of Professional Conduct and the Comments to those Rules.

B. **Scenario:** After your interview with Ms. Treadwell, she informs you of the Partnership's belief that, once it purchases the logo from Van Logo, the Partnership ought to be able to alter the logo in any way it pleases. She asks you to find out if the Partnership's belief is correct. You suspect that the Visual Artists Rights Act, 17 USCS § 106(A) ("VARA") may prevent your client from altering the logo. You also believe that Vincent Van Logo, who is not represented by an attorney, is unfamiliar with VARA. Assume that the Partnership does not want you to put anything in the contract about the alteration issue but informs you that they do intend to alter the logo.

C. **Format of Client Letter:** Address the letter to Marisa Treadwell. Begin the letter by summarizing the issue about which the Partnership has sought your advice. First explain whether VARA would prevent the Partnership from altering the logo. Then, if you believe that this scenario presents an ethical issue, explain the issue, your conclusion, and the rationale for your conclusion. Do the same for any business issue you identify.

D. Tone of Client Letter: Remember that the relationship between your firm and the Partnership is brand new. Your senior partner, Edwin Poe, expects that One Art eventually will become a famous band and that the One Art Partnership will send the firm a lot of additional legal work. In your letter, use a businesslike tone, but be sure to make the client feel that you have its best interests at heart.

E. Additional Instructions: Your professor may provide you with additional instructions regarding this assignment.

1D: MEMORANDUM FROM ASSOCIATES TO EDWIN POE, RE SUMMARY OF DEAL TERMS

Instructions

A. Summary: Using the notes from your interview with your client's general partner, Marisa Treadwell, draft a memorandum to Edwin Poe, summarizing the terms of the band logo purchase transaction. Assume that Edwin was not present at the client interview.

B. Format of Memorandum: Set up your memo as follows—

Hawthorn, Melville & Poe

MEMORANDUM

CONFIDENTIAL

TO: Edwin Poe

FROM: [Insert Your Name]

RE: Interview with Marisa Treadwell, September 25, 2013

SUBJECT: Band Logo Purchase Agreement

DATE: September 26, 2013

[Insert the text of the memo here, single-spaced. Use headings to help organize the material.]

C. **Collaboration:** If your professor permits, you and your classmates may share your client interview notes. Most likely, if you missed a deal fact, your classmate caught it. Through collaboration, you can fill in any information gaps you have, unless, of course, the client did not give you the information you need.

D. **Follow-Up Questions to Client:** In the course of writing this memo, you may find that you need to ask the client some additional questions. Please direct those questions to your professor, who will either consult the client and post the answers for the entire class or invite the client in for another interview.

E. **Identification of Legal Issues:** While drafting this memo, you may identify one or more legal issues that this transaction poses. If so, please identify those issues at the end of the memo so that Edwin becomes aware of them and can give you some direction regarding how to pursue them.

F. **Additional Instructions:** Your professor may provide you with additional instructions regarding this assignment.

1E: ASSEMBLING THE FRAME: DRAFTING THE TITLE, PREAMBLE, BACKGROUND, WORDS OF AGREEMENT, DEFINITIONS, AND SIGNATURE LINES

Instructions

A. **Summary:** Using the deal facts gathered from the client interview you conducted in Assignment 1B, you will draft the band logo purchase agreement's frame—the Title, Preamble, Background, Words of Agreement, Definitions, and Signature Lines.

B. **The "Frame" Metaphor:** Some parts of a contract are traditional and easily drafted using models. They create a "frame" for the business provisions of the contract. The Title, Preamble, Words of Agreement, and Signature Lines are rudimentary parts of the contract's frame. The Definitions and Background sections, while more difficult to draft, still should not contain covenants, conditions precedent, representations and warranties, and statements of discretionary authority—otherwise known as "operative" provisions. For that reason, the Background and Definitions sections are also part of the contract's frame, stabilizing it by adding more information about the deal and preparing the reader for the "picture" containing the operative provisions of the deal.

Professors who teach contract drafting use various images to convey what contract drafters do. Therefore, you may hear someone else refer to the "frame" as the "skeleton" of the contract and the "picture" as the "meat on the bones." If it helps you to think of the contract that way, please feel free to do so. The purpose of these metaphors is to help you break down the drafting process into manageable parts.

C. **The Preamble—An Example of Learning from a Model:** Provided that you have the correct information, you can draft a Preamble for the Band Logo Purchase Agreement by following the pattern of the Preamble in the model Leaf Disposal Services Agreement,[1] reprinted below.

LEAF DISPOSAL SERVICES AGREEMENT

Leaf Disposal Services Agreement made this 10th day of October 2007, between SpinGazer, Inc., a Delaware corporation with its principal place of business located at 1200 Ridge Avenue, Evanston, Illinois 60201 (the "Company"), and Fallen Leaves, Inc., an Illinois corporation with its principal place of business located at 2025 North Clark Street, Chicago, Illinois 60614 (the "Provider").

As a partnership, One Art Partnership does not necessarily have a "principal place of business." Instead, you can say "One Art Partnership, an Illinois general partnership with an office located at [insert address]." Since Vincent Van Logo is an individual (and not a corporation or partnership), you obviously do not need to identify where he is incorporated or where his principal place of business is located. For individuals, you simply say "an individual residing at [insert address]."

You must choose a shorthand nickname for each party and place the parenthetical containing the shorthand name *after* all of the identifying information about that party. Therefore, after the address of the partnership's office, you may insert (the "Partnership"), for example. If you call One Art Partnership, the "Partnership," then you will want to give Vincent Van Logo a nickname at the same level of generality. Perhaps for Van Logo, you will insert the parenthetical (the "Artist") after his address.

The placement of the shorthand names you choose for the parties, which function like in-text definitions, is very important. Perhaps it is hard to believe, but there could be more than one "One Art Partnership" or more than one "Vincent Van Logo" in the world. By placing the parenthetical after each of their addresses, you make it more likely that you have clearly identified the "One Art Partnership" and the "Vincent Van Logo" who are parties to this contract.

---

1. The entire model Leaf Disposal Services Agreement is included in Appendix 2.

When you draft the Preamble of your contract, pay careful attention to punctuation. The Preamble contains a lot of information and is difficult to read if not punctuated properly. Moreover, aside from the title, the Preamble is the very first thing that the reader will encounter in your contract. Even though it is formulaic, you can set a good tone by drafting it so that it reads smoothly. Proper punctuation helps.

Finally, you and your professor are likely to spend some time talking about what date you should insert in the Preamble. When is the contract "made"? Is it the same date when the contract is signed? Is this date different from the effective date of the term? Also, sometimes the date in the Preamble is preceded by the words "as of." Under what circumstances is it appropriate to use those words? Even a formulaic Preamble can present interesting questions that you are likely to bandy about in class.

D. **Title, Words of Agreement, and Signature Lines:** You and your professor will discuss what to call this contract. For the sake of convenience, I have referred to it as the *Band Logo Purchase Agreement,* but you are not required to use that title.

The Words of Agreement used in the model Leaf Disposal Services Agreement are simple. After the Background section, insert, "Accordingly, the parties agree as follows:". In most contracts, at about this point in the contract, you will see a lengthy "consideration" provision that sounds like complete gobbledygook. You and your professor are likely to discuss whether a formal statement of consideration is necessary when the contract itself makes it amply clear that consideration for the transaction does exist. The drafter of the Leaf Disposal Services Agreement has concluded that the contract does not require a formal statement of consideration.

You can easily imitate the Signature Lines and get them right. The Signature Lines from the Leaf Disposal Services Agreement are reprinted below.

AGREED:

SPINGAZER, INC.   **FALLEN LEAVES, INC.**

By: _____   By: _____
  Jackie Spingazer   Leif E. Liminator

Title: Director of Operations   Title: Supervisor

Since one of the parties to the Band Logo Purchase Agreement is a partnership and the other is an individual, you will need to adapt this format a bit. The names in boldfaced, all capital letters, above the Signature Lines are the formal names of the parties to the contract—not the shorthand names that you chose in the Preamble and used throughout the rest of the contract. So, where you see **SPINGAZER, INC.** and **FALLEN LEAVES, INC.**, above, you would substitute **ONE ART PARTNERSHIP** and **VINCENT VAN LOGO**.

> **Note:** Generally, it is a good idea to put your client's Signature Line first. Believe it or not, this sometimes matters to the client.

For "One Art Partnership," underneath the Signature Line, type "Marisa Treadwell," in upper and lowercase letters. Put the word "By" in front of her signature line. Then, under the Signature Line, type "General Partner." For "Vincent Van Logo," you do not need the word "By" in front of the Signature Line since he is signing on behalf of himself. Just re-type "Vincent Van Logo," in upper and lowercase letters, below his Signature Line. This may seem repetitious, but the names above the Signature Lines identify the parties to the contract and the names below the Signature Lines identify who signed the contract.

Finally, since Vincent Van Logo is an individual and does not have a title, you can eliminate the "Title" line under his signature.

E. **Background:** The purpose of the Background section is twofold—to put the Agreement in context and to express the intentions of the parties.

You may be accustomed to seeing this section called "Recitals" and containing a list of "WHEREAS" clauses ending with the crescendo "NOW THEREFORE" clause. Plain English drafters avoid those clauses like the plague. Instead, draft the Background section in smooth prose. This is probably the only place in the contract where you will get to tell a little story. Use it well. Who are the parties? What do they do? Why are they entering into this deal? The Background section should not be too long or too lopsided (containing more information about one party than the other).

The Background section is a place where you should avoid following your models too closely. It is not as formulaic as the Preamble, for example. Ask yourself: What do my readers need to know about the parties? About what happened before (if anything) and about what is about to happen (this transaction)?

Remember that you should not include any operative provisions in the Background section. Be very careful not to include any covenants, conditions precedent, representations and warranties, or statements of discretionary authority here. The courts generally will not give effect to operative language contained in a Background section. And, if you include a covenant in the Background section, you run the risk of forgetting to include it in the body of the contract, where it would actually obligate a party to do something.

Sometimes the parties want to clarify their intentions early in a contract. Even though the Background section should not contain operative provisions, it can contain a statement of the parties' intentions. Sometimes, if there is a contractual dispute, the court will give effect to a statement of intentions included in the Background section instead of, or in addition to, admitting parol evidence of those intentions.

F. **Definitions:** The model Leaf Disposal Services Agreement gives you some limited guidance about how to draft the definitions. It contains the prefatory language below.

As used in this Agreement, the terms defined in the preamble have their assigned meanings and the following terms have the meanings assigned to them in this Article.

If you have defined any terms, in-text, in the Background section, you must add the words "and in the Background section" to the prefatory language after the words "in the preamble." That way, you will not have to include any cross-references to those definitions in the Definitions article itself.

By looking at the model agreement, you will see that most definitions use the verb "means" or "includes but does not include." You will also see that in-text definitions found in the body of the contract (but not in the Preamble or Background section) are cross-referenced in the Definitions article, using the verb phrase "has the meaning assigned in."

You and your professor will discuss how to choose what to define and how to draft the definitions. Remember that definitions are declarations and should not contain any operative language—no covenants, conditions precedent, representations and warranties, or statements of discretionary authority. Think of a definition as a statement of what a term means whenever it appears capitalized in the contract. If you want a party to undertake any kind of obligation, you must include it in the body of the contract rather than in a definition.

Important Note About Drafting Definitions as Part of the Frame: In practice, lawyers hardly ever draft a complete Definitions article before they draft the rest of the contract. In a sense, asking you to draft the Definitions before you draft the rest of the contract is an artificial exercise. Nevertheless, it is a good exercise and it may save you some time and energy. It forces you, as a novice contract drafter, to think in advance about what terms you may need to define. You can draft a definition for the logo, for example, because you know that you will need to refer to it over and over again.

Moreover, drafting definitions in advance may prevent you from making the mistake of using too many in-text definitions. When a Definitions article contains too many cross-references to in-text definitions, the reader is forced to hop all over the contract to find out what things mean. Instead, by defining most terms in the Definitions article itself, you keep the reader happy by feeding her information. You also take the opportunity to educate her about the deal a bit before she launches into the contract. This idea of educating the reader may sound like a litigation drafting concept, but it holds true for contract drafting as well. As your reader moves into the contract, after reading a fully developed Definitions article, she is more likely to understand the rest of the contract.

If you remember to consider your audience(s), you will be more likely to achieve the goal of clear communication. Transactional attorneys who fail to consider their audience(s) give transactional attorneys a bad name.

G. **Additional Instructions:** Your professor may provide you with additional instructions regarding this assignment.

1F: FILLING IN THE PICTURE: DRAFTING THE CONTRACT'S OPERATIVE PROVISIONS

Instructions

A. **Summary:** Using the deal facts gathered from the client interview you conducted in Assignment 1B, draft all of the operative provisions of the Band Logo Purchase Agreement. The "operative" provisions do not include the "frame" of the contract—the Title, Preamble, Background, Words of Agreement, Definitions, and Signature Lines. This assignment assumes that you have already drafted the "frame" of the contract as part of Assignment 1E—or that your professor has asked you to skip that assignment and concentrate on "filling in the picture."

B. **Filling in the Picture:** To fill in the picture, you must draft all of the operative provisions of the contract and decide how to organize them. Your professor will help you develop the basic skills you need to take the terms of the deal and translate them into contract concepts—covenants, conditions precedent, representations and warranties, statements of discretionary authority, and declarations.[2]

   In practice, some attorneys call this *memorializing* the terms of the deal, which basically means getting the terms of the deal down on paper so that they have a legal effect. The paper (or contract) is the *memorial*. The parties should be able to turn to the contract whenever they have any questions about their rights and duties with regard to the particular transaction.

C. **Organization—Naming and Ordering the Articles and Sections:** Some provisions are traditionally placed in certain spots. For example, after the Definitions article, some drafters include a brief article containing the main covenants of the deal. One leading contract drafting expert, Tina L. Stark, calls this brief article the "subject matter performance provision."[3] The subject matter performance provision in the model Leaf Disposal Services Agreement is reprinted below.

Article III. Summary of Services and Fees

Section 3.01 Services and Fees. Subject to the provisions of this Agreement, the Provider shall perform the Services described in Article IV. To compensate the Provider for performing the Services, the Company shall pay the Provider the fees and reimburse the Provider for the expenses described in Article V.

The drafter of the model Leaf Disposal Services Agreement put the subject matter performance provision after the Term article. While the exact order of these provisions sometimes varies, remember that the subject matter performance provision, the Term, and the Closing articles should appear near the beginning of the contract.

   It is sometimes helpful to think of the subject matter performance provision as a thesis statement plus roadmap. It tells you the "main

---

2. Tina L. Stark, *Drafting Contracts: How and Why Lawyers Do What They Do* 9-10 (Aspen 2007) (describes the contract concepts as the "building blocks" of the contract and the process of converting business terms into contract concepts as a "translation skill").
   3. *Id.* at 39-40.

idea" (or "primary covenants") of the contract and points you to the places in the contract where you can find out more details about those covenants.

After the subject matter performance provision, the Term article, and the Closing article, the reader expects to find information about what the Partnership is buying and how much they are going to pay for it. Therefore, you must put those articles close to the beginning of the contract.

At the end of the contract, right before the Signature Lines, place the contract's boilerplate provisions (sometimes called *General Provisions*). The Termination and Dispute Resolution articles generally come right before the boilerplate.

So, with the parts of the contract in their traditional places, and allowing for some flexibility in their exact order, your contract (not including the frame) will look something like this:

Summary of Purchase and Compensation
Term
Closing (if any)
The Logo Design
Compensation
[OTHER TOPICS TO BE COVERED]
Dispute Resolution
Termination
General Provisions

One of the biggest challenges that a drafter faces is how to organize the business provisions not specifically listed above—that is, how to organize those "other topics to be covered." Start by making a list of every deal term not addressed in the named articles. Then, group those deal terms by topic and select a good name for the article covering that topic. Remember that "Partnership's Obligations" and "Artist's Responsibilities" are contract concepts, not topics. Moreover, if you use a heading like "Partnership's Obligations," you are indicating to the reader that all of the Partnership's obligations are contained under that heading. More likely, the Partnership's obligations are scattered throughout the contract.

Choose article names (and section names as well) that are specific and clear. Instead of "Partnership's Obligations" or "Artist's Responsibilities," for example, you may have articles called "Design Process" and "Permitted Uses of Logo." These articles may contain obligations and responsibilities of one or both parties.

If you find that you have a number of miscellaneous deal terms that do not seem to fit anywhere, give them another look before deciding to create single-section articles. Single-section articles (other than the subject matter performance provision and the Term article) can make the particular topic seem like an undeveloped afterthought or, conversely, give the particular topic too much weight. It is better to put the miscellaneous deal term into the article it relates to the most, even if it is not a perfect fit.

Once you have found a place for every deal term and named the articles you want to include in the contract, decide what order to put them in. Generally, place the articles in order from most important topic to least important topic. However, if you are describing a process, it may make more sense to put some of the articles in chronological order. There is no magic bullet of contract organization. However, it is very important to remember your audience(s). Ask yourself what your reader needs to know and when your reader needs to know it. Also, remember the terms of the deal. For example, if your client stressed that the Partnership's members are very concerned about their full participation in the logo design process, then you may want to move that topic up near the beginning of the contract for emphasis.

D. **Additional Instructions:** Your professor may provide you with additional instructions regarding this assignment.

1G: PUTTING THE PICTURE IN THE FRAME: FINISHING THE DRAFT CONTRACT

Instructions

A. **Summary:** This assignment applies only if you have already completed Assignments 1E and 1F. You will now insert the "picture" that you drafted in response to Assignment 1F into the "frame" that you drafted in response to Assignment 1E. The result will be one completed draft of a Band Logo Purchase Agreement (with a title that you have selected).

B. **The Process:** Inserting the picture into the frame is not merely a mechanical process. Once you have merged the two documents together, you must make sure that the picture fits the frame properly; in other words, you must review the draft contract as a whole and ask yourself at least the following questions:

- ☐ Is the Title I chose for the contract still appropriate?
- ☐ Have I consistently referred to the parties to the contract using the shorthand names that I gave them in the Preamble?
- ☐ Do the full party names in the Preamble (not the shorthand names) match the full party names above the Signature Lines?
- ☐ Does the date in the Preamble reflect the date when the contract is made? If this date is different from the effective date of the contract, have I clarified that in the body of the contract?
- ☐ Do the addresses in the Preamble match the addresses in the "Notice" provision included in the boilerplate?

☐ Did I include enough information in the Background section? Is there anything else that I may want to add to that section? Is there anything I may want to take out?

☐ Do I use my defined terms whenever it is appropriate? [*Note*: This is called "letting your defined terms do their work."]

☐ Did I remember to capitalize my defined terms in the body of the contract?

☐ Are there any lengthy phrases that I repeat more than once that could perhaps be defined terms?

☐ Are there any concepts that I repeat in different ways each time that I should perhaps be saying the same way each time? Would a defined term help?

☐ Are there any defined terms that I never use or use only once? (If so, you probably do not need to define that term.)

☐ Have I included a cross-reference to every in-text definition in the Definitions article? Are my definitions still in alphabetical order?

☐ Whenever I use a cross-reference, have I referenced the correct article or section?

☐ Have I used cross-references in the body of the contract to help the reader understand the relationship between parts of the contract?

☐ Are all of my article and section numbers in order? Does each have an appropriate heading?

☐ In the "Survivability" boilerplate provision, have I listed all of the sections of the contract that will survive the early termination of the contract or the end of the term?

☐ Do all of the parts of the contract work well together?

Once you have answered all of these questions and made any necessary adjustments to the contract, you can move into the editing and proofreading stage described next.

C. **Editing and Proofreading:** Using the Contract Drafting Checklist provided in Appendix 3, go back over your draft contract again. The checklist is set up to help you take the long view first. Think about the transaction. Have you captured all of the terms of the deal? Have you translated them into the correct contract concepts? Have you answered all questions about the rights and duties of the parties with regard to this transaction? Have you raised any questions without answering them? Is your contract well organized, coherent, and coordinated? Does it read smoothly? Is it easy to follow?

The checklist then asks you to look at some formatting issues that are directly related to readability. Review those issues, remembering also that well-chosen headings and the judicious use of "white space" enhance the readability of a contract. Do not remove headings or white space in order to make sure that you do not exceed the page limit for this assignment.

If you need guidance about how to avoid exceeding the page limit, seek your professor's help.

Following the checklist, now make sure that your contract contains all of the essential parts. Then, review each part. Finally, under the broad heading "Plain English," the checklist directs you to make sure that you have not made any grammatical, mechanical, or typographical errors.

Once you have gone through the checklist, prepare your contract for submission by proofreading it carefully, using the proofreading tips and tricks contained in Appendix 5. Finally, review your professor's instructions and verify that you have followed all of the directions regarding submitting the contract to your professor. There is something particularly disturbing about a transactional attorney who fails to follow directions. Failing to follow directions indicates that you are not detail oriented, which, in practice, can make your supervisor and your client mistrust you. It can also lead to a dangerous loss of credibility with the attorney representing the other side.

D. **Submitting the Contract:** Do one final thing before you submit your contract: Make sure that you are turning in a clean copy. That is, make sure that you have eliminated any highlighting or comments to yourself that you may have inserted during the drafting process. Practicing attorneys, both litigators and deal lawyers alike, can tell many war stories about forgetting to delete comments or critiques before filing documents or sending drafts to the other side. You do not want to make such an embarrassing mistake. You may also want to make sure that your document does not contain any hidden personal or metadata, such as information about when you finished the assignment. Check the software you are using to figure out how to eliminate that information.

E. **Additional Instructions:** Your professor may provide you with additional instructions regarding this assignment.

1H: MAKING CHANGES TO THE DRAFT CONTRACT: REDLINING

Instructions

A. **Summary:** Using the facts contained in the following memorandum from Edwin Poe, make the appropriate changes to the Band Logo Purchase Agreement. Apparently, Vincent Van Logo has hired an attorney. Mr. Poe's memorandum summarizes the conversation he had with Mr. Van Logo's attorney about the draft contract that Edwin sent him. Mr. Poe has consulted with your client's representative, Marisa Treadwell, and determined that all of the changes are acceptable to the Partnership.

B. **Making Changes to a Draft Reviewed by Opposing Counsel:** Now that opposing counsel has reviewed your draft contract, you should not make any changes to it without redlining those changes. Find the "Track Changes" (or equivalent function) on your computer and learn how to use it. Ideally, every word you delete should be struck through and every word you add should appear in red.

Make the changes mentioned in Mr. Poe's memo. Remember not to make any changes to the document without tracking them. In real life, you will quickly lose credibility with opposing counsel if you do not track all of your changes, because you will be breaking the unwritten code of honor that transactional attorneys follow. Track even the smallest change—even the correction of a minor misspelling.

C. **Turning in the Redlined Contract:** After you have reviewed the redlined contract to make sure that you took into account all of the changes mentioned in Mr. Poe's memo, submit it to your professor. This time, make sure that you submit the document *with* the changes showing. (This may be as simple as saving the document as "Final—Showing Markup.") Remember to rename the document, using the date and the initials "RL" to indicate that it is a redlined version.

D. **Additional Instructions:** Your professor may provide you with additional instructions regarding this assignment.

Hawthorn, Melville & Poe

MEMORANDUM

TO:	Associates
FROM:	Edwin Poe
RE:	Telephone Conference with Charlene Bronte, Attorney for Vincent Van Logo
DATE:	October 15, 2013

Charlene Bronte called to introduce herself as Vincent Van Logo's new attorney. She said that Vince and Marisa had gone out to dinner together and decided to make some changes to the contract. Of course, I checked with

Marisa, and she confirmed that she had agreed to everything that Charlene reported to me. So, your task is to put in the changes.

First, Vince does not want the Partnership to be able to use the logo on any CDs that One Art produces (or any associated CD art, like liner notes or CD covers) unless he gets a 5% royalty on the net profits. Initially, he thought it would be okay to let the Partnership use the logo that way free of charge, but he realized that he had missed a major revenue-generating opportunity. I wish that Marisa had not agreed to this provision, but it is a done deal.

We set the contract up so that, if the Partnership does not approve of the final test print, they don't have to make the final payment and the contract ends. Vince and Marisa agreed that he should be given one more chance to come up with a final test print meeting the Partnership's approval. Vince will have 14 days to do this and he will receive input from Marisa, who will gather input from the other members of the Partnership. He will then present the adjusted final test print for the Partnership's approval. If the Partnership does not approve it, then they will pay Vince one-half of the final payment, as opposed to none of it.

Marisa agreed to do another trademark search of the name "One Art." She admitted to Vince that the search they had done was not as thorough as she would have liked. (Was she drinking wine with dinner?) Marisa agreed to do another search no earlier than two weeks before the parties sign the contract.

Vince has agreed that, if he gets any discounts on the materials and services he purchases associated with designing the logo, he will pass them along to the Partnership, without any mark-up. (This applies to halftones, stats, photography, disks, illustrations, or related costs.) He also agreed to call in all of his favors from suppliers in order to get the best deals possible.

Marisa learned that Vince's tattoo business has really taken off. She's concerned that he'll be too busy to devote the necessary time to designing a really cool logo for One Art. Vince has agreed to turn his tattoo business entirely over to his assistant for 14 days in order to get a good start on the logo. Marisa thought that sounded like a good idea.

Marisa has agreed to provide Vince with copies of all of One Art's CDs in order to inspire him while he is working on the design. Vince will not have to pay anything for the CDs. She has also promised him a front row seat at One Art's first performance after the contract is signed. And, if he does a good job on the logo, One Art will let him use their name and a picture of their logo on his website in order to promote himself as a logo designer.

Please add these changes into the contract, using the redlining function so that I can see every addition or deletion you made. I would greatly appreciate it if you could turn this assignment around right away. Meanwhile, I will talk to Marisa about not meeting with Vince without her attorneys present until this contract has been signed. I don't want us to have to make additional changes—I especially don't want her agreeing to more things that are not advantageous to the Partnership.

The Band Performance Agreement

2A: THE WAIVER OF CONFLICT OF INTEREST AGREEMENT

Instructions

A. Summary: After reading the scenario below, you will draft a Waiver of Conflict of Interest Agreement, which you will ask your former client, One Art Partnership (the "Partnership"), to sign.

B. Scenario: It is now September 2015. Your new client is The Bell Jar Bar, Inc. (the "Company"). Your client contact is Sylvia P. Hughes, the president of the Company. The Company owns and operates a bar/music venue. Since drafting the Band Logo Purchase Agreement for the Partnership two years ago, you have not performed any additional legal work for the Partnership or any of its partners. Nevertheless, you have kept in touch with Marisa Treadwell; you have taken Ms. Treadwell out to lunch at least twice a year in order to maintain contact in case the Partnership were to find itself in a position to send your firm additional business.

The Company now wants to enter into a band performance agreement with the Partnership to engage One Art (the "Band") to perform regularly at The Bell Jar Bar. You remind your senior partner, Nate Hawthorn, that your firm represented the Partnership in the band logo purchase transaction and that your firm is still courting the Partnership as a client. Even though two years have passed since the band logo deal, Nate asks you to talk to your firm's conflicts administrator, who will help you determine if a conflict exists. The conflicts administrator determines that a conflict does exist.

Your client contact, Sylvia P. Hughes, has become friends with Marisa Treadwell, the lead singer and guitarist in the Band, and a member of the Partnership. Sylvia tells you that she has already told Marisa that she intended to contact your firm to seek representation in this deal. Sylvia believes that Marisa and the Partnership do not object to your firm representing the Company in this deal.

C. The Waiver of Conflict of Interest Agreement: Nate has asked you to do two things: (1) write a cover letter to the Partnership, explaining why you need its written consent to the firm's representation of the Company in this deal; and (2) draft a Waiver of Conflict of Interest Agreement, a copy of which you will enclose with your cover letter.

D. **Preparation for Drafting:** Your firm's conflicts administrator is new to the job and does not have a form Waiver of Conflict of Interest Agreement to give you. *You must complete this assignment without using any models, templates, or forms.*

Begin by looking at any guidance provided by the Model Rules of Professional Conduct regarding the "Client-Lawyer Relationship." More than one rule may be relevant to this issue. However, you are likely to find that Model Rule 1.9 ("Duties to Former Clients"), and its associated Comments, are right on point. Determine what constitutes "informed consent" and how best to confirm that you have obtained that informed consent in writing. Then draft the letter and the Waiver of Conflict of Interest Agreement (the "Waiver").

E. **Content of the Waiver:** Make sure that the Waiver contains a signature line for Nate Hawthorn and a signature line for Marisa Treadwell, who will sign on behalf of the Partnership. Use all of the basic contract drafting principles you have learned when you draft the Waiver. Do not forget about using contract drafting concepts like covenants and representations and warranties and expressing them with the appropriate verbs. For example, you may be tempted to have the Partnership "acknowledge" that it has been informed of a potential conflict and that it "understands" what it means. Consider having the Partnership "represent" and "warrant" these things instead. One exception: You may use the word "waives" instead of "shall waive" to capture the Partnership's covenant to waive the conflict.

Think carefully about how your cover letter and your Waiver work together. Are you going to include the information about the potential conflict in the cover letter and then refer to the letter in the Waiver? Will you be attaching the cover letter to the Waiver as an Exhibit? Or, do you want to inform the client of the conflict in the Waiver itself, so that attaching the cover letter is unnecessary? Use your best judgment, keeping in mind that the client must understand everything that you draft.

F. **Additional Consideration Re the Company:** Think about whether you should also write a letter to the Company, reminding them that your firm represented One Art Partnership with regard to a previously unrelated transaction. Let them know that you have sought the Partnership's waiver of any conflict of interest associated with your firm now representing the Company in the band performance agreement transaction. You may also want to consider whether to remind your new client that you are bound not to reveal any confidential information about your former client, One Art Partnership.

G. **Additional Instructions:** Your professor may provide you with additional instructions regarding this assignment.

2B: MEMORANDUM FROM ASSOCIATES TO HERMIONE MELVILLE, SENIOR PARTNER, RE SUMMARY OF DEAL TERMS

Instructions

A. **Summary:** Each of you must draft a memorandum to Hermione Melville, summarizing the information contained in the attached letter and memorandum from your client, Sylvia P. Hughes, the owner of The Bell Jar Bar (the "Bar") and the president of The Bell Jar Bar, Inc. (the "Company"). The Bar is a bar and music venue currently featuring experimental rock bands like One Art (the "Band"). The Company wants to engage the Band to play regularly at the Bar. Your senior partner, Nate Hawthorn, has decided to ask one of the other senior partners in the firm, Hermione Melville, to supervise your work on this transaction. Nate is busy with another transaction and wants the Company to get the attention it deserves. Therefore, Nate has introduced Hermione to Ms. Hughes. Hermione and Sylvia get along famously and are pleased to be working together on this band performance transaction.

   Like Nate, Hermione is very busy right now. Therefore, she would like you to draft a memorandum summarizing the terms of the deal for her.

B. **Format of Memorandum:** Set up your memo as follows—

Hawthorn, Melville & Poe

MEMORANDUM

CONFIDENTIAL

TO:	Hermione Melville
FROM:	[Insert Your Name]
RE:	Summary of Deal Terms
SUBJECT:	Band Performance Agreement Between The Bell Jar Bar, Inc., and One Art Partnership
DATE:	October 1, 2015

[Insert the text of the memo, single-spaced. Note that Hermione would like this memo to be organized a specific way. First, she wants you to summarize the deal facts. Then she wants you to list any legal issues that you think it may be necessary to research before drafting the contract. Finally, she wants you to make a list of additional questions that you want her to ask the client.]

To satisfy Hermione's expectations, the main headings in your memo should be:

  I. Known Deal Facts
  II. Potential Legal Issues
  III. Additional Questions for the Client

You may want to break up any one of the main sections into subsections with headings. This might be especially helpful to Hermione in Section I.

C. **Collaboration:** If your professor permits, you and your classmates may draft this memo (or parts of it) in pairs or in teams. Alternatively, you and your classmates may brainstorm about Sections II and III of the memo in class. Your professor will guide you regarding how much collaboration (if any) is appropriate on this assignment.

D. **Additional Instructions:** Your professor may provide you with additional instructions regarding this assignment.

The Bell Jar Bar, Inc.
2300 Ariel Lane
Chicago, Illinois 65432

September 28, 2015

Hermione Melville
Senior Partner
Hawthorn, Melville & Poe
1953 Contract Drafting Lane
Suite No. 1
Chicago, Illinois 65432

Dear Ms. Melville:

I am Sylvia P. Hughes, the President of The Bell Jar Bar, Inc. (the "Company"). I own and operate a bar/music venue called *The Bell Jar Bar,* located at the address shown on this letterhead (the "Bar"). My office is above the Bar.

I have heard high praise for your law firm. I don't know if you've done much work for bars or music venues but that doesn't matter to me as much as the fact that your firm is so highly regarded. I can certainly help you learn about our business, if need be.

I would like your assistance in drafting a performance contract between The Bell Jar Bar, Inc. and a great new experimental rock band called "One Art" (operating as the "One Art Partnership"). Believe it or not, the Company has never used a performance contract before. We are accustomed to handling everything with a mere handshake.

Forgive me for not meeting with you in person right now. I am in Sweden listening to a number of hot punk and metal bands who will be touring the United States next summer. I'm hoping to book them into the Bar, and, if your firm does a good job on the One Art agreement, I am very likely to be sending more business your way.

I am not an attorney (but I play one on T.V.—ha-ha), so I can't be sure that I covered all of the relevant points when I met with One Art's lead singer and partnership representative, Marisa Treadwell, last week. (She goes by "Risa.") After the meeting, I dictated the enclosed memo to you.

Sad to say, though we would like you to draft this contract yourself, we cannot afford to pay your hourly rate. I hope that you can delegate this project to some associates with lower billing rates. Of course, we'll pay for your time supervising their work and reviewing the final product.

FYI: As of yet, according to Risa, the One Art Partnership is not represented by counsel. She wants us to do the first draft of the contract and may later run it by her sister, who has just gotten her law degree. If her sister reviews the contract, it will be a bit like a surgeon operating on a family member, won't it?

After your crew gets a good start on the contract, I'd like to meet with them to answer any questions they might have. I'll be back in a week and will call you when I return.

I look forward to working with you and your team.

Sincerely,

Sylvia P. Hughes
Sylvia P. Hughes
President
The Bell Jar Bar, Inc.

CONFIDENTIAL/ATTORNEY CLIENT PRIVILEGE

MEMORANDUM

TO:	Hermione Melville, Senior Partner, Hawthorn, Melville & Poe
FROM:	Sylvia P. Hughes (President, The Bell Jar Bar, Inc.)
RE:	Performance Contract with One Art Partnership
DATE:	September 27, 2015

I own and run The Bell Jar Bar, which is located at the corner of Ariel Lane and Lazarus Avenue in Chicago, Illinois. (I am also president of the Illinois corporation through which the Bar does business—The Bell Jar Bar, Inc.—which is located at the same address. Our corporate office is upstairs.) We want to book the band One Art (operating as One Art Partnership) for a regular Saturday night gig.

I already met with the leader of the Band (and the Partnership's representative), Risa, and we hammered out most of the details. I'm dictating this memo, so I apologize if it's not the most coherent thing you've ever read.

The Bar needs an up and coming band like One Art to play every Saturday night and bring in a regular crowd. One Art already has a pretty good following, plus their newest member, Vincent Van Logo, plays the bagpipes, a rare but increasingly popular instrument for experimental rockers.

Anyway, the contract is for One Art to play at the Bar on 20 consecutive Saturdays, starting Saturday, November 14th. We're hoping for a huge turnout for One Art's debut at the Bar.

As the headliner, One Art will play two sets a night, one from 8:30 p.m. to 9:30 p.m. and one from 11:00 p.m. to 12:00 a.m. Since the sets are so short, they will not have any breaks during each hour on stage. We'll be responsible for hiring their opening acts, though Risa made some noises about wanting input into those decisions. I think she's afraid that we'll pick a band whose music is either too different from, or too similar to, One Art's music. I told her that we had to have final say on the opening acts, but I do want to give the Band some input. Perhaps your associates can figure out a way to make that happen.

I don't think One Art uses any pyrotechnics—thank goodness—and Risa said that the Band has been to shows at the Bar and likes our lighting system and our extremely creative lighting engineer. They trust her to design a great light show to accompany their performance.

However, the Band is much more particular about their sound. They have their own sound engineer and want to use him for all of their shows. I think that's reasonable as long as he's competent and the Band pays him out of their own pocket. I'd like our own sound engineer to be present during the shows and to take over if I determine that One Art's guy isn't doing a good job. (I have a very good ear.) Please make sure that the Band must continue to play if I replace their sound engineer during a show. If they walk out, they'll have to pay back their base fee for the night and they won't get their cut of that night's gate.

For the 20 Saturdays, we'll pay the Band a base fee of $1,000 a night. On top of that, we'll pay the Band 50% of the gate (that is, 50% of the net ticket receipts for the night). We typically deduct the cost of printing the tickets and the fees associated with tickets charged on major credit cards from the gross ticket receipts before giving a band its cut.

Also, the Bar holds about 550 people. We print 550 tickets for each night's performance. Risa agreed that the Band won't get any percentage of the gate on nights when we sell fewer than 200 tickets. That being said, if we sell

200 tickets, the initial 200 tickets sold will count toward the Band's cut of the gate. So, once the 200th ticket is sold, the Band gets 50% of the net ticket receipts for all tickets sold that night—including the initial 200 tickets.

One Art knows we're banking on them being a big draw. They've agreed to promote their Bell Jar nights on their website and to include a hyperlink to our website. Don't you think that they should also agree not to say bad things about the Bar during their engagement and for a while after it ends?

One Art wants some complimentary tickets for family and friends. I agreed to give them 15 tickets per night. They won't get any percentage of these "comped" tickets; nor will those tickets count toward the minimum 200 tickets required to be sold before they receive any percentage of the gate. Comped tickets are freebies, after all. Naturally, One Art has agreed that the Bar can also give free tickets to 15 family and friends. Those tickets will be treated the same way as those comped to the Band.

Risa's pretty smart. She wanted to pin down right away how much we are going to charge for the tickets. I'm okay with that, but I think we'd like the option to raise the ticket price for the rest of the engagement if the show sells out on five consecutive Saturdays. (A sellout means that we sell 520 tickets—remember that the other 30 tickets are comped to the family and friends of the Band and the Bar.) The initial ticket price will be $20. If the show sells out on five consecutive Saturdays, the ticket price for all of the following Saturdays will be $25. We'll keep the price at $25 per ticket for the rest of the engagement, no matter what. Risa and the Band can't complain that the higher ticket price keeps people away. They'll just have to work harder to prove that they are worth the price of admission.

I'm not supposed to discount any tickets unless I get the Band's approval first. I'll be asking for that approval quite a bit when I get started on my promotional campaign. We have to bring in some journalists and disc jockeys, for example.

Risa also asked me all kinds of questions about our insurance coverage. I told her we'd get insurance to cover the Band while they are at the Bar. She insisted that the Band won't perform unless they get a copy of our insurance policy before the beginning of the term—that is, on or before the 9th of November. I told her we'd provide them with a copy of a policy with $500,000 worth of coverage for personal injury and property damage. We'll add One Art's name as an additional insured for the date of each performance. That seemed to satisfy Risa, though she was adamant that the Band would not play unless they saw the policy with their own eyes at least three days before their debut.

I think One Art must be pretty strapped for cash right now. Risa asked if the Bar could advance them their first three $1,000 payments (their base fee for their first three Saturday performances) as soon as both parties have signed the contract. I agreed because I remember being a starving musician back in the days when my band, The Spelunking Frog, was trying to make it big. Anyway, Risa said that if the Band did not wind up playing on any one of those three Saturdays for any reason, they would pay that portion of the advance back to the Bar.

While One Art doesn't have a manager (other than Risa herself), apparently Maxwell Treadwell, Risa's brother (known as "Tree" because he's 6' 7" tall), handles their accounting. I agreed that Tree could watch over our ticket seller (though I think he'll have to duck his head to get into the box office). He can shadow the ticket seller whenever tickets are being sold and afterwards. That reminds me—tickets go on sale at 5 p.m. on the day of each performance. There are no advance ticket sales prior to that.

One Art seems to obsess over their sound. They want me to state that our sound system meets their specifications. When I asked what those specs were, I did not expect Risa to spew forth the following: a Midas sound console with at least 36 channels and a pre-fader listen feature; at least six auxiliary busses; five direct boxes; five Yamaha monitors; five AB International, 1,000-watt power amplifiers; and a variety of microphones (one AKG D 112, two EV RE 20s, five Beyer M 88s, six AKG C 414s, five Sennheiser MD 421s, and five Sennheiser 441s). I feel confident that we already have all this stuff in house, so I have no problem saying so in the contract. Some bands can be real whiners when it comes to the Bar's sound system. But I do respect One Art's quest for perfection!

I got a little fed up when Risa said that One Art wants to choose the background music that the Bar plays when the Bands are setting up, switching, or on break between sets. Come on! I told her that she was nitpicking and she backed down.

I did concede to her request to allow the Band to video and record part of a set for One Art's website. That seemed reasonable and it will probably benefit the Bar by leading to more ticket sales. One Art does have to let me know what they are planning to tape and when, and, of course, the taping will be all at One Art's expense. The Bar can veto the taping if it's scheduled at a particularly inconvenient time. And, I didn't mention this to Risa, but we have to be able to shut down the taping if it's interfering with our patrons' enjoyment of the show.

We're going to allow One Art to sell t-shirts, hats, and demo CDs on the premises before, during, and after each show, as long as all of the merchandise says "Now appearing at The Bell Jar Bar" somewhere where it's visible. A sticker is okay for the demo CDs since the cover art has already been printed. (However, Risa said that they are planning to make new t-shirts and hats. Therefore, they can have our tagline printed right on those items.)

Obviously, we'll take 10% of One Art's gross receipts for all merchandise sold at each performance; One Art can pay us in cash at the end of each night. Oh, and my husband, Teddy Hughes, will sit at the merch table with One Art's salesperson.

I guess both parties will have to settle up at the end of each night. The Bar will pay One Art its $1,000 base fee with a cashier's check (except for those first three nights, which we will have already advanced in a cashier's check at the beginning of the term). At the end of each Saturday's performance, Tree and our ticket seller will prepare and sign a ticket receipts record and present it to me. It will show the gross ticket receipts less the costs of printing the tickets and the fees for tickets purchased with major credit cards. The Bar will then pay the Band its percentage of the net ticket receipts in cash. Teddy and the Band's salesperson will prepare and sign a merchandise sales report and present it to Risa and Vince, who will then pay The Bell Jar Bar, Inc. its share of the merch sales in cash.

We need the Band to unload their equipment (musical instruments and amplifiers that they must provide themselves) each Saturday at 4 p.m. The sound check for One Art will be at 5:00 p.m. (one hour after load-in). The opening act will start playing at 7:30 p.m. Risa committed the Band to no more than 15 minutes switchover time after the opening act finishes, barring any unforeseen circumstances, of course.

The Bar will provide each Band member with free food and drink for the entire time they are present at the Bar for a performance, starting with the load-in time at 4 p.m. and ending one hour after the second set. While out in the general Bar area, the Band may order drinks and food off of the menu. Risa told me what the Band wanted to have backstage in the "green room" before, during, and after each show, and I burst out laughing. She requested that the refrigerator be stocked with two pitchers of Apple-tinis and a case of Goldschlager liqueur. She also asked for pâté de fois gras, caviar, and crackers. I'm not even sure it's legal to serve pâté in the city of Chicago!

I told Risa to stop being a prima donna and get real. We compromised. One hour before One Art's first set each night, the Bar will stock the refrigerator in the green room with two pitchers of dry Vodka martinis made with Ketel One vodka, 12 bottles of Heineken beer, 12 cans of Diet Coke, and 12 bottles of Fiji water. After the first set, the Bar will send a waiter back to the green room to take dinner orders (selected from the main menu). Also after the first set, there will be 12 Skinny Cow ice cream sandwiches available in the freezer. After the second set, the Bar will provide the Band with two bottles of chilled champagne (no particular brand—the cheapest we can find, if I have my way).

Risa then had the nerve to request that the Bar provide a masseuse for the Band members after the second set. I told her firmly, "No." She seemed so disappointed that I agreed we could re-negotiate about what food, drink, and other amenities the Bar will provide for the Band in the green room once One Art sells out five consecutive shows. That should give the Band an incentive to draw crowds!

The Bar wants to promote the Band's appearances at the Bar. Risa would rather hire an outside firm to do it (and charge the Bar, of course). I told her that I'd swear in the contract (if I have to) that I was the owner of my own advertising agency for nine years and that we specialized in promoting experimental rock bands appearing at clubs in Chicago. She was duly impressed. She agreed to allow the Bar to promote the Band's appearances as long as I handle all of the promotional activities myself. In other words, I, Sylvia P. Hughes, will promote the Band on behalf of The Bell Jar Bar, Inc.

The Band has some nicely done press kits—I've seen them—and they will supply us with 1,000 of them, free of charge. We will then arrange and pay for advertising on television and radio and in newspaper and other print media. We'll also pay to have a poster designed, printed, and distributed featuring One Art and its logo (which Van Logo apparently created before joining the Band). Risa said it was okay for one-quarter of each poster to mention the opening acts, but the rest of the poster must be dedicated to One Art. Makes good sense to me. Also, I got her to agree that the Band will cooperate with me by making themselves available for three personal appearances during the contract. I expect I'll ask them to go on television and radio shows or to sign autographs at the Centurion Shopping Mall.

The Bar expects to spend no more than $2,000 for promotional costs in the first two weeks of the Band's engagement. Promotional costs may include the cost of radio and TV ads as well as the cost of flyers (and other things like that). The Bar may spend more during those first few weeks if it chooses to. After those first two weeks, the Bar expects to spend a minimum of $300 per week on promotion, but the Bar may spend more than that.

The Bar has already booked the Band to appear at the Centurion Mall in Roman Park on the 5th Saturday of their engagement—10 a.m. until 12 p.m.—signing autographs. (The address of the Centurion Mall is 33330 N. Caesar Row; Chicago, Illinois 65432.) All of the Band members have agreed to appear and to behave in a reasonably pleasant and professional way. I bet you lawyers will have a picnic figuring out how to define that!

Risa was freaking out when she told me about a gig at the House of Experimental Rock where a fan jumped her as she was walking through the crowd to get to the stage for One Art's performance. He had scissors in his hand and she thought that he was going to stab her, but he really just wanted to cut off a lock of her hair. He had a collection of locks of hair from the heads of female experimental rockers. She was shaking all over when she told me this story, so I assured her that we will have ample security on duty to protect her and the other members of the Band. Besides, we won't make the Band enter through the crowd.

I lit up a cigarette at one point and Risa began hacking almost immediately. She then said that One Art couldn't play at the Bar at all unless the Bar is smoke-free. The Bar is officially smoke-free, but I don't usually enforce that rule; being a smoker myself, I'm not inclined to banish my fellow smokers to the street. But I was afraid that Risa and One Art would not sign, so I told her that the Bar is smoke-free and added that I would put up additional signs and specifically instruct our security guards to apprehend and eject smokers on Saturdays when One Art is scheduled to play.

Since Risa was coughing so hard, I got to thinking about her health and about what might happen if she got sick or if the Band couldn't perform for some other reason. If the Band cancels a performance, we won't pay the guaranteed $1,000 for that performance or, obviously, the percentage of the gate. If the performance can't happen because of a blizzard or terrorist attack or something like that, then we'd still pay the $1,000 but we'd extend the contract to add the number of performances missed—and, of course, we would not be required to pay the base fee for those additional performances (since we already paid it). No double dipping.

Maybe it would be a good idea for the Bar to have the right to automatically extend the contract—especially if One Art becomes extremely popular. Please work that into the contract somehow.

Though I didn't want to burst One Art's bubble, there's the slightest chance that they won't be successful at the Bar and that the Bar will want to terminate their contract early. I think that we should be permitted to do that if we sell fewer than 200 tickets for four consecutive performances. To cancel the contract, I'd have to send One Art a letter by overnight mail, signature requested, to arrive by the Friday before their next Saturday performance. If we do that, then the Bar shouldn't have to pay the Band a penny more.

I'm sure that there are lots of other reasons why the Bar might want to end the contract. Maybe your associates can brainstorm about that and put some of them in the contract. What if One Art radically changes its musical direction and begins playing pop music, for example? That kind of music just wouldn't fly at the Bar, which is noted for presenting punk, metal, and experimental bands whose music is edgy, and, frankly, a little bleak. (I mean if you've ever read that Elizabeth Bishop poem that One Art is named after, you know what I mean!)

Sorry this memo is getting so long. I did want to make sure you know that The Bell Jar Bar hasn't signed on to the American Federation of Musicians

(AFM) contract. Also, Risa told me that neither the Band nor any of its members is a member of AFM. I am relying on her statement because, if it's not true, the Bar will have to meet all kinds of bogus requirements imposed by the AFM.

Risa told me that the Amended One Art Partnership Agreement now authorizes her and Mr. Van Logo to sign contracts on behalf of the Partnership. I have the authority to sign contracts on behalf of The Bell Jar Bar, Inc. As soon as we agree to all of the contract's terms, I'll get Risa and Vince to sign and then I'll sign, too. We're not going to bother with a formal closing. But we'd like to get the agreement signed up as soon as possible—even though the contract's effective date should be November 9, 2015.

I didn't say anything to Risa about how we should resolve disputes. Just put in something less formal than going to court.

Other details: We'll provide a merch table and two chairs (one for Teddy) in the foyer of the Bar by 5 p.m. for every performance. Risa wants some protection if we fail to pay the Band. Okay. But the Band will have to give us some time to fix the problem. That way I can scramble around to find the money without worrying that they aren't going to show for their next performance. As for the Band members leaving the Band and new members joining, the Bar wants to be able to terminate the contract if either Risa or Vince leaves the Band during the engagement. As long as Risa and Vince are still in the Band, I don't think it matters if they add any new members, as long as their music doesn't change drastically. I hope we can get the Band to promise that it will continue to play experimental rock.

I'm sure you'll have some questions. I'm rushing off to a meeting, but I'll get in touch with you next week.

2C: E-MAIL FROM ASSOCIATE TO SENIOR PARTNER RE ANSWER TO POTENTIAL ETHICAL QUESTION

Instructions

A. **Summary:** You will analyze the scenario below in order to determine whether you or your firm may be violating any ethical rules if you cut a side deal with your client, The Bell Jar Bar, Inc. (the "Company"), whereby the Company engages you to perform freelance publicity work for One Art's appearances at The Bell Jar Bar. You will then draft an e-mail to your senior partner, Hermione Melville, answering the questions she has posed.

B. **Scenario:** Your firm represents The Bell Jar Bar, Inc. (the "Company"). The experimental rock band, One Art (the "Band"), has agreed to play at

The Bell Jar Bar (the "Bar") for 20 consecutive Saturday nights. Sylvia P. Hughes, your client contact, is handling the publicity for the Band's engagement at the Bar. You personally want to enter into a side deal with your firm's client, whereby the Company subcontracts the publicity work to your personal freelance publicity business, ExperiRock ("ER"). (Before you were a lawyer, you did public relations work for various experimental rock bands and you think you could do a very good job promoting the Band's appearances at the Bar. Plus, times are tough, and this is an opportunity for you to earn a little extra money.)

You asked your senior partner, Hermione Melville, whether you could approach the Company to propose that the Company subcontract the publicity work to ER. Hermione was not opposed to the idea, but she said that something did not quite smell right about it. She wondered if it presented a conflict of interest or an ethical issue either for you or for the firm. She also wants you to consider whether it presents any business or client relationship issues that the firm should weigh.

C. **Preparing the E-Mail to Senior Partner:** Find out the answers to all of Hermione Melville's questions. Review the Model Rules of Professional Conduct and the Comments to those rules for guidance.

Draft an e-mail to Hermione in which you explain any risks associated with ER performing the publicity work to promote the Band's performances at the Bar. Be sure to explain how you arrived at your conclusions.

D. **Tone of E-Mail:** Remember that you are drafting an e-mail to your senior partner, not to your best friend. Draft the e-mail in Plain English, using a professional tone. Do not use abbreviations or acronyms (like "OMG") and do not type in all caps for emphasis or insert any emoticons. Your e-mail should be only slightly less formal than a memorandum. Remember to carefully track how you arrived at your conclusions. Remember to spell check and proofread carefully.

E. **Additional Instructions:** Your professor may provide you with additional instructions regarding this assignment.

2D: ASSEMBLING THE FRAME: DRAFTING THE TITLE, PREAMBLE, BACKGROUND, WORDS OF AGREEMENT, DEFINITIONS, AND SIGNATURE LINES

Instructions

A. **Summary:** Using the deal facts contained in the memorandum from Sylvia P. Hughes to Hermione Melville (in Assignment 2B), draft the Band Performance Agreement's frame—the Title, Preamble, Background,

Words of Agreement, Definitions, and Signature Lines. In preparation for this assignment, you may also review the sample agreements referenced in Section B, Precedent, below.

B. **Precedent:** For this assignment, you may use the sample contracts cited below and only those sample contracts. This is a "canned precedent" assignment. In other words, in order to keep you focused on drafting rather than on searching for precedent, you are prohibited from using anything but the limited body (or "can") of precedent listed below. These are examples of the precedent you would be likely to find if you did your own search for band performance agreements on the Internet. You may not use any precedent other than the sample contracts listed here and any model contracts that your professor provides. If you do adapt or adopt any language from the samples provided, you must cite your source, even if you have not quoted it directly. Your professor will tell you what citation format she requires.

> *Caution # 1:* Remember that every contract "breaks the mold." That is, each contract memorializes the terms of a particular deal. If you rely too heavily on precedent, you are bound to make some serious mistakes.
>
> *Caution # 2:* View each sample contract with a critical eye, applying all of the contract drafting principles that you have learned so far.

Can of Precedent[4]

www.thunderbirdsband.com/images/PERFORMANCE_AGREE MENT.doc

http://www.gig-events-guide.co.uk/articles/gig-advice/example-contract. html

http://www.blues101.org/articles/contracts/htm

http://www.undercurrents.com/agreements/agreement-performance. html

http://www.musicbizacademy.com/articles/perfcontracts.htm
[*Note:* This is an article, not a sample contract.]

C. **The "Frame" Metaphor:** Some parts of a contract are traditional and easily drafted using models. They create a "frame" for the business provisions of the contract. The Title, Preamble, Words of Agreement, and Signature Lines are rudimentary parts of the contract's frame. The Definitions and Background sections, while more difficult to draft,

---

4. Your professor may substitute other citations for the ones included here.

still should not contain covenants, conditions precedent, representations and warranties, and statements of discretionary authority—otherwise known as "operative" provisions. For that reason, the Background and Definitions sections are also part of the contract's frame, stabilizing it by adding more information about the deal and preparing the reader for the "picture" containing the operative provisions of the deal.

A "model" contract is different from a "sample" contract in that a "model" is a contract worth imitating. Applying the basic contract drafting principles that you have learned so far, you may examine the samples in the "Can of Precedent," above, in order to determine if any elements of their frames are worthy of imitation. However, in drafting the frame of the Band Performance Agreement, you are most likely going to rely on the model Leaf Disposal Services Agreement or any other model agreement that your professor supplies. The precedent will become more useful when you fill in the picture of the contract, as required by Assignment 2E.

Professors who teach contract drafting use various images to convey what contracts drafters do. Therefore, you may hear someone else refer to the "frame" as the "skeleton" of the contract and the "picture" as the "meat on the bones." If it helps you to think of the contract that way, please feel free to do so. The purpose of these metaphors is to help you break down the drafting process into manageable parts.

D. **The Preamble: An Example of Learning from a Model:** Provided that you have the correct information, you can draft a Preamble for the Band Performance Agreement by following the pattern of the Preamble in the model Leaf Disposal Services Agreement, reprinted below.

LEAF DISPOSAL SERVICES AGREEMENT

Leaf Disposal Services Agreement made this 10th day of October 2007, between SpinGazer, Inc., a Delaware corporation with its principal place of business located at 1200 Ridge Avenue, Evanston, Illinois 60201 (the "Company"), and Fallen Leaves, Inc., an Illinois corporation with its principal place of business located at 2025 North Clark Street, Chicago, Illinois 60614 (the "Provider").

As a partnership, One Art Partnership does not necessarily have a "principal place of business." Instead, you can say "One Art Partnership, a partnership organized under the laws of Illinois with an office located at [insert address]." By placing the parenthetical shorthand name of the party after its office address, you make it more likely that you have clearly identified the "One Art Partnership" that is a party to this contract. The same goes for

The Bell Jar Bar, Inc. Clearly identify the party by placing the shorthand name for that party after the identifying information about that party.

When you draft the Preamble of your contract, pay careful attention to punctuation. The Preamble contains a lot of information and is difficult to read if not punctuated properly. Moreover, aside from the Title, the Preamble is the very first thing that the reader will encounter in your contract. Even though it is formulaic, you can set a good tone by drafting it so that it reads smoothly. Proper punctuation helps.

Finally, you and your professor are likely to spend some time talking about what date you should insert in the Preamble. When is the contract "made"? Is it the same date when the contract is signed? Is this date different from the effective date of the term? Also, sometimes the date in the Preamble is preceded by the words "as of." Under what circumstances is it appropriate to use those words? Even a formulaic Preamble can present interesting questions that you are likely to bandy about in class.

E. **Title, Words of Agreement, and Signature Lines:** You and your professor will discuss what to call this contract. For convenience sake, I have referred to it as the *Band Performance Agreement,* but you are not required to use that title.

The Words of Agreement used in the model Leaf Disposal Services Agreement are simple. After the Background section, insert "Accordingly, the parties agree as follows:". In most contracts, at about this point in the contract, you will see a lengthy "consideration" provision that sounds like complete gobbledygook. You and your professor are likely to discuss whether a formal statement of consideration is necessary if the contract itself makes it amply clear that consideration for the transaction does exist. The drafter of the Leaf Disposal Services Agreement has concluded that the contract does not require a formal statement of consideration.

You can easily imitate the Signature Lines and get them right. The Signature Lines from the Leaf Disposal Services Agreement are reprinted below.

AGREED:

SPINGAZER, INC.   **FALLEN LEAVES, INC.**

By: _____   By: _____
      Jackie Spingazer   Leif E. Liminator

Title: Director of Operations   Title: Supervisor

Since one party to the Band Performance Agreement is a partnership, you will need to adapt this format a bit. The names in boldfaced, all capital letters, above the Signature Lines are the formal names of the parties to the contract—not the shorthand names that you chose in the Preamble and used throughout the rest of the contract. So, where you see **SPINGAZER, INC.** and **FALLEN LEAVES, INC.**, above, you would substitute **THE BELL JAR BAR, INC.** and **ONE ART PARTNERSHIP.**

> **Note:** Generally, it is a good idea to put your client's signature line first. Believe it or not, this sometimes matters to the client.

For "One Art Partnership," insert a Signature Line for each general partner—one for Marisa Treadwell and one for Vincent Van Logo. Put the word "By" in front of each of their Signature Lines. Underneath each of their Signature Lines, type their names, in upper and lowercase letters, and the words "General Partner." For "The Bell Jar Bar, Inc.," follow the model, above.

F. **Background:** The purpose of the Background section is twofold—to put the Agreement in context and to express the intentions of the parties.

You may be accustomed to seeing this section called "Recitals" and containing a list of "WHEREAS" clauses ending with the crescendo "NOW THEREFORE" clause. Plain English drafters avoid those clauses like the plague. Instead, draft the Background section in smooth prose. This is probably the only place in the contract where you will get to tell a little story. Use it well. Who are the parties? What do they do? Why are they entering into this deal? The Background section should not be too long or too lopsided (containing more information about one party than the other).

The Background section is a place where you should avoid following your models too closely. It is not as formulaic as the Preamble, for example. Ask yourself: What do my readers need to know about the parties? About what happened before (if anything) and about what is about to happen (this transaction)?

Remember that you should not include any operative provisions in the Background section. Be very careful not to include any covenants, conditions precedent, representations and warranties, or statements of discretionary authority here. The courts generally will not give effect to operative language contained in a Background section. And, if you include a covenant in the Background section, you run the risk of forgetting to include it in the body of the contract, where it would actually obligate a party to do something.

Sometimes the parties want to clarify their intentions early in a contract. Even though the Background section should not contain operative provisions, it can contain a statement of the parties' intentions. Sometimes, if there is a contractual dispute, the court will give effect to a statement of intentions included in the Background section instead of, or in addition to, admitting parol evidence of those intentions.

G. **Definitions:** The model Leaf Disposal Services Agreement gives you some limited guidance about how to draft the definitions. It contains the prefatory language below.

As used in this Agreement, the terms defined in the preamble have their assigned meanings and the following terms have the meanings assigned to them in this Article.

If you have defined any terms, in-text, in the Background section, you must add the words "and in the Background section" to the prefatory language after the words "in the preamble." That way, you will not have to include any cross-references to those definitions in the Definitions article itself.

By looking at the model, you will see that most definitions use the verb "means" or "includes but does not include." You will also see that in-text definitions found in the body of the contract (but not in the Preamble or Background section) are cross-referenced here, using the verb phrase "has the meaning assigned in."

You and your professor will discuss how to choose what to define and how to draft the definitions. Remember that definitions are declarations and should not contain any operative language—no covenants, conditions, representations and warranties, or statements of discretionary authority. Think of a definition as a statement of what a term means whenever you encounter it used with a capital letter in the contract. If you want a party to undertake any kind of obligation, you must include it in the body of the contract rather than in a definition.

Important Note About Drafting Definitions: In practice, lawyers hardly ever draft a complete Definitions article before they draft the rest of the contract. In a sense, asking you to draft the Definitions before you draft the rest of the contract is an artificial exercise. Nevertheless, it is a good exercise and it may save you some time and energy. It forces you, as a novice contract drafter, to think in advance about what terms you may need to define. You can draft a definition of "performance," for example, because you know that you will need to refer to it over and over again.

Moreover, drafting definitions in advance will prevent you from making the mistake of using too many in-text definitions. When a Definitions article contains too many cross-references to in-text definitions, the reader is forced to hop all over the contract to find out what things mean. Instead, by defining most terms in the Definitions article itself, you keep the reader happy by feeding her information. You also take the opportunity to educate her about the deal a bit before she launches into the contract. This may sound like a litigation drafting concept, but it holds true for contract drafting as well. As your reader moves into the contract, after reading a fully developed Definitions article, she is more likely to understand the rest of the contract.

If you remember to consider your audience(s), you will be more likely to achieve the goal of clear communication. Transactional attorneys who fail to consider their audience(s) give transactional attorneys a bad name.

H. Additional Instructions: Your professor may provide you with additional instructions regarding this assignment.

2E: FILLING IN THE PICTURE: DRAFTING THE CONTRACT'S OPERATIVE PROVISIONS

Instructions

A. Summary: This assignment assumes that you have already drafted the "frame" of the contract as required by Assignment 2D—or that your professor has asked you to skip that assignment and concentrate on "filling in the picture." Using the deal facts contained in the memorandum from Sylvia P. Hughes to Hermione Melville (in Assignment 2B), draft all of the operative provisions of the Band Performance Agreement. The "operative" provisions do not include the "frame" of the contract—the Title, Preamble, Background, Words of Agreement, Definitions, and Signature Lines.

B. Preparation for Filling in the Picture: Before you begin to fill in the picture, you must do two things. First, review the Can of Precedent identified in Assignment 2D. Determine which topics are generally covered in a Band Performance Agreement and evaluate each contract to see if it contains any language that you think you may be able to adapt or adopt for use in your contract.

Second, if you have identified any legal issues presented by the transaction, then you must research them. Seek direction from your professor in order to avoid spending too much time on legal research. Your focus should be on drafting the contract.

C. **Filling in the Picture:** To fill in the picture, you must draft all of the operative provisions of the contract and decide how to organize them. Your professor will help you develop the basic skills you need to take the terms of the deal and translate them into contract concepts—covenants, conditions precedent, representations and warranties, statements of discretionary authority, and declarations.[5]

In practice, some call this *memorializing* the terms of the deal, which basically means getting the terms of the deal down on paper so that they have a legal effect. The paper (or contract) is the *memorial*. The parties should be able to turn to the contract whenever they have any questions about their rights and duties with regard to the particular transaction.

D. **Organization—Naming and Ordering the Articles and Sections:** Some provisions are traditionally placed in certain spots. For example, after the Definitions article, some drafters include a brief article containing the main covenants of the deal. One contract drafting expert, Tina L. Stark, calls this brief article the "subject matter performance provision."[6] The subject matter performance provision in the model Leaf Disposal Services Agreement is reprinted below.

Article III. Summary of Services and Fees

Section 3.01 Services and Fees. Subject to the provisions of this Agreement, the Provider shall perform the Services described in Article IV. To compensate the Provider for performing the Services, the Company shall pay the Provider the fees and reimburse the Provider for the expenses described in Article V.

The drafter of the model Leaf Disposal Services Agreement put the subject matter performance provision after the Term article. While the exact order of these provisions sometimes varies, remember that the

---

5. Tina L. Stark, *Drafting Contracts: How and Why Lawyers Do What They Do* 9-10 (Aspen 2007) (describes the contract concepts as the "building blocks" of the contract and the process of converting business terms into contract concepts as a "translation skill").
   6. *Id.* at 39-40.

subject matter performance provision, the Term, and the Closing articles should appear near the beginning of the contract.

It is sometimes helpful to think of the subject matter performance provision as a thesis statement plus roadmap. It tells you the "main idea" (or "primary covenants") of the contract and points you to the places in the contract where you can find out more details about those covenants.

After the subject matter performance provision, the Term article, and the Closing article, the reader expects to find information about what the Band is going to do and how much the Company is going to pay for the Band's services. Therefore, you must put the articles covering those topics close to the beginning of the contract.

At the end of the contract, right before the signature lines, place the contract's boilerplate provisions (sometimes called *General Provisions*). The Termination and Dispute Resolution articles generally come right before the boilerplate.

So, with the parts of the contract in their traditional places, and allowing for some flexibility in their exact order, your contract (not including the frame) will look something like this:

Summary of Services and Fees
Term
Closing (if any)
The Band's Performances
Fees and Expenses
[OTHER TOPICS TO BE COVERED]
Dispute Resolution
Termination
General Provisions

Note that the above italicized headings are offered as an example only. They are not set in stone. You are encouraged to draft your own appropriate headings for the articles you include in the contract.

One of the biggest challenges that a drafter faces is how to organize the business provisions not specifically listed above—that is, how to organize those "other topics to be covered." Start by making a list of every deal term not addressed in the named articles. Then group those deal terms by topic and select a good name for the article covering that topic. Remember that "Partnership's Obligations" and "Company's Responsibilities" are contract concepts, not topics. If you use a heading like "Partnership's Obligations," you are indicating to the reader that all of the Partnership's obligations are contained under that heading. More likely, the Partnership's obligations are scattered throughout the contract.

Choose article names (and section names as well) that are specific and clear. Instead of "Partnership's Obligations," for example, you may have articles or sections called "Publicity" and "Sale of Band Merchandise."

Either of these articles or sections may contain obligations and responsibilities of one or both parties.

If you find that you have a number of miscellaneous deal terms that do not seem to fit anywhere, give them another look before deciding to create single-section articles. Single-section articles (other than the subject matter performance provision and the Term article) can make the particular topic seem like an undeveloped afterthought or, conversely, give the particular topic too much weight. It is better to put the miscellaneous deal term into the article it relates to the most, even if it is not a perfect fit.

Once you have found a place for every deal term and named the articles you want to include in the contract, decide what order to put them in. Generally, place the articles in order from most important topic to least important topic. However, if you are describing a process, it may make more sense to put some of the articles in chronological order. There is no magic bullet of contract organization. However, it is very important to remember your audience(s). Ask yourself what your reader needs to know and when your reader needs to know it. Also, remember the terms of the deal. For example, if your client stressed that the Company was very concerned about the Band performing experimental rock music (as opposed to other kinds of music), then you may want to move that topic up near the beginning of the contract for emphasis.

E. **Boilerplate Provisions:** The memo from Sylvia P. Hughes to Hermione Melville may not contain all of the facts you need in order to select the appropriate boilerplate provisions to include in your contract. Follow your professor's instructions regarding which boilerplate to include. A valuable resource to help you understand the history and evolution of various boilerplate provisions is the book *Negotiating and Drafting Contract Boilerplate,* edited and co-authored by Tina L. Stark (American Lawyer Media 2003). Your professor may also ask you to complete Assignment 2G, which requires you to adjust the standard boilerplate language to address some of the parties' specific concerns.

F. **Additional Instructions:** Your professor may provide you with additional instructions regarding this assignment.

2F: PUTTING THE PICTURE IN THE FRAME: FINISHING THE DRAFT CONTRACT

Instructions

A. **Summary:** You will now insert the "picture" that you drafted in response to Assignment 2E into the "frame" that you drafted in response to Assignment 2D. The result will be one completed draft of a Band Performance Agreement (with a title that you have selected).

B. The Process: Inserting the picture into the frame is not merely a mechanical process. Once you have merged the two documents together, you must make sure that the picture fits the frame properly; in other words, you must review the draft contract as a whole and ask yourself at least the following questions:

- ☐ Is the Title I chose for the contract still appropriate?
- ☐ Have I consistently referred to the parties to the contract using the shorthand names that I gave them in the Preamble?
- ☐ Do the full party names in the Preamble (not the shorthand names) match the full party names above the Signature Lines?
- ☐ Does the date in the Preamble reflect the date when the contract is made? If this is different from the effective date of the contract, have I clarified that in the body of the contract?
- ☐ Do the addresses in the Preamble match the addresses in the "Notice" provision included in the boilerplate?
- ☐ Did I include enough information in the Background section? Is there anything else that I may want to add to that section? Is there anything I may want to take out?
- ☐ Do I use my defined terms whenever it is appropriate? [*Note:* This is called "letting your defined terms do their work."]
- ☐ Did I remember to capitalize my defined terms in the body of the contract?
- ☐ Are there any lengthy phrases that I repeat more than once that could perhaps be defined terms?
- ☐ Are there any concepts that I repeat in different ways each time that I should perhaps be saying the same way each time? Would a defined term help?
- ☐ Are there any defined terms that I never use or use only once? (If so, you probably do not need to define that term.)
- ☐ Have I included a cross-reference to every in-text definition in the Definitions article? Are my definitions still in alphabetical order?
- ☐ Whenever I use a cross-reference, have I referenced the correct article or section?
- ☐ Have I used cross-references in the body of the contract to help the reader understand the relationship between parts of the contract?
- ☐ Are all of my article and section numbers in order? Does each have an appropriate heading?
- ☐ In the "Survivability" boilerplate provision, have I listed all of the sections of the contract that will survive the early termination of the contract or the end of the term?
- ☐ Do all of the parts of the contract work well together?

Once you have answered all of these questions and made any necessary adjustments to the contract, you can move into the editing and proofreading stage described next.

C. **Editing and Proofreading:** Using the Contract Drafting Checklist provided in Appendix 3, go back over your draft contract again. The checklist is set up to help you take the long view first. Think about the transaction. Have you captured all of the terms of the deal? Have you translated them into the correct contract concepts? Have you answered all questions about the rights and duties of the parties with regard to this transaction? Have you raised any questions without answering them? Is your contract well organized, coherent, and coordinated? Does it read smoothly? Is it easy to follow?

The checklist then asks you to look at some formatting issues that are directly related to readability. Review those issues, remembering also that well-chosen headings and the judicious use of "white space" enhance the readability of a contract. Do not remove headings or white space in order to make sure that you do not exceed the page limit for this assignment. If you need guidance about how to avoid exceeding the page limit, seek your professor's help.

Following the checklist, now make sure that your contract contains all of the essential parts. Then, review each part. Finally, under the broad heading "Plain English," the checklist directs you to make sure that you have not made any grammatical, mechanical, or typographical errors.

Once you have gone through the checklist, prepare your contract for submission by proofreading it carefully, using the proofreading tips and tricks contained in Appendix 5. Finally, go back to the original assignment sheet and verify that you have followed all of the directions regarding submitting the contract to your professor. There is something particularly disturbing about a transactional attorney who fails to follow directions. Failing to follow directions indicates that you are not detail oriented, which, in practice, can make your supervisor and your client mistrust you. It can also lead to a dangerous loss of credibility with the attorney representing the other side.

D. **Submitting the Contract:** Do one final thing before you submit your contract. Make sure that you are turning in a clean copy. That is, make sure that you have eliminated any highlighting or comments to yourself that you may have used during the drafting process. Practicing attorneys, both litigators and deal lawyers, can tell many war stories about forgetting to delete comments or critiques before filing documents or sending drafts to the other side. You do not want to make such an embarrassing mistake. You may also want to make sure that your document does not contain any hidden personal or metadata, such as information about when you finished the assignment. Check the software you are using to figure out how to eliminate that information.

E. **Additional Instructions:** Your professor may provide you with additional instructions regarding this assignment.

2G: IN-CLASS WORKSHOP: BOILERPLATE PROVISIONS

Instructions

A. **Summary:** In pairs, triads, or larger teams (as directed by your professor), consider each business issue presented. Re-draft each basic boilerplate provision to address the business issue. You may sometimes decide that re-drafting the provision is not the best solution. If so, please suggest another solution.

B. **New Deal Facts:** This workshop introduces some new facts regarding the Band Performance Agreement that you are drafting. You must incorporate these new deal facts into the final draft of your contract.

C. **Caveat:** This workshop does not address all of the boilerplate provisions that you should include in the contract.

D. **Source of the Basic Boilerplate Provisions:** Each basic boilerplate provision is taken from *Drafting Contracts: How and Why Lawyers Do What They Do*, by Tina L. Stark (Aspen 2007), cited as "Stark, *Drafting Contracts*." Remember that, in Tina Stark's words, the standard provisions "are not paradigms of perfect drafting." Rather, they are "intended to give you a sense of the provisions that you will typically see." Stark, *Drafting Contracts* 167. In drafting your answer, you may also wish to consult *Negotiating and Drafting Contract Boilerplate*, edited and co-authored by Tina L. Stark (American Lawyer Media 2003).

E. **Additional Instructions:** Your professor may provide you with additional instructions regarding this assignment.

EXERCISE I: ASSIGNMENT AND DELEGATION

BUSINESS ISSUE: The Bell Jar Bar, Inc. (the "Company") is in the process of forming a subsidiary called BJB Entertainment ("BJB") that will handle booking and promotion of all musical acts for the Company. The subsidiary is likely to be up and running by the tenth Saturday of One Art's engagement. Your client wants to be able to assign its rights and delegate its duties to BJB so that BJB can pay the Band, receive the money from the gate and the merch sales, and promote the Band's appearance at The Bell Jar Bar.

The Band is willing to agree to let the Company assign its rights and delegate its duties to BJB. However, the Band wants to make sure that BJB will assume in writing the Company's obligation to perform.

Meanwhile, the Company is adamantly opposed to allowing the Band to assign any of its rights or delegate any of its duties, except if the Band loses a member and replaces that member with another individual (and assuming that the lost member is not Marisa or Vince).

STANDARD PROVISION:

Assignment and Delegation. This Agreement cannot be assigned or delegated by the parties.

(Stark, *Drafting Contracts* 170-172.)

REVISED PROVISION (OR OTHER SOLUTION):

EXERCISE II: GOVERNING LAW

BUSINESS ISSUE: The Company is an Illinois corporation operating only in Illinois. However, Sylvia P. Hughes believes that New York law is more beneficial to bar owners and would like New York law to apply. (She recently read an article about the benefits of New York's dram shop liability laws to bar owners.) The Band, a partnership organized under Illinois law, is insisting that Illinois law should govern.

STANDARD PROVISION:

Governing Law. This Agreement is to be governed by and construed in accordance with the laws of [insert name of state], without regard to its conflict of law principles.

(Stark, *Drafting Contracts* 173-174.)

REVISED PROVISION (OR OTHER SOLUTION):

EXERCISE III: NOTICE

BUSINESS ISSUE: Your client is concerned that it may sometimes need to notify the Band of its need to cancel a performance very quickly—more quickly than by mail or even by e-mail. (What if the very hot punk band "Death by Text Message" comes to town and is available to play on Saturday night and it's the Thursday before, for example?) Under circumstances like these, Sylvia would like to be able to call Risa or Vince directly to notify the Band of the need to cancel. Sylvia would like the notice to be effective upon her speaking to Risa or Vince live or via voicemail. She is willing to confirm the notice with an e-mail. She wants it to be clear exactly when the notice becomes effective.

STANDARD PROVISION:

>**Notice.** All notices under this Agreement shall be given in writing.
>(Stark, *Drafting Contracts* 175-176.)

REVISED PROVISION (OR OTHER SOLUTION):

EXERCISE IV: SEVERABILITY

BUSINESS ISSUE: In Illinois, it is unlawful to sell, serve, deliver or give alcoholic beverages to a person under 21 years of age. Violation of this provision is a Class A Misdemeanor. The penalty is a minimum $500 fine (maximum $2,500) and may include a jail sentence of up to one year. Also, the Illinois Liquor Control Commission can fine a bar or suspend or revoke its liquor license.

Assume that some of the members of One Art are not 21 years of age. Could a court or agency find any provisions of the Band Performance Agreement to be illegal? Which ones? What if a court or agency rules that One Art cannot play at the Bar at all because some of its members are under the age of 21?

STANDARD PROVISION:

>**Severability.** If any provision of this Agreement is illegal or unenforceable, that provision is severed from this Agreement and the other provisions remain in force.
>(Stark, *Drafting Contracts* 176-177.)

REVISED PROVISION (OR OTHER SOLUTION):

EXERCISE V: MERGER/INTEGRATION

BUSINESS ISSUE: Before entering into this Agreement—during the course of their negotiations—the Company and the Band signed a Non-Disclosure Agreement (dated September 20, 2015), prohibiting both parties from disclosing any Confidential Information revealed to the other party. Both parties agreed not to disclose the other party's Confidential Information for two years. Both parties want the Non-Disclosure Agreement to remain in effect. However, they still want to include a Merger provision in this Agreement.

STANDARD PROVISION:

>**Merger.** This Agreement states the full agreement between the parties and supersedes all prior negotiations and agreements.
>(Stark, *Drafting Contracts* 178-179.)

REVISED PROVISION (OR OTHER SOLUTION):

2H: SIDE LETTER RE SPECIAL BENEFIT PERFORMANCE OF BAND

Instructions

A. **Summary:** Your client, The Bell Jar Bar, Inc. (the "Company"), has asked you to draft a "side letter" memorializing a new, but not completely unrelated agreement it has struck with One Art Partnership (the "Partnership"). Your client does not want to terminate the performance agreement already in place (the "Agreement"); nor does it want to push the Partnership into terminating the Agreement.

B. **Scenario:** The Company has been asked to provide the musical entertainment and the venue for a benefit. The benefit will raise money for an organization called "Young and Rocking Musicians," also known as "YARM." The Company has asked One Art (the "Band") if they would be willing to perform at the benefit for free and the Band has agreed, with some caveats. Read the attached letter from Sylvia P. Hughes to Marisa Treadwell and Vincent Van Logo. Read also the attached e-mail string between Sylvia and your senior partner, Hermione Melville.

C. **Side Letters, in General:** Do not look for an example of a "side letter" on the Internet or in forms books. Instead, with your professor's guidance, think this through.

Side letters are generally used to clarify an issue in a contract or to address an issue that the parties have failed to cover in the contract. Collective bargaining agreements, for example, often have numerous side letters that become a part of the main agreement.

Clients like the Company will sometimes request that you draft a side letter because they believe that it will take you less time than drafting a separate contract and will therefore cost them less money (since you generally are billing them by the hour).

D. **Drafting the Side Letter:** Address the side letter from your client, Sylvia P. Hughes, to Marisa Treadwell and Vincent Van Logo, the general partners of the Partnership.

> **Note:** If you know that the Partnership is represented by an attorney, then you—as attorney for the Company—have an ethical obligation

not to contact the Partnership (or any of its partners) directly. However, Sylvia can communicate directly with Marisa and Vince because the parties are not prohibited from talking to each other directly.

It is a good idea to think about a side letter as being a contract in its own right. Ask yourself what the consideration is for the Band's services at the benefit. Make sure that you clarify that the side letter concerns a bargained-for exchange by describing that exchange in the body of the letter.

Note: You can accomplish this without including an archaic statement of consideration that is full of meaningless gobbledygook!

Think first about the Agreement and how the side letter will work with the Agreement. Include language clarifying that the side letter does not override the Agreement; nor is the side letter superseded by the Agreement. The side letter is, in effect, a written agreement amending the Agreement in certain limited ways.

In order to make sure that the side letter does not get lost or overlooked, make sure that you provide for it to be attached to and incorporated into the Agreement. Then follow through, making sure that both your client and the Partnership receive new copies of the Agreement with the signed Side Letter attached as an exhibit. (This is what you would do in real life. Your professor will let you know whether he wants you to do this for purposes of this assignment.)

Remember to include language stating that this side letter is the only amendment to the Agreement and that the remainder of the Agreement's provisions will remain in effect. Include signature and date lines for parties (and title lines for the Company's representative, Sylvia P. Hughes, as well as title lines for Marisa Treadwell and Vincent Van Logo, the Partnership's general partners.) Sylvia will sign and date the letter, fill in her title, and mail it to the Partnership to obtain the signatures of both general partners. The letter should include instructions for her to sign and return the letter to Sylvia as soon as possible. Remember to inform Sylvia that the side letter is not effective until it is signed by both parties.

E. **Additional Instructions:** Your professor may provide you with additional instructions regarding this assignment.

The Bell Jar Bar, Inc.
2300 Ariel Lane
Chicago, Illinois 65432

December 14, 2015

Marisa Treadwell & Vincent Van Logo
General Partners
One Art Partnership
1953 Percussion Avenue
Chicago, Illinois 65431

Dear Risa and Vince:

As you know, I have agreed to provide the musical entertainment and the venue for a benefit intended to raise money for "Young and Rocking Musicians" (YARM), an organization that funds scholarships for kids under the age of 16 who want to learn how to play rock music. The benefit is to take place on Wednesday, January 13, 2016. When we spoke, you agreed to perform at the benefit free of charge, under certain conditions.

You assured me that the Band is free to play on the date of the benefit. You agreed to play for no charge, but you want to be one of the headliner bands. You also want to play second-to-last or last, as you believe that is a prominent position on the roster. Although every member of every other band will be required to wear the YARM fluorescent green t-shirts that the Company will provide, you asked that you be permitted to wear your usual performance clothing. I agreed.

I also agreed that you can set up a merch table and sell your merch, without the Company taking any cut, as long as you donate $1 of every purchase to YARM.

Finally, you are willing to alter some of your lyrics to remove bad words since it will be an all-ages show and a benefit for a children's organization. You also said that you would allow some of the children to come up on stage to look at your musical instruments and talk to you while you are setting up.

The Company agreed to put some additional delicacies in the green room on the night of the benefit and on every one of your regular performance nights after the benefit, including a red velvet cake and the makings of root beer floats (made with diet root beer and fat-free, vanilla frozen yogurt).

I am going to ask the Company's attorneys to draw up a side letter capturing the terms of our deal. They may also need to add other language protecting the Company's rights—if, for example, you were to perform at the benefit and then decide that you are too tired to show up for the regular Saturday night performance three days later. Also, since they *are* lawyers, you can expect the letter to contain some other legal mumbo-jumbo. But I will try to rein them in.

Thanks so much for agreeing to perform for the YARM benefit. I will send you more information later. You can call me if you have any additional questions.

Sincerely yours,

Sylvia P. Hughes
Sylvia P. Hughes
President
The Bell Jar Bar, Inc.

E-Mail String Between Sylvia P. Hughes and Hermione Melville

From:	Sylvia P. Hughes	Sent: 12/17/2015, 7:30 a.m.
To:	Hermione Melville	
Cc:		
Subject:	Side Letter to Band Performance Agreement with One Art Partnership	

Hermione:

By now you've had a chance to read the letter I faxed over to you. In the letter, I remembered to warn Marisa and Vince that the side letter you draw up is likely to contain some legal mumbo-jumbo (no offense to you, of course). Anyway, I did that because I was concerned about some of the things they asked for and about how put out they seemed to be because I was asking them to do something for free.

So, when you draft the side letter, please make sure that you add in a clause terminating the entire contract if the Band does not show up to play the benefit. If they bail out, then I will be too angry with them to continue the relationship.

Thanks,
Sylvia

* * *

From:	Hermione Melville	Sent: 12/17/2015, 7:45 a.m.
To:	Sylvia P. Hughes	
Cc:		
Subject:	Side Letter to Band Performance Agreement with One Art Partnership	

Sylvia:

Having One Art play at the benefit seems very important to you. We can add in the termination provision you request, but I'm not sure it will fly.

Did you put any limitations around what kind of merch the Band can sell? I know that at least one of their t-shirts contains an image of a nude man along with a sentence containing the "F" word on the back.

Hermione

* * *

From:	Sylvia P. Hughes	Sent: 12/17/2015, 8:30 a.m.
To:	Hermione Melville	
Cc:		
Subject:	Side Letter to Band Performance Agreement with One Art Partnership	

Hermione:

Good thinking. I hadn't thought about that t-shirt. Go ahead and
put something about it in the side letter and I'll see what I can do on this
end to get them to agree. They didn't have much problem with adjusting
the song lyrics, so I doubt if they will refuse to keep the t-shirt out of the
merch sales.

Hey—I just received confirmation that a more famous band, "Explosive Brains,"
is willing to headline the benefit. That pushes One Art down to being the No. 2
headliner and the second-to-last act. I don't think they'll have much problem
with that because I'm sure they respect the status of Explosive Brains.
However, please make the side letter explicitly state that One Art will play
second-to-last, as befits their status as the second headliner.

Thanks,
Sylvia

* * *

From:	Hermione Melville	Sent: 12/17/2015, 8:45 a.m.
To:	Sylvia P. Hughes	
Cc:		
Subject:	Side Letter to Band Performance Agreement with One Art Partnership	

Sylvia:

Did you work out any other details about the benefit performance with the
Band? How long are they supposed to play, for example? When are they
supposed to arrive for a sound check? When are they supposed to arrive to set
up? Can they come early to hear the rest of the bands play? Is it a sit-down
dinner? Are you providing dinners for the musicians?

Let me know.

Thanks,
Hermione

Hawthorn, Melville & Poe. Then delete the e-mail and destroy any copies of it.

* * *

From: Sylvia P. Hughes   Sent: 12/17/2015, 9:30 a.m.

To: Hermione Melville

Cc:

Subject: Side Letter to Band Performance Agreement with One Art
             Partnership

Hermione:

We didn't talk about that stuff. Here's what to put in: The Band is invited to the whole benefit, so they will be able to eat dinner and listen to the other bands play. The sound check is at 4:30 p.m. They should be ready to set up at 10 p.m. and will play one long set from 10:00 p.m. to 11:00 p.m. (Explosive Brains will play from 11:00 p.m. to midnight.) The benefit begins at 7:00 p.m.

Hope that helps.

* * *

From: Hermione Melville   Sent: 12/17/2015, 9:45 a.m.

To: Sylvia P. Hughes

Cc:

Subject: Side Letter to Band Performance Agreement with One Art
             Partnership

Sylvia:

Thank you. That's very helpful. We'll have the side letter ready by tomorrow.

By the way, our firm would like to buy a table at the benefit, so be sure to send us an invitation.

Hermione

error, please return it with the title "received in error" to Hermione Melville at Hawthorn, Melville & Poe. Then delete the e-mail and destroy any copies of it.

* * *

From: Sylvia P. Hughes   Sent: 12/17/2015, 10:30 a.m.

To: Hermione Melville

Cc:

Subject: Side Letter to Band Performance Agreement with One Art Partnership

Hermione:

Thank you so much. Yes, your firm is at the top of our list.

Regards,
Sylvia

Assignment 3

The Band Management Services Agreement

3A: NON-DISCLOSURE AGREEMENT: DRAFTING THE DEFINITIONS OF CONFIDENTIAL INFORMATION

Instructions

A. **Summary:** In Assignment 3E, you will be assigned to represent either the One Art Partnership (the "Partnership") or We Brake For Musicians, Inc., a music management company (the "Manager"). Ultimately, you will negotiate and draft a band management services agreement embodying the negotiated terms of the deal. (Read General Information for Both Parties, which follows.)

   Before the parties can negotiate further, they need a non-disclosure agreement ("NDA") to protect any confidential information that they may disclose to each other during the course of the negotiations. This assignment requires you to draft the definitions of the "Partnership's Confidential Information" and the "Manager's Confidential Information." You will later incorporate these definitions into the NDA (as part of Assignment 3B).

B. **Using Precedent:** You may review any non-disclosure agreements you can locate in order to determine how "Confidential Information" is generally defined. However, definitions of Confidential Information contained in non-disclosure agreements are notoriously full of meaningless language that does not take into account what information actually is going to be disclosed by each party during the course of their negotiations. You must closely examine any precedent you find, tailor it to the terms of your deal (that is, to what kinds of confidential information the parties to this deal are likely to disclose to each other), and translate it into Plain English.

C. **Focus:** The purpose of this brief exercise is to make you focus on who is going to disclose what to whom. In law practice, as in-house counsel at a corporation, for example, you may find the vice president of sales standing at your office door five minutes before a scheduled meeting, demanding that you prepare an NDA. You may have most of the NDA already prepared in a template. But the most important thing is for you to identify what information your client is going to disclose and for what purpose. You would not want your client to reveal a marketing strategy, for example, if you have not included "marketing strategy" in the list of things considered Client's Confidential Information. Nor would you want the other side to use the information about your client's marketing strategy for any purpose other than the particular project about which the parties are negotiating.

You must also be very careful to describe as specifically and narrowly as possible the information that the other party is going to reveal to your client. Parties will frequently bring their own NDAs to meetings and attempt to get other parties to agree not to disclose a wide range of information, much of which is simply not confidential. Limit your client's risk by limiting the kind of information your client agrees not to disclose.

D. **Procedure and Format:** Think about what you know about the transaction. What confidential information has your client most likely already disclosed to the other side? What confidential information is your client likely to disclose to the other side during the course of the continuing negotiation? Make a list of these specific items. Your goal is to avoid using a vague definition like "any information that has commercial value to the Partnership [or the Manager]."

Draft two separate definitions as described below:

"Partnership's Confidential Information" includes [insert list of specific items], and [catchall phrase].

"Manager's Confidential Information" includes [insert list of specific items], and [catchall phrase].

The "catchall phrase" is designed to make sure that your definition covers things that you have not listed but that are similar to the items in your list. For example, your catchall phrase could be something like "and any other similarly sensitive or proprietary information revealed by the Partnership during the negotiations." You can do better than that! Look at the precedent you have gathered to see if you can find a definition of Confidential Information that employs a better catchall phrase.

After you say what each party's Confidential Information includes, you must put in the standard exceptions to the definition of Confidential Information, which generally cover things like "information that has previously entered the public domain." You can easily find out what these standard exceptions are by looking at almost any non-disclosure agreement.

Introduce these exceptions by stating: "Neither the Partnership's nor the Manager's Confidential Information includes [insert standard exceptions]."

E. Additional Instructions: Your professor may provide you with additional instructions regarding this assignment.

General Information for Both Parties

It is January 2019.

The experimental rock band, One Art ("One Art" or the "Band"), has come a long way from the days when its lead singer and guitarist, Marisa Treadwell, suggested that the Band purchase the artwork for its logo from their favorite tattoo artist, Vincent Van Logo. As you know, the many-talented Vince later joined the Band. The combination of Marisa's gravelly voice and Vince's electric bagpipes thrilled audiences at The Bell Jar Bar (the "Bar") so much that The Bell Jar Bar, Inc. (the "Company") extended the Band's engagement for 32 additional consecutive Saturdays. The Band's banner year at the Bar launched their career. (They have hired an attorney as the first member of their "entourage.")

This past summer, Risa and Vince attended a House of Blues concert headlined by "The Mars Volta," one of their favorite bands. During the switchover time between the opening and featured acts, Vince went to the bar to get Risa another dry martini and struck up a conversation with a man named Harmon E. Brake. It turns out that Harmon is the president of a music management company called "We Brake For Musicians, Inc." (the "Manager"). Vince could not believe his good fortune! Harmon, who had been to the Bar to hear One Art on more than one occasion, said that his company would love to have the Band as a client. Moreover, he personally would be interested in managing the Band.

Vince brought Harmon over to meet Risa, where they talked until The Mars Volta began to play. Afterwards, Risa, Vince, and Harmon continued talking until the security guards kicked them out. As they said their goodbyes in the parking lot, Harmon handed Risa one of his business cards and said, "Have your attorney call our attorney and we'll hammer out a deal." Risa smiled and pocketed the card. She and Vince agree about Harmon: In addition to being smart and savvy, he has great taste in music. Moreover, given the name of his company, he has a good sense of humor. These are all qualities that One Art is looking for in a personal manager.

The Manager is an Illinois corporation with its principal place of business located at 720 W. Musicality Place, Suite 8342, Chicago, Illinois 65432. It is a privately held corporation with 50 employees. The Manager is strictly a management company. It does not own a record company, a production company, or a music publishing company. Nor is it a licensed talent agency. The Manager currently has no intention of owning a record company, a production company, or a music publishing company, or of becoming a licensed talent agency.

The Band still has the same members as it did when the One Art Partnership initially entered into the Band Performance Agreement with the Company. The Band still operates as the One Art Partnership, an Illinois partnership. It is now located at Ferris Wheel View Condominiums, 55550 N. Riparian Drive, Suite 9200, Chicago, Illinois 65432. This is the residence of Marisa Treadwell and Vincent Van Logo. The Band is now a member of the American Federation of Musicians union.

3B: NON-DISCLOSURE AGREEMENT: DRAFTING THE OPERATIVE PROVISIONS

Instructions

A. **Summary:** This assignment assumes that you have completed Assignment 3A and that you now have in hand the definitions of Partnership's Confidential Information and Manager's Confidential Information. Using those definitions, you will complete the Non-Disclosure Agreement ("NDA") that the parties will sign before they begin negotiating the terms of the Band Management Services Agreement. The attorneys for the Partnership and the Manager have met and agreed upon the operative terms that they want to include in the NDA. The Manager's attorney assigned a junior associate to take notes during this meeting (copy follows). Marisa Treadwell and Vincent Van Logo have read the notes and believe that they accurately represent what the parties agreed to at the meeting.

B. **Using Precedent:** You may review any NDAs you can locate in order to help you determine how NDAs look and what provisions they generally contain. (You may want to refer to the same NDAs you used when drafting the definitions of Confidential Information in Assignment 3A.) You must apply everything you know about good contract drafting to any language you adopt or adapt from the available precedent. For example, remember to use "shall" for covenants and to draft in the active voice. Say "The Partnership shall not disclose the Manager's Confidential Information" as opposed to "The Manager's Confidential Information shall not be disclosed by the Partnership."

Remember, also, to eliminate all legalese from any precedent you use. Do not develop the lawyerly bad habit of using two or even three words when one strong word will do. For example, say "The Manager shall not disclose the Partnership's Confidential Information" as opposed to "The Manager shall not reveal, disseminate, or disclose the Partnership's Confidential Information."

Note: Reasonable people may disagree about whether "disseminate" carries a different meaning from "reveal" and "disclose" and should therefore be included. Always ask yourself if all of the words in your list are necessary to carry your meaning. (Certainly "reveal" and "disclose" are synonymous. Eliminate one of them.)

C. **Organization of the Non-Disclosure Agreement:** Draft a Preamble for the NDA, just as you would for any other contract. Follow the model Leaf Disposal Services Agreement Preamble shown below.

LEAF DISPOSAL SERVICES AGREEMENT

Leaf Disposal Services Agreement made this 10th day of October 2007, between SpinGazer, Inc., a Delaware corporation with its principal place of business located at 1200 Ridge Avenue, Evanston, Illinois 60201 (the "Company"), and Fallen Leaves, Inc., an Illinois corporation with its principal place of business located at 2025 North Clark Street, Chicago, Illinois 60614 (the "Provider").

Since the One Art Partnership is a partnership and not a corporation, identify it as "an Illinois general partnership with an office located at [insert address]." For the Manager, follow the model, above.

For the Background section in your NDA, do not succumb to blindly following precedent by inserting a number of "WHEREAS" clauses culminating in the big "NOW, THEREFORE" clause. Instead, simply insert a brief description of why the parties are going to be revealing confidential information to each other. What does the Partnership want to discuss with the Manager? In the Background section, you may want to create an in-text definition of "Services" that you can use throughout the NDA. Remember that your client is entering into an NDA to protect information revealed to your client during the negotiations about the Services.

After the Preamble, you should include the words, "Accordingly, the parties agree as follows," unless you determine that it may be important to use a fuller statement of consideration in this NDA. Since both parties are exchanging Confidential Information, and both parties are agreeing not to disclose that information, the consideration for the contract is inherent in the contract itself. But, because the consideration for an NDA may not be as obvious as it is for a purchase or services agreement, you may want to include a statement like, "Accordingly, in consideration of the mutual promises contained in this Agreement, the parties agree as follows." Do not revert to gobbledygook by adding the words "and other good and valuable consideration, the receipt and sufficiency of which is hereby mutually acknowledged." Keep it simple.

After the statement of consideration, organize the remainder of the NDA as follows:

Definitions
Term
Basic Non-Disclosure Obligations
[Other Operative Provisions]
General Provisions
Signature Lines

Draft the basic non-disclosure obligations before you cover any other operative provisions. You will find precedent in which the drafters describe both parties' non-disclosure obligations in one section or paragraph. In order to avoid the difficulties of the "Both parties shall not" construction—including having to define "Disclosing Party" and "Recipient"—try drafting one section containing the Partnership's non-disclosure obligations and another section containing the Manager's non-disclosure obligations.

After you draft the parties' basic non-disclosure obligations, you must decide what other operative provisions you need to cover and organize them in a logical way. For example, you will want to talk about what happens to the Confidential Information when the Term ends. You may want to cover this topic near the end of the contract, since it addresses what is to happen at the end of the parties' relationship. When considering how to organize the "other operative provisions," keep your audience in mind. You still have to consider an audience wider than just the parties' signators and the parties' attorneys. Remember that other executives working for the Manager may have a "need to know" the Partnership's Confidential Information, for example. Therefore, those other executives may have to see the NDA so that they understand their own non-disclosure obligations.

Next, look at the precedent you have located to determine what kind of boilerplate provisions generally appear in an NDA. Most NDAs have merger/integration and choice-of-law provisions, for example. Some have severability provisions as well. Think about your client's needs. If you believe that any other boilerplate should be included to address your client's needs, put it in. For example, perhaps several years after signing the NDA, your client will need to disclose the other party's Confidential Information to a third party. If you think that might happen, you may want to include an amendment and modification clause so that it might be possible to shorten the NDA's term.

D. **Formatting the Non-Disclosure Agreement:** After the Definitions article, you can use simple numbered paragraphs with headings to format the NDA. So, for example, the "Term" and "Non-Disclosure Obligations" sections might look like this:

1. **Term.** This Agreement begins on [insert date] and ends [insert date].
2. **Partnership's Duty Not to Disclose Manager's Confidential Information.** [Insert body of provision].
3. **Manager's Duty Not to Disclose Partnership's Confidential Information.** [Insert body of provision].

E. **One Final Note About the Nature of Confidential Information:** Remember that parties can reveal confidential information both orally and in writing. In other words, much of what the parties say to each other may never be put down in a document but may still constitute confidential information. Do not make the mistake of assuming that confidential information is only contained in written documents. Be sure that your NDA takes this into account.

F. **Additional Instructions:** Your professor may provide you with additional instructions regarding this assignment.

From the desk of:

Roberto Frost

Subject: Notes of Meeting Between One Art Partnership and We Brake For Musicians, Inc.

Re: Terms of Non-Disclosure Agreement (Band Management Services Agreement)

Date: January 5, 2019

* * *

The Partnership asked that the Manager stamp any document considered to contain the Manager's Confidential Information with the word "Confidential." The Manager explained that it would not be possible to ensure that all of its employees involved in the negotiation (and preparation for the negotiation) remember to stamp documents "Confidential." The Manager has a broad universe of people to control. Therefore, the Manager does not want to accept the risk that some of the Manager's Confidential Information might not be considered confidential just because someone forgot to stamp it.

Since the Partnership's partners, attorneys, and financial advisors are likely to be the only ones who handle documents containing the Partnership's Confidential Information, the Partnership can easily stamp any documents containing the Partnership's Confidential Information with the word "Confidential" in the upper right-hand corner. Marisa Treadwell and Vincent Van Logo agreed to do this.

The Partnership asked that the Manager only share the Partnership's Confidential Information (whether contained in documents or otherwise) with people in the Manager's employ who have some genuine need to know what the documents contain. The Manager agreed. Both parties agreed that those Manager employees with a "need to know" include at least Harmon E. Brake, his assistant, the Manager's attorneys, and the Manager's Accountant. At this time, it is not possible for the Manager to identify exactly who else may need to see the documents containing the Partnership's Confidential Information.

The Manager knows that the Partnership will want to share some of the Partnership's Confidential Information with its attorneys, and, of course, its financial advisors. The Partnership agreed not to disclose the Manager's Confidential Information to anyone else unless it gets the Manager's written permission first.

Both the Partnership and the Manager agree that they will show the NDA to everyone on the permitted list and get those individuals to sign an acknowledgment stating that they have read the NDA and understand that they are undertaking the same obligations as the signators. Both the Manager and the Partnership also agreed that, if they have to show the other party's Confidential Information to anyone not on the permitted list, they will get that person to agree not to disclose the information and have that person sign a similar acknowledgment.

The Partnership wants to make sure that entering into this NDA does not bind it to enter into a contract with the Manager for band management services. The Manager has the same concern—i.e., that the NDA not bind the Manager to perform management services for the Partnership—and would like to include some language to that effect in the NDA. Both parties want this language to be prominent in the NDA.

There was much discussion about how long the duties not to disclose should last. The parties finally agreed that the non-disclosure obligations should last for five years after the negotiation is completed, if the negotiation does not result in a contract. If the negotiation does result in a contract, then the parties want the non-disclosure obligations to last for the life of the contract plus five years and not to be superseded by the contract.

For both parties, the duties not to disclose the Confidential Information will include the obvious—not disclosing to anyone but those on the permitted list—as well as protecting the other party's Confidential Information just as the recipient would protect its own. Also, the parties are only going to use the Confidential Information in connection with the project at hand—the negotiation of the Band Management Services Agreement between the Partnership and the Manager. Both parties want the NDA to state the reason why they are disclosing the information to each other—to evaluate whether or not to enter into that Band Management Services Agreement.

After the parties finish negotiating, if they decide not to enter into a contract, both parties must return each other's Confidential Information immediately. The parties agreed to deliver by messenger the Confidential Information contained in documents. If the parties do enter into a contract, a party can keep the documents containing the Confidential Information until the other party requests its return. All Confidential Information must be returned by messenger within five business days of the other party's request. Alternatively, the party holding the Confidential Information may destroy the documents and provide an Affidavit of Destruction, signed by the Partnership or the Manager, as appropriate.

If either the Partnership or the Manager is compelled to produce the other party's Confidential Information by a court order or subpoena, then the compelled party will let the other party know right away by telephone and e-mail. That way the owner of the Confidential Information can decide whether to move for a protective order or take some other action to prevent its disclosure. The Manager was particularly adamant about this point.

Finally, both parties want the existence of the NDA and its contents to remain confidential, except that the parties may show it to people on the permitted list, who will also agree to keep its existence and contents confidential.

3C: PREPARATION FOR THE NEGOTIATION OF THE BAND MANAGEMENT SERVICES AGREEMENT

Part I: Finding, Evaluating, and Using the Relevant Precedent

Instructions

A. **Summary:** Re-read the General Information for Both Parties included in Assignment 3A. You will now search for contracts that will be likely to help you draft a Band Management Services Agreement. Once you locate the relevant precedent, you will review it and begin creating a negotiation prep sheet.

B. **Resources:** You may look for precedent in the library and on the Internet. You may not purchase any forms, whether from a store or online. You may not use any precedent in your own files (from a previous job or a summer position) or any precedent you obtain from an attorney. Finally, you may not use any contracts obtained from other students who have taken this class. Pretend that the library and the Internet are your only resources.

C. **What to Look For:** When you look for precedent in the litigation context, you try to find cases that are as close to your case as possible. If your case is about intentional infliction of emotional distress and involves one neighbor terrorizing another by putting dead insects and snakes on the other neighbor's doorstep, you would be very happy to find another case with nearly identical facts. If that case turns out to be in the same jurisdiction as yours, you would be even happier. Most likely, you will have to settle for cases with similar or analogous facts — and you may need to look beyond your jurisdiction.

In the transactional context, when you look for precedent, focus first on what kind of contract you are being asked to draft. For the purpose of this assignment, you want to find band management services agreements. While it may be helpful to find a band management services agreement about a rock band that plays experimental music and a place that is both a bar and a music venue, it is not as important to find a contract with nearly identical facts as it might be if you were trying to prove a case in the litigation context. Moreover, while searching for precedent in the transactional context, you do not have to be as conscious of jurisdictional issues, though you do have to familiarize yourself with any laws that affect your deal (as you will do in Assignment 3D).

D. **How to Find It:** If you love books and libraries, you may be tempted to start looking for precedent there. However, unless you do not own a computer or cannot connect to the Internet, looking for books in the library would not be the most efficient way to begin.

Begin by surfing the Web. You may choose to do a general search, using the search engine of your choice, or to go to LEXIS or WESTLAW to see what forms are available there. One very good online source of sample contracts is www.onecle.com (click on Business Contracts). There, you will find thousands of actual contracts used by businesses for various purposes. Another good online source of sample contracts is Findlaw.com (click on Learn about the Law; Small Business; then Business Forms and Contracts). Remember that the "samples" you find on these sites are "samples," and not "models." For more about what that distinction means, see Section E, Reviewing and Evaluating Precedent, below.

When you surf the Web seeking relevant precedent, start with a narrow search and then broaden it out. For example, you may want to start by searching for "rock band management services agreement." From there, you might move on to "band management services agreement." If you still do not feel as if you have found enough precedent, ask yourself what kinds of contracts are similar to a band management services agreement. Perhaps searching for "musician management contracts" will reveal some precedent containing useful provisions. Since "agreement" and "contract" are used interchangeably, be sure to search for both terms.

Do not forget to search LEXIS and WESTLAW. Both have databases containing contract forms.

If you prefer working with actual books, go to your law library and locate the "forms" books. Skim through the tables of contents or indexes to determine if the books contain any relevant forms.

E. **Reviewing and Evaluating Precedent:** Once you have located eight or ten relevant contracts, begin to review them. Ask yourself at least the following questions about each contract:

- ☐ How relevant is the precedent?
  - ☐ Is it a rock band management services contract?
  - ☐ Is it a musician management contract?
  - ☐ Is it a contract from the United States (as opposed to the United Kingdom or another country, with different contract drafting methods and formats)?
- ☐ How is the agreement formatted?
  - ☐ Does it contain all of the essential parts of a contract?
  - ☐ If it does not contain all of the essential parts, what is omitted?
- ☐ What topics are covered?
  - ☐ Does the agreement cover any topics that you would not have thought to cover?
- ☐ How is the agreement organized?
  - ☐ What appears to be the organizing principle behind the placement of topics in the agreement? Importance? Chronology? Something else?
- ☐ Is it easy to find things in the agreement?
- ☐ Does the agreement read smoothly?
- ☐ Did the drafters use the appropriate verbs to express contract concepts?
- ☐ Did the drafters use the active voice?
- ☐ Did the drafters use Plain English throughout? In parts?
  - ☐ Are there any places in the agreement that are heavy with legalese?
- ☐ Does anything in the agreement strike you as being particularly well drafted or handled?

After you finish reading through all of the relevant precedent you have found, rate the agreements on a scale of 1 to 5, with 1 signifying "best" and 5 signifying "useless." Make a note of which contracts contain "good language" about particular topics. The "good language" standard does not necessarily mean "well-drafted" language; you may just appreciate the way the drafters handle a particular issue as opposed to the way they write about it. Perhaps, for example, you find an agreement that requires the band to cooperate in specific ways with the manager's efforts to promote their music. The drafters may be the worst culprits when it comes to using legalese. Nevertheless, make a note of the language because it contains an interesting idea that you may want to include in your own contract.

After you have rated the contracts, look at the entire batch of precedent once again and make a list of the main topics covered in the agreements. If most of the agreements cover "Manager's Presence for Performances," for example, then you will most likely need to cover that topic when you negotiate and draft the Band Management Services Agreement between One Art Partnership and We Brake For Musicians, Inc. If one agreement contains a provision that none of the other agreements contains, you may have found a provision particular to the transaction at issue in that agreement.

F. **Using the Relevant Precedent:** When you draft your contract, you may decide to adopt or adapt some language from the relevant precedent you found. If so, you must remember the following principles:

1. **Every deal is its own deal.** This means that no matter how close the relevant precedent seems to the deal you are negotiating, your deal is a different deal. On the surface level, the parties' names and addresses are different. On a deeper level, your deal may include many facts that are different from the deal memorialized in the precedent. Maybe, for example, the Partnership wants the Manager to engage a subcontractor to give the Partnership advice about One Art's public image. You must remember to tailor the precedent to the facts of your deal.

2. **Cutting and pasting numbs the mind.** It is tempting to cut and paste. Resist the temptation. If you re-type the language instead, you are more likely to notice things about how it is drafted—like the way the drafters used "null and void" instead of just "void." Or the fact that none of the parties is mentioned in a sentence purporting to obligate one of the parties to do something. If you simply cut and paste the language and rely on yourself to catch and fix those things in the editing and proofreading stage, you are missing a golden, immediate opportunity. The best example of the way cutting and pasting numbs the mind is this: Many students make the mistake of cutting and pasting a piece of precedent from another contract and forgetting to change the names of the parties. When the reader,

used to seeing the "the Partnership" and "the Manager," suddenly comes across "the Buyer" and "the Seller," she stumbles. If she is grading the contract, she takes off points.

3. **The naked drafter rules the world.** No, I am not advocating that you draft in the nude. I am advocating that you learn how to draft without relying on precedent. If you master the skill of translating deal terms into contract concepts (covenants, conditions precedent, representations and warranties, declarations, and statements of discretionary authority), then you will be able to draft a contract without having any precedent at hand. When your client asks you to put a unique provision in the contract, you will be the "can-do" lawyer—that is, the lawyer who can draft the provision on the spot without needing a precedential crutch. Exercising your naked drafting skills will make you feel smart, efficient, creative, and, yes, powerful! Moreover, when you decide to use precedent, you will have the skills necessary to help you analyze and improve the language in the provisions you decide to adopt or adapt.

4. **Mine the precedent for ideas, not language.** The best way to use precedent is to help you "see" how a contract like the one you are attempting to draft generally "looks." Reviewing some relevant precedent is a good way to get started on drafting a contract that seems daunting. In other words, with the facts of your own deal foremost in your mind, you can use precedent to help you figure out what terms to define, what topics to cover, and in what order to cover them. You can also use precedent to help you discover whether you ought to include certain provisions because they are traditionally included in this type of contract or because they are required by law. (Of course, you must still do enough legal research to satisfy yourself that you have covered any legal issues the contract raises.)

Finally, ask your professor if she wants you to cite to any precedent you use. If so, find out what citation format she prefers.

G. **The Negotiation Prep Sheet:** After you have located some good, relevant precedent, use it to help you prepare for the negotiation of the Band Management Services Agreement between the Partnership and the Manager. Create a three-column table entitled *Negotiation Prep Sheet.* Label the first column "Topic," the second column "Description," and the third column "Position." Since you do not yet know which client you represent, leave the third column blank. In the first column, list the topics covered in the precedent. In the second column, insert some details about each topic. Your negotiation prep sheet will look something like this:

NEGOTIATION PREP SHEET

Topic	Description	Position
Partnership's duty to cooperate with Manager's publicity efforts	Covers showing up for photography and video sessions, signing autographs at public appearances, providing biographical data and history of the Band	
Etc.	Etc.	

When you finish filling in columns 1 and 2 of your negotiation prep sheet, you will have a living document that you can revise in light of the legal research you do in response to Assignment 3D and the confidential instructions you receive from your client as part of Assignment 3E.

H. **Collaboration:** Your professor may permit you to collaborate with your classmates in locating, reviewing, and evaluating precedent as well as in creating the first negotiation prep sheet. If you do collaborate with your classmates on this assignment, you will get to see how different people approach the task of finding precedent. Which search engines do your classmates use? How do they word their first search? Their second search? Their third? Do they begin with LEXIS or WESTLAW? When they find something useful, how do they record it? Do they bookmark it? Copy the URL into a Word document? Print it out in hard copy? Do they make any spot judgments about the quality of the precedent they find? Do they dwell on one contract or continue searching until they have gathered a number of relevant contracts? And so on. . . . You will inevitably get some great ideas from your classmates. But the most valuable part of the collaboration lies in observing someone else's "process." It may open your mind!

I. **Additional Instructions:** Your professor may provide you with additional instructions regarding this assignment.

3D: CONTINUED PREPARATION FOR THE NEGOTIATION OF THE BAND MANAGEMENT SERVICES AGREEMENT

Part II: Researching the Legal Issues

Instructions

A. **Summary:** This assignment assumes that you have completed Assignment 3C. First, re-read the General Information for Both Parties included in Assignment 3A. In further preparation for your negotiation, you will now research the legal issues impacting the Band Management Services Agreement between One Art Partnership (the "Partnership") and We Brake For Musicians, Inc. (the "Manager"). You will research the legal issues that you identified when locating, reviewing, and evaluating the relevant precedent, as well as research any other legal issues that you have identified yourself or that your professor has identified for you. You will then revise the negotiation prep sheet, adding new topics and descriptions that address these legal issues.

B. **What to Look For:** When you reviewed and evaluated the relevant precedent, you may have found that several sample contracts contained references to particular statutes or regulations. Begin there. For example, if you have found any band management services agreements in which the manager is also to serve as a booking agent, you probably noticed that those agreements contain boilerplate (or other provisions) that addresses the issue of booking agents being required to hold licenses.

   Do not hesitate to research other legal issues that you or your professor have identified, even if you do not find them addressed in the relevant precedent. Remember that you have located "sample contracts," not models. Perhaps the additional legal research you do will uncover some key points that the sample contracts simply failed to cover.

> **Caveat:** Do not let yourself get too caught up in legal research. You are not striving to become an expert. Do enough research to satisfy yourself that you are competent to draft the contract—and rely on your professor to supply additional expertise, if need be.

C. **How to Find It:** By now, you know how to find statutes and regulations. Start with the primary sources: the statutes and regulations cited in the precedent. Then delve into any other legal issues you have uncovered. Is it appropriate, for example, to include a "key person" provision in the contract, restricting the Manager's right to fire that key person?

D. **The Negotiation Prep Sheet:** When you feel you have a pretty good grasp of the legal issues you have identified, add them to the negotiation prep sheet. Remember to include citations in your descriptions, since you may want to revisit these issues when you are negotiating or drafting.

E. **Collaboration:** Your professor may permit you to collaborate with your classmates in conducting the legal research this assignment requires. If so, you will benefit from seeing how someone else approaches a problem. Observing your classmates' "process" may make you decide to change your own way of doing things. Even if watching your classmates in action merely confirms that your own process is more effective, you are still likely to benefit from talking about the legal issues while you are researching them. In a good collaborative environment, participants take turns being the striker and the flint. When a striker is applied to flint, sparks fly. Sometimes you will raise a question (acting as the striker) and your classmate will propose an answer (acting as the flint), and sometimes, vice versa. You will both benefit from the sparks!

F. **Additional Instructions:** Your professor may provide you with additional instructions regarding this assignment.

3E: NEGOTIATION OF THE BAND MANAGEMENT SERVICES AGREEMENT: LETTER OF INTENT AND TERM SHEET

Instructions

A. **Summary:** For this assignment, you will represent either One Art Partnership (the "Partnership") or We Brake For Musicians, Inc. (the "Manager"). As you know from reading the General Information for Both Parties included in Assignment 3A, the Partnership wants to engage the Manager (the "Manager") to manage One Art (the "Band") and the solo careers of the Band's individual members. Your task is to negotiate the deal and draft the contract between the Partnership and the Manager.

B. **Assume No Conflict of Interest:** If you represent the Manager in this deal, you can assume that there is no conflict of interest in your representing the Manager against the Partnership, even though you may have represented the Partnership in connection with a previous deal. Alternatively, you may pretend that you have never represented the Partnership in the past.

C. **The Negotiation:** Your professor will tell you which party you represent and which of your classmates will be your opposing counsel. Your professor will also give you some Confidential Instructions from your client.

Logistics:
1. Begin by re-reading the General Information for Both Parties included in Assignment 3-A. Then read the Confidential Instructions from your client.
2. After carefully reviewing the Confidential Instructions from your client, revise the Negotiation Prep Sheet you prepared in response to Assignments 3C and 3D to add any topics mentioned in the Confidential Instructions but not listed on your negotiation prep sheet. If you know what your client's position is with regard to a particular issue, insert that information in the "Position" column.

> **Note:** If you do not know what your client's position is with regard to a particular issue—and you believe it is an issue that the contract ought to cover—make a note to ask your client about it.

3. Complete your negotiation prep sheet by asking your professor to answer any questions you have about your client's position on the issues. Your professor may choose to tell you what your client's position is, or allow you to decide what your client's position ought to be. Either way, be sure to complete the negotiation prep sheet before moving on to the next step.
4. Prepare to negotiate. Study your negotiation prep sheet and tweak it, if necessary. You will bring this sheet with you to the negotiation.
5. Talk to your opposing counsel to schedule a mutually convenient time and place for the negotiation. Make sure that you find a quiet place where you will not be disturbed and will not encounter other pairs of negotiators from your class. Allow at least two hours for your first negotiation session.
6. Do not show your negotiation prep sheet or the Confidential Instructions you received from your client to your opposing counsel (or any other students who represent the opposing party) at any time before, during, or after the negotiation. During the negotiation, you will use the information in your Confidential Instructions as your guide to your client's wishes. You will naturally and judiciously reveal some of the information to your opposing counsel during the course of the negotiation in order to achieve your client's objectives.
7. Your Confidential Instructions may or may not contain information about your client's wishes regarding every issue you need to cover in the contract. For example, your Confidential Instructions do not address every boilerplate provision that you may want to include in the contract. If you do not know what your client wants, ask your professor or negotiate for what you believe will be in your client's best interests.

8. During the negotiation, you and your opposing counsel should pre-pare a "Term Sheet," which will ultimately be attached to your Letter of Intent ("LOI") and should look something like this:

ATTACHMENT A TO LETTER OF INTENT

Issue	Terms

---

9. In this negotiation, you MUST reach an agreement. While the nego-tiation itself is not graded, you will receive extra points for being especially thorough and for devising creative solutions to disputed issues between the parties.
10. If you need access to your client during the negotiation, please con-tact your professor. If you and your opposing counsel reach a stale-mate on any issues, please contact your professor.
11. If you do not finish your negotiation in one sitting, schedule another mutually convenient time to meet. Remember that you are likely to continue negotiating during the drafting process.

D. **Drafting the Letter of Intent:** Once you have completed your negotiation, you and your opposing counsel must draft one Letter of Intent ("LOI") and submit it to your professor. Your professor will decide whether to grade the LOI itself, but he may simply want to refer to the LOI when grading your contract. Therefore, if you and your opposing counsel change any signifi-cant terms contained in the LOI during subsequent negotiations, your professor may ask you to revise the LOI and re-submit it.

DRAFTING THE LETTER OF INTENT

(A Mini-Assignment within the Negotiation Assignment)

1. Draft an LOI. You will attach the term sheet that you created during your negotiation to the LOI as Exhibit A.

2. Address the LOI to your professor.

---

3. Do not use any precedent to draft the LOI. Draft in Plain English. Do not include anything that looks like a covenant. This is not a contract. See No. 4, below.

4. The most important thing to keep in mind is that you do not want your opposing counsel to be able to say that the LOI is a binding contract whether your negotiations fall through or your negotiations result in a signed contract. The LOI contains preliminary terms, some of which are likely to change over time. Make sure that you emphasize that the LOI is not a binding contract by featuring this point prominently in the LOI.

5. State that the letter describes the terms that the Partnership and the Manager have discussed about the project and include a brief description of the project. Mention that the terms are attached in Exhibit A.

6. Clarify that the parties are not bound by any of the terms in the term sheet unless they sign a contract including those terms.

7. Clarify that when the parties sign the letter they are not acquiring any rights or undertaking any obligations, and, especially, that they are not promising to enter into a contract with the other party.

8. Include a paragraph reminding the Partnership and the Manager that they are bound by the Non-Disclosure Agreement ("NDA") they signed before they began negotiating this deal and that the NDA prohibits them from disclosing the existence or terms of this LOI. Alternatively, you can include non-disclosure obligations in the LOI. (However, since the LOI is not a contract, any covenants you include in it arguably are not enforceable.)

9. Insert signature lines for both parties. This is another reason to include the language about the LOI not being a contract. The LOI is likely to look like a contract because both parties sign it.

10. Remember to attach the term sheet to the LOI before submitting the LOI to your professor.

E. **Additional Instructions:** Your professor may provide you with additional instructions regarding this assignment.

3F: PREPARATION OF TALKING POINTS FOR MEETING WITH SENIOR PARTNER RE POTENTIAL ETHICAL QUESTION

Instructions

A. **Summary:** For the purposes of this assignment, assume that your firm represents One Art Partnership (the "Partnership") and you are negotiating a Band

Management Services Agreement whereby We Brake For Musicians, Inc. (the "Manager") agrees to manage the careers of One Art (the "Band") and its individual members. After reviewing the scenario below, you will prepare talking points for a meeting with your senior partner, Hermione Melville.

B. **Scenario:** Your client contacts are Marisa Treadwell and Vince Van Logo. You meet frequently with Risa and Vince, but you never meet with each of the other individual band members, even though the contract you are negotiating provides that the Manager is going to manage the Band's career as well as all of the band members' solo careers. You do distribute copies of the draft contract to all of the Band members through Risa and Vince.

C. **Analysis:** Your senior partner, Hermione Melville, has asked you to analyze this scenario to determine whether you may be violating any ethical rules by not communicating individually with the band members other than Risa and Vince. Explain your answer by citing specific portions of the Model Rules of Professional Conduct and the Comments to those rules. Are there any additional steps you should take to assure that you are communicating appropriately with the band members other than Risa and Vince?

D. **Preparation of Talking Points:** "Talking Points" are simply notes that you prepare for yourself to structure your discussion with your senior partner. You do not have to draft them using any particular format. That being said, it is a good idea to use headings and bullet points to keep yourself on track—especially if you get nervous talking to your supervisor. Include a brief statement of the issue. Then summarize what you have concluded and how you reached those conclusions. Conclude with "action points" in which you recommend how to proceed.

E. **Additional Instructions:** Your professor may provide you with additional instructions regarding this assignment.

3G: DRAFTING THE BAND MANAGEMENT SERVICES AGREEMENT

The Frame and the Picture

Instructions

A. **Summary:** Once you have completed your negotiations and drafted and submitted your LOI (as described in Assignment 3E), you will draft the Band Management Services Agreement, memorializing the terms of the deal that you negotiated with your opposing counsel. The two of you will turn in one completed contract.

B. **The Frame and the Picture:** Unlike what you did with the Band Logo Purchase and the Band Performance Agreements in this sequence, you will not draft the frame and the picture of the contract separately. Since we will not repeat the instructions for drafting the frame and the picture here, you may want to review Assignments 1E and 1F or Assignments 2D and 2E.

C. **The Drafting Process:** In the real world, one of you would probably prepare the entire first draft and submit it to your opposing counsel, who would edit it and redline the changes. You would review her edits and decide whether to accept or reject each of them. You might then send another redlined version to her, showing additional edits that you have made. This back-and-forth process may carry you through many drafts.

For this assignment, I recommend that you and your opposing counsel consider operating as you would in the real world. This can work in the law school context if one of you has more time and fewer pending deadlines than the other. Ideally, the least busy person would prepare the entire first draft and submit it to the busier person for review. The back-and-forth editing and redlining process can then proceed.

Realistically, you and your opposing counsel are more likely to divide up the work of preparing the first draft so that the bulk of it does not fall on one student's shoulders. If you do divide the contract into parts, you will have to allow a lot of extra time before the contract is due for the two of you to make sure that the parts work together well. For example, you will need to make sure that both of you have used the same defined terms and that you have used them to mean the same things. This is trickier than you think, so you should try to complete a full draft as early in the process as possible. That way, the two of you can review, edit, redline, and repeat as often as you need to in order to produce a seamless, polished product.

Remember that your goal is to produce a contract that sounds as if it were written by one person, not two. If one of you drafts in Plain English and the other peppers his language with legalese, your contract will be split into two distinct halves. Alternatively, if the two of you have divided up the work so that you each have responsibility for drafting alternating articles within the contract, the reader is likely to feel like she is on a seesaw. Strive to draft with a consistent voice. To accomplish this, both of you will have to read the entire contract more than once. I recommend reading it out loud to each other and listening for the places where the language becomes more elevated or slips into legalese. The two of you can then work together to translate those passages into Plain English.

D. **Incomplete Confidential Instructions:** You may not have received any confidential instructions from your clients about some of the topics in your negotiation prep sheet (see Assignments 3C and 3D). Address any questions about your client's position on particular issues to your professor, who will either provide you with additional confidential instructions or give you permission to decide what would be in your client's best interests. Because this is a "simulated assignment," you may have to use your imagination. Do not go so far as to make up wildly improbable deal facts, but do feel free to be a little creative.

Include any boilerplate provisions appropriate for this particular deal, as well as any boilerplate provisions that your professor suggests are necessary. Remember to negotiate about the language of the boilerplate provisions. While you may not have confidential instructions addressing every piece of boilerplate, you can imagine what your clients' concerns might be and address them. For example, if you represent the Partnership and do not have any confidential instructions about delegation of performance, think about whether the Partnership would want the Manager to be able to delegate its performance to another party. Most likely the Partnership does not want the Manager to have the right to delegate its performance since the Partnership has already developed such a good relationship with the Manager. Therefore, you may want to negotiate to adjust the standard anti-delegation language (which allows a party to delegate only with the written consent of the other party) to address the Partnership's concern. In other words, you may want to draft stronger anti-delegation language to indicate that the Partnership would never even entertain the Manager's request for permission to delegate.

E. **Use of Precedent for Drafting the Band Management Services Agreement:** As you know if you completed Assignment 3C, you may use any forms or templates you can find in the library or on the Internet. You may not purchase any forms, whether from a store or online. You may not use any precedent in your own files (from a previous job or a summer position) or any precedent you obtain from an attorney. *Finally, you may not use any contracts obtained from other students who have taken this class.* Pretend that the library and the Internet are your only resources.

See Assignment 3C for some tips on how to locate, review, evaluate, and use the available precedent.

F. **Provisions Addressing Legal Issues:** Be sure to address in the contract any specific things that the parties must do in order to comply with the law. If you know that you need to address booking agent licensing issues, for example, spell out the parties' specific rights and obligations. Avoid the easy cop-out of saying, "The Partnership and the Manager shall abide by all booking agent licensing statutes and regulations," or words to that effect. If you try to simplify your task this way, it will be apparent that you did not take the time and care necessary to determine which licensing statutes and regulations apply, if any. Moreover, including language requiring your clients to abide by all statutes and regulations is, in effect, redundant; that is, it simply amounts to your clients' promises to obey the law, which your clients must do even if they are not contractually bound. If there is a legal issue that you must address, include specific provisions that give the parties clear guidance about their rights and duties.

G. **Grading:** Unless your professor tells you otherwise, both you and your opposing counsel will receive the same grade on the contract you submit.

H. **Additional Instructions:** Your professor may provide you with additional instructions regarding this assignment.

The
TOY AND GAME INVENTOR
Sequence

Assignment 1

The Toy Purchase Agreement

1A: ENGAGEMENT LETTER BETWEEN ATTORNEY AND CLIENT

Instructions

A. **Summary:** You will draft an engagement letter/retainer agreement between your law firm and a new client.

B. **Background:** You are an associate at the law firm of Payne & Associates. Victoria ("Tory") B. Green and her best friend, Troy Gardner, have formed The T-4 Partnership ("T-4") and plan to open a store called "Tory and Troy's Treehugger Toys." The store will be a specialty toy store, selling toys that are made with "green" materials and toys that are designed to teach kids about science, nature, ecology, and preserving the environment.

Tory and Troy are getting ready to purchase a large part of their toy inventory from Truly Green Toys, Inc. ("TGT"). They have asked your firm to draft the toy purchase agreement between T-4 and TGT. Tory's grandparents, who are both retired attorneys, advised Tory to get an engagement letter in place before your firm starts working on the contract.

Payne & Associates, being a bit behind the times, has never required its clients to sign an engagement letter or retainer agreement. The senior partner, Sue Payne, has resisted formalizing client relationships in this way. Sue now wants you to draft an engagement letter that she can present to Tory and Troy to communicate basic information about how the attorney/client relationship between T-4 and the firm is likely to work.

Sue wants the engagement letter to be a contract that both parties will sign, but she does not want it to be so formal that it frightens Tory and Troy away. She wants you to strike just the right tone—businesslike with a touch of warmth.

C. **No Use of Precedent:** Sue does not want you to use other engagement or retainer letters that you find through a library or Internet search or through any other means. She would like to see what you can draft without using any precedent. She believes that, if you are not influenced by what other firms have already done, you will produce something fresh, creative, well written, and tailored to this particular client's needs.

D. **Legal Research:** In preparation for completing this assignment, please read *Brian Dowling v. Chicago Options Associates, Inc. et al. (DLA Piper Rudnick Gray Cary (US), LLP)*, 226 Ill. 2d 277, 875 N.E.2d 1012 (Ill. 2007).

E. **Draft Specific to This Attorney/Client Relationship:** Sue does not want you to create a "form" engagement letter/retainer agreement to be used for all of the firm's clients. She wants you to focus on this particular client. If you do a good job, perhaps Sue will ask you to create a "form" later. Right now, Sue's main concern is that you cover the issues listed in the table below and that you capture the terms that Sue already has communicated to Tory and Troy.

F. **Table of Issues and Terms:** Sue prepared this quick list of the issues that the engagement letter should cover and the terms upon which your firm and T-4 have reached agreement. The issues appear in no particular order.

Issue	Terms
Who firm works for	The T-4 Partnership (Tory and Troy are equal partners)
End of representation	When final bill is paid; note that the $2,000 retainer is deducted from the first bill
When work will begin	Upon receipt of signed engagement letter and check for $2,000 security retainer
Initial consultation (Sue already met with Tory)	Charge Sue's regular rate; they met for one hour; Tory may not expect this charge
Fees	Senior Partner Payne—$225 per hour Associate (any level)—$170 per hour Paralegal (any level)—$80 per hour
Refund of unused fees	Will refund unused fees (if any)
Security retainer (intended to secure payment of fees for future services the firm is expected to perform)	$2,000; will be applied to first bill

Issue	Terms
Trust account (separate from firm's property; remains client's property until firm applies it to charges for services actually rendered)	Will put the $2,000 security retainer in client trust account
Detail in bills	Will show who performed the work, how much time was spent (rounded up to the tenth of an hour), brief description of the work performed
Phone calls	We bill for time spent on calls received and made— at reduced hourly rate (reduce attorney or paralegal's rate by 5%)
Scope of services	Draft contract for purchase of toys from Truly Green Toys, Inc.; no more than that; if they want more, then we must draft an amendment to the engagement letter or they must sign another engagement letter
Changes to personnel	Can substitute associates and paralegals, without client's consent
Attorney/client privilege	Explain it briefly; make sure they know that they should not share info with third parties and destroy privilege; especially note that they must not forward e-mails to anyone
Client's obligations to firm	Cooperate Tell us everything about the deal Provide any supporting documents needed Be available; reachable through multiple means Pay bill within 30 days of receipt
Termination by firm	If client doesn't pay in timely fashion or if there's a breakdown in the attorney/client relationship (spell out what this means a bit—client fails to fulfill its obligations, other causes, such as client wanting attorney to do something that might violate ethical obligations)

Issue	Terms
Invoices	Sent out on the 15th of each month
Expenses	Client pays for travel expenses (for airline trips) and overnight mail; no markup, just a pass-through
Overhead expenses	Not billed to client
E-mails	We bill for reading and responding at regular hourly rate
Termination by client	Can terminate at any time; no refund if the retainer has been spent; must pay fees for services already rendered; firm will prepare final invoice
Division of labor and billing	Associates will do initial client interview and first draft of contract We bill for associates' time, plus partner supervisory time Partner will not attend client interview but will review associates' work and communicate with client
Core billing	Time spent reviewing facts, creating drafts, reviewing drafts, communicating with clients, communicating with opposing counsel, all other activities related to representation
Qualifications of attorneys	All will be licensed to practice law in Illinois We'll state that everyone working on the matter is competent; add in "with appropriate supervision" for associates and paralegals
Dowling v. Chicago Options	Include whatever the court requires about the security retainer to assure that the client is fully informed about how the money will be handled
Governing law	Illinois
Increase in hourly billing rates	Occurs at the beginning of each new year, no matter what; will apply to T-4 if services are still being rendered at beginning of year

Issue	Terms
Business hours of firm	6:30 a.m. to 6:30 p.m.; but give Tory and Troy Sue's cell phone number [make up this number]
Disputing a bill	Must contact Sue Payne by mail or telephone within 14 days of receipt of invoice
Potential conflict of interest	We conducted a conflict search based on the info the client supplied and turned up no conflict
Overhead expenses	Not billed to client
Customer service	Can expect us to work hard and to keep client informed; let us know if we are not doing that
Signatures required	Victoria B. Green and Troy Gardner (on behalf of T-4) and Sue Payne (on behalf of your firm)

G. Further Instructions for Drafting Engagement Letter: Sue wants the engagement letter to come from Sue herself. She would like you to draft it using a personal, somewhat informal tone, without including any slang and without sounding unprofessional. Unlike most other contracts you will draft, you may use personal pronouns in this letter. Refer to Sue as "I" and to Tory and Troy as "you." (Refer to "Payne & Associates as the "Firm" and The T-4 Partnership as "T-4.") Victoria B. Green and Troy Gardner will sign on behalf of T-4. *Note:* T-4's address is 246810 Sheridan Road, Evanston, Illinois 60202.

Remember that your main audience for the engagement letter is the partners of T-4—a duo with very little experience in business and almost no experience with attorney/client relationships. You must make sure that you communicate clearly so that Tory and Troy understand everything in the letter. Encourage them to ask Sue questions before signing the letter if there is anything that they do not understand.

In order to keep the engagement letter from sounding too formal, you may use "will" instead of "shall" for covenants throughout the letter.

Please divide the letter into sections and use boldfaced headings to help T-4. Think about how best to organize the information you convey.

> *Note:* You may not use a table, except perhaps to summarize the information about the individuals working on the matter and their hourly rates.

After Sue's signature (with her title and the date), include a statement from Tory and Troy, acknowledging that they have read the letter, understand it, and agree to its terms. Then put lines for T-4's signature and the date. Under the signature line for T-4, spell out Victoria B. Green's name, in upper and lowercase letters. Insert another signature line for Troy Gardner. Put the word "By" in front of both Tory and Troy's signature lines. Under each of their names, put the title "Partner."

One final word: Strive to keep the engagement letter simple, straightforward, and brief. This letter should provide you with an excellent opportunity to practice the skill of drafting in Plain English. Your main goal is to communicate clearly so that the client understands how the attorney/client relationship is supposed to work.

H. **Additional Instructions:** Your professor may provide you with additional instructions regarding this assignment.

1B: THE CLIENT INTERVIEW

Instructions

A. **Summary:** You are going to meet Victoria B. Green, one of the partners in The T-4 Partnership. She and her partner, Tory Gardner, are going to open a specialty toy store — that is, a store that sells toys made from "green" materials as well as toys designed to teach kids about science, nature, ecology, and preserving the environment. You will interview Ms. Green in order to find out the terms of the toy purchase transaction that she has negotiated between T-4 and Truly Green Toys, Inc. ("TGT").

B. **Preparation for the Client Interview:** After you read the following memorandum from Sue Payne, please read Appendix 1, Ten Tips for Interviewing a Client About a Transaction. Since your client's business and website are fictional, you will not be able to do any research about T-4, Tory Green, or Troy Gardner ahead of time. However, as a backdrop for the client interview, you should do a small amount of research about the toy store business and "green" toys. Remember that you may not search for any toy purchase agreements, as that would violate the prohibition against using precedent on this assignment (see Section D, Precedent, below). Brainstorm about what provisions you think ought to be included in a contract for the purchase of toys to be used as inventory in a toy store. Then prepare a list of questions to ask your client.

C. **Legal Expertise and Research:** In practice, you should not draft a contract in an area in which you have no legal expertise unless you acquire the expertise or seek help from another attorney who possesses it. Rule 1.1 of the Model Rules of Professional Conduct states:

> *Competence.* A lawyer shall provide competent representation to a client. Competent representation requires the legal knowledge,

skill, thoroughness and preparation reasonably necessary for the representation.

Comment 2 to MRPC Rule 1.1 clarifies that "[a] lawyer can provide adequate representation in a wholly novel field through necessary study" or "through the association of a lawyer of established competence in the field in question." For the purposes of this assignment, you may assume that your senior partner has the requisite legal expertise to serve as your guide. You may not do any legal research in connection with this assignment unless your professor instructs you to do so.

D. Precedent: In preparation for the client interview, you may not use any sample contracts, forms, templates, or models (collectively, "precedent") other than any model contracts provided by your professor.

> **Note:** Because most transactional attorneys have some relevant precedent in hand when drafting a contract, you will be permitted to use precedent in some subsequent drafting assignments.

E. Additional Access to Client: After the in-class interview, you may need to obtain more information from Ms. Green. Collect your questions and e-mail them to your professor, who may (a) pass them along to Ms. Green, or (b) arrange for Ms. Green to come into class for another interview.

F. Additional Instructions: Your professor may provide you with additional instructions regarding this assignment.

Payne & Associates

MEMORANDUM

TO:	Associates
FROM:	Sue Payne
RE:	New Client (The T-4 Partnership)
DATE:	September 23, 2013

As many of you know, I have six young grandchildren. Needless to say, we spend a lot of time in toy stores. A few months ago, I took the kids to the Toy and Game Expo at the McCormick Center. There, I met Tory Green and her business partner, Troy Gardner. They were attending the Expo to scope out toys for the new toy store they are planning to open.

Tory and Troy formed an Illinois partnership called The T-4 Partnership ("T-4"). They have named their store "Tory and Troy's Treehugging Toys" (the "Store") to reflect the store's theme; they'll be selling toys made from "green" materials as well as toys designed to teach kids about science, nature, ecology, and preserving the environment.

Naturally, I saw a client development opportunity here. I told Tory and Troy about our firm and they asked if we might be able to draft a toy purchase agreement between T-4 and Truly Green Toys, Inc. ("TGT"), a company from which T-4 hopes to purchase a large part of the Store's inventory. T-4 can't really afford my rates, but they can afford yours. Therefore, Tory will be coming into the office to meet with you about the details.

I don't know much about TGT, except that T-4's contact at TGT is a sales representative named Will I. Cheeter. TGT is an Illinois corporation with its principal place of business located in Naperville, Illinois, at 56 Organic Avenue, 60563. So far, TGT is not represented by an attorney.

Note: T-4's address is 246810 Sheridan Road, in Evanston, Illinois 60202. This is the address of Tory's residence. *Note also:* Tory's formal name is Victoria B. Green, though she insists that we call her "Tory."

Please interview Tory to find out the terms of the deal that she has struck between T-4 and TGT.

1C: LETTER TO CLIENT RE POTENTIAL ETHICAL QUESTION

Instructions

A. **Summary:** Analyze the scenario presented below in order to determine whether you or your firm will be violating any ethical rules if you personally enter into a side deal to handle Truly Green Toys, Inc.'s part of the advertising and publicity for Earth Month at Tory and Troy's Treehugger Toys. Think also about whether the scenario presents any business issues. Draft a letter to Victoria B. Green, explaining why you personally can or cannot handle the publicity and advertising for the Earth Month events.

B. **Scenario:** Your firm represents the The T-4 Partnership ("T-4") with regard to the toy store purchase agreement that T-4 is entering into with Truly Green Toys, Inc. ("TGT"). Your firm's client contact is Victoria B. Green, one of T-4's partners. (Victoria has asked you to call her "Tory.") TGT has agreed to help the toy store with the advertising and publicity for the toy store's Earth Month events. Tory knows that, in a former life, you did public relations work for various retail stores — including several small toy stores. She knows that TGT is likely to subcontract out the advertising and publicity for Earth Month, and she wants to know if you could serve as the subcontractor. You think you could do a very good job. Additionally, your firm has been hit very hard by the recession and you fear that you are going to be laid off sometime before the end of next year. Handling the publicity for the toy store's Earth Month events would give you the opportunity to tune up your public relations skills and earn some extra money to put away for the future.

C. **Format of Client Letter:** Assume that, after you analyzed the issues presented by the scenario, you talked with your senior partner, Sue Payne. She advised you to write a letter to the firm's client, T-4. Address the letter to Victoria B. Green. Begin the letter by summarizing the issues. Then, if you believe that this scenario presents an ethical issue, explain the issue, your conclusion, and the rationale for your conclusion. Do the same for any business issue you identify.

D. **Tone of Client Letter:** Remember that the relationship between your firm and T-4 is brand new. Your senior partner, Sue Payne, expects that T-4 eventually will become a very successful business and that Tory and Troy will send the firm a lot of additional legal work. In your letter, use a businesslike tone, but be sure to make the client feel that you have its best interests at heart.

E. **Additional Instructions:** Your professor may provide you with additional instructions regarding this assignment.

1D: MEMORANDUM FROM ASSOCIATES TO SUE PAYNE, SENIOR PARTNER, RE SUMMARY OF DEAL TERMS

Instructions

A. **Summary:** Using the notes from your interview with Victoria B. Green, draft a memorandum to Sue Payne, summarizing the terms of the toy purchase transaction between The T-4 Partnership and Truly Green Toys, Inc. Assume that Sue was not present at the client interview.

B. **Format of Memorandum:** Set up your memo as follows—

Payne & Associates

MEMORANDUM

CONFIDENTIAL

TO: Sue Payne

FROM: [Insert Your Name]

RE: Interview with Victoria B. Green, September 5, 2013

SUBJECT: Toy Purchase Agreement

DATE: September 6, 2013

[Insert the text of the memo here, single-spaced. Use headings to help organize the material.]

C. **Collaboration:** If your professor permits, you and your classmates may share your client interview notes. Most likely, if you missed a deal fact, your classmate caught it. Through collaboration, you can fill in any information gaps you have, unless, of course, the client did not give you the information you need.

D. **Follow-Up Questions to Client:** In the course of writing this memo, you may find that you need to ask the client some additional questions. Please direct those questions to your professor, who will either consult the client and post the answers for the entire class or invite the client in for another interview.

E. **Identification of Legal Issues:** While drafting this memo, you may identify one or more legal issues that this transaction poses. If so, please identify those issues at the end of the memo so that Sue becomes aware of them and can give you some direction regarding how to pursue them.

F. **Additional Instructions:** Your professor may provide you with additional instructions regarding this assignment.

1E: ASSEMBLING THE FRAME: DRAFTING THE TITLE, PREAMBLE, BACKGROUND, WORDS OF AGREEMENT, DEFINITIONS, AND SIGNATURE LINES

Instructions

A. **Summary:** Using the deal facts gathered from the client interview you conducted in Assignment 1B, you will draft the Toy Purchase Agreement's frame—the Title, Preamble, Background, Words of Agreement, Definitions, and Signature Lines.

B. **The "Frame" Metaphor:** Some parts of a contract are traditional and easily drafted using models. They create a "frame" for the business provisions of the contract. The Title, Preamble, Words of Agreement, and Signature Lines are rudimentary parts of the contract's frame. The Definitions and Background sections, while more difficult to draft, still should not contain covenants, conditions precedent, representations and warranties, and statements of discretionary authority—otherwise known as "operative" provisions. For that reason, the Background and Definitions sections are also part of the contract's frame, stabilizing it by adding more information about the deal and preparing the reader for the "picture" containing the operative provisions of the deal.

Professors who teach contract drafting use various images to convey what contract drafters do. Therefore, you may hear someone else refer to the "frame" as the "skeleton" of the contract and the "picture" as the "meat on the bones." If it helps you to think of the contract that way, please feel free to do so. The purpose of these metaphors is to help you break down the drafting process into manageable parts.

C. **The Preamble—An Example of Learning from a Model:** Provided that you have the correct information, you can draft a Preamble for the toy purchase agreement by following the pattern of the Preamble in the model Leaf Disposal Services Agreement, reprinted below.[1]

LEAF DISPOSAL SERVICES AGREEMENT

Leaf Disposal Services Agreement. made this 10th day of October 2007, between SpinGazer, Inc., a Delaware corporation with its principal place of business located at 1200 Ridge Avenue, Evanston, Illinois 60201 (the "Company"), and Fallen Leaves, Inc., an Illinois corporation with its principal place of business located at 2025 North Clark Street, Chicago, Illinois 60614 (the "Provider").

---

1. The entire model Leaf Disposal Services Agreement is included in Appendix 2.

As a partnership, The T-4 Partnership ("T-4") does not necessarily have a "principal place of business." Instead, you can say "The T-4 Partnership, an Illinois partnership with an office located at [insert address]." For Truly Green Toys, Inc., an Illinois corporation, follow the model, above.

You must choose a shorthand nickname for each party and place the parenthetical containing the shorthand name *after* all of the identifying information about that party. Therefore, after the address of the partnership's office, you may insert "("T-4")," for example. If you call The T-4 Partnership, "T-4," then you will want to give Truly Green Toys, Inc. a nickname at the same level of generality. Perhaps for Truly Green Toys, Inc., you will insert the parenthetical "("TGT")" after its address.

The placement of the shorthand names you choose for the parties, which function like in-text definitions, is very important. Perhaps it is hard to believe, but there could be more than one "The T-4 Partnership" or more than one "Truly Green Toys, Inc." in the world. By placing the parenthetical after each entities' address, you make it more likely that you have clearly identified the "The T-4 Partnership" and the "Truly Green Toys, Inc." that are parties to this contract.

When you draft the Preamble of your contract, pay careful attention to punctuation. The Preamble contains a lot of information and is difficult to read if not punctuated properly. Moreover, aside from the title, the Preamble is the very first thing that the reader will encounter in your contract. Even though it is formulaic, you can set a good tone by drafting it so that it reads smoothly. Proper punctuation helps.

Finally, you and your professor are likely to spend some time talking about what date you should insert in the Preamble. When is the contract "made"? Is it the same date when the contract is signed? Is this date different from the effective date of the term? Also, sometimes the date in the Preamble is preceded by the words "as of." Under what circumstances is it appropriate to use those words? Even a formulaic Preamble can present interesting questions that you are likely to bandy about in class.

D. **Title, Words of Agreement, and Signature Lines:** You and your professor will discuss what to call this contract. For the sake of convenience, I have referred to it as the *Toy Purchase Agreement*, but you are not required to use that title.

The Words of Agreement used in the model Leaf Disposal Services Agreement are simple. After the Background section, insert, "Accordingly, the parties agree as follows:". In most contracts, at about this point in the contract, you will see a lengthy "consideration" provision that sounds like complete gobbledygook. You and your professor are likely to discuss whether a formal statement of consideration is necessary when the contract itself makes it amply clear that consideration for the transaction does exist. The drafter of the Leaf Disposal Services Agreement has concluded that the contract does not require a formal statement of consideration.

You can easily imitate the Signature Lines and get them right. The Signature Lines from the Leaf Disposal Services Agreement are reprinted below.

AGREED:

SPINGAZER, INC.   **FALLEN LEAVES, INC.**

By: _____   By: _____
    Jackie Spingazer   Leif E. Liminator

Title: Director of Operations   Title: Supervisor

Since one of the parties to the Toy Purchase Agreement is a partnership, you will need to adapt this format a bit. The names in boldfaced, all capital letters, above the Signature Lines are the formal names of the parties to the contract—not the shorthand names that you chose in the Preamble and used throughout the rest of the contract. So, where you see **SPINGAZER, INC.** and **FALLEN LEAVES, INC.**, above, you would substitute **THE T-4 PARTNERSHIP** and **TRULY GREEN TOYS, INC.**

> **Note:** Generally, it is a good idea to put your client's Signature Line first. Believe it or not, this sometimes matters to the client.

For "The T-4 Partnership," put in two Signature Lines, one for Victoria B. Green and one for Troy Gardner. Underneath each of their Signature Lines, type their names, in upper and lowercase letters. Put the word "By" in front of each of their Signature Lines. Then, under their Signature Lines, type "Partner." For "Truly Green Toys, Inc.," follow the model. Note that the names above the Signature Lines identify the parties to the contract and the names below the Signature Lines identify who signed the contract.

E. **Background:** The purpose of the Background section is twofold—to put the Agreement in context and to express the intentions of the parties.

You may be accustomed to seeing this section called "Recitals" and containing a list of "WHEREAS" clauses ending with the crescendo

"NOW THEREFORE" clause. Plain English drafters avoid those clauses like the plague. Instead, draft the Background section in smooth prose. This is probably the only place in the contract where you will get to tell a little story. Use it well. Who are the parties? What do they do? Why are they entering into this deal? The Background section should not be too long or too lopsided (containing more information about one party than the other).

The Background section is a place where you should avoid following your models too closely. It is not as formulaic as the Preamble, for example. Ask yourself: What do my readers need to know about the parties? About what happened before (if anything) and about what is about to happen (this transaction)?

Remember that you should not include any operative provisions in the Background section. Be very careful not to include any covenants, conditions precedent, representations and warranties, or statements of discretionary authority here. The courts generally will not give effect to operative language contained in a Background section. And, if you include a covenant in the Background section, you run the risk of forgetting to include it in the body of the contract, where it would actually obligate a party to do something.

Sometimes the parties want to clarify their intentions early in a contract. Even though the Background section should not contain operative provisions, it can contain a statement of the parties' intentions. Sometimes, if there is a contractual dispute, the court will give effect to a statement of intentions included in the Background section instead of, or in addition to, admitting parol evidence of those intentions.

F. **Definitions:** The model Leaf Disposal Services Agreement gives you some limited guidance about how to draft the definitions. It contains the prefatory language below.

As used in this Agreement, the terms defined in the preamble have their assigned meanings and the following terms have the meanings assigned to them in this Article.

If you have defined any terms, in-text, in the Background section, you must add the words "and in the Background section" to the prefatory language after the words "in the preamble." That way, you will not have to include any cross-references to those definitions in the Definitions article itself.

By looking at the model agreement, you will see that most definitions use the verb "means" or "includes but does not include." You will also see that in-text definitions found in the body of the contract (but not in the Preamble or Background section) are cross-referenced in the Definitions article, using the verb phrase "has the meaning assigned in."

You and your professor will discuss how to choose what to define and how to draft the definitions. Remember that definitions are declarations and should not contain any operative language — no covenants, conditions precedent, representations and warranties, or statements of discretionary authority. Think of a definition as a statement of what a term means whenever it appears capitalized in the contract. If you want a party to undertake any kind of obligation, you must include it in the body of the contract rather than in a definition.

Important Note About Drafting Definitions as Part of the Frame: In practice, lawyers hardly ever draft a complete Definitions article before they draft the rest of the contract. In a sense, asking you to draft the Definitions before you draft the rest of the contract is an artificial exercise. Nevertheless, it is a good exercise and it may save you some time and energy. It forces you, as a novice contract drafter, to think in advance about what terms you may need to define. You can draft a definition of "green toy," for example, because you know that you will need to use that term over and over again.

Moreover, drafting definitions in advance may prevent you from making the mistake of using too many in-text definitions. When a Definitions article contains too many cross-references to in-text definitions, the reader is forced to hop all over the contract to find out what things mean. Instead, by defining most terms in the Definitions article itself, you keep the reader happy by feeding her information. You also take the opportunity to educate her about the deal a bit before she launches into the contract. This idea of educating the reader may sound like a litigation drafting concept, but it holds true for contract drafting as well. As your reader moves into the contract, after reading a fully developed Definitions article, she is more likely to understand the rest of the contract.

If you remember to consider your audience(s), you will be more likely to achieve the goal of clear communication. Transactional attorneys who fail to consider their audience(s) give transactional attorneys a bad name.

G. Additional Instructions: Your professor may provide you with additional instructions regarding this assignment.

1F: FILLING IN THE PICTURE: DRAFTING THE CONTRACT'S OPERATIVE PROVISIONS

Instructions

A. **Summary:** Using the deal facts gathered from the client interview you conducted in Assignment 1B, draft all of the operative provisions of the toy purchase agreement between The T-4 Partnership ("T-4") and Truly Green Toys, Inc. ("TGT") The "operative" provisions do not include the "frame" of the contract—the Title, Preamble, Background, Words of Agreement, Definitions, and Signature Lines. This assignment assumes that you have already drafted the "frame" of the contract as part of Assignment 1E—or that your professor has asked you to skip that assignment and concentrate on "filling in the picture."

B. **Filling in the Picture:** To fill in the picture, you must draft all of the operative provisions of the contract and decide how to organize them. Your professor will help you develop the basic skills you need to take the terms of the deal and translate them into contract concepts—covenants, conditions precedent, representations and warranties, statements of discretionary authority, and declarations.[2]

   In practice, some attorneys call this *memorializing* the terms of the deal, which basically means getting the terms of the deal down on paper so that they have a legal effect. The paper (or contract) is the *memorial.* The parties should be able to turn to the contract whenever they have any questions about their rights and duties with regard to the particular transaction.

C. **Organization—Naming and Ordering the Articles and Sections:** Some provisions are traditionally placed in certain spots. For example, after the Definitions article, some drafters include a brief article containing the main covenants of the deal. One leading contract drafting expert, Tina L. Stark, calls this brief article the "subject matter performance provision."[3] The subject matter performance provision in the model Leaf Disposal Services Agreement is reprinted below.

---

2. Tina L. Stark, *Drafting Contracts: How and Why Lawyers Do What They Do* 9-10 (Aspen 2007) (describes the contract concepts as the "building blocks" of the contract and the process of converting business terms into contract concepts as a "translation skill").
   3. *Id.* at 39-40.

Article III. Summary of Services and Fees

Section 3.01 Services and Fees. Subject to the provisions of this Agreement, the Provider shall perform the Services described in Article IV. To compensate the Provider for performing the Services, the Company shall pay the Provider the fees and reimburse the Provider for the expenses described in Article V.

The drafter of the model Leaf Disposal Services Agreement put the subject matter performance provision after the Term article. While the exact order of these provisions sometimes varies, remember that the subject matter performance provision, the Term, and the Closing articles should appear near the beginning of the contract.

It is sometimes helpful to think of the subject matter performance provision as a thesis statement plus roadmap. It tells you the "main idea" (or "primary covenants") of the contract and points you to the places in the contract where you can find out more details about those covenants.

After the subject matter performance provision, the Term article, and the Closing article, the reader expects to find information about what T-4 is purchasing and how much it is going to pay for it. Therefore, you must put those articles close to the beginning of the contract.

At the end of the contract, right before the Signature Lines, place the contract's boilerplate provisions (sometimes called *General Provisions*). The Termination and Dispute Resolution articles generally come right before the boilerplate.

So, with the parts of the contract in their traditional places, and allowing for some flexibility in their exact order, your contract (not including the frame) will look something like this:

Summary of Purchase and Payment
Term
Closing (if any)
The Toy Purchase
Fees
[OTHER TOPICS TO BE COVERED]
Dispute Resolution
Termination
General Provisions

Note that the above italicized headings are offered as an example only. They are not set in stone. You are encouraged to draft your own appropriate headings for the articles you include in the contract.

One of the biggest challenges that a drafter faces is how to organize the business provisions not specifically listed above—that is, how to organize those "other topics to be covered." Start by making a list of every deal term not addressed in the named articles. Then group those deal terms by topic and select a good name for the article covering that topic. Remember that "T-4's Obligations" and "TGT's Responsibilities" are contract concepts, not topics. Moreover, if you use a heading like "T-4's Obligations," you are indicating to the reader that all of T-4's obligations are contained under that heading. More likely, T-4's obligations are scattered throughout the contract.

Choose article names (and section names as well) that are specific and clear. Instead of "T-4's Obligations" or "TGT's Responsibilities," for example, you may have articles called "Toy Ordering Process" and "Advertising and Marketing of Earth Month." These articles may contain obligations and responsibilities of one or both parties.

If you find that you have a number of miscellaneous deal terms that do not seem to fit anywhere, give them another look before deciding to create single-section articles. Single-section articles (other than the subject matter performance provision and the Term article) can make the particular topic seem like an undeveloped afterthought or, conversely, give the particular topic too much weight. It is better to put the miscellaneous deal term into the article it relates to the most, even if it is not a perfect fit.

Once you have found a place for every deal term and named the articles you want to include in the contract, decide what order to put them in. Generally, place the articles in order from most important topic to least important topic. However, if you are describing a process, it may make more sense to put some of the articles in chronological order. There is no magic bullet of contract organization. However, it is very important to remember your audience(s). Ask yourself what your reader needs to know and when your reader needs to know it. Also, remember the terms of the deal. For example, if your client stressed that The T-4 Partnership is very concerned about making sure that the toys it purchases from Truly Green Toys, Inc. are made from "green" materials, then you may want to move that topic up near the beginning of the contract for emphasis.

D. **Additional Instructions:** Your professor may provide you with additional instructions regarding this assignment.

1G: PUTTING THE PICTURE IN THE FRAME: FINISHING THE DRAFT CONTRACT

Instructions

A. **Summary:** This assignment applies only if you have already completed Assignments 1E and 1F. You will now insert the "picture" that you drafted in response to Assignment 1F into the "frame" that you drafted in response to Assignment 1E. The result will be one completed draft of a Toy Purchase Agreement (with a title that you have selected).

B. **The Process:** Inserting the picture into the frame is not merely a mechanical process. Once you have merged the two documents together, you must make sure that the picture fits the frame properly; in other words, you must review the draft contract as a whole and ask yourself at least the following questions:

☐ Is the Title I chose for the contract still appropriate?

☐ Have I consistently referred to the parties to the contract using the shorthand names that I gave them in the Preamble?

☐ Do the full party names in the Preamble (not the shorthand names) match the full party names above the Signature Lines?

☐ Does the date in the Preamble reflect the date when the contract is made? If this date is different from the effective date of the contract, have I clarified that in the body of the contract?

☐ Do the addresses in the Preamble match the addresses in the "Notice" provision included in the boilerplate?

☐ Did I include enough information in the Background section? Is there anything else that I may want to add to that section? Is there anything I may want to take out?

☐ Do I use my defined terms whenever it is appropriate? [*Note:* This is called "letting your defined terms do their work."]

☐ Did I remember to capitalize my defined terms in the body of the contract?

☐ Are there any lengthy phrases that I repeat more than once that could perhaps be defined terms?

☐ Are there any concepts that I repeat in different ways each time that I should perhaps be saying the same way each time? Would a defined term help?

☐ Are there any defined terms that I never use or use only once? (If so, you probably do not need to define that term.)

☐ Have I included a cross-reference to every in-text definition in the Definitions article? Are my definitions still in alphabetical order?

☐ Whenever I use a cross-reference, have I referenced the correct article or section?

☐ Have I used cross-references in the body of the contract to help the reader understand the relationship between parts of the contract?

☐ Are all of my article and section numbers in order? Does each have an appropriate heading?

☐ In the "Survivability" boilerplate provision, have I listed all of the sections of the contract that will survive the early termination of the contract or the end of the term?

☐ Do all of the parts of the contract work well together?

Once you have answered all of these questions and made any necessary adjustments to the contract, you can move into the editing and proofreading stage described next.

C. **Editing and Proofreading:** Using the Contract Drafting Checklist provided in Appendix 3, go back over your draft contract again. The checklist is set up to help you take the long view first. Think about the transaction. Have you captured all of the terms of the deal? Have you translated them into the correct contract concepts? Have you answered all questions about the rights and duties of the parties with regard to this transaction? Have you raised any questions without answering them? Is your contract well organized, coherent, and coordinated? Does it read smoothly? Is it easy to follow?

The checklist then asks you to look at some formatting issues that are directly related to readability. Review those issues, remembering also that well-chosen headings and the judicious use of "white space" enhance the readability of a contract. Do not remove headings or white space in order to make sure that you do not exceed the page limit for this assignment. If you need guidance about how to avoid exceeding the page limit, seek your professor's help.

Following the checklist, now make sure that your contract contains all of the essential parts. Then review each part. Finally, under the broad heading "Plain English," the checklist directs you to make sure that you have not made any grammatical, mechanical, or typographical errors.

Once you have gone through the checklist, prepare your contract for submission by proofreading it carefully, using the proofreading tips and tricks contained in Appendix 5. Finally, review your professor's instructions and verify that you have followed all of the directions regarding submitting the contract to your professor. There is something particularly disturbing about a transactional attorney who fails to follow directions. Failing to follow directions indicates that you are not detail oriented, which, in practice, can make your supervisor and your client mistrust you. It can also lead to a dangerous loss of credibility with the attorney representing the other side.

D. **Submitting the Contract:** Do one final thing before you submit your contract: Make sure that you are turning in a clean copy. That is, make sure that you have eliminated any highlighting or comments to yourself that you may have inserted during the drafting process. Practicing attorneys, both litigators and deal lawyers alike, can tell many war stories about forgetting to delete comments or critiques before filing documents or sending drafts to the other side. You do not want to make such an embarrassing mistake. You may also want to make sure that your document does not contain any hidden personal or metadata, such as information about when you finished the assignment. Check the software you are using to figure out how to eliminate that information.

E. **Additional Instructions:** Your professor may provide you with additional instructions regarding this assignment.

1H: MAKING CHANGES TO THE DRAFT CONTRACT: REDLINING

Instructions

A. **Summary:** Using the facts contained in the following memorandum from Sue Payne, make the appropriate changes to the Toy Purchase Agreement. Apparently, Truly Green Toys, Inc. ("TGT") has hired an attorney. Ms. Payne's memorandum summarizes the conversation she had with TGT's attorney about the draft contract that Ms. Payne sent to TGT. Ms. Payne has consulted with your client's representative, Victoria B. Green, and determined that all of the changes are acceptable to The T-4 Partnership ("T-4").

B. **Making Changes to a Draft Reviewed by Opposing Counsel:** Now that your opposing counsel has reviewed your draft contract, you should not make any changes to it without redlining those changes. Find the "Track Changes" (or equivalent function) on your computer and learn how to use it. Ideally, every word you delete should be struck through and every word you add should appear in red.

Make the changes mentioned in Sue's memo. Remember not to make any changes to the document without tracking them. In real life, you will quickly lose credibility with opposing counsel if you do not track all of your changes, for you will be breaking the unwritten code of honor that transactional attorneys follow. Track even the smallest change—even the correction of a minor misspelling.

C. **Turning in the Redlined Contract:** After you have reviewed the redlined contract to make sure that you took into account all of the changes mentioned in Sue's memo, submit it to your professor. This time, make sure that you submit the document *with* the changes showing. (This may be as simple as saving the document as "Final Showing Markup.") Remember to rename the document, using the date and the initials "RL" to indicate that it is a redlined version.

D. Additional Instructions: Your professor may provide you with additional instructions regarding this assignment.

Payne & Associates

MEMORANDUM

CONFIDENTIAL

TO: Associates

FROM: Sue Payne, Senior Partner

RE: Opposing Counsel's Review of Toy Purchase Agreement

DATE: October 5, 2013

Tory Green recently had a long lunch with Will I. Cheeter, the sales representative for Truly Green Toys, Inc. ("TGT"). Tory and Will discussed the draft contract that our firm sent to Mr. Cheeter's attention at TGT. Now, TGT has an attorney, who called to inform me about certain changes that Tory and Will allegedly agreed to over lunch. I ran all of these changes by Tory over the phone, and she confirmed that she has agreed to all of them. Please make the changes and send me a redlined draft.

Tory and Will agreed that it's not fair to TGT to say that TGT's prices are not subject to change under any circumstances. TGT is always revising its manufacturing processes to make them more eco-friendly. Sometimes these measures make it more expensive to manufacture certain toys. If TGT can prove to The T-4 Partnership ("T-4") that a new manufacturing process has raised the cost of manufacturing a particular toy, then TGT may raise the price of that toy by no more than 5%. TGT will have to produce documentation to T-4, demonstrating that the manufacturing process has become more expensive due to measures taken to make the process more eco-friendly.

As it turns out, TGT's "fleet" of hybrid trucks only includes two trucks. T-4 agreed that TGT can use non-hybrid trucks to deliver toys to T-4 if TGT's two hybrid trucks are unavailable. T-4 does not want to have to wait for the availability of the hybrid trucks. T-4 will still pay for the shipping if it becomes necessary to substitute a hybrid truck.

Tory agreed to reduce the number of miles in the exclusivity clause from 200 to 100. Cheeter convinced her that T-4 was restricting TGT's ability to grow its business, and Tory has a soft heart.

TGT wants T-4 to specify which toys T-4 wants TGT to donate for the play area of the store. Tory was happy to hear that. She knows that her partner, Troy, will enjoy choosing those toys, since the play area is going to be his project.

TGT proposed having a special "TGT Toys Day" every quarter at the toy store. On that day, TGT will send its mascot, "TGT Man" to the store and he will give out eco-friendly bags and demonstrate some of TGT's toys. He will also raffle off one TGT Toy worth at least $50, which TGT will donate. Everyone who comes to the store that day will receive a raffle ticket and the raffle will be held before the store closes at 6 p.m. that evening. Tory apparently loved this idea.

T-4 asked TGT to send a representative to the store to train T-4's sales people about how to operate and market TGT's toys. TGT agreed to do this—at no cost to T-4—before the store opens and then again six months later.

Finally, TGT agreed that T-4 would not have to display a sign identifying TGT's toys in the store. Both parties recognized that TGT's logo is brightly colored and prominent on all of TGT's packaging. Therefore, the sign is superfluous.

Assignment 2

The Movie Location and Product Placement Agreement

2A: THE WAIVER OF CONFLICT OF INTEREST AGREEMENT

Instructions

A. **Summary:** After reading the scenario below, you will draft a Waiver of Conflict of Interest Agreement, which you will ask your former client, This Is Just To Say, Inc. ("JTS") to sign.

B. **Scenario:** It is now October 2015. It has been approximately two years since your firm represented The T-4 Partnership ("T-4") with regard to the toy purchase agreement between T-4 and Truly Green Toys, Inc. ("TGT"). Since then, Tory and Troy's Treehugger Toys (the "Store") has become a huge success. Victoria B. Green and Troy Gardner, T-4's partners, have dissolved the partnership and formed a corporation called Green-Gardner Toy Company (the "Toy Company"). They recently contacted your senior partner, Sue Payne, to see if your firm could draft a Movie Location and Product Placement Agreement for them. Apparently, a movie production company called "This Is Just To Say, Inc." (the "Producer") wants to: (a) use the Store as a location for a movie, and (b) show two action figures created by Troy in the movie. Sue was very happy that the Toy Company brought your firm some new business, but, at the same time, she had a nagging suspicion that your firm may have represented the Producer in the past. When Sue checked the firm's records, she found that your firm had reviewed a commercial real estate lease for the Producer six years ago. Sue and the firm's conflicts administrator have determined that the firm must seek a waiver from the Producer in order to represent the Toy Company with regard to the Movie Location and Product Placement Agreement between the Toy Company and the Producer.

C. **The Waiver of Conflict of Interest Agreement:** Sue has asked you to do two things: (1) write a cover letter to the Producer, explaining why you need its written consent to the firm's representation of the Toy Company in this deal; and (2) draft a Waiver of Conflict of Interest Agreement, a copy of which you will enclose with your cover letter.

D. **Preparation for Drafting:** Your firm's conflicts administrator is new to the job and does not have a form Waiver of Conflict of Interest Agreement to give you. *You must complete this assignment without using any models, templates, or forms.*

Begin by looking at any guidance provided by the Model Rules of Professional Conduct regarding the "Client-Lawyer Relationship." More than one rule may be relevant to this issue. However, you are likely to find that Model Rule 1.9 ("Duties to Former Clients"), and its associated Comments, are right on point. Determine what constitutes "informed consent" and how best to confirm that you have obtained that informed consent in writing. Then draft the letter and the Waiver of Conflict of Interest Agreement (the "Waiver").

E. **Content of the Waiver:** Make sure that the Waiver contains a signature line for Sue Payne (on behalf of the firm) and a signature line for Mia Kandu, the Producer's location manager (on behalf of the Producer). Use all of the basic contract drafting principles you have learned when you draft the Waiver. Do not forget about using contract drafting concepts like covenants and representations and warranties and expressing them with the appropriate verbs. For example, you may be tempted to have the Producer "acknowledge" that it has been informed of a potential conflict and that it "understands" what it means. Consider having the Producer "represent" and "warrant" these things instead. One exception to the verb rules regarding covenants: You may use the word "waives" instead of "shall waive" to capture the Producer's covenant to waive the conflict.

Think carefully about how your cover letter and your Waiver work together. Are you going to include the information about the potential conflict in the cover letter and then refer to the letter in the Waiver? Will you be attaching the cover letter to the Waiver as an Exhibit? Or, do you want to inform the Producer of the conflict in the Waiver itself, so that attaching the cover letter is unnecessary? Use your best judgment, keeping in mind that the Producer must understand everything that you draft.

F. **Additional Consideration Re the Company:** Think about whether you should also write a letter to the Toy Company, informing them that your firm represented the Producer with regard to a previously unrelated transaction. Let them know that you have sought the Producer's waiver of any conflict of interest associated with your firm now representing the Toy Company in the movie location and product placement transaction. You may also want to consider whether to remind the Toy Company that you are bound not to reveal any confidential information about your former client, the Producer.

G. **Additional Instructions:** Your professor may provide you with additional instructions regarding this assignment.

2B: MEMORANDUM FROM ASSOCIATES TO SUE PAYNE, SENIOR PARTNER, RE SUMMARY OF DEAL TERMS

Instructions

A. **Summary:** Each of you must draft a memorandum to Sue Payne, summarizing the deal terms to be included in the Movie Location and Product Placement Agreement between your client, Green-Gardner Toy Company (the "Toy Company"), and This Is Just To Say, Inc. (the "Producer"), a movie production company. Before drafting your memorandum to Sue, please review the following documents: (a) memorandum from Sue Payne, senior partner, Payne & Associates; (b) letter from Tory Green-Gardner; (c) transcript of a meeting between Tory Green-Gardner and Mia Kandu; (d) e-mail string between Tory Green-Gardner and Mia Kandu; and (e) draft Location and Product Placement Release Agreement provided to Tory Green-Gardner by the Producer.

B. **Format of Memorandum:** Set up your memo as follows—

Payne & Associates

MEMORANDUM

CONFIDENTIAL

TO:	Sue Payne
FROM:	[Insert Your Name]
RE:	Summary of Deal Terms
SUBJECT:	Movie Location and Product Placement Agreement Between Green-Gardner Toy Company and This Is Just To Say, Inc.
DATE:	October 7, 2015

[Insert the text of the memo, single-spaced. Note that Sue would like this memo to be organized a specific way. First, she wants you to summarize the deal facts. Then she wants you to list any legal issues that you think it may be necessary to research before drafting the contract. Finally, she wants you to make a list of additional questions that you want her to ask the client.]

To satisfy Sue's expectations, the main headings in your memo should be:

I. Known Deal Facts
II. Potential Legal Issues
III. Additional Questions for the Client

You may want to break up any one of the main sections into subsections with headings. This might be especially helpful to Sue in Section I.

C. **Collaboration:** If your professor permits, you and your classmates may draft this memo (or parts of it) in pairs or in teams. Alternatively, you and your classmates may brainstorm about Sections II and III of the memo in class. Your professor will guide you regarding how much collaboration (if any) is appropriate on this assignment.

D. **Additional Instructions:** Your professor may provide you with additional instructions regarding this assignment.

Payne & Associates
357 East Chicago Avenue
Chicago, Illinois 60202
312-503-0000
Payne.S@lawfirm.com

Partners
Sue Payne

Associates
Students

MEMORANDUM

TO: Associates

FROM: Sue Payne

RE: Green-Gardner Toy Company

DATE: October 4, 2015

Remember Tory and Troy's Treehugger Toys? Back in 2013, we drafted a toy purchase agreement for The T-4 Partnership when they were just getting ready to open their toy store and wanted to buy a bunch of "green" toys from Truly Green Toys, Inc. As you may know, the toy store—which is affectionately known as "Treehuggers"—has been a huge success. T-4 has been dissolved.

Its former general partners, Victoria B. Green and Troy Gardner, have formed Green-Gardner Toy Company, an Illinois corporation. Treehuggers, now located in Chicago, is apparently the "go-to" place for eco-conscious parents. Not only have the store's green and discovery toys been a big hit, but Tory and Troy's efforts to educate and interact with the community are drawing a continuous stream of customers.

(As an aside, I don't know why Tory and Troy dropped out of our sight for so long. If some of you had stayed in touch with them, perhaps they would have hired us to help them dissolve their partnership and form their corporation. Or maybe they would have asked us to review the real estate sales contract when their company bought the building and surrounding property where the toy store is now located.)

By the way, Tory and Troy got married and they both changed their last names to "Green-Gardner." Tory tells me that her interest in Troy grew steadily after the end of her unfortunate fling with Will I. Cheeter. Cheeter publicly disgraced her at the Chicago Toy Fair's Benefit by bringing Barbie Dahl, a notorious designer of toxic toys, as his date. Apparently, Troy has always been in love with Tory. He was just waiting for the right opportunity to take their friendship to the next level.

Over the years, Troy has devoted most of his time and attention to developing the play area and storytime theater at Treehuggers. I took my grandchildren to the Chicago store to check it out. As we entered the store, we saw green toys on the left and discovery toys on the right, but Troy's play area/storytime theater, directly ahead, really captured our attention.

Tory and Troy hold monthly educational events at the store to teach kids (and their parents) about science, nature, and protecting the environment. But what Treehuggers has become most famous for are the two action figure characters that Troy invented and manufactures himself from recycled plastic water bottles and discarded cell phone and computer parts. He calls one character "Glenna the Go-Green Goddess" and the other character "Trey the Treehugging Troll."

Troy writes stories about the adventures of Glenna and Trey and performs them in the theater. I gather that kids from all over Chicago come to hear these stories and to purchase their own Glenna and Trey action figures. (So, there's another business opportunity we missed! Tory tells me that Troy sought and obtained all of the intellectual property rights necessary to protect his characters and their stories. Wish they'd sent that legal business our way.)

I am giving you all of this information as background for your next project. Tory sent me a letter a few days ago. Luckily, the Green-Gardner Toy Company now needs our services. I've enclosed Tory's letter, along with some other documents for you to review. After you look over these materials, please get me a draft of the contract between Tory and Troy's company and the film production company, This Is Just To Say, Inc. (the "Producer"). Apparently, the Producer wants to use Treehuggers as a location for a movie. Moreover, the Producer has agreed to show the Glenna and Trey action figures in the movie—a "product placement" similar to those you sometimes see for various soft drinks and other items like automobiles and designer sunglasses. Maybe if you do a great job on this contract, Tory and Troy will continue to use us as their legal counsel for Green-Gardner Toy Company. Let me know if you need any additional information. I can always give Tory a call.

October 1, 2015

Green-Gardner Toy Company
[Tory and Troy's Treehugger Toys]
52313 N. Clark Street
Chicago, Illinois 60640
312-555-5555
e-mail: T&TGreenGardner@toystore.com

Sue Payne
Payne & Associates
357 E. Chicago Avenue
Chicago, Illinois 60611

Dear Sue:

I have some exciting news. Tory and Troy's Treehugger Toys is going to be used as a location for a movie! Although we haven't worked together for quite some time, I'd like your firm to help us finalize the contract.

Here's the story: Three months ago, a suspicious looking man came into the store and spent a lot of time looking around. When I noticed him jotting down notes on a legal pad, I got a little nervous and sent Troy over to ask him what he was doing. He identified himself as Abel Finder, a location scout for a movie production company called "This Is Just To Say, Inc." ("JTS" for short.) Troy couldn't really believe it, so he asked him for his business card.

When Troy introduced me to Abel and told me the name of the company he works for, I laughed because I am familiar with the poem by William Carlos Williams—the one the company is named after. (It's that short poem with the guy kind of apologizing for eating the plums someone was saving to eat for breakfast.) In fact, I have a copy of the poem on the bulletin board outside of my office. Choosing a name like that shows that the company has a good sense of humor.

Anyway, Abel said that he thought our store would be a good place to film several key scenes in a romantic comedy that JTS is making. He asked me if he could take some pictures of the inside and outside of the store and wondered when he could come back with some other folks like the producer, director, and designer. I let him take the pictures he wanted and invited him to come back the following week for breakfast with myself and Troy.

We live right above the store. So, Abel brought the producer, director, and designer over and—after Troy gave them the grand tour of the store (inside and out)—they came upstairs and I fed them my superb egg-white omelets. We had a very nice time. They seemed quite interested in using our store for the movie and we let them know that we were interested, too, but that we wanted to be paid. I guess lots of people think getting their name in the movie's credits is enough, but that could never compensate us for the business we'll lose on days when they are shooting.

Abel and his group left to catch a plane back to Los Angeles. They said that they would talk on the plane and let us know if the store seemed like the right location. If they decided to use the store, they would send a location manager to work out the details with us, including negotiating a contract.

To make a long story short, JTS decided that they want to use the store. I had a very long meeting with JTS's location manager, Mia Kandu, on September 1st. Initially, I tried to take notes, but things were going too fast for me. Finally, I asked Mia if I could tape record our conversation, and she agreed. So, for your convenience, I had my secretary type up a transcript of the tape.

Along with the transcript, I'm sending you some follow-up correspondence I had with Mia via e-mail. Also, I'm enclosing the draft contract that Mia sent me. I was shocked that it was so poorly written and contained so few of the details we discussed, and I told her so. She said something like, "Well, why don't you give it to your attorneys? They can put in some changes and then we can send it back to our legal department."

It looks to me like you guys will have to re-draft the entire contract. For what it's worth, I think we have a lot of leeway because I overheard Mia talking to Abel on her cell phone and his voice boomed through the phone. He was shouting, "We HAVE TO HAVE that store."

I look forward to seeing the contract you draft. Please call me when it's ready. Meanwhile, I hope that all is well with you and your family and your lovely dog, Annabelle.

Sustainably yours,

Victoria B. Green-Gardner

Victoria B. Green-Gardner

**Transcript of Meeting Between Tory Green-Gardner and
Mia Kandu: September 1, 2015**

Tory	Well, I guess I'd like to know more about the movie. What's it about? Who's going to star in it? That sort of thing.
Mia	I can't tell you very much about it. Actually, it's better for you not to know too much. That way the public won't find out and there won't be too much chaos when we start filming. In fact, I'm really not supposed to talk to you about the movie at all without getting you to sign a Confidentiality Agreement. [A pause; some paper shuffling.] Oh yeah, here it is.
Tory	Okay. No big deal. I'll sign it. [A pause; a search for a pen; the scratchy sound of Tory signing the Confidentiality Agreement.]
Mia	Thank you. The movie is probably going to be called "Please Wink Back." At least that's the current title. It's about a nerdy toy store owner—a man—who tries online dating because he wants to fall in love. On one of the online services, you can read someone's profile and send them a "Wink" if you like what you see. If that person "Winks" back, then usually you start up an e-mail conversation and eventually progress to dating. This nerdy guy, Walter, is going to meet a number of women who come into the toy store to see him after he "winks" at them online.
Tory	So the movie's about a toy store owner—kind of like Troy!

Mia	Oh no. It's not based on Troy or any other real person. We need you to understand that and will want something in the contract to assure that you do.
Tory	Sure, sure. I was just kidding. Do you have any idea of when you want to get started and how long you are going to need the Store? We have some concerns about making sure we get through the holiday season first.
Mia	Well, we have a lot of things to do before we can get started. And we anticipated your issue about the holiday season. We'll be ready to get set up at the Store on January 11th [2016]. Would that work?
Tory	Yes, I think so, but it kind of cuts into our post-holiday sales. We can have a New Year's Super Sale, or something like that, so that we're ready for you when you get here on the 11th. How long will you be around? We can't close the Store for more than a month. We'd lose too much business and a lot of momentum. Our customers bring their kids here for monthly educational events. Tory and I teach them about science and nature and protecting the environment. I don't want the filming to interfere with those events.
Mia	I understand completely. We are going to need the Store until we finish filming the scenes and I estimate that will be at least 28 days for the initial filming. Let's say we think we may be able to finish, including take-down, by February 14th [2016]. That doesn't include post-production things like re-takes and additional scenes. We'll have to be able to come back to do those.
Tory	Could we keep the Store open on the weekends during the filming?
Mia	No, I don't think that would work. The Store will always have to be closed during the filming, which will take place every day of the week, even on holidays (if there are any in that time frame). So much goes in to setting things up. It just wouldn't be economical to take it all down and put it up again.
Tory	Well, what parts of the Store are you going to need access to? You know, we live upstairs and I sure don't want anyone filming anything up there.

Mia	We'd like you to give us access to the whole toy store, inside and out. We can make sure that doesn't include your living quarters. But we have to be able to use your power outlets, your water supply, your parking lot, and everything inside the Store—that includes your shelving and displays and the toys themselves. (Of course, we'll be responsible for getting permission from the manufacturers to show the toys in the movie—at least for any toys that get prominently shown.) You have a public restroom, too, don't you?
Tory	Yes, we do. We have to because there are so many little kids who come in here and really have to go! [Pause.] Oh, about showing the toys. Troy made up these fantastic characters and created action figures for them. Glenna the Go-Green Goddess and Trey the Treehugging Troll. Could we show those in the movie? That would certainly boost their sales.
Mia	I don't see why not. Sure. Sure. But you'll have to grant us the right to show them and you'll have to guarantee that Troy owns the intellectual property rights in them and, if we get sued because he doesn't, then you have to pay the damages, plus our attorney's fees.
Tory	Sounds kind of harsh. But okay, as long as you can promise not to disparage poor Glenna and Trey? And not to show them doing anything violent or not eco-friendly?
Mia	Of course. But it's doubtful we'll have them "do" anything. We usually just have one of the movie's characters pick the object up or show it to another character, or something like that. We can't commit to more than that. And we won't pay you anything extra for showing Glenna and Trey. Often, the product's manufacturers pay us for product placements!
Tory	Well, that's not happening here. What else should we be talking about?
Mia	We're also going to have to have your permission to change the place a bit if it's necessary. We'll put everything back the way we found it, of course.
Tory	What would you need to change? I thought you loved the Store as a location because of its charm.

Mia	Yes. Indeed. I'm just talking about stuff like maybe trimming trees so we can get our equipment through. And we don't want to use the name of your store, so we'll make up a sign and lay it over your sign. We can do that without damaging your sign at all. You'll still get a movie credit that includes the real name of your store.
Tory	Wait, before we talk about the credit, let me make sure I understand you about the changes you might need to make. Will they involve painting the Store, for example? Troy and I spent a lot of time picking out the colors and I feel certain that he'd have a fit if you tried to change that—even temporarily.
Mia	We can promise not to change the colors of the Store. We are satisfied with those. Is there anything else you're concerned about?
Tory	I wouldn't want you to make any structural changes to the Store—like knocking out a wall or a window. Do you think you'd have to do that?
Mia	I've done some preliminary measurements and don't think that will be necessary. However, we may need to take the doors off of their hinges in order to get some of our equipment through the doorways. We'll put them back the way we found them. I am really talking about changes that will make the filming possible and make each shot look good. Nothing major.
Tory	Okay. We can agree to non-structural, minor changes, as long as you don't change the look of the Store too much. Especially the colors. Wow. We have so much to cover. What about that movie credit we're going to get? What will it say?
Mia	Well, it usually says something like: "Filmed by permission on location at Tory and Troy's Treehugger Toys." Will that do?
Tory	Yes, I like that, but could we add "in Chicago, Illinois"?

Mia	No problem. And we could also put a link to your website on the movie's promotional website. That's routine and won't cost you a dime. (We won't pay to do it either. It's entirely up to you whether you want it up there.)
Tory	Now, about the money. We want to be paid for every day when you have any kind of access to the Store for making the film. We'd like at least $1,500 per day. That will help compensate for some of the business we're going to lose.
Mia	Sorry. That's a little bit higher than what we usually pay. I can get you $1,000 per day, maybe $1,100 per day, but that's about it.
Tory	We can't take a penny less than $1,100 per day.
Mia	It's a deal!
Tory	Good. Whew. That part was easy enough. Now I want to know how you're going to protect our property while your crew is here. Do you have insurance? We want you to add us as an additional insured and to show us the certificate of insurance before you begin filming at the Store.
Mia	Yes, of course. We do have insurance. We have to. I'm pretty sure that the Chicago Film Office requires us to have insurance. Don't know exactly what the requirements are, but I'll check it out and we'll put it in the contract. And we'll get you those certificates before we start filming at the Store.
Tory	Oh yeah, one of my neighbors told me that the Chicago Film Office has a bunch of regulations you'll have to follow if you want to film at our Store. Do you know what those are?
Mia	I have one of my people finding out. I know we have to have some police supervision to control the car and foot traffic. I'm not sure if we need fire department personnel because we don't need to use any pyrotechnics, but it's possible that our lighting is so intense it's considered a fire hazard. Oh, and they have some wacky requirement about drafting a leaflet to notify the neighbors of what's happening before it happens. Have you heard about that one?

Tory	No. But I really like the idea. I want you to do that. I'd like to have the right to review it and approve of it before you distribute it, too. We have such a good relationship with the community.
Mia	We'll do whatever the Chicago Film Office requires us to do and we'll also draft the leaflet and let you see it before we distribute it.
Tory	Yes, I want to see it, but I also want to have some time to make changes to it. Can you agree to let me do that? I know the community very well and I can help ease the tension a bit.
Mia	Sure. As long as your changes don't go too far. We don't want to go too much beyond what the City requires.
Tory	Of course. I think you'll like my changes, though. [Pause.] And you'll pay any fees that Chicago requires you to pay to the City from your pocket and not from ours?
Mia	Of course. We also want to apply for the Illinois Production Tax Credit. Will you and Troy agree to do anything you need to do to help us secure that credit?
Tory	Sure. We'll help with that as long as it doesn't require us to lie about anything. By the way, I have a few golden doodle puppies—Gus and Gert—and a pair of lovebirds—Bill and Coo—upstairs. Do you think that you'll be making much noise?
Mia	Oh yes. We'll definitely be making noise. Not explosions or anything as loud as that. But a film production crew makes noise. It's inevitable.
Tory	I guess I'll have to drop the dogs off at a kennel and send the lovebirds to my Mom's house. Will JTS pay for the kennel? It costs $35 a day per dog.
Mia	Yes, we can do that. Let's call it the daily kennel fee, or something like that.
Tory	Thank you so much. I do love my pets!

Mia	I want to make sure that I let you know how much flexibility we're going to need. I don't know how much you know about the filmmaking business, but it is possible that we could film all of the parts we need to film at your Store and then wind up not using any of them. We might decide to produce the film without those scenes. Or, we might decide not to finish the film at all. I'd like to cover that in the contract so that it's very clear.
Tory	Okay. I get it. I remember hearing actors on talk shows discuss certain scenes they filmed that never made it into their movies—they wound up "on the cutting room floor" as they say. But we'd still get paid in full, wouldn't we?
Mia	Yes. As long as we finish the filming.
Tory	Good. [Pause.] I did do a little research before our meeting. Let's focus a bit on some really practical stuff.
Mia	Okay.
Tory	What time of day will you start filming? And when will you finish? As I mentioned, we live upstairs, and we're not planning on staying in a hotel during the shooting.
Mia	We will start at 7 a.m. and shoot until 7 p.m. on an average day, but there are a lot of days when we'll go well beyond 7 p.m.
Tory	Oh, that's a problem for us. We like to have our dinner at 8 p.m. and we've gotten used to it being pretty quiet. I'm beginning to think this is going to be way more disruptive than I originally thought it would be.
Mia	Don't worry. We can try our best to limit the amount of overtime hours or warn you two when we need to stay late so you can go out to dinner.
Tory	I'm not sure that's good enough. We don't eat out much because there aren't any good organic restaurants nearby. Isn't it pretty standard for you to pay us an hourly overtime rate on days when you use the Store past 7 p.m.?

Mia	Okay. You got me on that one. We can pay $50 per hour of overtime.
Tory	I don't know where that number comes from. If you're paying us $1,100 a day, then that's about $92 per hour for regular hours. I think you should pay us more when you inconvenience us more. I'd like you to pay at least $100 per overtime hour.
Mia	Would $75 per overtime hour work?
Tory	You drive a hard bargain. I think Troy would want input on this one.
Mia	Are you saying that you don't really have the authority to agree to everything we've been talking about?
Tory	No, no. I definitely have the authority to agree to everything. But both of us will be signing the contract. What about you? Am I really talking to the right person or am I going to find out that only the director is permitted to agree to the things we've talked about today?
Mia	I have the authority to agree to everything. But, actually, it's the producer who is going to sign the contract. So, what about it? $75 per hour for overtime hours?
Tory	Okay, okay. I don't want to sweat the small stuff.
Mia	Good. So let's talk about some more big things. JTS is going to own all of the intellectual property related to the film. To put that in layman's—oh, forgive me—in laywoman's terms, we will own the film plus any still photos and sound recordings and anything else we create to promote the film (like a website, for example). Oh, and if I didn't say it before, you have to give us the exclusive right to advertise and promote the film and exhibit the film all over the world—heck, all over the universe!
Tory	Gosh, I hope you're going to make the Store look good!

Mia	Well, actually, we intend to do that, but we can't commit to it. And you must agree not to sue us for defamation or libel or invasion of privacy or anything like that because we depict the Store in a way that doesn't make you happy.
Tory	Ouch! I don't like that very much. Can I discuss it with my husband?
Mia	I understand. Let's table that for now. When you talk to him, please explain that we intend to depict the Store in a positive light, but that we can't guarantee it. If you can't agree not to sue us because of how we depict the Store, that's a deal breaker for us. I don't want to have to look for another location, so I hope you can agree.
Tory	As you said, let's table that for now. Again, I don't mean to obsess about the little details, but I'm still thinking about practical stuff. Who is going to come to our property? Do you have any idea how many people it might be?
Mia	Those are really good questions. We'll have at least 50 people around every day when the filming is in full swing. We need you to grant access to our personnel and our contractors so that they can bring in cameras and lighting equipment. And, also, we'll have to bring in food and drink and props. We'll need someplace for the actors to get prepped and to rest when they're not on the set. Your parking lot is big enough for three small trailers that can serve as dressing rooms. We'd like to tent the rest of the parking lot so we can feed people out there. And since it's winter, we'll have to heat that tent.
Tory	Yes, that sounds fine. But where is everyone going to park? I don't think our neighborhood can absorb that many cars.
Mia	We can alleviate that somewhat by bussing people in. The producer and director and other key personnel such as cast members will still want to drive their own cars, though. We'll have a valet park the cars somewhere in the neighborhood.
Tory	Okay. That sounds pretty reasonable. And you'll pay for all of this stuff, including the bussing, the trailers, the food and drink, the valet, the heated tent?

Mia	Yes. We'll pay for it all. And since your public restrooms are so small, we'll even bring in some portable toilets..
Tory	So smelly! But, yes, that's acceptable, as long as you pay for them. [Pause.] Now I need a break. Would you like a cup of tea?
Mia	Sure. But I'll need to go to my car to make a few phone calls.
TORY AND MIA TOOK A BREAK. TORY MADE TEA AND MIA TOOK HER CUP TO HER CAR WITH HER.	
Tory	This is hard work, but I'm kind of enjoying it, I must admit. Now that you've had a moment to relax, will you tell me who you've hired to play Walter, the toy store owner? I hope it's Brad Pitt!
Mia	I wish! Although it would be a little difficult to make him look nerdy. No. But—and remember that you are bound by the Confidentiality Agreement you signed not to reveal this to anyone but your husband and your attorney—we're trying to get Matt Damon.
Tory	Oh, that would be so cool! Who's your second choice?
Mia	Our second choice is an unknown actor named Brendan Finn Donnelley. He's a fashion model and a professional squash player.
Tory	Well, I really hope you get Matt. [Pause. Shuffling of papers.] I took some notes during our break. And I talked to Troy, too, about that "depiction of the Store" issue. We've decided to trust you, but we do want you to say somewhere in the contract that you intend to depict the Store in a positive way consistent with the Store's mission, or something like that. That's the only way we'd be able to agree not to sue you if the way you depict the Store doesn't make us happy. Will that work?
Mia	Yes, we can put something about our good intentions in the contract somewhere.

Tory	I think you mentioned something about being able to come back for re-takes and additional scenes? How would that work?
Mia	Yes, re-takes and additional scenes, if need be. We'd give you some notice in advance and you'd tell us if it's convenient. Then we'd troop back in with all the people and the stuff. You'd have to grant us access sporadically for up to a year after we finish the initial filming. We usually give at least 48 hours of notice before we come back in.
Tory	We'll want 7 days' notice, especially to prepare our customers and our neighbors for the additional upheaval.
Mia	4 days.
Tory	6 days.
Mia	5 days.
Tory	Okay. 5 days' notice. Please notify us by phone and you must reach one of us—you can't just leave a voicemail.
Mia	We need another alternative if you don't answer your phone. How about if we call your attorney and notify you through him or her?
Tory	Yes, I think that either of those methods would work. If we find the timing is inconvenient, then we will say so. And then what?
Mia	We have to request an alternative time at least two weeks later and you must accept that time. If one year from completion of the initial filming is going to expire and we still haven't finished with the re-takes and additional scenes because of your objections to our suggested times, then you have to extend the one year re-take period so we can finish those things. We need them in order to finish the film.
Tory	Sounds good.
Mia	By the way, your company does own this building and the property it sits on, including the parking lot, right?

Tory	Yes, we do. When we first started our business, we rented a store in Evanston, but we soon outgrew it and found we could afford to buy this place. We really love it. You obviously do, too, or Abel Finder wouldn't have recommended you use it for your movie.
Mia	I feel as if you are going somewhere with this.
Tory	Yes. A few times you've said that if JTS moved or changed anything, they would put it back the way it was. I was thinking about that promise and I began to feel the way a landlord must feel when she rents out an apartment. How can I be sure that you are going to live up to that promise? That's why I think a security deposit makes some sense. We'd have the money in hand to fix anything you didn't fix and, if everything is fine, then we'd refund the money within 14 days after the completion of the initial filming. And, just like a landlord, we'd be able to deduct a reasonable cleaning fee.
Mia	That might work. How much were you thinking of?
Tory	How about $5,000? Who knows what kind of damage all that equipment and all of those people can do?
Mia	That's too steep. Let's say three days' fees—or $3,300—as security deposit.
Tory	Fine. As long as you pay it with a cashier's check when you send us the signed contract. (I guess every payment you make should be in a cashier's check, to be safe.) What else should we be thinking about?
Mia	Fine. [Pause.] We'll need to build in some flexibility in the dates in case there is a change in the production schedule or in case of weather problems or some other act of God or man (like a terrorist attack) that might prevent us from completing the film on schedule.
Tory	If something like that happens, we'll talk and agree upon another schedule. Doesn't that make sense? Say, that brings something else to mind. When are we going to get paid? Will you pay up front? At the end of each day that you use the Store? When?

Mia	We like to pay when all of the work is completed. That's our standard procedure, except for the security deposit, which we'll pay up front.
Tory	Let's make sure that we're on the same page about this. When you say "when all of the work is completed," are you saying that we'll have to wait until the end of that year in which you can come back and do re-takes? I think you really mean that we'll get paid for the initial filming on the completion date of the initial filming. We'll get paid at the end of the one-year period for any additional days when you have done re-takes and additional scenes. Correct?
Mia	You got that right. Very good.
Tory	When you do finish the initial filming, how long will it take you to break everything down and put everything back and be gone?
Mia	No more than three days. Of course, you get paid for those days. But those days—called *Strike Days*—are paid at a discounted rate of 1/2 of the regular daily rate. It makes sense because there are fewer people on site—only about 20—and a lot less commotion—especially since the stars of the movie are gone.
Tory	Okay. You know, speaking of discounts, I have some ideas about ways that you could get us to lower the regular daily rate. I want to think about it a little more and send you an e-mail tomorrow. I think we can get your costs down considerably if you'll agree to do a few affirmative things.
Mia	Sounds mysterious. I'll look forward to getting your e-mail. [Pause while Mia takes a cell phone call.] I've really got to wrap up this meeting. Is there anything else?
Tory	Oh, dear. Yes, there's lots more. Let's see what we can get through before you have to leave. What if something goes wrong and one of us has to terminate the contract? I know that good contracts are all about good relationships, after all.

Mia	Once we start filming, we can't let you stop us. That sounds pretty harsh. Let me rephrase. What I mean is that if we breach the contract you can sue us for money but you can't seek a court order to stop the production or the distribution of the film.
Tory	I'm not comfortable with that. I want us to have some kind of process in place to handle disputes. We should agree to take our disputes to a mediator on the list provided by the Chicago Lawyers for the Creative Arts.
Mia	But we have to agree on the definition of "dispute," don't we? I don't think we want to go to mediation if you get mad because we're making too much noise when we arrive in the morning, for example. A "dispute" should be limited to something that is a material breach of the contract. Like if we make a structural change to the Store. That's a pretty bad breach and should go immediately to mediation. And all production should stop as soon as you notify us of the potential breach.
Tory	I don't know. I think your example is bad. If you start knocking down walls, we will have to terminate the contract immediately. I think we can let our attorneys work out some definition of material breach that lets either of us terminate the contract immediately under certain circumstances. You'll want to terminate immediately, for example, if we significantly alter the Store so that it no longer suits your purposes. Right?
Mia	I see what you're saying. Yes, in fact we want your company to state in the contract that the store is pretty much the same as it was when Abel Finder found it. [Pause.] What about if we try to handle disputes that are not material breaches of the contract informally at first? Perhaps you contact me and we meet to have tea and talk things through. If that doesn't work, we take the dispute to a mediator recommended by the Chicago Lawyers for the Creative Arts, as you suggested.
Tory	I like that. Let's pick neutral ground where we can meet if we need to talk about one of those informal disputes. How about The Mythical Beast Café, in Evanston? I can get you the address. And, for material breaches, we'll leave that up to the lawyers to define those.

Mia	Yes, to the Mythical Beast. And yes to the lawyers working out the material breach stuff.
Tory	Troy wants to make sure that we aren't liable for any damages or loss to your equipment while you have it on our property.
Mia	I can see that, but, of course, you would be liable if you damaged it willfully or because you were being careless. Or because one of your animals defecated on it, for example.
Tory	Eeew. I'm putting the dogs in a kennel, remember? And now you've gone all lawyerly on me. I'm not sure what that stuff about willfulness and carelessness means. I'll have my lawyer decide if it's reasonable to agree to that.
Mia	A few more things before I go. Abel is waiting for me at another Chicago location. There are no children or other guests allowed on the premises during production unless they're part of our crew.
Tory	How are you going to prevent that? We won't invite anyone, but we can't be responsible if somebody shows up to watch. Don't you filmmakers always draw a crowd? If you get Matt Damon to play Walter, don't you think that every woman on the block will want to see him?
Mia	We're fine with you agreeing not to invite anyone. The other stuff is just crowd control. I believe that is what we'll be paying Chicago's finest (the police officers) to do.
Tory	I was wondering. Can we see the movie before you release it? We might want to suggest some changes.
Mia.	Nope. Sorry. That's another deal breaker for us. You have to agree that you have no approval rights. You don't get to see the film until it's released in the theaters. Is that going to be a problem for you?

Tory	I guess not. But I do have a few things I don't want to happen on our premises during the filming. These are deal breakers for us: No pyrotechnics, no access to our living quarters upstairs, no access to the roof (it's rather delicate), and no use of alcohol or drugs on site. Have your cast parties off site, please. We'd like to come and drink with you at a local restaurant to celebrate, but we don't want you doing it here. Agreed?
Mia	Of course. No problem. What about smoking? Our crew members—well, some of them just can't quit. Can we have a designated smoking area?
Tory	I'm not sure you can. We wouldn't object, as long as it was at the far end of the parking lot. But I don't know exactly what Chicago's non-smoking ordinance says. Can you find out?
Mia	Yes. We'll comply with whatever it says. I sure hope it allows our people to smoke somewhere.
Tory	Can you make sure you put some kind of boards down to cover the floors where lots of folks are going to be walking and where your heavy equipment has to go? I worked long and hard to refurbish those hardwood floors—they're the original oak and just gorgeous.
Mia	I know! We'll do what we can to protect them with boards and pads.
Tory	I guess we'll have to define "normal wear and tear" somehow in the contract. Oh, and on a totally unrelated topic, do you know anything about how we handle these payments for tax purposes? I know I shouldn't be asking you this, but I just thought you might know.
Mia	I believe you have to declare the payments we make to you as income on your taxes. We are going to want you to indemnify us if you don't pay those taxes and the IRS comes after us.
Tory	Of course. We'll declare the money. We don't want any trouble from the IRS. One other thing before you go. What about the Screen Actors Guild? JTS has signed onto the SAG union contract, hasn't it? (I did see that on the Internet.) Will that affect our contract?

| Mia | Yes, we've signed onto the SAG agreement, but you don't have to worry about that. It just regulates what we pay our people. [Cell phone rings again.] And, on that note, I must go. I'll have our lawyer draft up a contract and send it to you. |
| Tory | Good. Thanks a lot. I'll e-mail you about my little proposition to lower the daily regular rate tomorrow. I think you'll find it worth some serious consideration. |

E-Mail String Between Victoria B. Green-Gardner and Mia Kandu

To: Mia Kandu   Sent: 9/2/15, 8:30 a.m.

From: Victoria B. Green-Gardner

Subject: Possible Discount on Basic Daily Rate

Hi Mia.

I really enjoyed our meeting yesterday. Thanks for spending so much time going over the details.

As promised, I'm sending along my thoughts about something JTS could do in order to lower the $1,100 basic daily rate for using the Store as a location. By now, you've spent enough time at the Store to know that Troy and I are especially fond of "green" toys and of "greenness" in general. We are committed to minimizing our own negative impact on the environment and to teaching kids how to be "green" as well.

So, do you think that JTS would consider providing an employee designated as the "Green Production Assistant"? That person would be dedicated to minimizing the environmental impact of your film. JTS would pay and supervise the person and we could agree about that person's duties.

Let me know what you think.

Sustainably Yours,

Tory

* * *

Reply from: Mia Kandu   Sent: 9/2/15, 9:12 a.m.

To: Victoria B. Green-Gardner

Re: Possible Discount on Basic Daily Rate

Good Morning, Tory.

Wow! So this is your mysterious proposal. I'm interested in hearing more. JTS has never done anything like have a Green Production Assistant before, but we're a young, eco-friendly bunch, so we might be willing to try it. Give me a basic outline of what you'd expect that person to do. And, of course, how much would you lower the basic daily rate?

Thanks, Mia

* * *

To: Mia Kandu   Sent: 9/2/15, 11:14 a.m.

From: Victoria B. Green-Gardner

Subject: Possible Discount on Basic Daily Rate

Mia—Sorry I couldn't get back to your sooner. Things are crazy around here today. We're having a sale on beach toys and every Mom and Dad in the neighborhood has been in here snatching up our pails and shovels made from recycled plastic grocery bags. Troy's back in the play room/storytime theater area performing stories featuring his action figures—Glenna the Go-Green Goddess and Trey the Treehugging Troll. I've been waiting on all of the customers myself. (Everyone else is on vacation.)

Enough about that. The Green Production Assistant (can we call this person the "GPA"?) would be responsible for seeing that there are at least two refuse stations with five cans each. They'd be labeled paper, metal, plastic, compost, and landfill. (Paper would be "clean" paper; soiled plates, utensils, paper cups, and napkins are considered landfill.) The GPA would also bring in water stations with 5-gallon jugs of water where the cast and crew could fill up their own water bottles (perhaps JTS has some with their logo on them) instead of using bottled water and creating so much waste. (It's a good idea to have people put their names on their water bottles with permanent markers, too.)

The cans would have to be lined with biodegradable clear bags—so the GPA can sort stuff if the cast and crew dump items into the wrong refuse cans. Also, the GPA would have to arrange for the refuse to be carted away at the end of each day in some energy efficient way.

How does that sound so far?

Sustainably Yours,

Tory

*   *   *

Reply from:	Mia Kandu	Sent: 9/2/15, 1:05 p.m.

To:	Victoria B. Green-Gardner

Re:	Possible Discount on Basic Daily Rate

Dear Tory:

It doesn't sound that practical because I think most of the waste accumulated will be from food. The craft services and catering companies we usually use aren't very eco-minded. We can't change that since we have such a good deal with them. How would the GPA control them? Any ideas?

*   *   *

To:	Mia Kandu	Sent: 9/2/15, 3:30 p.m.

From:	Victoria B. Green-Gardner

Subject:	Possible Discount on Basic Daily Rate

Mia:

I understand the problem. What about supplying craft services and the caterers with compostable utensils, cups, plates, bowls, and napkins? That would be a big help. Oh, but that brings up another important item. Education! The GPA would have to educate everyone—the whole cast and crew, including craft services and catering—about what it means to be a green production. The GPA would come in at the beginning and talk to everyone (briefly) about what to put in which trash cans and how to use the water stations.

I would want the GPA to be hired a few weeks before filming starts at the Store. That way, the GPA could have some time to evaluate the location and figure out where to put the refuse cans and the water stations.

Yours in Greenness,

Tory

*   *   *

Reply from: Mia Kandu   Sent: 9/2/15, 3:45 p.m.

To: Victoria B. Green-Gardner

Re: Possible Discount on Basic Daily Rate

Okay, Mia, so tell me what the lower rate would be. Then I can take this to the Producer and Director and we can decide whether we're willing to do it.

*   *   *

To: Mia Kandu   Sent: 9/2/15, 4:12 p.m.

From: Victoria B. Green-Gardner

Subject: Possible Discount on Basic Daily Rate

Mia—If JTS agrees to do everything I've mentioned, we'll reduce the basic daily rate to $900 a day. And we'll go even lower if your GPA proves to be effective.

Tory

*   *   *

Reply from: Mia Kandu   Sent: 9/2/15, 4:15 p.m.

From: Victoria B. Green-Gardner

Re: Possible Discount on Basic Daily Rate

Tory—Please stop teasing me like this. What goals would the GPA have to meet? How would we measure the GPA's effectiveness?

Mia

*   *   *

To: Mia Kandu   Sent: 9/2/15, 4:25 p.m.

From: Victoria B. Green-Gardner

Subject: Measuring the GPA's Effectiveness

My Dear Mia:

I did not intend to tease you. Troy and I want to be involved in measuring the GPA's effectiveness half way through the initial filming. Before filming begins, we could get together with you (or anyone else you designate) and write up some goals for the GPA. Having those goals in place from the beginning would be a prerequisite for JTS getting the chance to further lower the basic daily rate.

Halfway through the filming at the Store, Troy and I would sit down with the GPA and go over the goals and determine whether they've been met. We'd then send you an e-mail lowering the basic daily rate further by anywhere from $100 to $500 per day, depending on the GPA's effectiveness rating.

Sound good?

* * *

Reply from:	Mia Kandu	Sent: 9/2/15, 5:13 p.m.
To:	Victoria B. Green-Gardner	
Re:	Possible Discount on Basic Daily Rate	

OMG! My head is spinning. I'm signing off for today, but I am going to think more about this and get back to you in the morning.

Mia

* * *

To:	Mia Kandu	Sent: 9/3/15, 6:00 a.m.
From:	Victoria B. Green-Gardner	
Subject:	Your Agreement to Green Filmmaking!	

Dear Mia:

I guess the subject line of this e-mail is rather optimistic. I'm up very early today, excited by the prospect of working with you to see that JTS makes the right decision and commits itself to going green, at least in a small way.

Since you seemed so overwhelmed by my green suggestions yesterday afternoon, why don't you have your lawyers leave them out of the draft contract and I'll have our lawyers put them in? I just need to get you to confirm that JTS has agreed to everything we've "spoken" about in these e-mails. Last night, I went over everything with Troy and he, too, was enthusiastic—especially since his characters, Glenna and Trey, are going to be shown in the film.

Don't you think that JTS would like to put something in the movie credits about its commitment to green filmmaking? Wouldn't that get you some additional good publicity? "Please Wink Back" will not only be a delightful romantic comedy, but it will be a film made by environmentally responsible people. If you have any trouble selling this idea to your bosses, tell them to think about their children and their grandchildren, who are learning all about going green in school. Wouldn't the producer and director like to brag about how they hired a GPA on one of their films? It makes them sound so cool!

I hope to hear back from you soon.

In Green We Trust,

Tory

*   *   *

Reply from: Mia Kandu   Sent: 9/3/15, 2:16 p.m.

To: Victoria B. Green-Gardner

Re: Your Agreement to Green Filmmaking!

Tenacious Tory:

I just got out of a very long meeting. JTS agrees to hire a GPA and have that person do everything you mentioned. Hurray.

Mia

*   *   *

To: Mia Kandu   Sent: 9/3/15, 2:30 p.m.

From: Victoria B. Green-Gardner

Subject: Clarification

Hi Mia.

I laughed when you called me "Tenacious Tory."

Just to clarify, JTS will hire the GPA a few weeks before filming begins at the Store and the GPA will perform the duties we spoke about. And JTS will also pay for all of the materials and supplies the GPA will need to carry out those duties, right? Also, JTS is going to allow Troy and me to help the GPA set goals. We'll also get to evaluate whether the GPA has met those goals halfway through the filming schedule at the Store. If she or he has met the goals, then we'll further reduce the basic daily rate accordingly.

Finally, our lawyer will add these things into the contract draft that your lawyer supplies.

Okay? Are you smiling out there?

Tory :)

*   *   *

Reply from: Mia Kandu   Sent: 9/3/15, 2:40 p.m.

To: Victoria B. Green-Gardner

Re: Clarification

Hi Tory.

That sounds about right to me. You can expect to have our draft in your hands in five or six days.

I may seem like I'm not very "green," but I do buy all of my clothes at a vintage clothing store.

Looking forward to working with you on finalizing the contract,

Mia Kandu

Location and Product Placement Release Agreement Between This Is Just To Say, Inc. and Green Gardner Toy Store, Inc.

WHEREAS, This Is Just To Say, Inc. wants to film part of its movie, "Please Wink Back" at a toy store and believes that Treehuggers is an appropriate site; and

WHEREAS, This Is Just To Say, Inc. also wants to show the Glenna and Trey dolls in the movie and Green Gardner is desirous of said result;

NOW THEREFORE, in consideration of the mutual promises contained herein, and for good and valuable consideration, the receipt and sufficiency of which is hereby acknowledged, confirmed, agreed, and recognized by all parties, it is agreed that:

Green Gardner hereby grants to JTS, its successors, assigns and licensees, the right to photograph, reproduce, and use (either accurately or with such liberties as deemed necessary) the exteriors and interiors of the premises located at 52313 North Clark Street, Chicago, Illinois 60640, and to bring personnel and equipment onto the premises and remove same. JTS agrees to pay Green Gardner a basic daily fee of $1,100 per day for said rights, unless otherwise agreed. JTS is responsible for paying Gardner Green $100 per hour for every hour after 7 p.m. that JTS continues filming (the "Overtime Fee").

JTS may have access to the premises on or about January 11, 2016, and may continue access thereof until the completion of the proposed scenes and work, estimated to require about 30 consecutive days, exclusive of set-up and take-down. However, in the event of illness of actors, director, or other essential artists and crew, or weather conditions, or any other occurrence beyond JTS's control, preventing JTS from starting work on the date designated above, or in the event of damaged or imperfect film or equipment, JTS shall have the right to use the premises at a later date to be mutually agreed upon.

This Location Release Agreement is in connection with the motion picture tentatively entitled "Please Wink Back" and includes the right to re-use the photography in connection with other motion pictures as JTS, its successors, assigns and licensees will elect, and, in connection with the exhibition, advertising and promotion thereof, in any manner whatsoever and at any time in any part of said universe.

JTS agrees to hold Green Gardner harmless and free from any claims for damage or injury arising during JTS's occupancy of the premises and arising out of JTS's negligence thereon, and to leave the premises in as good order and condition as when received by Green Gardner, provided, reasonable wear and tear, and use herein permitted excepted and acknowledged by Gardner Green to be negligible.

Green Gardner acknowledges that, in photographing the premises, JTS is not in any way depicting or portraying Tory or Troy in the motion picture, either directly or indirectly. Neither Tory nor Troy will assert or maintain against JTS any claim of any kind or nature whatsoever, including, without limitation, those based upon invasion of privacy or other civil rights, defamation, libel or slander, in connection with the exercise of the permission herein granted. Green-Gardner grants JTS the right to use its products, Glenda and Tree (two action figures created by the owner) in the film and to use them in a positive way rather than in a manner disparaging of their essences. JTS does not have to pay for this right, as GG recognizes and affirms.

Green Gardner swears that Green Gardner is the owner(s) and/or authorized representative(s) of the premises, and that Green Gardner has the authority to grant JTS the permission and rights herein granted, and that no one else's permission is required.

This Agreement supersedes all other agreements of the parties, which are all subsumed herein.

Signature of Owner or Authorized Agent:

_____

Date: _____

2C: E-MAIL FROM ASSOCIATES TO CLIENT RE ANSWER TO POTENTIAL ETHICAL QUESTION

Instructions

A. **Summary:** You represent Green-Gardner Toy Company (the "Toy Company"). Analyze the scenario described below to determine whether your firm will be violating any ethical rules if you follow your client's instructions and do not point out the mistake in the draft contract prepared by the attorney representing This Is Just To Say, Inc. (the "Producer"). Consider also whether there are any business reasons in favor of pointing out the mistake. Draft an e-mail to Victoria B. Green-Gardner, summarizing your answer and recommending a course of action.

B. **Scenario:** After a lengthy meeting and lively e-mail correspondence with Tory Green, Mia Kandu directed the Producer's attorney to send Tory a draft contract. In reviewing the draft contract and checking it against the transcript of Tory's meeting with Mia, you find that it contains a mistake about the hourly overtime fee that the Producer has agreed to pay whenever the filming goes later than 7 p.m. (The draft says that the overtime fee is $100 per hour; the parties agreed during their meeting to an overtime fee of $75 per hour.) This mistake benefits your client (the Toy Company) and does not amount to a large amount of money for a film production company like the Producer.

   When Tory reviewed the draft contract before sending it to your partner, she noticed the mistake, too. She has since told you that she doesn't think Mia or the Producer's attorney will catch the error and she does not want to alert them to it.

C. **Preparing the E-Mail to Client:** In your brief e-mail to the client, emphasize the legal and business risks for the client over any potential ethical risks to you, the attorney. Use your judgment about how much to include regarding the potential ethical risks. Perhaps you will have to explain those risks to convince the client to change its position.

   Take every step you can to assure that your e-mail remains confidential and protected by the attorney/client privilege. Send it only to Victoria B. Green-Gardner. Mark it "Confidential: Attorney/Client Privilege." Explicitly request that Tory not forward the e-mail to anyone else, which could destroy the e-mail's privileged status. At the end of the e-mail, include a standard notification-to-unintended-recipients box like the following:

This communication is from Payne & Associates. E-mail text or attachments may contain information that is confidential and may also be privileged. This communication is for the exclusive use of the intended recipient(s). If you have received this communication in error, please return it with the title "received in error" to Sue Payne, at Payne & Associates (payne.s.@lawfirm.com) Then delete the e-mail and destroy any copies of it.

D. Tone of E-Mail: Remember that you are drafting an e-mail to the client, not to your best friend. Draft the e-mail in Plain English, using a professional tone. Do not use abbreviations or acronyms (like "OMG") and do not type in all caps for emphasis or insert any emoticons. Your e-mail to the client should be only slightly less formal than a letter to the client. You are writing the e-mail presumably because it's faster to write and faster to send than a formal letter. While it might be better to communicate the results of your review via telephone, your client wants a written record for its files.

Remember to always keep your audience in mind. Tory is a business owner and entrepreneur, not a lawyer. Explain everything in terms that she may be able to understand.

E. Additional Instructions: Your professor may provide you with additional instructions regarding this assignment.

2D: ASSEMBLING THE FRAME: DRAFTING THE TITLE, PREAMBLE, BACKGROUND, WORDS OF AGREEMENT, DEFINITIONS, AND SIGNATURE LINES

Instructions

A. Summary: Each of you must draft the "frame" of the Toy Purchase Agreement, using the information contained in the documents in Assignment 2B. The frame includes the Title, Preamble, Background, Words of Agreement, Definitions, and Signature Lines.

B. Legal Research: As you may know, in practice, you should not draft a contract in an area in which you have no legal expertise unless you acquire the expertise or seek help from another attorney who possesses it. See the Model Rules of Professional Conduct, Rule 1.1, Competence (with Comment). For the purposes of this assignment, you will focus on contract drafting rather than on legal research. Your professor will provide you with the legal expertise you need or direct you to another reliable source.

C. **Precedent:** For this assignment, you may use the sample contracts cited below and only those sample contracts. This is a "canned precedent" assignment. In other words, in order to keep you focused on drafting rather than on searching for precedent, we are restricting you to the use of a limited body (or "can") of precedent. These are examples of the precedent you would be likely to find if you did your own Internet search. You may not use any precedent other than the Draft Location and Product Placement Release Agreement that This Is Just To Say, Inc. provided to Tory Green-Gardner, the sample contracts listed here, and any model contracts that your professor provides. If you do adapt or adopt any language from the samples provided, then you must cite your source, even if you have not quoted it directly. Your professor will tell you what citation format she requires.

> **Caution # 1:** Remember that every contract "breaks the mold." That is, each contract memorializes the terms of a particular deal. If you rely too heavily on precedent, you are bound to make some serious mistakes.
>
> **Caution # 2:** View each sample contract with a critical eye, applying all of the contract drafting principles that you have learned thus far.

Can of Precedent[4]

http://www.cifvf.ca/English/locationrelease.eng_Final.pdf
http://www.rrhobbs.us/locationcontract.doc
http://www.vlaa.org/assets/documents/SampleLocationAgreement.pdf
http://filmmakeriq.com/development/contracts-and-law/588-free-film-contracts-and-forms.html
http://rtf.utexas.edu/sp/groups/public/@commrtf/documents/form/prod75_027287.pdf

---

D. **The "Frame" Metaphor:** Some parts of a contract are traditional and easily drafted using models. They create a "frame" for the business provisions of the contract. The Title, Preamble, Words of Agreement, and Signature Lines are rudimentary parts of the contract's frame.

---

4. Your professor may substitute other citations for the ones included here.

The Definitions and Background sections, while more difficult to draft, still should not contain covenants, conditions precedent, representations and warranties, and statements of discretionary authority—otherwise known as "operative" provisions. For that reason, the Background and Definitions sections are also part of the contract's frame, stabilizing it by adding more information about the deal and preparing the reader for the "picture" containing the operative provisions of the deal.

A "model" contract is different from a "sample" contract in that a "model" is a contract worth imitating. Applying the basic contract drafting principles that you have learned so far, you may examine the samples in the "Can of Precedent," above, in order to determine if any elements of their frames are worthy of imitation. However, in drafting the frame of the Movie Location and Product Placement Agreement, you are most likely going to rely on the model Leaf Disposal Services Agreement or any other "model" agreement that your professor has supplied. The precedent will become more useful when you fill in the picture of the contract, as required by Assignment 2E.

Professors who teach contract drafting use various images to convey what contracts drafters do. Therefore, you may hear someone else refer to the "frame" as the "skeleton" of the contract and the "picture" as the "meat on the bones." If it helps you to think of the contract that way, please feel free to do so. The purpose of these metaphors is to help you break down the drafting process into manageable parts.

E. **The Preamble: An Example of Learning from a Model:** Provided that you have the correct information, you can draft a Preamble for the Movie Location and Product Placement Agreement by following the pattern of the Preamble in the model Leaf Disposal Services Agreement, reprinted below.

LEAF DISPOSAL SERVICES AGREEMENT

Leaf Disposal Services Agreement made this 10th day of October 2007, between SpinGazer, Inc., a Delaware corporation with its principal place of business located at 1200 Ridge Avenue, Evanston, Illinois 60201 (the "Company"), and Fallen Leaves, Inc., an Illinois corporation with its principal place of business located at 2025 North Clark Street, Chicago, Illinois 60614 (the "Provider").

Since both parties to the Movie Location and Product Placement Agreement are corporations, you can draft the Preamble by closely following the model. Note that you must include the state in which each company is incorporated, as well as the addresses of their principal places of business. Insert shorthand names for each party after all of the identifying information about each party. Believe it or not, there could be more than one "Green-Gardner Toy Company" or "This Is Just To Say, Inc." Inserting the shorthand names for the parties in the right place assures that you have correctly identified the parties to this contract.

Choose shorthand names for the parties that are on the same level of generality. For example, if you select "GGT" for the Green-Gardner Toy Company, then you should probably select "JTS" for This Is Just To Say, Inc. If you want to avoid using acronyms, you may use "the Toy Company" for the Green-Gardner Toy Company and "the Producer" for This Is Just To Say, Inc.

When you draft the Preamble of your contract, pay careful attention to punctuation. The Preamble contains a lot of information and is difficult to read if not punctuated properly. Moreover, aside from the Title, the Preamble is the very first thing that the reader will encounter in your contract. Even though it is formulaic, you can set a good tone by drafting it so that it reads smoothly. Proper punctuation helps.

Finally, you and your professor are likely to spend some time talking about what date you should insert in the Preamble. When is the contract "made"? Is it the same date when the contract is signed? Is this date different from the effective date of the term? Also, sometimes the date in the Preamble is preceded by the words "as of." Under what circumstances is it appropriate to use those words? Even a formulaic Preamble can present interesting questions that you are likely to bandy about in class.

F. **Title, Words of Agreement, and Signature Lines:** You and your professor will discuss what to call this contract. For the sake of convenience, I have referred to it as the *Movie Location and Product Placement Agreement*, but you are not required to use that title.

The Words of Agreement used in the model Leaf Disposal Services Agreement are simple. After the Background section, insert, "Accordingly, the parties agree as follows:". In most contracts, at about this point in the contract, you will see a lengthy "consideration" provision that sounds like complete gobbledygook. You and your professor are likely to discuss whether a formal statement of consideration is necessary if the contract itself makes it amply clear that consideration for the transaction does exist. The drafter of the Leaf Disposal Services Agreement has concluded that the contract does not require a formal statement of consideration.

You can easily imitate the Signature Lines and get them right. The Signature Lines from the Leaf Disposal Services Agreement are reprinted below.

AGREED:

SPINGAZER, INC.   **FALLEN LEAVES, INC.**

By: _____   By: _____
     Jackie Spingazer   Leif E. Liminator

Title: Director of Operations   Title: Supervisor

Since both parties to the Movie Location and Product Placement Agreement are corporations, you should follow the model closely. The names in boldface, all capital letters, above the Signature Lines are the formal names of the parties to the contract—not the shorthand names that you chose in the Preamble and used throughout the rest of the contract. So, where you see **SPINGAZER, INC.** and **FALLEN LEAVES, INC.**, above, you would substitute **GREEN-GARDNER TOY COMPANY** and **THIS IS JUST TO SAY, INC.**

> **Note:** Generally, it is a good idea to put your client's signature line first. Believe it or not, this sometimes matters to the client.

For "Green-Gardner Toy Company," insert a signature line for Victoria B. Green-Gardner and for "This Is Just To Say, Inc.," insert a signature line for Mia Kandu. Put the word "By" in front of each of their Signature Lines. Underneath each of their Signature Lines, type their names, in upper and lowercase letters. Then, insert their titles.

G. **Background:** The purpose of the Background section is twofold—to put the Agreement in context and to express the intentions of the parties.

You may be accustomed to seeing this section called "Recitals" and containing a list of "WHEREAS" clauses ending with the crescendo "NOW THEREFORE" clause. Plain English drafters avoid those clauses like the plague. Instead, draft the Background section in smooth prose. This is probably the only place in the contract where you will get to tell a little story. Use it well. Who are the parties? What do they do? Why are they entering into this deal? The Background section should not be too long or too lopsided (containing more information about one party than the other).

The Background section is a place where you should avoid following your models too closely. It is not as formulaic as the Preamble, for example. Ask yourself: What do my readers need to know about the parties? About what happened before (if anything) and about what is about to happen (this transaction)?

Remember that you should not include any operative provisions in the Background section. Be very careful not to include any covenants, conditions precedent, representations and warranties, or statements of discretionary authority here. The courts generally will not give effect to operative language contained in a Background section. And, if you include a covenant in the Background section, you run the risk of forgetting to include it in the body of the contract, where it would actually obligate a party to do something.

Sometimes the parties want to clarify their intentions early in a contract. Even though the Background section should not contain operative provisions, it can contain a statement of the parties' intentions. Sometimes, if there is a contractual dispute, the court will give effect to a statement of intentions included in the Background section instead of, or in addition to, admitting parol evidence of those intentions.

H. Definitions: The model Leaf Disposal Services Agreement gives you some limited guidance about how to draft the definitions. It contains the prefatory language below.

As used in this Agreement, the terms defined in the preamble have their assigned meanings and the following terms have the meanings assigned to them in this Article.

If you have defined any terms, in-text, in the Background section, you must add the words "and in the Background section" to the prefatory language after the words "in the preamble." That way, you will not have to include any cross-references to those definitions in the Definitions article itself.

By looking at the model agreement, you will see that most definitions use the verb "means" or "includes but does not include." You will also see that in-text definitions found in the body of the contract (but not in the preamble or Background section) are cross-referenced here, using the verb phrase "has the meaning assigned in."

You and your professor will discuss how to choose what to define and how to draft the definitions. Remember that definitions are declarations and should not contain any operative language—no covenants, conditions, representations and warranties, or statements of discretionary authority. Think of a definition as a statement of what a term means whenever you encounter it used with a capital letter in the contract. If you want a party to undertake any kind of obligation, you must include it in the body of the contract rather than in a definition.

> ***Important Note About Drafting Definitions:*** In practice, lawyers hardly ever draft a complete Definitions article before they draft the rest of the contract. In a sense, asking you to draft the Definitions before you draft the rest of the contract is an artificial exercise. Nevertheless, it is a good exercise and it may save you some time and energy. It forces you, as a novice contract drafter, to think in advance about what terms you may need to define. You can draft a definition of the "location," for example, because you know that you will need to refer to it over and over again.
>
> Moreover, drafting definitions in advance will prevent you from making the mistake of using too many in-text definitions. When a Definitions article contains too many cross-references to in-text definitions, the reader is forced to hop all over the contract to find out what things mean. Instead, by defining most terms in the Definitions article itself, you keep the reader happy by feeding her information. You also take the opportunity to educate her about the deal a bit before she launches into the contract. This may sound like a litigation drafting concept, but it holds true for contract drafting as well. As your reader moves into the contract, after reading a fully developed Definitions article, she is more likely to understand the rest of the contract.

If you remember to consider your audience(s), you will be more likely to achieve the goal of clear communication. Transactional attorneys who fail to consider their audience(s) give transactional attorneys a bad name.

I. **Additional Instructions:** Your professor may provide you with additional instructions regarding this assignment.

2E: FILLING IN THE PICTURE: DRAFTING THE CONTRACT'S OPERATIVE PROVISIONS

Instructions

A. **Summary:** This assignment assumes that you have already drafted the "frame" of the contract as required by Assignment 2D—or that your professor has asked you to skip that assignment and concentrate on "filling in the picture." Using the deal facts contained in the documents in

Assignment 2B, draft all of the operative provisions of the Movie Location and Product Placement Agreement. The "operative" provisions do not include the "frame" of the contract—the Title, Preamble, Background, Words of Agreement, Definitions, and Signature Lines.

B. **Preparation for Filling in the Picture:** Before you begin to fill in the picture, you must do two things. First, review the Can of Precedent identified in Assignment 2D. Determine which topics are generally covered in a Movie Location and Product Placement Agreement and evaluate each contract to see if it contains any language that you think you may be able to adapt or adopt for use in your contract.

Second, if you have identified any legal issues presented by the transaction, then you must research them. Seek direction from your professor in order to avoid spending too much time on legal research. Your focus should be on drafting the contract.

C. **Filling in the Picture:** To fill in the picture, you must draft all of the operative provisions of the contract and decide how to organize them. Your professor will help you develop the basic skills you need to take the terms of the deal and translate them into contract concepts—covenants, conditions precedent, representations and warranties, statements of discretionary authority, and declarations.[5]

In practice, some call this *memorializing* the terms of the deal, which basically means getting the terms of the deal down on paper so that they have a legal effect. The paper (or contract) is the *memorial.* The parties should be able to turn to the contract whenever they have any questions about their rights and duties with regard to the particular transaction.

D. **Organization—Naming and Ordering the Articles and Sections:** Some provisions are traditionally placed in certain spots. For example, after the Definitions article, some drafters include a brief article containing the main covenants of the deal. One contract drafting expert, Tina L. Stark, calls this brief article the "subject matter performance provision."[6] The subject matter performance provision in the model Leaf Disposal Services Agreement follows.

---

5. Tina L. Stark, *Drafting Contracts: How and Why Lawyers Do What They Do* 9-10 (Aspen 2007) (describes the contract concepts as the "building blocks" of the contract and the process of converting business terms into contract concepts as a "translation skill").
6. *Id.* at 39-40.

Article III. Summary of Services and Fees

Section 3.01 Services and Fees. Subject to the provisions of this Agreement, the Provider shall perform the Services described in Article IV. To compensate the Provider for performing the Services, the Company shall pay the Provider the fees and reimburse the Provider for the expenses described in Article V.

The drafter of the model Leaf Disposal Services Agreement put the subject matter performance provision after the Term article. While the exact order of these provisions sometimes varies, remember that the subject matter performance provision, the Term, and the Closing articles should appear near the beginning of the contract.

It is sometimes helpful to think of the subject matter performance provision as a thesis statement plus roadmap. It tells you the "main idea" (or "primary covenants") of the contract and points you to the places in the contract where you can find out more details about those covenants.

After the subject matter performance provision, the Term article, and the Closing article, the reader expects to find information about what the Green-Gardner Toy Company is going to provide and how much This Is Just To Say, Inc. is going to pay. Therefore, you must put the articles covering those topics close to the beginning of the contract.

At the end of the contract, right before the Signature Lines, place the contract's boilerplate provisions (sometimes called *General Provisions*). The Termination and Dispute Resolution articles generally come right before the boilerplate.

So, with the parts of the contract in their traditional places, and allowing for some flexibility in their exact order, your contract (not including the frame) will look something like this:

Summary of Services and Fees
Term
Closing (if any)
The Location
The Product Placement
Fees and Expenses
[OTHER TOPICS TO BE COVERED]
Dispute Resolution
Termination
General Provisions

Note that the above italicized headings are offered as an example only. They are not set in stone. You are encouraged to draft your own appropriate headings for the articles you include in the contract.

One of the biggest challenges that a drafter faces is how to organize the business provisions not specifically listed above — that is, how to organize those "other topics to be covered." Start by making a list of every deal term not addressed in the named articles. Then, group those deal terms by topic and select a good name for the article covering that topic. Remember that "Toy Company's Obligations" and "Producer's Responsibilities" are contract concepts, not topics. If you use a heading like "Toy Company's Obligations," you are indicating to the reader that all of the Toy Company's obligations are contained under that heading. More likely, the Toy Company's obligations are scattered throughout the contract.

Choose article names (and section names as well) that are specific and clear. Instead of "Toy Company's Obligations," for example, you may have articles or sections called "Restrictions on Location Use" and "Modifications to the Location." Either of these articles or sections may contain obligations and responsibilities of one or both parties.

If you find that you have a number of miscellaneous deal terms that do not seem to fit anywhere, give them another look before deciding to create single-section articles. Single-section articles (other than the subject matter performance provision and the Term article) can make the particular topic seem like an undeveloped afterthought or, conversely, give the particular topic too much weight. It is better to put the miscellaneous deal term into the article it relates to the most, even if it is not a perfect fit.

Once you have found a place for every deal term and named the articles you want to include in the contract, decide what order to put them in. Generally, place the articles in order from most important topic to least important topic. However, if you are describing a process, it may make more sense to put some of the articles in chronological order. There is no magic bullet of contract organization. However, it is very important to remember your audience(s). Ask yourself what your reader needs to know and when your reader needs to know it. Also, remember the terms of the deal. For example, if your client stressed that it was very concerned about the Producer maintaining green production standards, then you may want to move that topic up near the beginning of the contract for emphasis.

E. **Boilerplate Provisions:** The documents may not contain all of the facts you need in order to select the appropriate boilerplate provisions to include in your contract. Follow your professor's instructions regarding which boilerplate to include. A valuable resource to help you understand the history and evolution of various boilerplate provisions is the book *Negotiating and Drafting Contract Boilerplate*, edited and co-authored by Tina L. Stark (American Lawyer Media 2003). Your professor may also ask you to complete Assignment 2G, which requires you to adjust the standard boilerplate language to address some of the parties' specific concerns.

F. Additional Instructions: Your professor may provide you with additional instructions regarding this assignment.

2F: PUTTING THE PICTURE IN THE FRAME: FINISHING THE DRAFT CONTRACT

Instructions

A. Summary: You will now insert the "picture" that you drafted in response to Assignment 2E into the "frame" that you drafted in response to Assignment 2D. The result will be one completed draft of a Movie Location and Product Placement Agreement (with a title that you have selected).

B. The Process: Inserting the picture into the frame is not merely a mechanical process. Once you have merged the two documents together, you must make sure that the picture fits the frame properly; in other words, you must review the draft contract as a whole and ask yourself at least the following questions:

- ☐ Is the Title I chose for the contract still appropriate?
- ☐ Have I consistently referred to the parties to the contract using the shorthand names that I gave them in the Preamble?
- ☐ Do the full party names in the Preamble (not the shorthand names) match the full party names above the Signature Lines?
- ☐ Does the date in the Preamble reflect the date when the contract is made? If this is different from the effective date of the contract, have I clarified that in the body of the contract?
- ☐ Do the addresses in the Preamble match the addresses in the "Notice" provision included in the boilerplate?
- ☐ Did I include enough information in the Background section? Is there anything else that I may want to add to that section? Is there anything I may want to take out?
- ☐ Do I use my defined terms whenever it is appropriate? [*Note:* This is called "letting your defined terms do their work."]
- ☐ Did I remember to capitalize my defined terms in the body of the contract?
- ☐ Are there any lengthy phrases that I repeat more than once that could perhaps be defined terms?
- ☐ Are there any concepts that I repeat in different ways each time that I should perhaps be saying the same way each time? Would a defined term help?
- ☐ Are there any defined terms that I never use or use only once? (If so, you probably do not need to define that term.)

☐ Have I included a cross-reference to every in-text definition in the Definitions article? Are my definitions still in alphabetical order?

☐ Whenever I use a cross-reference, have I referenced the correct article or section?

☐ Have I used cross-references in the body of the contract to help the reader understand the relationship between parts of the contract?

☐ Are all of my article and section numbers in order? Does each have an appropriate heading?

☐ In the "Survivability" boilerplate provision, have I listed all of the sections of the contract that will survive the early termination of the contract or the end of the term?

☐ Do all of the parts of the contract work well together?

Once you have answered all of these questions and made any necessary adjustments to the contract, you can move into the editing and proofreading stage described next.

C. **Editing and Proofreading:** Using the Contract Drafting Checklist provided in Appendix 3, go back over your draft contract again. The checklist is set up to help you take the long view first. Think about the transaction. Have you captured all of the terms of the deal? Have you translated them into the correct contract concepts? Have you answered all questions about the rights and duties of the parties with regard to this transaction? Have you raised any questions without answering them? Is your contract well organized, coherent, and coordinated? Does it read smoothly? Is it easy to follow?

The checklist then asks you to look at some formatting issues that are directly related to readability. Review those issues, remembering also that well-chosen headings and the judicious use of "white space" enhance the readability of a contract. Do not remove headings or white space in order to make sure that you do not exceed the page limit for this assignment. If you need guidance about how to avoid exceeding the page limit, seek your professor's help.

Following the checklist, now make sure that your contract contains all of the essential parts. Then, review each part. Finally, under the broad heading "Plain English," the checklist directs you to make sure that you have not made any grammatical, mechanical, or typographical errors.

Once you have gone through the checklist, prepare your contract for submission by proofreading it carefully, using the proofreading tips and tricks contained in Appendix 5. Finally, go back to the original assignment sheet and verify that you have followed all of the directions regarding submitting the contract to your professor. There is something particularly disturbing about a transactional attorney who fails to follow directions. Failing to follow directions indicates that you are not detail oriented, which, in practice, can make your supervisor and your client mistrust you. It can also lead to a dangerous loss of credibility with the attorney representing the other side.

D. **Submitting the Contract:** Do one final thing before you submit your contract: Make sure that you are turning in a clean copy. That is, make sure that you have eliminated any highlighting or comments to yourself that you may have used during the drafting process. Practicing attorneys, both litigators and deal lawyers, can tell many war stories about forgetting to delete comments or critiques before filing documents or sending drafts to the other side. You do not want to make such an embarrassing mistake. You may also want to make sure that your document does not contain any hidden personal or metadata, such as information about when you finished the assignment. Check the software you are using to figure out how to eliminate that information.

E. **Additional Instructions:** Your professor may provide you with additional instructions regarding this assignment.

2G: IN-CLASS WORKSHOP: BOILERPLATE PROVISIONS

Instructions

A. **Summary:** In pairs, triads, or larger teams (as directed by your professor), consider each business issue presented. Re-draft each basic boilerplate provision to address the business issue. You may sometimes decide that re-drafting the provision is not the best solution. If so, please suggest another solution.

B. **New Deal Facts:** This workshop introduces some new facts regarding the Movie Location and Product Placement Agreement that you are drafting. You must incorporate these new deal facts into the final draft of your contract.

C. **Caveat:** This workshop does not address all of the boilerplate provisions that you should include in the contract.

D. **Source of the Basic Boilerplate Provisions:** Each basic boilerplate provision is taken from *Drafting Contracts: How and Why Lawyers Do What They Do*, by Tina L. Stark (Aspen 2007), cited as "Stark, *Drafting Contracts.*" Remember that, in Tina Stark's words, the standard provisions "are not paradigms of perfect drafting." Rather, they are "intended to give you a sense of the provisions that you will typically see." Stark, *Drafting Contracts* 167.

> **Note:** In drafting your answer, you may also wish to consult *Negotiating and Drafting Contract Boilerplate*, edited and co-authored by Tina L. Stark (American Lawyer Media 2003).

E. **Additional Instructions:** Your professor may provide you with additional instructions regarding this assignment.

EXERCISE I: ASSIGNMENT AND DELEGATION

BUSINESS ISSUE: This Is Just To Say, Inc. (the "Producer") is in the process of forming a subsidiary called Rom-Com Corporation ("Rom-Com"), which will produce and manage all of the romantic comedies that the Producer decides to film. The subsidiary is likely to be up and running by the middle of April 2016. The Producer wants to be able to assign its rights (such as its rights of access) and delegate its duties to Rom-Com so that Rom-Com can complete the film tentatively entitled "Please Wink Back," pay the Green-Gardner Toy Company (the "Toy Company"), and meet all of the Producer's other obligations under the Agreement.

The Toy Company is willing to let the Producer assign its rights and delegate its duties to Rom-Com but only to Rom-Com and not to any other company or subsidiary. However, the Toy Company wants to make sure that Rom-Com will assume the Producer's obligations in writing.

Meanwhile, the Producer remains adamantly opposed to allowing the Toy Company to assign any of its rights or delegate any of its duties. (Assume that this is a reasonable position for the Producer to take, given the unique nature of the toy store and the action figures involved in this deal.)

STANDARD PROVISION:

Assignment and Delegation. This Agreement cannot be assigned or delegated by the parties.

(Stark, *Drafting Contracts* 170-172.)

REVISED PROVISION (OR OTHER SOLUTION):

EXERCISE II: GOVERNING LAW

BUSINESS ISSUE: The Toy Company is an Illinois corporation operating only in Illinois. The Producer is a Delaware corporation with its principal place of business in California. As the Toy Company's attorney, you want Illinois law to apply because it is the law with which you and your client are most familiar. The Producer wants California law to apply because it is generally more favorable to filmmakers than the law of any other state. The parties are still arguing about this point.

What can you do to solve this problem?

STANDARD PROVISION:

Governing Law. This Agreement is to be governed by and construed in accordance with the laws of [insert name of state], without regard to its conflict of law principles.

(Stark, *Drafting Contracts* 173-174.)

REVISED PROVISION (OR OTHER SOLUTION):

EXERCISE III: NOTICE

BUSINESS ISSUE: If either party commits a material breach of the contract, the non-breaching party wants to be able to notify the breaching party of its desire to terminate the contract immediately by telephone. Both parties would like this kind of notice to be effective upon the representative of the non-breaching party speaking to the representative of the breaching party either live or via voicemail. The non-breaching party would then confirm the notice with an e-mail. Both parties want it to be clear exactly when the notice becomes effective.

STANDARD PROVISION:

Notice. All notices under this Agreement shall be given in writing.
(Stark, *Drafting Contracts* 175-176.)

REVISED PROVISION (OR OTHER SOLUTION):

EXERCISE IV: SEVERABILITY

BUSINESS ISSUE: Illinois is considering passing a new statute prohibiting out-of-state filmmakers from using Illinois locations unless they pay the State of Illinois a fee of $1 million per film (the "State Convenience Fee"). Both parties know about this proposed legislation. If this statute is passed during the Term, the Producer will not be able to pay the State Convenience Fee. Therefore, it will be illegal for the Filmmaker to continue filming at the Store.

What language can you add to the Severability provision to make it clear that the contract will terminate if a key provision is severed because it is illegal or unenforceable?

STANDARD PROVISION:

Severability. If any provision of this Agreement is illegal or unenforceable, that provision is severed from this Agreement and the other provisions remain in force.

(Stark, *Drafting Contracts* 176-177.)

REVISED PROVISION (OR OTHER SOLUTION):

_____

EXERCISE V: MERGER/INTEGRATION

BUSINESS ISSUE: Before entering into this Agreement—at the beginning of her first long meeting with Mia Kandu—Tory signed a Confidentiality Agreement (dated September 1, 2015) prohibiting the Toy Company from disclosing anything about its negotiations with the Producer (see agreement, reprinted below). The Producer insists that this Confidentiality Agreement should not be superseded by the Agreement, but still wants to include a Merger provision in the Agreement.

STANDARD PROVISION:

Merger. This Agreement states the full agreement between the parties and supersedes all prior negotiations and agreements.

(Stark, *Drafting Contracts* 178-179.)

* * *

Confidentiality Agreement

I, Victoria B. Green-Gardner, on behalf of Green-Gardner Toy Company (the "Toy Company"), hereby agree not to disclose to anyone but my spouse and my attorney anything about the Toy Company's negotiations with This Is Just To Say, Inc. (the "Producer") regarding the Producer's potential use of the Toy Company's property as a location for its film tentatively entitled "Please Wink Back."

GREEN-GARDNER TOY COMPANY

By: *Victoria B. Green-Gardner*

Dated: 9/1/2015

Witnessed by: *Mia Kandu*

* * *

REVISED PROVISION (OR OTHER SOLUTION):

EXERCISE VI: WAIVER OF JURY TRIAL

BUSINESS ISSUE: If the Toy Company and the Producer end up going to trial regarding anything related to the Agreement, the Toy Company wants to make sure that the Producer has no right to a jury trial. (Tory and Troy had a bad experience with a jury trial when T-4 had to sue Truly Green Toys, Inc. ("TGT") and Will I. Cheeter for misrepresentation and breach of warranty after Tory and Troy discovered that most of TGT's toys did not meet all of their "green" criteria. Cheeter used his considerable charm to convince the jury that the toys were "green enough.")

Tory has persuaded the Producer that the Producer should give up its right to trial by jury.

Re-draft the Waiver of Jury Trial provision to make it more likely than not that the court will enforce it.

> **Note:** If your textbook does not contain any information about how to draft a Waiver of Jury Trial, you may need to do a small amount of legal research on this issue.

STANDARD PROVISION:

> **Waiver of Jury Trial.** [Insert Party Name] waives its right to trial by jury in all matters involving this Agreement.
>
> (Stark, *Drafting Contracts* 175.)

REVISED PROVISION (OR OTHER SOLUTION):

2H: SIDE LETTER RE DOG'S APPEARANCE IN FILM

Instructions

A. **Summary:** Your client, the Green-Gardner Toy Company (the "Toy Company"), has asked you to draft a "side letter" memorializing a new, but not completely unrelated agreement it has struck with This Is Just To Say, Inc. (the "Producer"). Your client does not want to terminate the

Movie Location and Product Placement Agreement already in place (the "Agreement"); nor does it want to push the Producer into terminating the Agreement.

B. **Scenario:** Recently, the screenwriter revised the screenplay of the film and gave the film's main character, Walter, a dog. Apparently, the screenwriter wants a mechanism whereby Walter's thoughts can be revealed to the audience. Now, while working alone at the toy store, Walter frequently speaks aloud to his dog. Mia Kandu met Tory and Troy's two adorable golden doodles during the negotiations about the Movie Location and Product Placement Agreement. Mia wants to kill two birds with one stone by having one of the dogs co-star in the film (and eliminating the kennel fee for that dog). Tory and Troy agreed that the largest of their golden doodles, Gus, can co-star in the film. To learn about the facts of the deal, read the attached letter from Mia Kandu to Tory and Troy Green-Gardner.

C. **Side Letters, in General:** Do not look for an example of a "side letter" on the Internet or in forms books. Instead, with your professor's guidance, think this through.

   Side letters are generally used to clarify an issue in a contract or to address an issue that the parties have failed to cover in the contract. Collective bargaining agreements, for example, often have numerous side letters that become a part of the main agreement.

   Clients like the Toy Company will sometimes request that you draft a side letter because they believe that it will take you less time than drafting a separate contract and will therefore cost them less money (since you generally are billing them by the hour).

D. **Drafting the Side Letter:** Address the side letter from your client's representative, Victoria B. Green-Gardner, to the Producer's representative, Mia Kandu.

> **Note:** If you know that the Producer is represented by an attorney, then you—as attorney for the Toy Company—have an ethical obligation not to contact the Producer directly. However, Tory can communicate with Mia because the parties are not prohibited from talking to each other directly.

It is a good idea to think about a side letter as being a contract in its own right. Ask yourself what the consideration is for the dog's appearance in the film. Make sure that you clarify that the side letter concerns a bargained-for exchange by describing that exchange in the body of the letter.

> **Note:** You can accomplish this without including an archaic statement of consideration that is full of meaningless gobbledygook!

First, think about the Agreement and how the side letter will work with the Agreement. Include language clarifying that the side letter does not override the Agreement; nor is the side letter superseded by the Agreement. The side letter is, in effect, a written agreement amending the Agreement in certain limited ways.

In order to make sure that the side letter does not get lost or overlooked, make sure that you provide for it to be attached to and incorporated into the Agreement. Then, follow through, making sure that both the Toy Company and the Producer receive new copies of the Agreement with the signed Side Letter attached as an exhibit. (This is what you would do in real life. Your professor will let you know whether she wants you to do this for purposes of this assignment.)

Remember to include language stating that this side letter is the only amendment to the Agreement and that the remainder of the Agreement's provisions will remain in effect. Include signature and date lines for the parties (and title lines for their representatives, Victoria B. Green-Gardner and Mia Kandu). Tory will sign and date the letter, fill in her title, and mail it to Mia, who will sign on behalf of the Producer. The letter should include instructions for Mia to sign and return the letter to Tory as soon as possible. Remember to inform Tory that the side letter is not effective until it is signed by both parties.

E. **Additional Instructions:** Your professor may provide you with additional instructions regarding this assignment.

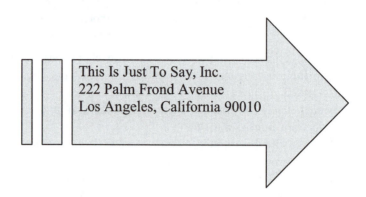

This Is Just To Say, Inc.
222 Palm Frond Avenue
Los Angeles, California 90010

December 14, 2015
Tory Green-Gardner
Green-Gardner Toy Company
Tory and Troy's Treehugger Toys
52313 N. Clark Street
Chicago, Illinois 60640

Dear Tory:

As I mentioned when we spoke, the screenwriter has added a dog to the script and we think that your golden doodle, Gus, is perfect for the part. You asked me to put the details in a letter, so here it is. Please do have your attorney change this into a side letter to our existing Movie Location and Product Placement Agreement.

In response to my question, you told me that Gus is a pure-bred golden doodle. What that means is that his Mom was 100% standard poodle and his Dad was 100% golden retriever. I am relying on that statement since our dog trainer believes that a pure-bred golden doodle is the only dog with the right temperament for this movie.

I promised that Gus will appear in 55% of the scenes in which the character "Walter" appears. I also said that the percentage would remain constant even after editing. In other words, while some scenes with Gus in them will wind up on the cutting room floor, Gus will still appear in 55% of the "Walter" scenes that ultimately wind up in the film.

You'll be present while Gus is on set, but you will not serve as Gus's trainer or acting coach. Our dog trainer, Ida Gimmepaw, will be Gus's trainer and acting coach. You'll be present during all training and coaching sessions. And we'll be sure to follow all of the laws, rules, and regs about using animals in films. No animal will be harmed during this production.

We will still pay to put Gus's sister, Gert, in a kennel during the filming, as originally promised. However, when Gus is rehearsing or is on set, you will not have to put him in a kennel, so we'll be relieved of paying his kennel fees for those days. We'll let you know at least 24 hours in advance of what Gus's filming schedule will be.

You will have Gus groomed by a reputable groomer before his first day of filming. You should ask the groomer to do a "puppy cut," and to leave Gus's beard as long as possible. (There are some lines in the script about his beard.) By the way, you won't get to read the script in advance. The only thing I can tell you is that we won't be requiring Gus to do anything out of the ordinary—that is, anything that a normal, healthy dog doesn't regularly do. Mostly, it will just be shots of his face looking up into Walter's face.

The dog trainer won't give Gus any treats containing lamb, as you have told us that he is allergic to lamb. The dog trainer will never shout at or hit Gus.

On days when you can't be present on the set with Gus, your husband, Troy, will substitute for you. On days when Gus is supposed to be present, Gus will be present, except if he is sick enough to go to the vet. We want a doctor's note if Gus is absent.

We are going to pay you $2,100 for Gus's appearance in the movie. We'll also pick up Gus's grooming costs for the entire production time period, including the initial grooming and all subsequent grooming during the initial filming and for any re-take period.

You will not get to see the rushes and we ask you to refrain from making suggestions while on set. Your role is to simply bring Gus to the set, watch the filming, and take Gus away after his part of the filming is finished.

We have the right to change Gus's name for purposes of the film. I expect that the screenwriter will come up with a more appropriate name, but I don't know what it will be. You do not have veto rights on the doggy character's name.

You'll cooperate by letting us use Gus in all of the promotional materials for the film, including the film's trailer, television commercials, print ads, and other similar things. Oh, and if the movie gets a four-star rating when PEOPLE magazine reviews it and the review mentions the dog, we'll pay you an additional $1,000 for Gus's appearance in the film.

That about sums it up. Please send me the side letter ASAP.

Yours,

Mia Kandu

Mia Kandu
Location Manager

The Toy and Game License Agreement

3A: NON-DISCLOSURE AGREEMENT: DRAFTING THE DEFINITIONS OF CONFIDENTIAL INFORMATION

Instructions

A. **Summary:** Assignment 3A requires you and your opposing counsel to negotiate and draft a license agreement between Troy Green-Gardner, one of the former owners and operators of Tory and Troy's Treehugger Toys, and Even Greener Toys and Games, a company that manufactures, distributes, markets, and sells toys and games designed to help people learn how to reduce their impact on the environment. In Assignment 3E, you will be assigned to represent either the toy and game inventor, Troy Green-Gardner (the "Inventor"), or the toy manufacturer and distributor, Even Greener Toys and Games (the "Company").

Read the General Information for Both Parties, which follows below.

The parties began discussing Troy's inventions without having a non-disclosure agreement ("NDA") in place. They now need an NDA to protect any confidential information that they have previously disclosed to each other and that they may disclose to each other during the course of their continuing negotiations. This assignment requires you to draft the definitions of the "Inventor's Confidential Information" and the "Company's Confidential Information." You will later incorporate these definitions into the NDA (as part of Assignment 3B).

B. **Using Precedent:** You may review any NDAs you can locate in order to determine how "Confidential Information" is generally defined. However, definitions of Confidential Information contained in NDAs are notoriously full of meaningless language that does not take into account what information actually is going to be disclosed by each party during the course of their negotiations. You must closely examine any precedent you find, tailor it to the terms of your deal (that is, to what kinds of confidential information the parties to this deal are likely to disclose to each other), and translate it into Plain English.

C. **Focus:** The purpose of this brief exercise is to make you focus on who is going to disclose what to whom. In law practice, as in-house counsel at a corporation, for example, you may find the vice president of sales standing at your office door five minutes before a scheduled meeting, demanding that you prepare an NDA. You may have most of the NDA already prepared in a template. But the most important thing is for you to identify what information your client is going to disclose and for what purpose. You would not want your client to reveal a marketing strategy, for example, if you have not included "marketing strategy" in the list of things considered Client's Confidential Information. Nor would you want the other side to use the information about your client's marketing strategy for any purpose other than the particular project about which the parties are negotiating.

You must also be very careful to describe as specifically and narrowly as possible the information that the other party is going to reveal to your client. Parties will frequently bring their own NDAs to meetings and attempt to get other parties to agree not to disclose a wide range of information, much of which is simply not confidential. Limit your client's risk by limiting the kind of information your client agrees not to disclose.

D. **Procedure and Format:** Think about what you know about the transaction. What confidential information has each client most likely already disclosed to the other side? What confidential information is each client likely to disclose to the other side during the course of the continuing negotiation? Make a list of these specific items. Your goal is to avoid using a vague definition like "any information that has commercial value to the Inventor [or the Company]."

Draft two separate definitions as described below:

"Inventor's Confidential Information" includes [insert list of specific items], and [catchall phrase].
"Company's Confidential Information" includes [insert list of specific items], and [catchall phrase].

The "catchall phrase" is designed to make sure that your definition covers things that you have not listed but that are similar to the items in your list. For example, your catchall phrase could be something like "and any other similarly sensitive or proprietary information revealed by the Inventor [or the Company] during the negotiations." You can do better than that! Look at the precedent you have gathered to see if you can find a definition of Confidential Information that employs a better catchall phrase.

After you say what each party's Confidential Information includes, you must put in the standard exceptions to the definition of Confidential Information, which generally cover things like "information that has previously entered the public domain." You can easily find out what these standard exceptions are by looking at almost any non-disclosure agreement.

Introduce these exceptions by stating: "Neither the Inventor's nor the Company's Confidential Information includes [insert standard exceptions]."

E. Additional Instructions: Your professor may provide you with additional instructions regarding this assignment.

General Information for Both Parties

It is January 2019.

This Is Just To Say, Inc. (the "Producer") never completed the film tentatively entitled "Please Wink Back." Unfortunately, the Producer re-wrote the script and added a scene in which some fireworks go off when the woman of Walter's dreams finally walks into Tory and Troy's Treehugger Toys (the "Toy Store") and their eyes meet. The fireworks set off a devastating fire that destroyed the entire building. No one was hurt. The cast and crew evacuated. Tory and Troy were out shopping for organic groceries at the time. Fortunately, their two lovebirds were visiting Tory's Mom. Their two golden doodle dogs were at the grocery store with Tory and Troy, playing in the dog playground out back.

To make a long story short, the Green-Gardner Toy Company ultimately sued the Producer for violating the provision in their contract prohibiting the use of pyrotechnics. The parties settled the matter for a large amount of money. Now Tory and Troy own a small home in Evanston, Illinois, and another home in Norway, one of the most eco-friendly countries in the world. Tory was so traumatized by the destruction of the Toy Store (and their upstairs residence) that she spends most of her time in Norway, attending yoga classes, reading poetry, and taking Gus and Gert for long walks. (Yes, she has moved the dogs to Norway.) Troy, on the other hand, spends most of his time in Evanston with only the lovebirds for his companions. He now believes that he is ready to plunge back into business.

Remember the two action figures that Troy created? Glenna the Go-Green Goddess ("Glenna") and Trey the Treehugging Troll ("Trey") (collectively, the "Characters")? Even before the fire in the Toy Store, Troy had applied for and received U.S. patents—both utility and design patents—on the Characters.

> **Note:** A patent gives an inventor like Troy the right to exclude others from making, using, or selling his invention. Troy obtained a utility patent on the Characters because of their unique composition; you will recall that they are made from recycled plastic water bottles and discarded cell phone and computer parts. Troy obtained a design patent on the Characters to protect their appearance, as opposed to their structure.

Before the fire, Troy had also registered the Characters' names and figures as trademarks. Fortunately, Troy kept his prototypes of Glenna and Trey in a locked, fireproof vault in the basement of the Toy Store. The prototypes survived, and Troy has continued the storytelling tradition by entertaining large groups of small children and their parents with Glenna/Trey stories at the Evanston Community Center once a month.

Troy has also invented a board game featuring the Characters. He is tentatively calling it "Glenna and Trey's Go-Green Challenge" (the "Game"). He has registered this name as a trademark. He has also obtained a certificate of copyright registration for the written rules of the game. Briefly, the players accompany Glenna and Trey on their mission to reduce the carbon footprints of various imaginary manufacturers. Each player adopts a manufacturer and is faced with challenges particular to that manufacturer's product and business—things like how to limit air and water pollution, how to manage wasted materials, and how to use energy more efficiently. By following Glenna and Trey's example, each player earns money, raises the CEO's consciousness, and implements significant changes at the manufacturer's plant. Ultimately, the player who reduces its manufacturer's carbon footprint the most wins the game.

The game board, game pieces, and game cards are all made from recycled paper and plastic. The game comes with a simple "carbon footprint journal and calculator" that Troy has created, using the engineering degree he acquired from M.I.T. many years ago (and before he became an accountant, financial advisor, and toy store owner). Troy applied for and obtained U.S. patents (both utility and design) on the game and the carbon footprint journal/calculator.

Just recently, Troy began to look for a company to manufacture, distribute, market, and sell the Characters and the Game. He was about to hire an agent to help him when he happened to meet David Henry Thoreau at the local organic grocery store. Mr. Thoreau was engaged in a passionate conversation about green manufacturing with one of the other customers. When Troy introduced himself and added some insightful remarks to the conversation, Mr. Thoreau greeted him heartily with the words, "Great to meet you, Troy. You obviously know what you're talking about. Call me Hank."

Hank is the Director of Product Acquisition and Inventor Relations for a toy and game company he founded five years ago called Even Greener Toys and Games ("EGTAG" or the "Company"). EGTAG is an Illinois corporation with its office, manufacturing plant, and warehouse located at 4323 Walden Pond Parkway, Chicago, Illinois 60629. EGTAG is in the business of developing, manufacturing, distributing, marketing, and selling toys and games designed to help people learn how to reduce their impact on the environment. EGTAG sells toys and games to toy store and other retailers, but not to individual consumers. EGTAG is committed to using green manufacturing techniques. Its motto is "Go green. Then go even greener."

When Hank told Troy about his profession, Troy bought him a cup of coffee at the nearby Fair Trade Coffee Bar so that they could enjoy a lengthy discussion about the future of toys and games. Troy told Hank about his own background and hinted that he had some inventions he would like to present to Hank's company.

In a subsequent meeting on January 2, 2019, in a conference room at EGTAG, Hank and Troy met to discuss Troy's inventions. Troy did not want to share too much because he was not sure he could trust Hank to keep the information confidential. At the end of the meeting, Hank expressed EGTAG's desire to review Troy's ideas further. Troy and Hank agreed that they should get a non-disclosure agreement in place before sharing any additional confidential information with each other. Hank asked Troy if, once the non-disclosure agreement is drafted and signed, Troy would be willing to take the Characters and the Game off of the market while the Company completed its review and made a final decision. Troy said that he would be glad to do it, especially because EGTAG offered him a "holding fee" of $5,000.

During the week that followed their meeting, Hank and Troy negotiated and signed a non-disclosure agreement. On January 14, 2019, Troy received the attached Option Agreement by express mail, overnight delivery. Troy signed it on January 14, 2019, and returned it to EGTAG by messenger that afternoon, instructing the messenger to wait for a return envelope. Ninety minutes later, the messenger returned to Troy's home in Evanston and handed him an envelope from Hank. Hank had enclosed a Company check for Troy in the amount of $5,000. The 30-day review period began.

On February 11, 2019, EGTAG notified Troy that it wants to negotiate the terms of a license agreement between the Company and Troy regarding Troy's inventions—the Characters and the Game. The Company informed Troy that it had just hired a new attorney and that he could expect to hear from that attorney very soon.

Option Agreement Between Troy Green-Gardner and Even Greener Toys and Games

This Agreement made on **1/14/19**, between Troy Green-Gardner (hereinafter "Inventor"), and Even Greener Toys and Games (hereinafter, "Company").

WHEREAS, Inventor has invented two action figures, Glenna the Go-Green Goddess and Trey the Treehugging Troll, and a game tentatively entitled, Glenna and Trey's Go-Green Challenge (hereinafter, "Items"), and

WHEREAS, Inventor has presented the Items to Company for evaluation and possible licensing; and

WHEREAS, the Company wishes to review and evaluate said Items:

Now Therefore It Is Hereby Agreed as Follows:

Inventor shall let Company examine and evaluate Items for a period of 30 days, commencing on the date of this Agreement and ending on February 13, 2019. Inventor represents and warrants that it owns all intellectual property in the Items and has the ability to grant an exclusive license for said Items manufacture and sale. Inventor agrees that it will not license or disclose the Items during the 30-day review period to any other person or entity. Inventor agrees that if Company wants to license the Items, Inventor will enter into a mutually negotiated and satisfactory licensing agreement regarding the Items with Company.

In consideration of the foregoing, Company agrees to pay Inventor the sum of **$5,000**, along with other good and valuable consideration, the receipt and sufficiency of which is hereby acknowledged. If Company decides to license the Items, it will so notify Inventor by written confirmation sent to Inventor's residence no later than the 30th day. Both parties agree that they will then negotiate a license agreement. In that event, the Company may apply the **$5,000** holding fee against any royalties payable under the executed license agreement. If the Company does not elect to license the Items, then the Inventor shall keep the entire **$5,000** payable hereunder.

IN WITNESS WHEREOF, the parties have executed this Agreement as of the date first written above.

INVENTOR   COMPANY

Troy Green-Gardner   By: *David Henry Thoreau*
Troy Gardner   David Henry Thoreau
                                      Title: Director of Product
                                      Acquisition and Inventor Relations

3B: NON-DISCLOSURE AGREEMENT: DRAFTING THE OPERATIVE PROVISIONS

Instructions

A. **Summary:** This assignment assumes that you have completed Assignment 3A and that you now have in hand the definitions of Inventor's Confidential Information and Company's Confidential Information. Using those definitions, you will complete the Non-Disclosure Agreement ("NDA") that the parties will sign before they continue discussing the inventions and begin negotiating the terms of the Toy and Game License Agreement. The attorneys for the Inventor and the Company have met and agreed upon the operative terms that they want to include in the NDA. The Company's attorney assigned a junior associate to take notes during this meeting (copy attached). Troy Green-Gardner and David Henry Thoreau (Director of Product Acquisition and Inventor Relations for Even Greener Toys and Games) have read the notes and believe that they accurately represent what the parties agreed to at the meeting.

B. **Using Precedent:** You may review any non-disclosure agreements you can locate in order to help you determine how non-disclosure agreements look and what provisions they generally contain. (You may want to refer to the same non-disclosure agreements you used when drafting the definitions of Confidential Information in Assignment 3A.) You must apply everything you know about good contract drafting to any language you adopt or adapt from the available precedent. For example, remember to use "shall" for covenants and to draft in the active voice. Say "The Inventor shall not disclose the Company's Confidential Information" as opposed to "The Company's Confidential Information shall not be disclosed by the Inventor."

Remember, also, to eliminate all legalese from any precedent you use. Do not develop the lawyerly bad habit of using two or even three words when one strong word will do. For example, say "The Company shall not disclose the Inventor's Confidential Information" as opposed to "The Company shall not reveal, disseminate, or disclose the Inventor's Confidential Information."

> **Note:** Reasonable people may disagree about whether "disseminate" carries a different meaning from "reveal" and "disclose" and should therefore be included. Always ask yourself if all of the words in your list are necessary to carry your meaning. (Certainly "reveal" and "disclose" are synonymous. Eliminate one of them.)

C. **Organization of the Non-Disclosure Agreement:** Draft a Preamble for the NDA, just as you would for any other contract. Follow the model Leaf Disposal Services Agreement Preamble shown below.

LEAF DISPOSAL SERVICES AGREEMENT

Leaf Disposal Services Agreement made this 10th day of October 2007, between SpinGazer, Inc., a Delaware corporation with its principal place of business located at 1200 Ridge Avenue, Evanston, Illinois 60201 (the "Company"), and Fallen Leaves, Inc., an Illinois corporation with its principal place of business located at 2025 North Clark Street, Chicago, Illinois 60614 (the "Provider").

Since Troy Green-Gardner is an individual (not a corporation), identify him as "an individual who resides at [INSERT ADDRESS]. For the Company, follow the model, above.

For the Background section in your NDA, do not succumb to blindly following precedent by inserting a number of "WHEREAS" clauses culminating in the big "NOW, THEREFORE" clause. Instead, simply insert a brief description of why the parties are going to be revealing confidential information to each other. What does the Inventor want to discuss with the Company? In the Background section, you may want to create an in-text definition of "Project" that you can use throughout the NDA. Remember that your client is entering into an NDA to protect information revealed to your client during the negotiations about the Project.

After the Preamble, you should include the words, "Accordingly, the parties agree as follows," unless you determine that it may be important to use a fuller statement of consideration in this NDA. Since both parties are exchanging Confidential Information, and both parties are agreeing not to disclose that information, the consideration for the contract is inherent in the contract itself. But, because the consideration for an NDA may not be as obvious as it is for a purchase or services agreement, you may want to include a statement like, "Accordingly, in consideration of the mutual promises contained in this Agreement, the parties agree as follows." Do not revert to gobbledygook by adding the words "and other good and valuable consideration, the receipt and sufficiency of which is hereby mutually acknowledged." Keep it simple.

After the statement of consideration, organize the remainder of the NDA as follows:

Definitions
Term
Basic Non-Disclosure Obligations
[Other Operative Provisions]
General Provisions
Signature Lines

Draft the basic non-disclosure obligations before you cover any other operative provisions. You will find precedent in which the drafters describe both parties' non-disclosure obligations in one section or paragraph. In order to avoid the difficulties of the "Both parties shall not" construction— including having to define "Disclosing Party" and "Recipient"—try drafting one section containing the Inventor's non-disclosure obligations and another section containing the Company's non-disclosure obligations.

After you draft the parties' basic non-disclosure obligations, you must decide what other operative provisions you need to cover and organize them in a logical way. For example, you will want to talk about what happens to the Confidential Information when the Term ends. You may want to cover this topic near the end of the contract, since it addresses what is to happen at the end of the parties' relationship. When considering how to organize the "other operative provisions," keep your audience in mind. You still have to consider an audience wider than just the parties' signators and the parties' attorneys. Remember that other executives working for the Company may have a "need to know" the Inventor's Confidential Information, for example. Therefore, those other executives may have to see the NDA so that they understand their own non-disclosure obligations.

Next, look at the precedent you have located to determine what kind of boilerplate provisions generally appear in an NDA. Most NDAs have merger/integration and choice-of-law provisions, for example. Some have severability provisions as well. Think about your client's needs. If you believe that any other boilerplate should be included to address your client's needs, put it in. For example, perhaps several years after signing the NDA, your client will need to disclose the other party's Confidential Information to a third party. If you think that might happen, you may want to include an amendment and modification clause so that it might be possible to shorten the NDA's term.

D. **Formatting the Non-Disclosure Agreement:** After the Definitions article, you can use simple numbered paragraphs with headings to format the NDA. So, for example, the "Term" and "Non-Disclosure Obligations" sections might look like this:

1. **Term.** This Agreement begins on January 10, 2019 and ends [insert date].
2. **Inventor's Duty Not to Disclose Company's Confidential Information.** [Insert body of provision].
3. **Company's Duty Not to Disclose Inventor's Confidential Information.** [Insert body of provision].

E. **One Final Note About the Nature of Confidential Information:** Remember that parties can reveal confidential information both orally and in writing. In other words, much of what the parties say to each other may never be put down in a document but may still constitute confidential information. Do not make the mistake of assuming that confidential information is only contained in written documents. Be sure that your NDA takes this into account.

F. **Additional Instructions:** Your professor may provide you with additional instructions regarding this assignment.

From the Desk of: Lowell Auden

Subject: Notes of Meeting Between Troy Green-Gardner and Even Greener Toys and Games

Re: Terms of Non-Disclosure Agreement (Toy and Game License Agreement)

Date: January 7, 2019

The Inventor asked that the Company stamp any document considered to contain the Company's Confidential Information with the word "Confidential." David Henry Thoreau explained that it would not be possible to ensure that all of the Company's employees involved in the negotiation (and preparation for the negotiation) remember to stamp documents "Confidential." The Company has a broad universe of people to control. Therefore, the Company does not want to accept the risk that some of the Company's Confidential Information might not be considered confidential just because someone forgot to stamp it.

Since the Inventor's spouse, attorneys, and financial advisors are likely to be the only ones who handle documents containing the Inventor's Confidential Information, the Inventor can easily stamp any documents containing the Inventor's Confidential Information with the word "Confidential" in the upper right-hand corner. Troy agreed to do this.

The Inventor asked that the Company only share the Inventor's Confidential Information (whether contained in documents or otherwise) with people in the Company's employ who have some genuine need to know what the documents contain. The Company agreed. Both parties agreed that those Company employees with a "need to know" include at least David Henry Thoreau, the Company's attorneys, and the Company's accountant. At this time, it is not possible for the Company to identify exactly who else may need to see the documents containing the Inventor's Confidential Information.

The Company knows that the Inventor will want to share some of the Company's Confidential Information with his spouse, his attorneys, and, of course, his financial advisors. The Inventor agreed not to disclose the Company's Confidential Information to anyone else unless it gets the Company's written permission first.

Both the Inventor and the Company agree that they will show the NDA to everyone on the permitted list and get those individuals to sign an acknowledgment stating that they have read the NDA and understand that they are undertaking the same obligations as the signators. Both the Inventor and the Company also agreed that, if they have to show the other party's

Confidential Information to anyone not on the permitted list, they will get that person to agree not to disclose the information and have that person sign a similar acknowledgment.

The Inventor wants to make sure that entering into this NDA does not bind it to enter into a toy and game license agreement with the Company. The Company has the same concern—i.e., that the NDA not bind the Company to enter into a toy and game license agreement with the Inventor—and would like to include some language to that effect in the NDA. Both parties want this language to be prominent in the NDA.

There was much discussion about how long the duties not to disclose should last. The parties finally agreed that the non-disclosure obligations should last for five years after the negotiation is completed, if the negotiation does not result in a contract. If the negotiation does result in a contract, then the parties want the non-disclosure obligations to last for the life of the contract plus five years and not to be superseded by the contract.

For both parties, the duties not to disclose the Confidential Information will include the obvious—not disclosing to anyone but those on the permitted list—as well as protecting the other party's Confidential Information just as the recipient would protect its own. Also, the parties are only going to use the Confidential Information in connection with the project at hand—the negotiation of the Toy and Game License Agreement between the Inventor and the Company. Both parties want the NDA to state the reason why they are disclosing the information to each other—to evaluate whether or not to enter into that Toy and Game License Agreement.

After the parties finish negotiating, if they decide not to enter into a contract, both parties must return each other's Confidential Information immediately. The parties agreed to deliver by messenger the Confidential Information contained in documents. If the parties do enter into a contract, a party can keep the documents containing the Confidential Information until the other party requests their return. All Confidential Information must be returned by messenger within five business days of the other party's request. Alternatively, the party holding the Confidential Information may destroy the documents and provide an Affidavit of Destruction, signed by the Inventor or the Company, as appropriate.

If either the Inventor or the Company is compelled to produce the other party's Confidential Information by a court order or subpoena, then the compelled party will let the other party know right away by telephone and e-mail. That way the owner of the Confidential Information can decide whether to move for a protective order or take some other action to prevent its disclosure. The Company was particularly adamant about this point.

Finally, both parties want the existence of the NDA and its contents to remain confidential, except that the parties may show it to people on the permitted list, who will also agree to keep its existence and contents confidential.

3C: PREPARATION FOR THE NEGOTIATION OF THE TOY AND GAME LICENSE AGREEMENT

Part I: Finding, Evaluating, and Using the Relevant Precedent

Instructions

A. **Summary:** Re-read the General Information for Both Parties included in Assignment 3A. You will now search for contracts that will be likely to help you draft a Toy and Game License Agreement. Once you locate the relevant precedent, you will review it and begin creating a negotiation prep sheet.

B. **Resources:** You may look for precedent in the library and on the Internet. You may not purchase any forms, whether from a store or online. You may not use any precedent in your own files (from a previous job or a summer position) or any precedent you obtain from an attorney. Finally, you may not use any contracts obtained from other students who have taken this class. Pretend that the library and the Internet are your only resources.

C. **What to Look For:** When you look for precedent in the litigation context, you try to find cases that are as close to your case as possible. If your case is about intentional infliction of emotional distress and involves one neighbor terrorizing another by putting dead insects and snakes on the other neighbor's doorstep, you would be very happy to find another case with nearly identical facts. If that case turns out to be in the same jurisdiction as yours, you would be even happier. Most likely, you will have to settle for cases with similar or analogous facts—and you may need to look beyond your jurisdiction.

   In the transactional context, when you look for precedent, focus first on what kind of contract you are being asked to draft. For the purpose of this assignment, you want to find toy and game license agreements. While it may be helpful to find a toy and game license agreement about green toys and eco-friendly board games, it is not as important to find a contract with nearly identical facts as it might be if you were trying to prove a case in the litigation context. Moreover, while searching for precedent in the transactional context, you do not have to be as conscious of jurisdictional issues, though you do have to familiarize yourself with any laws that affect your deal (as you will do in Assignment 3D).

D. **How to Find It:** If you love books and libraries, you may be tempted to start looking for precedent there. However, unless you do not own a computer or cannot connect to the Internet, looking for books in the library would not be the most efficient way to begin.

Begin by surfing the Web. You may choose to do a general search, using the search engine of your choice, or to go to LEXIS or WESTLAW to see what forms are available there. One very good online source of sample contracts is www.onecle.com (click on Business Contracts). There, you will find thousands of actual contracts used by businesses for various purposes. Another good online source of sample contracts is Findlaw.com (click on Learn about the Law; Small Business; then Business Forms and Contracts). Remember that the "samples" you find on these sites are "samples," and not "models." For more about what that distinction means, see Section E, Reviewing and Evaluating Precedent, below.

When you surf the Web seeking relevant precedent, start with a narrow search and then broaden it out. For example, you may want to start by searching for "toy and game license agreements." From there, you might move on to "toy license agreements" or "game license agreements." If you still do not feel as if you have found enough precedent, ask yourself what kinds of contracts are similar to toy and game license agreements. Perhaps searching for "license agreements" will reveal some precedent containing useful provisions. Since "agreement" and "contract" are used interchangeably, be sure to search for both terms.

Do not forget to search LEXIS and WESTLAW. Both have databases containing contract forms.

If you prefer working with actual books, go to your law library and locate the "forms" books. Skim through the tables of contents or indexes to determine if the books contain any relevant forms.

E. **Reviewing and Evaluating Precedent:** Once you have located eight or ten relevant contracts, begin to review them. Ask yourself at least the following questions about each contract:

☐ How relevant is the precedent?
    ☐ Is it a toy and game license agreement?
    ☐ Is it a toy license agreement? A game license agreement?
    ☐ Is it a contract from the United States (as opposed to the United Kingdom or another country, with different contract drafting methods and formats)?
☐ How is the agreement formatted?
    ☐ Does it contain all of the essential parts of a contract?
    ☐ If it does not contain all of the essential parts, what is omitted?

☐ What topics are covered?
  ☐ Does the agreement cover any topics that you would not have thought to cover?
☐ How is the agreement organized?
  ☐ What appears to be the organizing principle behind the placement of topics in the agreement? Importance? Chronology? Something else?
☐ Is it easy to find things in the agreement?
☐ Does the agreement read smoothly?
☐ Did the drafters use the appropriate verbs to express contract concepts?
☐ Did the drafters use the active voice?
☐ Did the drafters use Plain English throughout? In parts?
  ☐ Are there any places in the agreement that are heavy with legalese?
☐ Does anything in the agreement strike you as being particularly well drafted or handled?

After you finish reading through all of the relevant precedent you have found, rate the agreements on a scale of 1 to 5, with 1 signifying "best" and 5 signifying "useless." Make a note of which contracts contain "good language" about particular topics. The "good language" standard does not necessarily mean "well-drafted" language; you may just appreciate the way the drafters handle a particular issue as opposed to the way they write about it. Perhaps, for example, you find an agreement that requires an inventor to sign a morals clause, assuring that the inventor will not invent any lewd toys and games during the life of the contract. Perhaps the manufacturer also agreed to a similar morals clause for itself. The drafters may have filled the provision with legalese. Nevertheless, make a note of the language because it contains an interesting idea that you may want to include in your own contract.

After you have rated the contracts, look at the entire batch of precedent once again and make a list of the main topics covered in the agreements. If most of the agreements cover "Inventor's Approval Process," for example, then you will most likely need to cover that topic when you negotiate and draft the Toy and Game License Agreement between the Inventor and the Company. If one agreement contains a provision that none of the other agreements contains, you may have found a provision particular to the transaction at issue in that agreement.

F. **Using the Relevant Precedent:** When you draft your contract, you may decide to adopt or adapt some language from the relevant precedent you found. If so, you must remember the following principles:

1. **Every deal is its own deal.** This means that no matter how close the relevant precedent seems to the deal you are negotiating, your deal is a different deal. On the surface level, the parties' names and addresses are different. On a deeper level, your deal may include many facts that

are different from the deal memorialized in the precedent. Maybe, for example, the Inventor wants the Company to engage a consultant to give the Inventor advice about how to make the products more marketable. You must remember to tailor the precedent to the facts of your deal.

2. **Cutting and pasting numbs the mind.** It is tempting to cut and paste. Resist the temptation. If you re-type the language instead, you are more likely to notice things about how it is drafted—like the way the drafters used "null and void" instead of just "void." Or the fact that none of the parties is mentioned in a sentence purporting to obligate one of the parties to do something. If you simply cut and paste the language and rely on yourself to catch and fix those things in the editing and proof-reading stage, you are missing a golden, immediate opportunity. The best example of the way cutting and pasting numbs the mind is this: Many students make the mistake of cutting and pasting a piece of precedent from another contract and forgetting to change the names of the parties. When the reader, used to seeing the "the Inventor" and "the Company," suddenly comes across "the Licensee" and "the Licensor," she stumbles. If she is grading the contract, she takes off points.

3. **The naked drafter rules the world.** No, I am not advocating that you draft in the nude. I am advocating that you learn how to draft without relying on precedent. If you master the skill of translating deal terms into contract concepts (covenants, conditions precedent, representations and warranties, declarations, and statements of discretionary authority), then you will be able to draft a contract without having any precedent at hand. When your client asks you to put a unique provision in the contract, you will be the "can-do" lawyer—that is, the lawyer who can draft the provision on the spot without needing a precedential crutch. Exercising your naked drafting skills will make you feel smart, efficient, creative, and, yes, powerful! Moreover, when you decide to use precedent, you will have the skills necessary to help you analyze and improve the language in the provisions you decide to adopt or adapt.

4. **Mine the precedent for ideas, not language.** The best way to use precedent is to help you "see" how a contract like the one you are attempting to draft generally "looks." Reviewing some relevant precedent is a good way to get started on drafting a contract that seems daunting. In other words, with the facts of your own deal foremost in your mind, you can use precedent to help you figure out what terms to define, what topics to cover, and what order to cover them in. You can also use precedent to help you discover whether you ought to include certain provisions because they are traditionally included in this type of contract or because they are required by law. (Of course, you must still do enough legal research to satisfy yourself that you have covered any legal issues the contract raises.)

Finally, ask your professor if she wants you to cite to any precedent you use. If so, find out what citation format she prefers.

G. **The Negotiation Prep Sheet:** After you have located some good, relevant precedent, use it to help you prepare for the negotiation of the Toy and Game License Agreement between the Inventor and the Company. Create a three-column table entitled *Negotiation Prep Sheet*. Label the first column "Topic," the second column "Description," and the third column "Position." Since you do not yet know which client you represent, leave the third column blank. In the first column, list the topics covered in the precedent. In the second column, insert some details about each topic. Your negotiation prep sheet will look something like this:

NEGOTIATION PREP SHEET

Topic	Description	Position
Inventor's duty to cooperate with Company's publicity efforts	Covers showing up for toy demonstrations and conferences, allowing his image to be used in photographs and videos, and allowing the products to be placed in films	
Etc.	Etc.	

When you finish filling in columns 1 and 2 of your negotiation prep sheet, you will have a living document that you can revise in light of the legal research you do in response to Assignment 3D and the confidential instructions you receive from your client as part of Assignment 3E.

H. **Collaboration:** Your professor may permit you to collaborate with your classmates in locating, reviewing, and evaluating precedent as well as in creating the first negotiation prep sheet. If you do collaborate with your classmates on this assignment, you will get to see how different people approach the task of finding precedent. Which search engines do your classmates use? How do they word their first search? Their second search? Their third? Do they begin with LEXIS or WESTLAW? When they find something useful, how do they record it? Do they bookmark it? Copy the

URL into a Word document? Print it out in hard copy? Do they make any spot judgments about the quality of the precedent they find? Do they dwell on one contract or continue searching until they have gathered a number of relevant contracts? And so on. . . . You will inevitably get some great ideas from your classmates. But the most valuable part of the collaboration lies in observing someone else's "process." It may open your mind!

I. **Additional Instructions:** Your professor may provide you with additional instructions regarding this assignment.

3D: CONTINUED PREPARATION FOR THE NEGOTIATION OF THE TOY AND GAME LICENSE AGREEMENT

Part II: Researching the Legal Issues

Instructions

A. **Summary:** This assignment assumes that you have completed Assignment 3C. First, re-read the General Information for Both Parties included in Assignment 3A. In further preparation for your negotiation, you will now research the legal issues impacting the Toy and Game License Agreement between Troy Green-Gardner (the "Inventor") and Even Greener Toys and Games (the "Company"). You will research the legal issues that you identified when locating, reviewing, and evaluating the relevant precedent as well as any other legal issues that you have identified yourself or that your professor has identified for you. You will then revise the negotiation prep sheet, adding new topics and descriptions that address these legal issues.

B. **What to Look For:** When you reviewed and evaluated the relevant precedent, you may have found that several sample contracts contained references to particular statutes or regulations. Begin there. For example, if you have found any toy and game license agreements that deal with copyright ownership issues, you may want to begin by looking at Title 17 of the U.S. Code (Copyrights).

Do not hesitate to research other legal issues that you or your professor have identified, even if you do not find them addressed in the relevant precedent. Remember that you have located "sample contracts," not models. Perhaps the additional legal research you do will uncover some key points that the sample contracts simply failed to cover.

> *Caveat:* Do not let yourself get too caught up in legal research. You are not striving to become an expert. Do enough research to satisfy yourself that you are competent to draft the contract—and rely on your professor to supply additional expertise, if need be.

C. **How to Find It:** By now, you know how to find statutes and regulations. Start with the primary sources: the statutes and regulations cited in the precedent. Then delve into any other legal issues you have uncovered.

D. **The Negotiation Prep Sheet:** When you feel you have a pretty good grasp of the legal issues you have identified, add them to the negotiation prep sheet. Remember to include citations in your descriptions, since you may want to revisit these issues when you are negotiating or drafting.

E. **Collaboration:** Your professor may permit you to collaborate with your classmates in conducting the legal research this assignment requires. If so, you will benefit from seeing how someone else approaches a problem. Observing your classmates' "process" may make you decide to change your own way of doing things. Even if watching your classmates in action merely confirms that your own process is more effective, you are still likely to benefit from talking about the legal issues while you are researching them. In a good collaborative environment, participants take turns being the striker and the flint. When a striker is applied to flint, sparks fly. Sometimes you will raise a question (acting as the striker) and your classmate will propose an answer (acting as the flint). And sometimes, vice versa. You will both benefit from the sparks!

F. **Additional Instructions:** Your professor may provide you with additional instructions regarding this assignment.

3E: NEGOTIATION OF THE TOY AND GAME LICENSE AGREEMENT: LETTER OF INTENT AND TERM SHEET

Instructions

A. **Summary:** For this assignment, you will represent either Troy Green-Gardner (the "Inventor") or Even Greener Toys and Games (the "Company"). As you know from reading the General Information for Both Parties included in Assignment 3A, the Inventor wants to license his characters (Glenna and Trey) and his board game (Glenna and Trey's Go-Green Challenge) to the Company. The Company is in the business of manufacturing, distributing, marketing, and selling toys and games designed to help people learn how to reduce their impact on the environment. The Company wants to obtain a license from the Inventor. Your task is to negotiate the deal and draft the Toy and Game License Agreement between the Inventor and the Company.

B. **Assume No Conflict of Interest:** If you represent the Company in this deal, you can assume that there is no conflict of interest in your representing the Company against the Inventor, even though you may have represented the Green-Gardner Toy Company and The T-4 Partnership in connection with some previous transactions. Alternatively, you may pretend that you have never represented the Green-Gardner Toy Company or The T-4 Partnership in the past.

C. **The Negotiation:** Your professor will tell you which party you represent and which of your classmates will be your opposing counsel. Your professor will also give you some Confidential Instructions from your client.

Logistics:

1. Begin by re-reading the General Information for Both Parties included in Assignment 3A. Then read the Confidential Instructions from your client.

2. After carefully reviewing the Confidential Instructions from your client, revise the negotiation prep sheet you prepared in response to Assignments 3C and 3D to add any topics mentioned in the Confidential Instructions but not listed on your negotiation prep sheet. If you know what your client's position is with regard to a particular issue, insert that information in the "Position" column.

> **Note:** If you do not know what your client's position is with regard to a particular issue—and you believe it is an issue that the contract ought to cover—make a note to ask your client about it.

3. Complete your negotiation prep sheet by asking your professor to answer any questions you have about your client's position on the issues. Your professor may choose to tell you what your client's position is, or allow you to decide what your client's position ought to be. Either way, be sure to complete the negotiation prep sheet before moving on to the next step.

4. Prepare to negotiate. Your professor may provide you with a handout about how to negotiate a contract. Review the handout. Study your negotiation prep sheet and tweak it, if necessary. You will bring this sheet with you to the negotiation.

5. Talk to your opposing counsel to schedule a mutually convenient time and place for the negotiation. Make sure that you find a quiet place where you will not be disturbed and will not encounter other pairs of negotiators from your class. Allow at least two hours for your first negotiation session.

6. Do not show your negotiation prep sheet or the Confidential Instructions you received from your client to your opposing counsel (or any other students who represent the opposing party) at any time before, during, or after the negotiation. During the negotiation, you will use the information in your Confidential Instructions as your guide to

your client's wishes. You will naturally and judiciously reveal some of the information to your opposing counsel during the course of the negotiation in order to achieve your client's objectives.

7. Your Confidential Instructions may or may not contain information about your client's wishes regarding every issue you need to cover in the contract. For example, your Confidential Instructions do not address every boilerplate provision that you may want to include in the contract. If you do not know what your client wants, ask your professor or negotiate for what you believe will be in your client's best interests.

8. During the negotiation, you and your opposing counsel should prepare a "Term Sheet," which will ultimately be attached to your Letter of Intent ("LOI") and should look something like this:

ATTACHMENT A TO LETTER OF INTENT

Issue	Terms

---

9. In this negotiation, you MUST reach an agreement. While the negotiation itself is not graded, you will receive extra points for being especially thorough and for devising creative solutions to disputed issues between the parties.

10. If you need access to your client during the negotiation, please contact your professor. If you and your opposing counsel reach a stalemate on any issues, please contact your professor.

11. If you do not finish your negotiation in one sitting, schedule another mutually convenient time to meet. Remember that you are likely to continue negotiating during the drafting process.

D. Drafting the Letter of Intent: Once you have completed your negotiation, you and your opposing counsel must draft one LOI and submit it to your professor. Your professor will decide whether to grade the LOI itself, but he may simply want to refer to the LOI when grading your contract. Therefore, if you and your opposing counsel change any significant terms contained in the LOI during subsequent negotiations, your professor may ask you to revise the LOI and re-submit it.

DRAFTING THE LETTER OF INTENT

(A Mini-Assignment within the Negotiation Assignment)

1. Draft an LOI. You will attach the term sheet that you created during your negotiation to the LOI as Exhibit A.

2. Address the LOI to your professor.

3. Do not use any precedent to draft the LOI. Draft in Plain English. Do not include anything that looks like a covenant. This is not a contract. See No. 4, below.

4. The most important thing to keep in mind is that you do not want your opposing counsel to be able to say that the LOI is a binding contract whether your negotiations fall through or your negotiations result in a signed contract. The LOI contains preliminary terms, some of which are likely to change over time. Make sure that you emphasize that the LOI is not a binding contract by featuring this point prominently in the LOI.

5. State that the letter describes the terms that the Inventor and the Company have discussed about the project and include a brief description of the project. Mention that the terms are attached in Exhibit A.

6. Clarify that the parties are not bound by any of the terms in the term sheet unless they sign a contract including those terms.

7. Clarify that when the parties sign the letter they are not acquiring any rights or undertaking any obligations and, especially, that they are not promising to enter into a contract with the other party.

8. Include a paragraph reminding the Inventor and the Company that they are bound by the Non-Disclosure Agreement ("NDA") they signed when negotiating this deal and that the NDA prohibits them from disclosing the existence or terms of this LOI. Alternatively, you can include non-disclosure obligations in the LOI. (However, since the LOI is not a contract, any covenants you include in it arguably are not enforceable.)

9. Insert signature lines for both parties. This is another reason to include the language about the LOI not being a contract. The LOI is likely to look like a contract because both parties sign it.

10. Remember to attach the term sheet to the LOI before submitting the LOI to your professor.

E. **Additional Instructions:** Your professor may provide you with additional instructions regarding this assignment.

3F: PREPARATION OF TALKING POINTS FOR MEETING WITH SUE PAYNE, SENIOR PARTNER, RE POTENTIAL ETHICAL QUESTION

Instructions

A. **Summary:** For the purposes of this assignment, assume that your firm represents Troy Green-Gardner (the "Inventor") and that you are negotiating a Toy and Game License Agreement between the Inventor and Even Greener Toys and Games (the "Company"). After reviewing the scenario below, you will prepare talking points for a meeting with your senior partner, Sue Payne.

B. **Scenario:** As you know, Troy's wife, Tory, has moved to Norway to recuperate from the trauma she experienced when the building housing Tory and Troy's Treehugger Toys burned down. Recently, in the midst of your negotiations with the Company, Troy told you that his wife may be returning to the United States for a visit soon and that he wants you to wrap up the negotiations and draft the contract quickly. Troy's goal is to sign the contract before she arrives so that she cannot have any input into the deal.

   You begin putting pressure on your opposing counsel to get the contract ready for signing. Your opposing counsel complains about this pressure and asks: "What's going on? Why are you pushing so hard to get this done all of a sudden?" You tell your opposing counsel that Troy's wife is about to get back into town and that your client fears she may interfere with the deal.

C. **Analysis:** Your senior partner, Sue Payne, thinks that you may have violated an ethical rule by telling your opposing counsel about Tory Green-Gardner's imminent return to the States and Troy's fear that she could interfere with the deal. Sue has asked you to analyze this scenario to determine whether you violated any ethical rules. She wants you to explain your answer by citing specific portions of the Model Rules of Professional Conduct and the Comments to those rules. If you determine that you did violate an ethical rule, is there anything you can do to fix this problem? If you decide that you did not violate any ethical rules, have you raised any business issues that you now need to address? (Assume that your opposing counsel is now more nervous about her client entering into this deal, for example.)

D. **Preparation of Talking Points:** "Talking Points" are simply notes that you prepare for yourself to structure your discussion with your senior partner. You do not have to draft them using any particular format. That being said, it is a good idea to use headings and bullet points to keep yourself on track—especially if you get nervous talking to your supervisor. Include a brief statement of the issue. Then summarize what you have concluded and how you reached those conclusions. Conclude with "action points" in which you recommend how to proceed.

E. **Additional Instructions:** Your professor may provide you with additional instructions regarding this assignment.

3G: DRAFTING THE TOY AND GAME LICENSE AGREEMENT

The Frame and the Picture

Instructions

A. **Summary:** Once you have completed your negotiations and drafted and submitted your LOI (as described in Assignment 3E), you will draft the Toy and Game License Agreement memorializing the terms of the deal that you negotiated with your opposing counsel. The two of you will turn in one completed contract.

B. **The Frame and the Picture:** Unlike what you did with the Toy Purchase and the Movie Location and Product Placement Agreements in this sequence, you will draft the frame and the picture of the contract together. Since we will not repeat the instructions for drafting the frame and the picture here, you may want to review Assignments 1E and 1F or Assignments 2D and 2E.

C. **The Drafting Process:** In the real world, one of you would probably prepare the entire first draft and submit it to your opposing counsel, who would edit it and redline the changes. You would review his edits and decide whether to accept or reject each of them. You might then send another redlined version to him, showing additional edits that you have made. This back-and-forth process may carry you through many drafts.

For this assignment, I recommend that you and your opposing counsel consider operating as you would in the real world. This can work in the law school context if one of you has more time and fewer pending deadlines than the other. Ideally, the least busy person would prepare the entire first draft and submit it to the busier person for review. The back-and-forth editing and redlining process can then proceed.

Realistically, you and your opposing counsel are more likely to divide up the work of preparing the first draft so that the bulk of it does not fall on one student's shoulders. If you do divide the contract into parts, you will have to allow a lot of extra time before the contract is due for the two of you to make sure that the parts work together well. For example, you will need to make sure that both of you have used the same defined terms and that you have used them to mean the same things. This is trickier than you think, so please try to complete a full draft as early in the process as possible. That way, the two of you can review, edit, redline, and repeat as often as you need to in order to produce a seamless, polished product.

Remember that your goal is to produce a contract that sounds as if it were written by one person, not two. If one of you drafts in Plain English and the other peppers her language with legalese, your contract will be split into two distinct halves. Alternatively, if the two of you have divided up the work so that you each have responsibility for drafting alternating articles within the contract, the reader is likely to feel like she is on a seesaw. Strive to draft with a consistent voice. To accomplish this, both of you will have to read the entire contract more than once. I recommend reading it out loud to each other and listening for the places where the language becomes more elevated or slips into legalese. The two of you can then work together to translate those passages into Plain English.

D. **Incomplete Confidential Instructions:** You may not have received any confidential instructions from your clients about some of the topics in your negotiation prep sheet (see Assignments 3C and 3D). Address any questions about your client's position on particular issues to your professor, who will either provide you with additional confidential instructions or give you permission to decide what would be in your client's best interests. Because this is a "simulated assignment," you may have to use your imagination. Do not go so far as to make up wildly improbable deal facts, but do feel free to be a little creative.

Include any boilerplate provisions appropriate for this particular deal as well as any boilerplate provisions that your professor suggests are necessary. Remember to negotiate about the language of the boilerplate provisions. While you may not have confidential instructions addressing every piece of boilerplate, you can imagine what your clients' concerns might be and address them. For example, if you represent the Company and do not have any confidential instructions about delegation of performance, think about whether the Company would want the Inventor to be able to delegate his performance to another party. Most likely the Company does not want the Inventor to have the right to delegate his performance since the Inventor is the creator of the characters that the Company wants to license. On the other hand, the Inventor may not have a problem with the Company assigning its rights or delegating its duties to a third party, as long as that party agrees, in writing, to accept the assignment and delegation. Therefore, you may want to negotiate to adjust the standard anti-delegation and anti-assignment language to specifically address both parties' concerns.

E. **Use of Precedent for Drafting the Toy and Game License Agreement:** As you know if you completed Assignment 3C, you may use any forms or templates you can find in the library or on the Internet. You may not purchase any forms, whether from a store or online. You may not use any precedent in your own files (from a previous job or a summer position) or any precedent you obtain from an attorney. *Finally, you may not use any contracts obtained from other students who have taken this class.* Pretend that the library and the Internet are your only resources.

See Assignment 3C for some tips on how to locate, review, evaluate, and use the available precedent.

F. **Provisions Addressing Legal Issues:** Be sure to address in the contract any specific things that the parties must do in order to comply with the law. If you know that you need to address copyright issues, for example, spell out the parties' specific rights and obligations. Avoid the easy cop-out of saying, "The Inventor and the Company shall abide by copyright law," or words to that effect. If you try to simplify your task this way, it will be apparent that you did not take the time and care necessary to determine which specific sections of the Copyright Act (Title 17 of the U.S. Code) apply, if any. Moreover, including language requiring your clients to abide by all statutes and regulations is, in effect, redundant; that is, it simply amounts to your clients' promises to obey the law, which your clients must do even if they are not contractually bound. If there is a legal issue that you must address, include specific provisions that give the parties clear guidance about their rights and duties.

G. **Grading:** Unless your professor tells you otherwise, both you and your Opposing Counsel will receive the same grade on the contract you submit.

H. **Additional Instructions:** Your professor may provide you with additional instructions regarding this assignment.

Appendices

Appendix *1*

Ten Tips for Interviewing a Client About a Transaction

1. Interview the client contact who has first-hand information.

   - This may sound obvious. However, sometimes the vice president of sales will call you even though it is the regional sales representative who is doing the deal. You will to talk to the regional sales representative to get the information you need, though you may want to keep the vice president of sales in the loop.
   - For the assignments in this book, I connect you with the appropriate client contact in every instance. Nevertheless, you should keep in mind that, in practice, this will not always be the case.

2. Prepare for the client interview by finding out everything you can about the client's business beforehand.

   - First, talk to the attorney who originated the business. What does she know about her client's business? (And what does she already know about the deal?)
   - If the client has a website, thoroughly familiarize yourself with it.
   - Look for general information about your client's field on the Internet or at the library. For example, assume you know that your client makes plastic bottles for soda, using a process called *injection blow molding,* and that your client wants to lease a plant where it can perform this process. Then, before you meet with the client, you should try to learn about the injection blow molding process. How large is the necessary equipment? What materials are used? How are the materials delivered? Nowadays, you may even be able to find a video on the Internet demonstrating the injection blow molding process.
   - Additionally, never underestimate the value of asking your client to tell you about his business. You will learn a lot, and your questions will put your client at ease. This will give you a chance to demonstrate what you have learned about the client's business during your research. Your research will have given you the language you need to have a meaningful dialogue with the client.
   - For the assignments in this book, you will need to learn about some businesses—art, professional golf, toy store management, or rock

music, for example. If the parameters of the assignment allow, you may do some research about the business and locate a glossary of terms to help you understand the jargon that is second nature to your client. If your client is a member of the Ladies Professional Golf Association (LPGA), you may want to find out what that membership entails. Moreover, if your LPGA client tells you that she wants the putting green she's purchasing to have "fringe" you will feel better if you don't have to ask her what that word means.

3. Recognize the difference between interviewing a client about a pending transaction and interviewing a client about a problem that may (or has already) resulted in litigation.

    -   This is related to the difference between representing a client in litigation and representing a client regarding a deal. As Tina L. Stark points out, "The analytical skill of translating the business deal into contract concepts fundamentally differs from the analytical skill that litigators use. Litigators take the law and apply it to the facts to create a persuasive argument. . . . Deal lawyers start from the business deal. The terms of the business deal are the deal lawyers' facts."[1]
    -   When interviewing a client about a potential litigation problem, simply asking the client "What happened?" is likely to get you very far. The client's natural urge to tell the story will take over. When interviewing a client about a pending transaction, if you simply say "What's the transaction about?" your client is likely to give you a general outline of the deal, which will require you to work harder to elicit details.

4. When the client consults you, first figure out where the client is on what George Kuney calls "The Deal Timeline," a "chain of events that characterizes most transactions. . . ."[2]

    -   For example, if your client, Company X, is going to purchase a large piece of equipment, has it already selected the vendor? Or has it merely solicited proposals from various vendors? If Company X has already selected a vendor, has it spoken with the vendor about the deal terms? Have Company X and the vendor agreed upon any (or all) of the deal terms?
    -   For the purposes of the main contract drafting assignments in each sequence provided in this book, your client is already pretty far along on the Deal Timeline. For the first main contract drafting assignment, you are interviewing a client who has already selected a vendor (or

---

1. Tina L. Stark, *Drafting Contracts: How and Why Lawyers Do What They Do* 10 (Aspen 2007).

2. George W. Kuney, *The Elements of Contract Drafting with Questions and Clauses for Consideration*, 2d ed., 3-5 (Thomson West 2006).

purchaser) and agreed upon most of the terms of the deal. For the second main contract drafting assignment, you will be using documents that summarize the terms of the deal already negotiated by the client. By contrast, in the third and final contract drafting assignment, you enter the Deal Timeline at an earlier point in time. You know some of your client's wishes (from the Confidential Instructions provided), but you will have the opportunity to negotiate, with the client's objectives as your guide.

5. Use your knowledge of where the client is on the Deal Timeline to help you decide how to approach the client during the interview. As Kuney advises, "Clarify your client's expectations of your role early in the process to avoid confusion and client dissatisfaction."[3]

   - If the client clearly telegraphs that the deal terms are set, you should question the client about those terms and keep your advisory cap in your hand until you have a clear sense of the whole deal.
   - If, during the interview, the client sounds unsure about certain deal terms and asks you what you think, you can don your advisory cap (if you have the expertise to answer the question) or you can tell the client that you want to get a sense of the whole deal before you answer the question. You may also tell the client that the question requires some additional digging (i.e., research).
   - A law student interviewing a client late in the Deal Timeline frequently uses an adversarial tone, making statements like, "I don't think you should have agreed to keep that information confidential," or "Did you ever consider that agreeing to that provision could wipe out your business?" I advise the student to interview the client in a cordial, professional way and avoid statements and questions that put the client on the defensive. If the client has already agreed to the deal terms, initially, the student should act as a fact finder, much as he would in a discovery deposition — asking open-ended questions and focusing on gathering information, rather than on advising and shaping the deal.

6. Prepare a list of questions while keeping in mind that the end product will be a contract.

   - Use what you know about the essential parts of a contract to help you determine what questions to ask the client. This does not mean that you begin the interview by asking the client for all of the information that you need to include in the contract's preamble. Obviously, if you barely know the client, you do not want to begin the interview by

---

3. Kuney, at 4.

asking a question like "Where is the vendor incorporated?" Begin by finding out a general outline of the deal. If the client wants to engage a software consultant to design a new accounting program, for example, ask what your client wants the consultant to do and how much your client is going to pay for the consultant's services.

- As mentioned in Tip 3, above, your discussion of the deal is unlikely to progress in a linear fashion, the way a discussion of a litigation problem often does. Your client's story may not lend itself naturally to narrative. You must drill down to get the details.

- Since you know that both parties to the deal are going to undertake some obligations (covenants), you will want to find out what those are. Is your client's obligation only the obligation to pay? Or is your client also obliged to provide materials and labor for the project? What are the vendor's obligations beyond providing the primary services?

- If the parties have talked prior to your client contacting you, did either party make any statements (representations and warranties) designed to induce the other side to enter into the deal?

- Is there anything that either party must do or refrain from doing (condition precedent) prior to the execution of the contract or prior to, for example, the other party making a payment during the contract's term?

- Are there any processes that the parties need to design and spell out? For example, if your client may approve or disapprove of the other party's work (discretionary authority) before the other party is paid, what does the approval process look like?

- Are there any key words that you must define in order for the parties to be "on the same page"? For example, in a Snow Removal Services Agreement, the parties may need to define what they mean by "snow removal" or, even, the elusive word "snow."

- If you have a contract drafting checklist like the one provided in Appendix 3, go over it before interviewing the client. While you may not get all of the information you need during the initial interview, you should try to get enough information to prepare an initial draft of the contract.

7. Ask follow-up questions to elicit more detailed information.

- In at least one way, interviewing a client about a transaction is similar to examining a witness in a deposition or at trial. When training litigators, supervising attorneys or professors often say, "You take your witness as you find him." In other words, if you represent the plaintiff and you are examining the defendant or the defendant's witness—that is, a witness you did not prepare for testimony—you may be facing a witness who is reticent, angry, loquacious, vague, meandering, meek, or [insert any number of other adjectives]. You take your witness as you find him. In other words, you have to adapt your style of questioning so that you can get what you want from the witness. When interviewing a client about a transaction, you take your witness as you find her. Is she reticent? If so, you will have to try to make her more comfortable (and perhaps less reticent) and then you will have to ask her a lot of follow-up questions. Does he meander? You will have to rely on your excellent people skills to get him back on track without making him angry or defensive.

- In the client interview you conduct for the first main contract drafting assignment in each sequence in this book, challenge yourself to suspend your disbelief and treat the person playing the role of the client as a real client. If she is shy, for example, you will have to ask more questions in order to break through her shell and find out the terms of the deal. If you embrace the simulated client interview, you can use it as an opportunity to practice in a safe setting—where making mistakes won't hurt you.

8. Take good notes during the client interview.

- Does this go without saying? Sometimes a new attorney is so nervous during a client interview that she is unable to listen to the client and take good notes at the same time. If at all possible, ask someone else to be present to supplement your own note taking.
- If you are asked to draft the contract in a team, you may designate one or more person to take notes during the client interview. In my experience, even though all teams are present during the same client interview, the team members' notes differ significantly. It reminds me of the game of telephone, in which one person whispers a message to the next person and that person whispers it to another person and so on, until, at the end of a line of ten people, the message has changed completely. The moral is: listen carefully, take good notes, and don't be afraid to ask for clarification either during the interview or afterwards.

9. At the end of the interview, find out how best to contact your client and establish a deadline for producing the first draft of the contract.

- Does your client contact want to continue in that role or does he want to give you the name of another client contact?
- If your client wants to continue in that role, what is the best way for you to contact him, and how available will he be between now and the impending deadline?
- Ask your client when he would like you to produce a first draft of the contract for his review.
- Establish whether your client wants to meet again to discuss the draft or if she would prefer to communicate about the draft by phone or e-mail.

- If you need your client to gather any additional information, remind him of that at the end of the meeting and tell him that you can send him a confirming e-mail if that would be helpful.
- For the purposes of the assignments in this book, if you need to communicate with your client, you will have to contact your professor. Ideally, you would have access to a real client, but a simulation does have its limitations.

10. Show your client that you are a deal facilitator, not a deal killer. (But that does not mean you are "a mere scrivener.")

- If your client contact is enthusiastic about the deal, you should allow her enthusiasm to be infectious, at least initially. Otherwise, she may view you as a deal killer rather than a deal facilitator. This can have a high cost, especially if she decides not to bring you in on any other deals. If you are an in-house attorney, your client contact may decide to avoid the legal department altogether and resort to cutting and pasting from fully negotiated contracts she used in other deals. Although she will soon learn the dangers of this shortcut, she may contact you too late in the process—that is, she may ask for your help after she has already unwittingly agreed to a provision detrimental to the Company.
- Once you have learned the deal facts, you can demonstrate to your client that you are more than a "mere scrivener"—that is, one who merely takes dictation without thinking about the legal or business issues involved in the deal. As Tina Stark so eloquently states:

> Drafting contracts is more than translating the business deal into contract concepts and writing clear, unambiguous contract provisions. Sophisticated drafting requires a lawyer to understand the transaction from a client's business perspective and to add value to the deal. Looking at a contract from the client's perspective means understanding what the client wants to achieve and the risks it wants to avoid. Adding value to the deal is a euphemism for finding and resolving business issues. These skills are problem-solving skills and are an integral component of a deal lawyer's professional expertise. . . .[4]

---

4. Tina L. Stark, *Drafting Contracts: How and Why Lawyers Do What They Do* 303 (Aspen 2007).

The Model Leaf Disposal Services Agreement

LEAF DISPOSAL SERVICES AGREEMENT

Leaf Disposal Services Agreement made this 10th day of October 2007, between SpinGazer, Inc., a Delaware corporation with its principal place of business located at 1200 Ridge Avenue, Evanston, Illinois 60201 (the "Company"), and Fallen Leaves, Inc., an Illinois corporation with its principal place of business located at 2025 North Clark Street, Chicago, Illinois 60614 (the "Provider").

Background

The Company designs and develops websites for artists and musicians. The Company owns the small building it occupies, as well as the large lot on which the building sits. There are forty mature, healthy trees on the lot. They include oak, maple, birch, chestnut, hickory, and gingko trees.

The Provider is in the business of collecting, removing, and disposing of fallen leaves for homeowners and businesses. The Provider is known for its ability to accomplish these tasks without using loud, gasoline-driven leaf blowers or other similar environmentally adverse equipment.

As part of its current "Go Green" initiative to take better care of the environment, the Company desires to hire the Provider to collect, remove, and dispose of the fallen leaves from its lot.

The Provider desires to help the Company with its "Go Green" initiative by using environmentally friendly methods to collect, remove, and dispose of the leaves from the Company's lot, in exchange for a fee.

Accordingly, the parties agree as follows:

Article I. Definitions

As used in this Agreement, the terms defined in the preamble have their assigned meanings and the following terms have the meanings assigned to them in this Article.

(a) **"Article [insert number]"** means the specified Article in this Agreement.

(b) **"Bag"** means a recyclable paper sack appropriate for the collection and removal of fallen leaves.

(c) **"Base Fee"** has the meaning assigned in Section 5.01.

(d) **"Company Material Breach"** has the meaning assigned in Section 10.06.

(e) **"Crew"** means the Provider's employees assigned to perform the Services.

(f) **"Cure Period"** has the meaning assigned in Section 10.03.

(g) **"Director of Operations"** means the Company's current Director of Operations, Jackie Spingazer, or her successor.

(h) **"Down Payment"** has the meaning assigned in Section 5.02(a).

(i) **"Environmentally Adverse Equipment"** includes any leaf collection, removal, or disposal machines that pollute the air, water, land, or general environment by emitting toxic gases, waste, heat, or loud noise. "Environmentally Adverse Equipment" does not include Hybrid Vehicles.

(j) **"Final Payment"** has the meaning assigned in Section 5.02(c).

(k) **"Hybrid Vehicle"** means a car or truck that uses a small combustion engine combined with an electric motor and a battery to reduce fuel consumption and tailpipe emissions.

(l) **"Inspection"** means a walk around the Lot to gather information facilitating an assessment of the quality of the Services.

(m) **"Inspection Report"** means a written assessment of the quality of the Services prepared as the result of an Inspection.

(n) **"Interim Payment"** has the meaning assigned in Section 5.02(b).

(o) **"Lot"** means the property owned by SpinGazer, Inc., at 1200 Ridge Road, Evanston, Illinois 60201, which measures 360 feet by 240 feet and is recorded at the Cook County Clerk's office as Lot No. 24-208756B.

(p) **"Notice"** has the meaning assigned in Section 11.03.

(q) **"Provider Material Breach"** has the meaning assigned in Section 10.01.

(r) **"Section [insert number]"** means the specified Section in this Agreement.

(s) **"Service Level Bonus Fee"** has the meaning assigned in Section 5.03.

(t) **"Services"** has the meaning assigned in Section 4.01.

(u) **"Supervisor"** means the Provider's employee, Leif E. Liminator.

(v) **"Term"** has the meaning assigned in Section 2.01.

Article II. Term

Section 2.01 Term. This Agreement begins on October 10, 2007, and ends on December 15, 2007 (the "Term"), unless terminated earlier in accordance with Article X.

Article III. Summary of Services and Fees

Section 3.01 Services and Fees. Subject to the Provisions of this Agreement, the Provider shall perform the Services described in Article IV. To compensate the Provider for performing the Services, the Company shall pay the Provider the fees and reimburse the Provider for the expenses described in Article V.

Article IV. Services

Section 4.01 Weekly Leaf Collection, Removal and Disposal. On Friday, October 12, 2007, and on each Friday of every week during the Term, the Provider shall collect the leaves that have fallen on the Lot, remove them from the Lot, and dispose of them (collectively, the "Services").

Section 4.02 Method of Leaf Collection. The Provider shall collect the leaves and put them into Bags. The Provider shall not use any Environmentally Adverse Equipment to collect the leaves and put them into Bags.

Section 4.03 Method of Leaf Removal. The Provider shall remove the Bags from the Lot by loading them into Hybrid Vehicles and carrying them away from the Lot.

Section 4.04 Method of Leaf Disposal. After removing the Bags from the Lot in the Hybrid Vehicles, the Provider shall empty the Bags, recycle the Bags, and dispose of the leaves without using any Environmentally Adverse Equipment.

Section 4.05 The Leaf Disposal Equipment. The Provider represents and warrants that it does not use Environmentally Adverse Equipment to dispose of any leaves that it collects in the course of its business. The Provider shall not use Environmentally Adverse Equipment to dispose of any leaves that it collects from the Lot.

Section 4.06 Timing for Services. Each Friday during the Term, the Provider shall:

(a) arrive at the Lot and begin collecting leaves after 10 a.m. and before 1 p.m.; and

(b) complete the leaf collection and removal before 5 p.m.

Section 4.07 Materials and Equipment. The Provider shall supply and pay for all materials and equipment necessary to perform the Services, except for the Bags. The Provider shall supply the Bags, but the Company shall reimburse the Provider for the cost of all Bags used in connection with the Services, in accordance with Sections 5.05 and 5.06.

Article V. Fees and Expenses

Section 5.01 The Base Fee. The Company shall pay the Provider a base fee of $3,000 for the Services (the "Base Fee").

Section 5.02 Payment Structure of Base Fee. The Company shall pay the Provider the Base Fee as follows:

(a) $500 concurrently with the execution and delivery of this Agreement (the "Down Payment");

(b) $1,500 in two equal installments of $750 each, the first installment due on November 1, 2007, and the second installment due on December 1, 2007 (collectively, the "Interim Payments"); and

(c) $1,000 on December 15, 2007 (the "Final Payment").

Section 5.03 Service Level Bonus Fee. If, pursuant to Section 8.02, the Company's Director of Operations rates the Provider's performance of Services as "Excellent" more than 50% of the time during the Term, then the Company shall pay the Provider a bonus of $500 (the "Service Level Bonus Fee").

Section 5.04 Payment Method for Base Fee and Service Level Bonus Fee. The Company shall pay the Down Payment, the Interim Payments, and the Final Payment to the Provider by mailing Company checks to the Provider by certified mail, return receipt requested. The Company shall pay the Service Level Bonus Fee to the Provider by delivering a Company check to the Supervisor by hand on the last day that the Provider performs the Services.

Section 5.05 Reimbursement for Cost of Bags. No later than ten days after the end of the Term, the Provider shall deliver an invoice to the Company detailing the number and cost of the Bags used to perform the Services. No later than ten days after receipt of the Provider's invoice, the Company shall reimburse the Provider for the cost of the Bags used to perform the Services.

Section 5.06 Payment Method for Reimbursement of Cost of Bags. The Company shall pay the reimbursement for the Bags to the Provider by mailing a Company check to the Provider by certified mail, return receipt requested.

Article VI. Exclusivity and Use of Company Name as Reference

Section 6.01 Exclusive Provider. During the Term, the Company shall not engage any individual or entity other than the Provider to provide leaf collection, removal, or disposal services for the Lot.

Section 6.02 Consequences of Violation of Exclusive Provider Provision. If the Company violates Section 6.01, then the Provider may terminate this Agreement immediately as described in Section 10.07.

Section 6.03 Use of Company Name as Reference. The Provider shall not use the Company's name as a reference without first obtaining the written approval of the Director of Operations.

Section 6.04 Consequences of Misuse of Company Name as Reference. If the Provider violates Section 6.03, then the Company may terminate this Agreement immediately as described in Section 10.02.

Article VII. Supervisory Continuity and Duties

Section 7.01 Key Supervisor Requirement. The Provider shall assign the Supervisor to be the only on-site supervisor of the Company's account for the entire Term.

Section 7.02 Supervisor's Duties. The Provider shall require the Supervisor to do the following each Friday during the Term:

(a) come to the Lot with the Crew;

(b) upon arrival, contact the Director of Operations;

(c) oversee all aspects of the Services;

(d) communicate with the Director of Operations if any problems needing the Company's attention arise during the performance of the Services;

(e) notify the Director of Operations when the Crew has completed the collection and removal of the leaves;

(f)   accompany the Director of Operations on the Inspection described in Section 8.01;

(g)   receive the Inspection Report from the Director of Operations; and

(h)   deliver the Inspection Report to the Provider.

Section 7.03 Consequences of Violation of Key Supervisor Requirement. If the Provider violates the Key Supervisor Requirement described in Section 7.01, then the Company may terminate this Agreement immediately in accordance with Section 10.02.

Article VIII. Quality Control

Section 8.01 Inspection. Each Friday during the Term, after the Crew finishes collecting the leaves and removing them to the Hybrid Trucks, the Company shall require its Director of Operations to conduct an Inspection.

Section 8.02 Determination of Quality. After each Inspection, the company shall require its Director of Operations to prepare an Inspection Report, rating the Services as "Excellent," "Satisfactory," or "Unsatisfactory" and deliver this document to the Supervisor by hand.

Section 8.03 Consequences of Unsatisfactory Rating. If the Director of Operations rates the Services as "Unsatisfactory," then the Company may terminate the Agreement unless the Provider cures the deficiency as described in Section 10.03.

Section 8.04 Consequences of Majority of Ratings Being Excellent. If the Director of Operations rates the Services as "Excellent" more than 50% of the time during the Term, then the Company shall pay the Provider the Service Level Bonus Fee described in Section 5.03.

Article IX. Status of Provider and Provider's Employees

Section 9.01 Provider's Independent Contractor Status. The Provider shall perform the Services as an independent contractor engaged under this Agreement and not as an employee of the Company. During the Term, the Provider shall: (a) remain a corporation in good standing; (b) maintain its own office; and (c) continue to service and solicit clients other than the Company. During the Term, the Provider shall not: (a) possess any authority to bind the Company; or (b) represent itself as an agent of the Company

Section 9.02 Provider's Employees. The Provider shall use its own employees to perform the Services. The Provider shall be responsible for payment of all federal, state, and local taxes and other fees arising out of the

Provider's performance of Services under this Agreement, including, but not limited to, income tax, payroll taxes, and worker's compensation and unemployment insurance premiums.

Section 9.03 Background Checks. The Provider represents and warrants that it has conducted background checks on each of its employees and that none of its employees has been convicted of a felony within the last ten years.

Section 9.04 No Subcontractors. The Provider shall not subcontract out any of the Services.

Article X. Termination Provisions

Section 10.01 Provider Material Breach. "Provider Material Breach" means the occurrence of any one or more of the following events during the Term:

(a)   the Provider removes the Supervisor from the Company's account;

(b)   the Provider fires the Supervisor;

(c)   the Provider uses the Company's name as a reference in violation of Section 6.03;

(d)   the Provider performs the Services in a way that endangers or negatively affects the productivity of the Company's employees;

(e)   the Provider uses Environmentally Adverse Equipment in performing the Services;

(f)   the Provider regularly fails to perform the Services as scheduled; or

(g)   the Provider fails to meet any other similarly significant requirements of this Agreement.

Section 10.02 Company's Right to Terminate Agreement for Provider's Material Breach. If one or more Provider Material Breaches occurs, the Company may terminate this Agreement immediately by giving Notice to the Provider.

Section 10.03 Company's Right to Terminate Agreement for Provider's Failure to Cure Unsatisfactory Performance. If, on any Friday during the Term, the Company's Director of Operations rates the Services as "Unsatisfactory" on the Inspection Report, then the Company shall give Notice to the Provider. If the Provider does not cure the deficiency within two days after receipt of Notice (the "Cure Period"), then the Company may terminate the Agreement immediately upon expiration of the Cure Period.

Section 10.04 Consequences of Company's Termination of Agreement. If the Company chooses to terminate this Agreement in accordance with Section 10.02 or Section 10.03, then the Provider shall:

(a)   retain one-half of the Down Payment;

(b)   refund to the Company one half of the Down Payment; and

(c)   refund to the Company any Interim Payments made.

Section 10.05 Method of Provider's Refunds to Company. The Provider shall refund the payments described in Section 10.04 to the Company by cashier's check delivered by certified mail, return receipt requested, no later than seven days after the Provider receives the Notice of termination.

Section 10.06 Company Material Breach. "Company Material Breach" means the occurrence of any one or more of the following events during the Term:

(a)   the Company fails to pay the Down Payment or any of the Interim Payments on or before the fourteenth day after the payment is due; or

(b)   the Company engages any other individuals or entities other than the Provider to perform leaf collection, removal, or disposal of fallen leaves from the Lot, in violation of Section 6.01.

Section 10.07 Provider's Right to Terminate Agreement for Company's Material Breach. If one or more Company Material Breaches occurs, the Provider may terminate this Agreement immediately by giving Notice to the Company.

Section 10.08 Consequences of Provider's Termination of Agreement. If the Provider chooses to terminate this Agreement in accordance with Section 10.07, then:

(a)   the Provider shall keep the Initial Down Payment and any Interim Payments made;

(b)   the Company shall pay the Provider any past due Interim Payments; and

(c)   the Company shall pay the Provider a pro-rata share of the Final Payment based on the number of days of Services actually provided prior to termination.

Section 10.09 Method of Company's Payments to Provider. The Company shall pay the Provider the payments described in Section 10.08 no later than five days after receipt of the Notice of termination, with a cashier's check delivered by certified mail, return receipt requested.

Section 10.10 No Further Obligations of the Parties. If either party exercises its right to terminate this Agreement in accordance with this Article, once the breaching party makes the refunds or payments specified in Sections 10.04 and 10.08, this Agreement terminates and the parties have no further rights or obligations under it.

Section 10.11 Reservation of Rights. By terminating this Agreement in accordance with this Article, neither party waives any of its rights to pursue any other available remedies, including, without limitation, the right to recover damages for harm suffered due to the other party's breach.

Article XI. General Provisions

Section 11.01 Assignment and Delegation. No party may assign any of its rights under this Agreement, except with the prior written consent of the other party. No party may delegate any performance under this Agreement.

Section 11.02 Choice of Law. The laws of the State of Illinois govern all matters arising out of or relating to this Agreement, including, without limitation, its validity, interpretation, construction, performance, and enforcement.

Section 11.03 Notices. Each party giving any notice ("Notice") pursuant to this Agreement shall give Notice in writing either: (a) by e-mail with a required delivery receipt to sender; or (b) by letter sent by overnight mail, next day delivery, signature required. Notices delivered by e-mail are deemed to have been received as of the time and date stamp on the delivery receipt to sender. Notices delivered by overnight mail are deemed to have been received as of the time and date on the signed receipt. Each party giving Notice shall address the Notice to the parties at the addresses appearing below.

The Company:	Jackie Spingazer
	Director of Operations
	SpinGazer, Inc.
	1200 Ridge Avenue
	Evanston, Illinois 60201
The Provider:	Leif E. Liminator
	Supervisor
	Fallen Leaves, Inc.
	2025 North Clark Street
	Chicago, Illinois 60614

Section 11.04 Severability. If any provision of this Agreement is determined to be invalid, illegal, or unenforceable, the remaining provisions of

this Agreement remain in full force, as long as the essential terms and conditions of this Agreement for each party remain valid, binding, and enforceable.

Section 11.05 Modification or Amendment. The parties may not modify or amend this Agreement, except by a written amendment signed by both parties.

Section 11.06 Merger. This Agreement constitutes the final agreement between the parties. All prior and contemporaneous negotiations and agreements between the parties on the matters contained in this Agreement are expressly merged into and superseded by this Agreement.

Section 11.07 Authority to Sign Agreement on Behalf of Company. The Company represents and warrants that its Director of Operations has the authority to sign this Agreement and bind the Company to its terms.

Section 11.08 Authority to Sign Agreement on Behalf of Provider. The Provider represents and warrants that its Supervisor has the authority to sign this Agreement and bind the Provider to its terms.

AGREED:

SPINGAZER, INC.   **FALLEN LEAVES, INC.**

By: _____   By: _____

    Jackie Spingazer   Leif E. Liminator

Title: Director of Operations   Title: Supervisor

Appendix *3*

Contract Drafting Checklist

Contract Drafting Checklist

Compiled by Professor Sue Payne, 2/25/08

I. General

☐ Accurately embodies negotiated terms
☐ Covers all relevant facts
☐ Parts of the Agreement are well coordinated—they all work together
☐ Defined terms prove their value and are consistently, appropriately used
☐ Cross-references are easy to follow and not too abundant
☐ Reads like good prose; clear, concise, smooth, well organized
☐ Reader ends up knowing all of the rights and duties of the parties
☐ Reader ends up with all significant questions answered
☐ Reader can understand the terms of the deal even though the reader is a third party

II. Format

☐ Font is Tahoma or comparable
☐ Font size is 12 point
☐ Article names use Roman numerals, centered, boldface
☐ Section names are regular numerals with decimals; numerals are keyed to Article names (e.g., Section 3.01 is the first section in Article III); boldface
☐ Heading of Section is indented after Section number; boldface
☐ Headings—initial caps of key words
☐ Pages are numbered at the bottom center
☐ Signature lines do not appear on a page without any text

III. Essential Parts

☐ Title
☐ Preamble
☐ Background
☐ Words of Agreement (Statement of Consideration)

☐ Definitions
☐ Action Sections
☐ Other Substantive Provisions
☐ Endgame
☐ General Provisions (Boilerplate)
☐ Signature Lines

IV. Review of Each Part

Title

☐ Appropriate for subject matter
☐ Not too general or too specific
☐ Not too long
☐ Initial caps of key words
☐ Centered; boldface

Preamble

☐ Nicknames for parties are at same level of generality
☐ Nicknames are placed appropriately (after all identifying information after the party)
☐ Full names of parties are correct
☐ State of incorporation and principal place of business (for company); residential address for individual
☐ If address included for one party, then address included for other party

Background

☐ Information not confidential or embarrassing to other party
☐ No covenants or other substantive provisions
☐ Puts Agreement in context but does not say too much

Words of Agreement (Statement of Consideration)

☐ No archaic language
☐ Short and sweet—"Accordingly, the parties agree as follows:"
☐ Appears at the end of the Background section; not set apart in separate section

Definitions

☐ Not circular; usually doesn't use the word itself to define the word
☐ No covenants or other operative provisions; each definition is a declaration only
☐ More than just the dictionary definition of a word
☐ Makes sense; doesn't define word in way so different from ordinary meaning that reader gets confused
☐ Terms that need to be defined are defined, especially if needed to clarify that parties agree to a particular meaning

☐ Nice balance between definitions in Definitions section and cross-references to in-text definitions
☐ Eliminates need to repeat a long group of words each time
☐ Description of Sale (or Services)
☐ Description of Payment/Compensation

Action Sections

☐ Term of the contract is described (with references to possible early terminations and extensions, if applicable)
☐ Closing Date is identified; time and place as well
☐ Closing Deliveries, if any, are specified
☐ Subject matter performance provision (parties covenant to perform the main subject matter of the contract)

Other Substantive Provisions

☐ Organized by topic, usually in order of importance (most to least)
☐ Utilizes contract concepts within each topic (*Note:* Do not use contract concepts as headings. Use topic headings, with appropriate sub-topics.)
☐ Within each topic, translates business terms into contract concepts:
    ☐ Covenants
    ☐ Representations and Warranties
    ☐ Conditions Precedent
    ☐ Statements of Discretionary Authority
    ☐ Uses correct verbs to indicate type of provision
    ☐ Not every contract concept appears under every topic

Endgame

☐ Section contains or references every endgame provision in Agreement—a snapshot of the Endgame
☐ Spells out all of the if/thens—good consequences; bad consequences
☐ Incorporates right to cure, if so agreed by the parties
☐ Spells out procedure for carrying out endgame
☐ Spells out what happens to the money and products or ongoing services if contract terminates early
☐ May include dispute resolution procedure

General Provisions (Boilerplate)

☐ Shows good judgment about choices made
☐ Appropriately adapts precedent used
☐ Appropriately cites precedent used (if required)
☐ Consistently utilizes defined terms from THIS Agreement

Signature Lines

☐ Uses correct, full names of parties
☐ Does not abbreviate names

☐ Does not use nicknames
☐ Formatted properly
☐ Contains prefatory language ("To evidence their agreement to the terms..." or "AGREED:")

V. Plain English

☐ Agreement is written in Plain English

AVOID THE FOLLOWING LANGUAGE ISSUES

☐ Archaic/elevated language
☐ Legalese
☐ Wordiness
☐ Choppy prose
☐ Passive voice
☐ Awkward phrases or sentences
☐ Inconsistency
☐ Vagueness
☐ Ambiguity
☐ Omission of articles ("a," "an," and "the")
☐ Incorrect verb tenses
☐ Use of nominalizations instead of strong verbs
☐ Double negatives
☐ Dangling modifiers
☐ Covenant language needed/not needed
☐ Discretionary authority language needed/not needed
☐ Condition precedent language needed/not needed
☐ Dual verbs (pick one)
☐ Dual adjectives (pick one)
☐ Wrong preposition choice
☐ Sentence fragments
☐ Run-on sentences
☐ Faulty parallel structure
☐ Inappropriate tone

AVOID PROOFREADING ERRORS AND TYPOGRAPHICAL ERRORS

☐ Missing words
☐ Extra words
☐ Missing word endings
☐ Spell check errors
☐ Failure to conform boilerplate to terms used in contract

AVOID PUNCTUATION ISSUES

☐ Commas in the wrong place
☐ Semicolons used incorrectly
☐ Colons used incorrectly
☐ Periods missing
☐ Tabulations punctuated improperly

Appendix *4*

What Deal Lawyers Say to Each Other: A Dictionary of Contract Negotiation and Drafting Slang[1]

ace in the hole: A powerful bargaining chip that the attorney is holding back; it carries so much weight that it is likely to tip the balance. *Example*: An in-house attorney negotiating an employment agreement with the Company's top candidate for CFO tells the Company's CEO, "I can still offer Mr. Smith a signing bonus. That's my ace in the hole."

any more room: Any authority to accept anything lower or to offer anything higher. *Example*: An attorney asks opposing counsel, "Are you sure you don't have any more room?"

belt and suspenders: Extra assurance, even if redundant. *Example*: An attorney says to opposing counsel, "My client is required not to violate the law. That provision stating that he won't discriminate on the basis of age is just a belt and suspenders."

boilerplate (just boilerplate): "Standard" provisions near the end of a contract, sometimes called *the fine print*. *Example*: An attorney says to opposing counsel, "I don't think you'll have any problems with the provision I'm going to add; it's just boilerplate." *Note*: The attorney intends for opposing counsel to accept the provision without reading it. He is implying that the provision is ordinary, fully vetted, and not usually changed.

bottom line: As low as you can go (presumably). *Example*: An attorney says to opposing counsel, "$10,000 is our bottom line." *Note*: Attorneys may say this when they don't really mean it.

bulletproof: Impenetrable; not capable of being evaded; no loopholes. *Example*: A Company tells its attorney, "I want this confidentiality clause to be bulletproof."

carve-out: An exception; limits a general prohibition in a specific way. *Example*: An attorney says to opposing counsel, "We agree that we won't directly solicit any of your employees, but we want a carve-out for employees who

---

1. This is a living, evolving document. Please send me more phrases and words, along with examples of how attorneys use them. I will add them to this "dictionary" and ask your professors to provide you with the revised document.

respond to one of our newspaper classified ads. That should not be considered soliciting."

caveat: A provision that qualifies or restricts another provision. *Example:* An attorney says to opposing counsel: "My client will agree not to disclose your client's confidential information, with the caveat that your client must clearly designate what information it considers to be confidential."

cowboy: A client who makes promises to the other side just to make the sale. (See also the definition of *pregnant*, below.) *Example:* One attorney colleague says to another attorney colleague (regarding one of the sales representatives), "Watch out for him. He's a cowboy." *Note:* Managing a cowboy can be difficult.

deal breaker (or show stopper): A provision that will cause the deal to fall through unless it's included or excluded from the contract. *Example:* Late in the negotiation process, with only one item in dispute, an attorney says to opposing counsel, "Is the change in control provision a deal breaker?"

deal killer: A derogatory term sometimes used by clients to describe attorneys they perceive as overly cautious and intrusive; alternatively, a provision similar to a deal breaker or show-stopper. *Example:* A sales representative tells the Company's CFO that the in-house attorney assigned to draft the contract is a deal killer.

drop-dead date: The date by which something must happen or the deal itself won't happen; alternatively, any fixed deadline within the contract that must be met or serious consequences will occur. *Example:* When negotiating an employment contract for an anxious executive with more than one job offer, the executive's attorney tells the opposing counsel, "We have to get this thing drafted and signed by May 1st. That's my client's drop-dead date."

everything but the kitchen sink: Used to express frustration when a lawyer overreaches and drafts a provision awarding her client a wide variety of rights. *Example:* One attorney colleague says to another, "Look what she put in here—everything but the kitchen sink."

eyeball it: Take a quick look at a document just to get the general outline of it. *Example:* One colleague says to another, "Just eyeball this contract once before we talk. Later, you can take whatever time you need to read it more carefully."

fur line it: Make a contract absolutely perfect, as if to give it a "fur lining." *Example:* A senior partner says to a junior partner, "The client doesn't have a lot of time or money, so just draft something quickly and don't fur line it."

go to the well again: Similar to "taking another bite of the apple"; an expression of frustration made when, near the end of a negotiation, an attorney adds something she forgot to put in earlier (or something that her client is suddenly demanding). *Example:* An attorney says to opposing counsel, "We already agreed on that language. Now you're just trying to go to the well again."

holding his cards close to the vest: A style of negotiating that involves not revealing very much to the other side. *Example:* A senior attorney tells her general counsel, "Attorney X is holding his cards so close to the vest that I don't really know Company Y's position on the key issue."

horse-trading: Giving in on one issue in order to get the other side to agree to another issue. *Example:* A lawyer says to her client, "If you really want the non-compete provision, we could probably horse-trade it for the audit provision they want."

in terrorem effect: The result of including a provision that may not be enforceable but may still deter a party from violating it. *Example:* An attorney tells his client, "I know that non-competes are not enforceable in California, but I'm putting it in anyway for the in terrorem effect." *Note:* There could ethical issues with drafting this way.

like taking candy from a baby: Easily negotiated; suggests that opposing counsel is naïve. *Example:* One colleague says to another, "He readily agreed to let our client assign the contract. It was like taking candy from a baby."

megillah (as in "the whole megillah"): Refers to a very important issue in a deal or a cluster of interrelated issues in a deal. *Example:* One colleague says to another, "If I concede on that point, then I'll be giving up the whole megillah."

massage the language: Change the language—usually includes more than minor revision; used when discussion of a complex concept is going nowhere; sounds like you may concede, but just means you are buying time to re-draft. *Example:* A lawyer says to opposing counsel, "I think I can come up with a way to describe the penalty for late delivery more clearly. Let me massage the language a bit and I'll get back to you."

may not fly: Speculation that the language may not be acceptable to the other party; used when you think the other side is going to object but your client is insisting the provision go in anyway. *Example:* A lawyer says to his client, "We can put in the exclusivity provision, but it may not fly."

mere scrivener: One who merely takes dictation and doesn't think about the legal or business issues. *Example:* A lawyer says to his client, "If you want me to draft a contract for you, you'll have to tell me everything about the deal. I am no mere scrivener." *Note:* It is unlikely that you would say this to your client in quite this way, although you may certainly think it.

nits: Small, insignificant changes to a document; "nits" are sometimes just "wordsmithing" (see below); "nits" sometimes include substantive changes that the drafter does not consider significant (or that the drafter considers significant but does not want the other side to know). *Example:* A lawyer says to opposing counsel, "I just have a few nits."

no-brainer: A point upon which it is easy to agree or concede. *Example:* An attorney says to opposing counsel, "Of course, we can put in a mutual non-disclosure provision. That's a no-brainer."

on the table/off the table: Indicates the status of a proposed term; if it remains on the table, then the offer is still open; if it has been taken off the table, then the offer has been withdrawn. *Example:* An attorney says to opposing counsel, "I'm not going to argue about the signing bonus anymore. We took that off the table yesterday."

overreaching: Going too far; trying to grab too much. *Example:* An attorney tells opposing counsel, "You're trying to prevent my client from working as a salesperson for any company in the world. That's overreaching!"

pass the red-face test: Used when a provision is significantly different from what was previously agreed upon; "red-face" refers to embarrassment. *Example:* One attorney colleague says to another, "I put in the termination-for-convenience that the other side wanted, but I added an early termination fee. Do you think that will pass the red-face test?"

pie-in-the-sky: Unreachable, unrealistic demands. *Example:* An attorney says to opposing counsel, "Yes, but that's your pie-in-the-sky demand. What is it your client *really* wants?"

playing hardball: Being a tough, seemingly immovable negotiator. *Example:* One attorney colleague says to another, "I'm just not getting anywhere on the discount for late delivery provision. Attorney X is really playing hardball."

posturing: Acting aggressive and unreasonable, just to get a reaction. *Example:* One attorney colleague says to another, "She keeps threatening to walk away from the deal. I know she's just posturing, but it's really not very productive."

pregnant: Similar to "the horse is already out of the barn"; already committed to an undesirable provision in the contract because the client spoke without consulting the attorney. *Example:* One attorney colleague says to another, "I don't want to put termination-for-convenience in the contract, but we're already pregnant."

quick and dirty: Something done quickly and not very thoroughly. *Example:* A senior partner tells an associate, "I need the contract right away. Just do a quick and dirty draft for now."

red herring: A provision put into the contract precisely so that there will be something to "horse-trade" later; alternatively, something put in the contract to deflect attention from something else. *Example:* An attorney tells opposing counsel, "That's just a red herring." Opposing counsel responds, "I don't agree, but I'll take it out if you give us the audit provision."

taking another bite of the apple: Used to express dismay when an attorney keeps on re-drafting provisions that both parties had agreed were already finalized. *Example:* An attorney says to opposing counsel, "But we already agreed to all of those provisions. I think you are just trying to take another bite of the apple."

tweak: Make minor changes to a provision in the contract; used when the change is insignificant or you want to make the other attorney believe you think the change is insignificant—that is, you are being a good guy, or this is something you can easily "give" on. *Example*: An attorney says to opposing counsel, "So you want to put some limits around my client's right to audit your books. I understand. Let me tweak the language a bit and get back to you."

unravel: To undo something or to do it over; used when a contract has already been signed but contains a provision that your client mistakenly included. *Example*: Your client (SVP of sales) agreed to limit the purchaser's liability for disclosure of confidential information to twice the amount paid for the services. However, your client forgot that he needed to get approval of such a provision from the CFO. The CFO finds out and asks you try to fix it. You say to the CFO and the SVP, "Now we'll have to try to unravel it."

win-win: A proposition that creates benefits for both sides. *Example*: An attorney says to opposing counsel, "Including this alternative dispute resolution provision is a win-win for both of our clients. It is likely to minimize everybody's litigation costs."

wordsmithing: Changing the words without changing the meaning; used when a lawyer makes editorial changes for no apparent reason other than personal whim. *Example*: An attorney says to opposing counsel, "I can understand the reason for some of these changes, but the rest just seem to be wordsmithing."

Appendix *5*

Proofreading Tips and Tricks

Introduction

When you're asked to turn in a "polished product," you can imagine that drafting a contract is like creating a diamond. Your first draft is carbon. As you apply large amounts of energy and pressure to each successive draft, you gradually transform that carbon into a flawless diamond. Then, you present it to the reader and the reader is dazzled!

To put it more plainly, when you proofread, you prepare a final draft to present to your reader. If you give your final draft "the special and patient attention"[1] that it deserves—that is, if you proofread carefully—you can produce an error-free (or nearly error-free) contract.

When you proofread your final draft, you should look for what are known as "surface errors." Generally, surface errors are errors involving spelling, punctuation, grammar, and word choice.[2] Surface errors also include "typographical" errors, such as doubling or omitting a word or a letter, and "formatting" errors, such as incorrect numbering or spacing.

Why is proofreading so difficult? Proofreading is so difficult because your mind often sees what you meant to write rather than what you actually wrote.[3] *Therefore, in order to be a good proofreader, you have to trick yourself into seeing what you actually wrote.*

Tips and Tricks: Six Categories

---

1. Focus

- Proofreading requires concentration. Find a quiet place. Focus. Some people are excellent multi-taskers, but it's best to try turning off your cell phone and iPod. Odds are that your proofreading will improve. On the

---

1. http://www.public.coe.edu/~wcenter/handouts_proofreading.php
2. http://www.indiana.edu/~wts/pamphlets/proofing_grammar.shtml
3. http://grammar.quickanddirtytips.com/proofreading.aspx

other hand, if you proofread better while listening to death metal music, then listen to death metal music while you proofread.

- Because proofreading requires concentration, it may be better to do it in small blocks of time.[4] Try proofreading the first five pages and then going out to lunch and proofreading the second five pages when you return.

---

2. Achieve Distance

- Finish the contract early and let it sit on a shelf for a day or two before you proofread it. (This may not be realistic, but at least try to let it sit on the shelf for a few hours.) This approach is also known as "achieving distance" or "viewing the contract with fresh eyes."

- Proofread your contract using a hard copy. Print out each draft in a different color. (This is supposed to trick your brain into thinking that you are proofreading an unfamiliar document.) If you proofread better on the computer screen, ignore this tip entirely.

---

3. Slow Yourself Down

- Read your contract out loud to yourself. Read your contract out loud to another person. Have someone else read your contract out loud to you. If you have the appropriate software, have your computer read your contract out loud to you.

- Read slowly. If you read at normal speed, your eyes may not have enough time to catch the errors.[5]

- Read your contract backwards, one sentence at a time. To catch spelling errors, read each sentence backwards, one word at a time (i.e., from right to

---

4. http://www.unc.edu/depts./wcweb/handouts/proofread.html
5. http://owl.english.purdue.edu/owl/resource/561

left). Read your contract in haphazard order[6]—that is, start in the middle and read random sections until you have finished reading all of them.

- Use a straight edge "screen" to reveal one line at time. (Try a piece of paper or a ruler.)

- Touch each word with a pencil as you are reading.

- Go through the contract and circle or highlight every punctuation mark. As you circle or highlight each punctuation mark, ask yourself whether you have used the correct punctuation.[7] (Pay particular attention to the punctuation in tabulated lists.)

4. Be Systematic

- Make a personalized proofreading checklist. Do this by going over your critiqued contracts and making a list of your errors.

- Make several "trips" through the contract, looking for a different type of error each time.

- If your deadline is two hours away and you have just finished the contract, prioritize your proofreading.[8] In other words, if you know that you tend to leave out articles before certain defined terms, proofread the contract for that error first.

5. Use Your Computer Wisely

- Do use a spell-checking function, but don't rely on it to catch all spelling errors.

---

6. http://www.public.coe.edu/?wcenter/handouts_proofreading.php
7. Id.
8. Id.

- Watch out for homonyms. Spell checkers do not catch these errors. If you type "principal" for "principle," a spell checker will not help you. Similarly, if you tend to type "fro" for "for," a spell checker will not help you.

- If you use a grammar checker, remember that each time a grammar checker flags an error, you have to use your own judgment to determine whether it is actually an error. If it is an error, then you have to figure out how to fix it yourself.

- Keep a list of words you tend to type incorrectly. Run a "search and replace" to fix these words. For example, you could search for "fro" if you tend to type it instead of "for."

- Search for each occurrence of a defined term and make sure that the defined term is capitalized.

---

6. Use Resources: A Dictionary and a Grammar Handbook

- If you are not sure whether you have chosen the correct word to express something, look it up in a dictionary.

- If you are not sure whether something is grammatically correct, look it up in a grammar handbook.

Decoding the Comments on Student Contracts: Some Samples with Illustrations[1]

Comment	Explanation/Illustration
Ambiguous	The drafter has written a phrase or a sentence that can mean more than one thing.
	Example: One drafter wrote—
	Section 4.02 Clients' Responsibilities. The Clients shall select the official to preside over the wedding ceremony, the menu, and the gifts for the bridal party.
	Interpretation 1: The Clients shall select the official, who is going to preside over the wedding ceremony, the menu, and the gifts for the bridal party.
	Interpretation 2: The Clients shall select: (a) the official to preside over the wedding ceremony; (b) the menu; and (c) the gifts for the bridal party.
	Note: The drafter intended the meaning contained in Interpretation 2.
	To clear up the ambiguity, the drafter could have tabulated the sentence as in Interpretation 2, above.
Archaic	The drafter has used old-fashioned language or an old-fashioned contract drafting convention.

1. This chart is not intended to contain an exhaustive list of every comment that a professor might make on a student's contract. It is intended to give students some idea of the kinds of comments they can expect to receive.

Comment	Explanation/Illustration
	Example: One drafter wrote—
	Section 7.09 Security. The Museum shall provide three (3) security guards for each Event.
	Using the parenthetical digit "(3)" after the prose "three" is an archaic drafting convention. The drafter should use the digit or the prose, but not both. The only exception to this is when drafting a provision referencing a very large sum of money. Then, the drafter may want to include both the digits and the prose to make sure that he does not omit any zeroes in the dollar figure.
AWK (Awkward)	This phrase or sentence sounds funny. It's hard to explain why. Perhaps the grammar is incorrect or the expression is not colloquial. In any event, if the drafter's first language is English, she may be able to spot an awkward phrase or sentence by reading it out loud (by doing what is, in effect, a "sound check").
	Example: One drafter wrote—
	If either party desires to raise a dispute with the other party, she shall provide Notice of such dispute within 5 days of awareness of the issue of concern.
	The second half of the quoted sentence is awkward. The professor may simply mark it that way, or he may explain that the drafter has strung together five prepositional phrases and four of them contain the preposition "of." Therefore, the phrase is wordy, convoluted, and contains an annoying echo—the repeated sound of the word "of."
Buried/hidden covenant or other substantive provision (in a Definition)	A definition is merely a declaration of what the parties agree a certain term means. It should not contain any substantive/operative provisions—no covenants, representations and warranties, conditions precedent, or statements of discretionary authority.

Comment	Explanation/Illustration
	The most frequent mistake that students make is to include a covenant in a definition and then forget to include the covenant in the body of the contract. A covenant in a definition is not an enforceable/operative provision. When the covenant contained in the definition is not immediately obvious to the drafter and reader, it is considered "buried" or "hidden."
	Example: One drafter wrote—
	"Consignment Record" means the document that both the Artist and the Gallery must prepare and sign upon delivery of the initial five sculptures and each subsequent delivery, containing title, description, medium, retail price and date of delivery to the Gallery.
	One of the hidden covenants is contained in the words "must prepare and sign," which is more than a mere declaration; rather, it is a promise—and an important one, too. Additionally, this definition mandates what the Consignment Record must contain.
	To correct this definition, the drafter can delete the covenants and say:
	"Consignment Record" means a document identifying the sculptures the Artist delivers to the Gallery.
	Later, the drafter can include the following covenants:
	The Artist shall prepare a Consignment Record. The Artist shall include in the Consignment Record the title, description, medium, retail price, and date of delivery of each sculpture the Artist delivers to the Gallery. The Artist and a representative of the Gallery shall both sign each Consignment Record.
Chop the snake	This sentence is too long. The drafter has probably crammed in too many ideas. She

Comment	Explanation/Illustration
	should try dividing it into more than one sentence or tabulating it (if appropriate).
	Example: One drafter wrote—
	Section 6.08 Automatic Renewal. Except for the Key Products, to which the Golfer's Endorsement applies during the Term of this Agreement, each Product to which the Golfer's Endorsement applied in any Contract Year is automatically eligible for the Golfer's Endorsement in the subsequent Contract Year unless the Golfer provides Notice to the Company within 90 days before December 31 that she does not want the Golfer's Endorsement to apply to a specific product.
	The drafter can begin making this sentence more readable by letting the defined term "Key Products" do its work, thereby eliminating the whole phrase "to which the Golfer's Endorsement applies during the Term of this Agreement." (That is, the defined term "Key Products" already presumably includes that concept.)
	One way the drafter could "chop the snake" is to divide this sentence into more than one section:
	Section 6.08 Automatic Renewal. Subject to the exception stated in Section 6.09, except for Key Products, each Product to which the Golfer's Endorsement applied in any Contract Year is automatically eligible for the Golfer's Endorsement in the subsequent Contract Year ("Automatic Renewal").
	Section 6.09 Exception to Automatic Renewal. If, at least 90 days prior to December 31, the Golfer provides Notice to the Company that she does not want the Golfer's Endorsement to apply to a specific Product, then the Endorsement is not subject to Automatic Renewal.

Comment	Explanation/Illustration
Colloquial/Slang	The drafter has used language that sounds more like spoken than written English. The tone is not appropriate for a contract. *Note:* Colloquial language is not to be confused with Plain English.
	Example: One drafter wrote—
	"**Chip**" means the technique golfers use when they find themselves within spitting distance of the green and they think they can just pop the ball up into the air and magically land it there.
	The drafter used a slang expression—"within spitting distance." The drafter also used language that may not be slang but is certainly too informal (and draws conclusions about what is in the golfers' heads)—"they think they can just pop the ball up into the air and magically land it there."
	The drafter can fix this provision by eliminating the colloquial language:
	"Chip" means the technique golfers use to hit the ball onto the green from a short distance away.
Comma splice	The drafter has used a comma to join together (or "splice together") two complete sentences. The comma should be a period or a semicolon. (In a contract, the drafter generally uses a period.)
	Example: One drafter wrote—
	Section 8.02 Accounting Sheet. The Bar shall submit an Accounting Sheet to the Band on the last day of each month, if the Bar fails to submit the Accounting Sheet by the due date, then the Band may terminate the contract as provided in Section 10.08.
	The drafter has joined two complete sentences with a comma (before "if"). The drafter can

Comment	Explanation/Illustration
	correct this by changing the comma to a period and starting the second sentence with "If."
Counterintuitive definition	The drafter has defined a term in a way that is so far away from the dictionary definition of the word that the reader can't get her head around it. In other words, a drafter can't define "Cat" to mean "a dog." *Example:* One drafter wrote— "Cash" means money from the One Art Partnership Bank Account. This definition is counterintuitive because the reader generally thinks of "cash" as money and not as money from a particular source. The drafter probably did not need to define this term at all. If she did, then she probably should have defined a unique term like "Partnership Cash." That way, she would not be going against the reader's ingrained definition of what "cash" means.
Dangling modifier	A dangling modifier is a phrase or clause that is placed too far away from the word or phrase it is intended to modify. *Example:* One drafter wrote— **"Special Materials"** means materials needed to display the Exhibited Works that are not used by the Gallery in the normal course of business. The drafter intends the clause "that are not used by the Gallery in the normal course of business" to modify "materials," not "the Exhibited Works." The drafter can generally fix a dangling modifier by moving it closer to the word or phrase it modifies or by re-drafting the sentence entirely. Since this example is a definition, the drafter can move the concept "needed to display the Exhibited Works" out of the definition.

Comment	Explanation/Illustration
	"Special Materials" means materials not used by the Gallery in the normal course of business.
	Later, the drafter can include a covenant:
	Section 4.02 Payment for Special Materials. The Artist shall pay for any Special Materials necessary to display the Exhibited Works.
Definition contains covenant	A definition is merely a declaration of what the parties agree a certain term means. A definition should not contain any substantive/operative provisions.
	Example: One drafter wrote—
	"Reception" means the event directly following the Ceremony during which a buffet dinner, wedding cake, and beverages will be served.
	The words beginning with "during which" contain a covenant—albeit a badly drafted covenant (written in passive voice and using the verb "will" rather than "shall"). The drafter should re-draft this definition, leaving out the covenant:
	"Reception" means the celebration following the ceremony.
	Later, in the body of the contract, the drafter should include covenants addressing what is supposed to happen at the reception:
	Section 8.05 Coordination of Reception. The Wedding Planner shall plan and coordinate the buffet dinner, champagne toast, and cake cutting ceremony for the Reception.
Don't make your heading do too much work	A heading is like a road sign. Readers use it to find their way but it is not an operative contractual provision. The provision ought to be able to stand on its own, without the reader referring back to the heading in order to figure out the provision's meaning.

Comment	Explanation/Illustration
	Example: One drafter wrote—
	Section 3.01 Content of the Logo. The Artist shall incorporate the theme of the poem "One Art" written by Elizabeth Bishop.
	The drafter can fix this problem by adding words to clarify the provision's meaning, so that the provision could stand alone without the heading.
	Section 3.01 Content of the Logo. The Artist shall incorporate into the Logo the theme of the poem "One Art" written by Elizabeth Bishop.
Don't drop article before defined terms	Reasonable contract drafters can disagree about this point. If the drafter omits articles before defined terms, the contract begins to sound like a telegram rather than a piece of prose. Moreover, most drafters drop articles inconsistently, leading the reader to wonder why the drafter sometimes uses the article and sometimes does not.
	Example: One drafter wrote—
	Section 6.06 Ownership of the Painting. Buyer is the sole owner of the Painting, and believes it to be worth at least $10,000.
	and
	Section 7.01 No Alterations. The Seller shall not make any changes to the Paperweight, except to clean the external glass or for regular maintenance of Paperweight.
	In the first example, the drafter drops the article before "Buyer" but includes the article before "Painting," both of which are defined terms. In the second example from the same contract, the drafter uses an article before the first instances of "Seller" and "Paperweight" but

Comment	Explanation/Illustration
	drops the article before the second instance of "Paperweight."
	The drafter can fix this problem by consistently using articles before defined terms or by consistently *not* using articles before defined terms. In my opinion, the first alternative is the best alternative. I believe that drafters should use articles to make the contract read smoothly. Not only is this easier on the reader, but it is easier on the drafter as well. Dropping the articles is unnatural and it is difficult to remember to do it consistently.
Echoing assignment sheet or client interview	Spoken English is different from written English. The documents and client interviews contain colloquial language that a drafter should not put into a contract.
	Example: One drafter wrote—
	Section 7.03 Contents of Consignment Record.
	The Consignment Record will contain the standard stuff, clearly identifying each piece by title, description, medium, and retail price. In a sense, the Consignment Record will serve as a receipt.
	The drafter lifted this language directly from one of the documents included in the assignment—a memorandum from the client. The drafter has to "do the drafting." In other words, he must translate the deal facts into contractual language.
	Section 7.03 Contents of Consignment Record.
	The Gallery shall prepare a Consignment Record that clearly identifies each piece by title, description, medium, and retail price. The Gallery shall present the Consignment

Comment	Explanation/Illustration
	Record to the Artist as a receipt after the Artist delivers the Sculptures.
Extra word	The drafter has included an extra word, most likely because she changed something and failed to edit and proofread carefully. *Example:* One drafter wrote— **Section 10.06 Access to the Green Room.** The Bar shall permit the Band to access to the Green Room. Perhaps the first "to"—the extra word—crept in because the drafter first wrote "The Bar shall permit the Band to access the Green Room before each Set." When she changed her mind and decided to say, "The Bar shall permit the Band access to the Green Room," she forgot to delete the first "to." The drafter can fix this problem by removing the extra word.
Factual error	The drafter has gotten the facts of the deal wrong. *Example:* One drafter representing the Golfer wrote— **Section 5.07 Dedicated Services.** The Sport Psychologist shall not offer his services to any clients other than the Golfer during the Term. This provision contains a factual error. The parties agreed that the Psychologist would be permitted to service other clients during the Term—in fact, the Psychologist must maintain other clients in order to help establish his status as an independent contractor (as opposed to the Golfer's employee). The drafter could have avoided this problem by reading and listening more carefully. Once he has included this provision in his draft, the

Comment	Explanation/Illustration
	Psychologist's attorney is likely to catch the error. However, if the Psychologist's attorney does not catch the error and the provision remains in the contract, both parties risk the Psychologist being deemed the Golfer's employee rather than an independent contractor.
Faulty parallel information in Preamble	In the Preamble, the drafter has supplied more information about one party than about the other party.
	Example: In a contract between two corporations, the Preamble states that Company A is "an Illinois corporation with its principal place of business located at 1234 Street, Plathville, Illinois." With regard to Company B, the Preamble states merely that it is "an Illinois corporation."
	The drafter can fix this problem by stating more specifically where Company B's principal place of business is located.
	Note: When one party is a corporation and the other party is an individual, then the parallel information about the individual is stated like this: "an individual who resides at 5678 Avenue, Bishoptown, Illinois."
Faulty parallel structure	The drafter has created a list of items, but not every item in the list has the same grammatical structure as the other items.
	Example: In the Background section of a contract, one drafter wrote—
	Plan-It with Planet's experience planning eco-friendly elements of weddings includes buying flowers from a local farmer, arranging for wedding guests to use public transportation, and used 100% recycled paper for menus and programs.

Comment	Explanation/Illustration
	The third item in the list is not parallel to the two items preceding it, which contain gerunds ("ing" verb forms). The drafter can fix this by changing "used" in the third item to "using."
Lacks precision	Precision = Clarity + Accuracy The drafter has written a provision that is either unclear, inaccurate, or both. *Example:* One drafter wrote— **Section 7.04 E-mail and Phone Communication.** PIP shall provide J & J with e-mails and phone calls for the duration of the Term at no additional charge. This provision lacks precision because it is unclear what the word "provides" means and it is not accurate to imply that PIP is going to provide for all of J & J's e-mails and phone calls *made to anyone* during the Term. The drafter did not tie this provision closely enough to this particular deal. The drafter can make this provision clear and accurate: **Section 7.04 E-mail and Phone Communication.** During the Term, PIP shall communicate with J & J about the Services by e-mail and by telephone for no additional charge.
Legalese	Legalese gives lawyers a bad name. The dictionary definition of legalese starts out sounding benign but ends up sounding malignant. Legalese is defined as "the specialized vocabulary of the legal profession, especially when considered to be overly complex or abstruse." The American Heritage Dictionary, 4th ed. (Houghton Mifflin Company 2000), at 1000. *Example:* One drafter wrote—

Comment	Explanation/Illustration
	"Deposit" means the payment to be effectuated by the Clients at the Closing.
	The drafter can fix this provision by eliminating the legalese "to be effectuated by" and substituting Plain English.
	"Deposit" means the payment that the Clients make at the Closing.
	Example: One drafter wrote—
	Section 1.01 Initial Term. The Artist hereby agrees to consign said Sculptures to said Gallery for a two-year period commencing on May 1, 2006, and ending on April 30, 2008, upon the terms and conditions hereinafter set forth.
	The drafter can fix this provision by eliminating the words "hereby," "said," and "upon the terms and conditions hereinafter set forth," and by changing the word "commencing" to "beginning."
	Section 1.01 Initial Term. The Artist shall consign the Sculptures to the Gallery for two years, beginning on May 1, 2006, and ending on April 30, 2008 (the "Initial Term").
Let your defined term do its work	The drafter has not made use of his defined term. Usually he is repeating words that he included in the definition of the term (and therefore does not need to repeat).
	Example: One drafter wrote—
	Section 2.01 Term. This Agreement begins on October 10, 2015, and ends on October 9, 2016 (the "Term").
	Later in the Agreement, every time the drafter used the word "Term," she included the words "of this Agreement." The in-text definition of "Term" has eliminated the need to repeat that word string.

Comment	Explanation/Illustration
Missing comma (after date)	The drafter has omitted the conventional comma that belongs after the year when a full date (month, day, and year) appears mid-sentence. *Example:* One drafter wrote— **Section 2.03 Closing.** The Closing will take place at The Everest Room, 440 South LaSalle Street, 40th Floor, Chicago, Illinois 60605, on April 30, 2009 at 7:00 p.m. The drafter can fix this error by putting a comma after "2009."
Missing commas (interruptive phrase)	The drafter has omitted the conventional commas that must surround a word or phrase interrupting the flow of a sentence. *Example:* One drafter wrote— **Section 2.01 Summary of Services and Fees.** The Golfer engages the Sport Psychologist to render services to the Golfer as described in Article IV of this Agreement below during the Term. The Golfer shall pay Bowker the fees for the services as described in Article V, below. The drafter has omitted the commas that should surround the word "below" in the first sentence. As a result, the reader gets derailed when she reaches that point in the sentence. The drafter can fix this problem by inserting a comma before and a comma after the word "below" in the first sentence.
Missing comma (at the end of introductory phrase)	The drafter has omitted the conventional comma that belongs at the end of an introductory phrase at the beginning of a sentence. *Example:* One drafter wrote— **Section 9.05 Approval Process.** Upon the end of the ten-day day period any product not disapproved is deemed to be approved.

Comment	Explanation/Illustration
	The drafter omitted a comma after the introductory phrase "Upon the end of the ten-day period." As a result, the reader gets derailed when she reads "period any product" and has to go back to pause after "period."
	The drafter can fix this problem by inserting a comma after the word "period."
Missing word	The drafter has omitted a word, most likely due to carelessness.
	Example: One drafter wrote—
	Section 3.03 Fifth Contract Year Compensation. The Company shall pay the Athlete an amount equal to the Athlete's compensation for Year 4 in the final year of the Term if the Company exercises its option to extend for a fifth Contract Year, described Article II.
	The drafter has omitted the word "as" before "described" and the word "in" before Article.
	The drafter can fix this problem by proofreading more carefully and adding in the missing words. It may be a good idea for this drafter to read the contract out loud in order to catch these kinds of errors.
Need defined term	The drafter keeps repeating a lengthy phrase that could be condensed into one word by using a defined term.
	Example: One drafter wrote—
	Section 4.04 Condition of Paperweight. The Seller shall keep the round glass blue, black, and gold sculpture, weighing 12 ounces, in essentially the same condition that the round glass, blue, black, and gold sculpture, weighing 12 ounces, was in when the Seller first viewed the round glass, blue, black, and gold sculpture, weighing 12 ounces.

Comment	Explanation/Illustration
	The drafter can fix this problem by making "Paperweight" a defined term. "Paperweight" means the round glass, blue, black, and gold sculpture, weighting 12 ounces, created by the Artist, and numbered 4-20098. *Note:* The drafter has added more information to be sure that she has clearly identified which paperweight is at issue.
Parts not working well together	The drafter has used a cross-reference to the wrong section or to a section that does not exist in the contract. *Example:* One drafter wrote— **Section 6.03. Review of Prototypes.** The Toy Company shall review each Prototype in accordance with the process described in Section 5.04. *Note:* Section 5.04 is entitled "Copyright Ownership." Obviously, the drafter cross-referenced to the wrong section. The "process" is described in Section 6.04. The drafter can fix this problem by proofreading carefully and paying special attention to the accuracy of her cross-references.
Passive voice	The drafter is using a verb in the passive voice. *Example:* One drafter wrote— **Section 4.01 Payment for Services.** The payment shall be made by the Buyer. The "do-er" of the action is not in front of the verb. In contracts, your goal usually is to assign, rather than avoid, responsibility. In litigation, we sometimes write, "The money was transferred by the Bank," if the Bank is our client and we want to deflect attention from the Bank. But the sentence, "The Bank transferred

Comment	Explanation/Illustration
	the money," is much stronger. It's in the active voice.
	The drafter can fix the above problem, by saying, "The Buyer shall pay the Seller $5,000 for the Services." This assigns responsibility for payment to the Buyer and also clarifies to whom the Buyer is going to make the payment.
Placement?	The drafter has put an Article or a Section in the wrong place.
	Example: One drafter put an Article describing the parties' auditing rights after the Article called "Services" but before the article called "Fees and Expenses." Auditing rights are not as important as "Fees and Expenses." Also, it makes more sense to talk about auditing rights after "Fees and Expenses" since fees and expenses are both likely to be topics of the audit.
	Example: One drafter put a section requiring the Band to do its sound check by 5:00 p.m. after a section requiring the Band to start playing its first set at 8 p.m. The drafter can organize this material chronologically to make it more readable.
Raises a questions (or questions)	The drafter has raised a question (or questions) without answering it (or them).
	Example: The drafter includes a covenant requiring the Purchaser of a car to pay the Seller $5,000 when the Seller delivers the car to the Purchaser. But the drafter does not say anything about the method, place, or timing of delivery or about whether the $5,000 is cash or a check. The reader wants to know the answers to these questions and ought to be able to find them in the contract.

Comment	Explanation/Illustration
	The drafter can fix this problem by providing the answers to the reader's questions within the contract.
Say the same thing in the same way	The drafter has used different words to describe the same thing. *Example:* One drafter wrote— **The Purchase and Sale.** Subject to the provisions of this Agreement, the Buyer shall purchase the Putting Green from the Seller, and the Seller shall sell the Putting Green to the Buyer and construct it in the Buyer's backyard. *Note:* Throughout this Agreement, the drafter uses the words "construct" and "install" interchangeably. And, in one place, the drafter says that the Seller is going to "construct and install." This confuses the reader, who begins to wonder if the two words mean the same thing or mean two different things. The drafter can fix this problem by using "construct" or "install" consistently throughout the agreement. If "construction" and "installation" are two different things, then the drafters can use them together but must use them consistently together or make them defined terms with distinct meanings.
Shorthand (DRAFT it!)	The drafter has failed to do the necessary drafting and is instead inappropriately relying on a heading or on the audience's knowledge of the deal. *Example:* One drafter wrote— **Section 3.01 Content of the Logo.** The Artist shall incorporate the theme of the poem "One Art" written by Elizabeth Bishop. The Fix: See "Don't make your heading do too much work," above.

Comment	Explanation/Illustration
Spell out the process	The drafter has failed to clarify how something is supposed to happen. Consequently, the drafter has raised questions in the reader's mind and left them unanswered.
	Example: In an endorsement contract, the drafter's client, a golfer, is entitled to approve of each outfit that the golf clothing company chooses for her to wear in each tournament. The drafter gives the golfer this right in the contract but fails to describe the steps for the approval process. When does the company present her with the clothing they have chosen? How does she express her approval/disapproval, and by when? How is the company to respond? Etc.
	The drafter can fix this problem by spelling out the approval process in detail within the contract.
Subject/verb agreement	The drafter has used a singular subject with a plural verb, or a plural subject with a singular verb.
	Example: One drafter wrote—
	Section 4.04 Cancellation for Incapacity. If the Company judges that one or more members of the Band are incapacitated to the point of not being able to perform, then the Company may cancel the performance.
	The drafter can fix this problem by changing the verb, as indicated below.
	Section 4.04 Cancellation for Incapacity. If the Company judges that one or more members of the Band *is* incapacitated to the point of not being able to perform, then the Company may cancel the performance.
The reader feels like she is in good hands	This is high praise, given to a contract (or part of a contract) that is written in an authoritative

Comment	Explanation/Illustration
	voice, using the appropriate contract concepts. The contract is well organized and reads smoothly. It contains no typographical errors. By the end of the second page, the reader feels she can relax and sit back to enjoy the ride.
Thoughtful drafting	The drafters came up with an interesting idea that solves a problem.
	Section 4.03 No Veto of Buyers. The Artist shall have no authority to veto or reject the sale of a Sculpture to a particular buyer. If the Artist has reason to believe, and does believe, that a potential buyer would infringe on her rights under the Copyright Law, the Art Dealer shall allow the Artist two days in which to find an alternate buyer or purchase the Sculpture herself.
	Here, the drafters recognized that the Artist may not be able to buy back the Sculpture. Therefore, they gave her the opportunity to find an alternate buyer.
Typographical error (major)	The drafter has made a typographical error that significantly changes the substantive meaning of a contractual provision.
	Example: One drafter wrote—
	Section 4.04. Conditions to Company's Obligations. All of the following conditions must have been satisfied or waived before the Band is obligated to close the transaction that this Agreement contemplates:
	(a) The Band must have delivered a copy of the Band's most recent partnership agreement, the Amended One Art Partnership Agreement, to the Company.
	Section 4.04 covers conditions to the Company's obligations to close. But the introductory language to this provision states that

Comment	Explanation/Illustration
	the conditions must have been satisfied or waived before *the Band* is obligated to close. The drafter can fix this problem by proofreading more carefully and replacing the words "before the Band is obligated to close" with "before *the Company* is obligated to close."
Vague	The drafter has used a word or a phrase that is not precise. Vagueness is different from ambiguity. Ambiguous phrases are subject to more than one specific interpretation. Vague phrases allow for a wide range of interpretations within a specific class. *Example:* One drafter wrote— **Section 2.05 Band's Rights to the Logo.** At the conclusion of the purchase transaction, the Artist assigns to the Band all rights to use the Logo in any manner the Band wishes. The phrase "at the conclusion of the purchase transaction" is vague. The reader might know what the drafter intends but cannot be sure. The drafter can fix this problem by clarifying her meaning. **Section 2.05 Band's Rights to the Logo.** When the Band makes the Final Payment, the Artist shall assign to the Band all rights to use the Logo in any manner the Band wishes.
Wordy	The drafter has used more words than necessary to communicate something. *Example:* One drafter wrote— **"Television Advertisement"** means a filmed Company commercial that is able to be shown on television. The drafter can fix this problem by eliminating unnecessary words.

Comment	Explanation/Illustration
	"Television Advertisement" means a filmed Company commercial that can be shown on television.
	Note: This drafter should also consider whether it is necessary to define this term at all.
Wrong verb choice	The drafter has used "shall" without a party name in front of it.
	Example: One drafter wrote—
	Section 9.01 Length of Set. The Band shall play two sets during each Performance for one hour each. The first set shall begin at 8:30 PM and end at 9:30 PM. The second set shall begin at 11:00PM and end at 12:00 PM.
	The drafter can fix this problem by using "will" instead of "shall" in the last two sentences, or, by defining "First Set" and "Second Set," thereby eliminating the need for the last two sentences.
	* * *
	The drafter has used "will" instead of "shall" for a covenant.
	Example: One drafter wrote—
	Section 3.02 Closing Celebration. PIP will provide an Eco-Friendly celebration at the Closing including wine from a local Illinois winery and cheese and fruit from a local Illinois farm.
	The drafter can fix this problem by using "shall" with the party name "PIP" to indicate that PIP is undertaking a covenant.
	* * *
	The drafter has used "means" with "does not include." Usually "means" stands alone.

Comment	Explanation/Illustration
	The verbs "includes" and "but does not include" are used together. *Example:* One drafter wrote— **"Band Equipment"** means all equipment necessary for the Band to perform Experimental Rock Music but does not include the Venue Equipment. The drafter can fix this problem by using the verb "includes" instead of "means."
Wrong word	The drafter has chosen the wrong word to communicate something. *Example:* One drafter wrote— **Section 5.09 Replacement Psychologist.** If the Replacement Psychologist charges Bennett an hourly rate rather than a flat rate as proscribed by Article 10 of this Agreement, then Bowker shall pay to Bennett the amount by which Replacement Psychologist's hourly rate exceeds $200 per hour. *Note:* The word "proscribed" means "prohibited." The drafter probably meant to use the word "prescribed," which means "dictated" or "required" in this context. The drafter can fix this problem by using the correct word ("prescribed") or by saying "required" instead.